A·N·N·U·A·L E·D·I·T·I·O·N·S

American Foreign Policy

06/07

Twelfth Edition

EDITOR

Glenn P. Hastedt

James Madison University

Glenn Hastedt received his Ph.D. from Indiana University. He is professor of political science at James Madison University, where he teaches courses on U.S. foreign policy, national security policy, and international relations. His special area of interest is on the workings of the intelligence community and the problems of strategic surprise and learning from intelligence failures. In addition to having published articles on these topics, he is the author of *American Foreign Policy: Past, Present, Future*; coauthor of *Dimensions of World Politics*; and editor and contributor to *Controlling Intelligence*. He has also published two volumes of readings, *Toward the Twenty-First Century* and *One World, Many Voices*.

Contemporary Learning Series

2460 Kerper Blvd., Dubuque, IA 52001

Visit us on the Internet
http://www.mhcls.com

Credits

1. **The United States and the World: Strategic Choices**
   Unit photo—© Department of Defense photo by Master Sgt. James Bowman, U.S. Air Force
2. **The United States and the World: Regional and Bilateral Relations**
   Unit photo—© Getty Images/PhotoLink
3. **The Domestic Side of American Foreign Policy**
   Unit photo—© Getty Images/PhotoLink/C. Borland
4. **The Institutional Context of American Foreign Policy**
   Unit photo—Courtesy of K. Jewell/U.S. House of Representatives.
5. **The Foreign Policy-Making Process**
   Unit photo—© Getty Images/PhotoLink/C. Lee
6. **U.S. International Economic Strategy**
   Unit photo—Photo courtesy of Department of State by Basil Shahin
7. **U.S. Military Strategy**
   Unit photo—© CORBIS/Royalty-Free
8. **The Iraq War and Beyond**
   Unit photo—Photo courtesy of U. S. Army by Sgt. 1st Class Johancharles Van Boers

Copyright

Cataloging in Publication Data
Main entry under title: Annual Editions: American Foreign Policy. 2006/2007.
1. U.S. Foreign Relations—Periodicals. I. Hastedt, Glenn P., comp. II. Title: American Foreign Policy.
ISBN 0–07–354585–6   658'.05   ISSN 1075–5225

Twelfth Edition

Cover image ©
Printed in the United States of America   1234567890QPDQPD987654   Printed on Recycled Paper

Editors/Advisory Board

Members of the Advisory Board are instrumental in the final selection of articles for each edition of ANNUAL EDITIONS. Their review of articles for content, level, currentness, and appropriateness provides critical direction to the editor and staff. We think that you will find their careful consideration well reflected in this volume.

EDITOR

Glenn P. Hastedt
James Madison University

ADVISORY BOARD

Linda S. Adams
Baylor University

Ralph G. Carter
Texas Christian University

Nader Entessar
Spring Hill College

Will Hazelton
Miami University

Christopher M. Jones
Northern Illinois University

James W. Peterson
Valdosta State University

George Poteat
Troy State University

Helen E. Purkitt
U.S. Naval Academy

Nathaniel Richmond
Utica College

J. Philip Rogers
San Antonio College

John T. Rourke
University of Connecticut, Storrs

Elizabeth Spalding
Claremont McKenna College

James C. Sperling
University of Akron

Michael J. Sullivan
Drexel University

Joseph E. Thompson
Villanova University

Caroline S. Westerhof
Florida Metropolitan University

Shelton Williams
Austin College

Stephen D. Wrage
U.S. Naval Academy

Staff

EDITORIAL STAFF

Larry Loeppke, Managing Editor
Susan Brusch, Senior Developmental Editor
Jay Oberbroeckling, Developmental Editor
Bonnie Coakley, Editorial Assistant

TECHNOLOGY STAFF

Luke David, eContent Coordinator

PERMISSION STAFF

Lenny J. Behnke, Permissions Coordinator
Lori Church, Permissions Coordinator
Shirley Lanners, Permissions Coordinator

PRODUCTION STAFF

Beth Kundert, Production Manager
Trish Mish, Production Assistant
Jade Benedict, Production Assistant
Kari Voss, Lead Typesetter
Jean Smith, Typesetter
Karen Spring, Typesetter
Sandy Wille, Typesetter
Tara McDermott, Designer
Maggie Lytle, Cover Graphics

Preface

This twelfth edition of *Annual Editions: American Foreign Policy* presents an overview of American foreign policy. Prior to September 11, 2001, the debate over the future of American foreign policy proceeded at a measured pace since few pressing threats to American national security seemed to exist. The foreign policy debate centered on selection strategies and tactics that could guide the United States in the transition period between the end of the cold war and the emergence of a post–cold war era. It was a debate largely conducted in the language of academics and it was one that did not engage large numbers of the American public. All of that has changed. After September 11, the conduct and content of American foreign policy is seen as important by virtually all Americans.

The immediate issue was combating and eradicating terrorism and the geographic focal point was Afghanistan and the target was the Taliban government and Osama bin Laden's al Qaeda terrorist organization. Few quarreled with the merits of this military undertaking either in the United States or abroad. This was not true for the Bush administration's next major foreign policy initiative when the war against terrorism was expanded to Iraq with the objective of removing Saddam Hussein from power. This successful military action was followed by an occupation marked by violence and political turmoil. Additional international challenges surfaced in short order. The most noteworthy being revelations concerning the North Korean and Iranian nuclear programs, and growing conflict over trade and monetary matters with China. As a consequence, we are now witnessing a wide-ranging debate over the strategic and tactical choices open to the United States in an era when it is the dominant (and some would say unchallenged) world power. To date this debate has produced far more questions than it has answers and it extends beyond questions of responding to terrorism and Iraq.

Annual Editions: American Foreign Policy 06/07 is divided into eight units. The first unit addresses questions of grand strategy. The second unit focuses on selected regional and bilateral relations. In the third unit, our attention shifts inward to the ways in which domestic forces affect the content of American foreign policy. The fourth unit looks at the institutions that make American foreign policy. In the fifth unit, the process by which American foreign policy is made is illustrated through accounts of recent foreign policy decisions. The sixth and seventh units provide an overview of the economic and military issues confronting the United States today. The final unit looks in depth at the issues surrounding the war in Iraq and its aftermath from a variety of different perspectives.

Together the readings in these eight units provide students with an up-to-date overview of key events in American foreign policy, the forces that shape it, and the policy problems on the agenda. The essays were chosen for their ability to inform students and to spark debate. They are not designed to advance any particular interpretation of American foreign policy.

I would like to thank Ian Nielsen for supporting the concept of an *Annual Editions: American Foreign Policy* many years ago. Also deserving of thanks are the many people at McGraw-Hill/Contemporary Learning Series who worked to make the project a success and those faculty on the Advisory Board who provided input on the selection of articles. In the end, the success of *Annual Editions: American Foreign Policy* depends upon the views of the faculty and students who use it. I encourage you to let me know what worked and what did not work so that each successive volume will be better than its predecessor. Please complete and return the postage-paid *article rating form* at the end of this book.

Glenn Hastedt

Glenn Hastedt

Editor

Contents

UNIT 1
The United States and the World: Strategic Choices

Unit Overview   xviii

The concepts in bold italics are developed in the article. For further expansion, please refer to the Topic Guide and the Index.

UNIT 2
The United States and the World: Regional and Bilateral Relations

The concepts in bold italics are developed in the article. For further expansion, please refer to the Topic Guide and the Index.

UNIT 3
The Domestic Side of American Foreign Policy

The concepts in bold italics are developed in the article. For further expansion, please refer to the Topic Guide and the Index.

UNIT 4
The Institutional Context of American Foreign Policy

UNIT 5
The Foreign Policy-Making Process

The concepts in bold italics are developed in the article. For further expansion, please refer to the Topic Guide and the Index.

UNIT 6
U.S. International Economic Strategy

The concepts in bold italics are developed in the article. For further expansion, please refer to the Topic Guide and the Index.

UNIT 7
U.S. Military Strategy

UNIT 8
The Iraq War and Beyond

The concepts in bold italics are developed in the article. For further expansion, please refer to the Topic Guide and the Index.

The concepts in bold italics are developed in the article. For further expansion, please refer to the Topic Guide and the Index.

Topic Guide

This topic guide suggests how the selections in this book relate to the subjects covered in your course. You may want to use the topics listed on these pages to search the Web more easily.

On the following pages a number of Web sites have been gathered specifically for this book. They are arranged to reflect the units of this *Annual Edition*. You can link to these sites by going to the student online support site at *http://www.mhcls.com/online/*.

ALL THE ARTICLES THAT RELATE TO EACH TOPIC ARE LISTED BELOW THE BOLD-FACED TERM.

Internet References

The following internet sites have been carefully researched and selected to support the articles found in this reader. The easiest way to access these selected sites is to go to our student online support site at *http://www.mhcls.com/online/*.

AE: American Foreign Policy 06/07

The following sites were available at the time of publication. Visit our Web site—we update our student online support site regularly to reflect any changes.

General Sources

Avalon Project at Yale Law School
http://www.yale.edu/lawweb/avalon/terrorism/terror.htm

The Avalon Project website feaures documents in the fields of law, history, economics, diplomacy, politics, government, and terrorism.

Center for Strategic and International Studies (CSIS)
http://www.csis.org

The Center for Strategic and International Studies (CSIS), which is a nonpartisan organization, has been dedicated to providing world leaders with strategic insights on, and policy solutions to, current and emerging global issues for 40 years. Currently, CSIS has responded to global terrorism threats by developing a variety of well-defined projects and responses that are available at this site.

The Federal Web Locator
http://www.infoctr.edu/fwl/

Use this handy site as a launching pad for the Web sites of federal U.S. agencies, departments, and organizations. It is well organized and easy to use for informational and research purposes.

Foreign Affairs
http://www.foreignaffairs.org

The *Foreign Affairs* site allows users to search the magazine's archives and provides access to the field's leading journals, documents, online resources, and so on. Links to dozens of other related Web sites are possible from here.

Institute for National Security Studies
http://www.usafa.af.mil/inss/occasion.htm

The full-text commissioned peer review reports on a variety of security topics affecting the United States and the world can be found at this Web site, sponsored by the Department of Defense.

International Information Programs
http://usinfo.state.gov

This wide-ranging page offered by the State Department provides definitions, related documentation, and a discussion of topics of concern to students of foreign policy and foreign affairs. It addresses today's hot topics as well as ongoing issues that form the foundation of the field. Many Web links are provided.

Oneworld.net
http://www.oneworld.net/section/partners/

Search this site for information and news about issues related to human sustainable development throughout the world. Information is available by topic or by country.

United Nations Home Page
http://www.un.org

Here is the gateway to information about the United Nations.

U.S. International Affairs
http://www.state.gov/www/regions/internat.html

Data on U.S. foreign policy around the world are available here. Some of the areas covered are arms control, economics and trade, international organizations, environmental issues, terrorism, current treaties, and international women's issues.

UNIT 1: The United States and the World: Strategic Choices

The Bulletin of the Atomic Scientists
http://www.bullatomsci.org

This site allows you to read more about the Doomsday Clock and other issues as well as topics related to nuclear weaponry, arms control, and disarmament.

The Henry L. Stimson Center
http://www.stimson.org

The Stimson Center, a nonprofit and (self-described) nonpartisan organization, focuses on issues where policy, technology, and politics intersect. Use this site to find assessments of U.S. foreign policy in the post–cold war world and to research many other topics.

International Network Information Center at University of Texas
http://inic.utexas.edu

This gateway has many pointers to international sites, organized into African, Asian, Latin American, Middle East, and Russian and East European subsections.

ISN International Relations and Security Network
http://www.isn.ethz.ch

Maintained by the Center for Security Studies and Conflict Research, this site is a clearinghouse for information on international relations and security policy. The many topics are listed by category (Traditional Dimensions of Security and New Dimensions of Security) and by major world regions.

UNIT 2: The United States and the World: Regional and Bilateral Relations

Inter-American Dialogue (IAD)
http://www.iadialog.org

This IAD Web site provides data on U.S. policy analysis, communication, and exchange in Western Hemisphere affairs. The organization has helped to shape the agenda of issues and choices in hemispheric relations.

Political Science RESOURCES
http://www.psr.keele.ac.uk/psr.htm

This is a link to sources available via European addresses. Listed by country name, it includes official government pages, official documents, speeches, elections, and political events.

Russian and East European Network Information Center
http://reenic.utexas.edu/reenic/index.html

Information ranging from women's issues to foreign relations and covering more than two dozen countries in Central and Eastern Europe and western Asia may be found here. Also check out

University of Texas/Austin's site on Broader Asia (*http://asnic.utexas.edu/asnic/index.html*) for more insight into bilateral/regional relations.

World Wide Web Virtual Library: International Affairs Resources

http://www.etown.edu/vl/

Extensive links are available here to help you learn about specific countries and regions, to research for various think tanks, and to study such vital topics as international law, development, the international economy, human rights, and peacekeeping.

UNIT 3: The Domestic Side of American Foreign Policy

American Diplomacy

http://www.unc.edu/depts/diplomat/

American Diplomacy is an online journal of commentary, analysis, and research on U.S. foreign policy and its results around the world. It provides discussion and information on current news, such topics as Life in the Foreign Service, and A Look Back.

Carnegie Endowment for International Peace (CEIP)

http://www.ceip.org

One of the most important goals of CEIP is to stimulate discussion and learning among both experts and the public on a range of international issues. This site provides links to the magazine *Foreign Policy,* to the Carnegie Moscow Center, and to descriptions of various programs.

RAND

http://www.rand.org

RAND, a nonprofit institution that works to improve public policy through research and analysis, offers links to certain topics and descriptions of RAND activities as well as major research areas (such as international relations and strategic defense policy).

UNIT 4: The Institutional Context of American Foreign Policy

Central Intelligence Agency (CIA)

http://www.cia.gov

Use this official CIA page to learn about many facets of the agency and to connect to other sites and resources.

The NATO Integrated Data Service (NIDS)

http://www.nato.int/structur/nids/nids.htm

NIDS was created to bring information on security-related matters within easy reach of the widest possible audience. Check out this Web site to review North Atlantic Treaty Organization documentation of all kinds, to read *NATO Review* magazine, and to explore key issues in the field of European security and transatlantic cooperation.

U.S. Department of State

http://www.state.gov/index.html

This State Department page is a must for any student of foreign affairs. Explore this site to find out what the department does, what services it provides, what it says about U.S. interests around the world, and much more.

United States Institute of Peace (USIP)

http://www.usip.org

The USIP, which was created by Congress to promote peaceful resolution of international conflicts, seeks to educate people and disseminate information on how to achieve peace.

U.S. White House

http://www.whitehouse.gov

This official Web page for the White House includes information on the President and Vice President and What's New. See especially The Virtual Library and Briefing Room for Hot Topics and latest Federal Statistics.

UNIT 5: The Foreign Policy-Making Process

Belfer Center for Science and International Affairs (BCSIA)

http://ksgwww.harvard.edu/csia/

BCSIA is the hub of the John F. Kennedy School of Government's research, teaching, and training in international affairs and is related to security, environment, and technology. This site provides insight into the development of leadership in policy making.

The Heritage Foundation

http://www.heritage.org

This page offers discussion about and links to many sites of the Heritage Foundation and other organizations having to do with foreign policy and foreign affairs.

National Archives and Records Administration (NARA)

http://www.nara.gov/nara/welcome.html

This official site, which oversees the management of all federal records, offers easy access to background information for students interested in the policy-making process, including a search of federal documents and speeches, and much more.

U.S. Department of State: The Network of Terrorism

http://usinfo.state.gov/products/pubs/

This Web site offers complete coverage from the American government's viewpoint regarding the war against terrorism. It provides a wealth of first-hand documentation and evidence.

UNIT 6: U.S. International Economic Strategy

International Monetary Fund (IMF)

http://www.imf.org

This Web site is essential reading for anyone wishing to learn more about this important body's effects on foreign policy and the global economy. It provides information about the IMF, directs readers to various publications and current issues, and suggests links to other organizations.

United States Agency for International Development

http://www.info.usaid.gov

Information is available here about broad and overlapping issues such as agriculture, democracy and governance, health, economic growth, and the environment in many regions and countries around the world.

United States Trade Representative

http://www.ustr.gov

The mission of the U.S. Trade Representative is presented on this site. Background information on international trade agreements and links to other sites may be accessed.

World Bank

http://www.worldbank.org

News (including press releases, summaries of new projects, and speeches), publications, and coverage of numerous topics regarding development, countries, and regions are provided at this Web site. It also contains links to other important global financial organizations.

UNIT 7: U.S. Military Strategy

Arms Control and Disarmament Agency (ACDA)
http://dosfan.lib.uic.edu/acda/

This archival ACDA page provides links to information on arms control and disarmament. Researchers can examine texts of various speeches, treaties, and historical documents. For further current information, go to the Bureau of Arms Control page at *http://state.gov/t/ac/.*

Counterterrorism Page
http://counterterrorism.com

A summary of worldwide terrorism events, groups, and terrorism strategies and tactics, including articles from 1989 to the present of American and international origin, plus links to related Web sites and graphs are available on this Web site.

DefenseLINK
http://www.defenselink.mil/news/

Learn about the Department of Defense at this site. News, publications, photos, and other related sites of interest are noted.

Federation of American Scientists (FAS)
http://www.fas.org

FAS, a nonprofit policy organization, maintains this site to provide coverage of such topics as terrorism and weapons of mass destruction.

Human Rights Web
http://www.hrweb.org

The history of the human rights movement, text on seminal figures, landmark legal and political documents, and ideas on how individuals can get involved in helping to protect human rights around the world can be found here.

UNIT 8: The Iraq War and Beyond

White House: Renewal in Iraq
http://www.whitehouse.gov/infocus/iraq/

View official White House reports, including presidential remarks on this site.

We highly recommend that you review our Web site for expanded information and our other product lines. We are continually updating and adding links to our Web site in order to offer you the most usable and useful information that will support and expand the value of your Annual Editions. You can reach us at: *http://www.mhcls.com/annualeditions/.*

UNIT 1

The United States and the World: Strategic Choices

Unit Selections

1. **Grand Strategy in the Second Term**, John Lewis Gaddis
2. **Hegemony on the Cheap**, Colin Dueck
3. **Reaganism v. Neo-Reaganism**, Richard Lowry
4. **The Eagle Has Crash Landed**, Immanuel Wallerstein
5. **Some Hard Truths about Multilateralism**, Jonathan Tepperman

Key Points to Consider

- Make a scorecard of the successes and failures of the Bush administration's foreign policy to date. Defend your choices and explain why these policies turned out as they did.

- Make a list of the five most important foreign policy problems facing the United States today. Defend your choices and explain why you ranked them in this order.

- Has the United States become a rogue superpower? Defend your answer.

- What principles do you think should guide American foreign policy in the future?

- How much and what type of responsibility does the United States have for maintaining world order?

- How helpful is the past as a guide to the future in constructing foreign policy strategies?

Student Website

www.mhcls.com/online

Internet References

Further information regarding these websites may be found in this book's preface or online.

The Bulletin of the Atomic Scientists
   http://www.bullatomsci.org

The Henry L. Stimson Center
   http://www.stimson.org

International Network Information Center at University of Texas
   http://inic.utexas.edu

ISN International Relations and Security Network
   http://www.isn.ethz.ch

Choice in foreign policy is always present. The September 11, 2001 terrorist attacks on the World Trade Center and on the Pentagon did not change this reality. The strong sense of national unity that followed these attacks momentarily quieted the debate on the proper conduct and content of American foreign policy but it did not end it. This debate was renewed as the George W. Bush administration moved toward war with Iraq and it has emerged with new force as the United States has entered into a period of occupation and reconstruction in Iraq. Much of the current debate is highly politicized. It focuses on assigning blame and responsibility for decisions already made and the nature of the current situation in Iraq. Still, in it we can also find evidence in this debate over the shape of the future world that the United States wishes to see come into existence and how to bring it about.

The strategic debate today is different from that—that long dominated the scene. For much of the cold war, the foreign policy debate focused on tactics. A consensus had formed around the policy of containment. But there were still choices. Rolling back the iron curtain was a minority view during the 1950s and cooperation with the Soviet Union was advocated by some during the immediate post–World War II period. In the late 1960s, détente emerged as a serious competitor to containment and succeeded in supplanting it for a brief period of time.

No single vision of American foreign policy emerged as dominant in the first decade of the post–cold war era. For some, the 1990s provided the United States with the long-awaited opportunity to walk away from the distracting and corrupting influence of international affairs and focus instead on domestic concerns and embrace traditional American values. For others, the 1990s represented a moment to be seized. Adherents to this perspective were divided over how to proceed. One group advocated replacing the strategies of conflict and confrontation of the cold war with ones designed to foster cooperation among states and to lift the human condition. A second group saw it as an opportunity to reorder the world in America's image—for it had won the cold war.

When he entered office, George W. Bush's administration's early initiatives suggested it would pursue a foreign policy based on unilateralist principles and favoring disengagement from global problem-solving efforts. This was evidenced in its withdrawal from the Kyoto protocol, its stated desire to extract the United States from involvement in the Balkans, negotiations with North Korea, and brokering a Middle East peace accord. Pursuit of a national ballistic missile defense system in face of global opposition further reinforced this perception.

The terrorist attacks of September 11 forced the Bush administration to reexamine its approach to foreign policy. Still pragmatic, now there is also present a strong sense of missionary zeal. Still unilateralist at heart, the administration now confronts demands that it work with the broader international community in order to achieve its foreign policy goals. Still reluctant to play the role of global policeman, it finds itself drawn much more deeply into regional and global disputes. The result has been a foreign policy that often seems at war with itself. At the same time it is self-confident, if not defiant, yet often appears to stumble as it moves forward.

The essays in this unit introduce us to the scope of the contemporary debate over the strategic choices open to the United States. The first article, "Grand Strategy in the Second Term" by John Lewis Gaddis asserts that the fundamental outlines of the Bush administration's first term foreign policy will be and should be continued. What is needed are modest midcourse corrections. The other essays in this section provide critiques of the administration's strategy. In "Hegemony on the Cheap," Colin Dueck criticizes Bush's pursuit of an ambitious Wilsonian agenda without adequate resources. Bush is not the first Wilsonian to error in this regard argues Dueck. "Reaganism v. Neo-Reaganism" argues that what is needed is a foreign policy grounded in conservative principles. The author argues that these can be found in Reaganism but not the neoconservative interpretation of Ronald Reagan's foreign policy. The next article, "The Eagle Has Crash Landed," raises the possibility that the United States has become a powerless superpower. The final essay, "Some Hard Truths about Multilateralism," argues that for domestic and international reasons it is harder for presidents to practice multilateralism than it is to praise it. As a result while the amount of cooperation in American foreign policy can improve it will not always be possible—no matter who is president.

Grand Strategy in the Second Term

John Lewis Gaddis

RECONSIDERATIONS

SECOND TERMS in the White House open the way for second thoughts. They provide the least awkward moment at which to replace or reshuffle key advisers. They lessen, although nothing can remove, the influence of domestic political considerations, since re-elected presidents have no next election to worry about. They enhance authority, as allies and adversaries learn—whether with hope or despair—with whom they will have to deal for the next four years. If there is ever a time for an administration to evaluate its own performance, this is it.

George W. Bush has much to evaluate: he has presided over the most sweeping redesign of U.S. grand strategy since the presidency of Franklin D. Roosevelt. The basis for Bush's grand strategy, like Roosevelt's, comes from the shock of surprise attack and will not change. None of F.D.R.'s successors, Democrat or Republican, could escape the lesson he drew from the events of December 7, 1941: that distance alone no longer protected Americans from assaults at the hands of hostile states. Neither Bush nor his successors, whatever their party, can ignore what the events of September 11, 2001, made clear: that deterrence against states affords insufficient protection from attacks by gangs, which can now inflict the kind of damage only states fighting wars used to be able to achieve. In that sense, the course for Bush's second term remains that of his first one: the restoration of security in a suddenly more dangerous world.

Setting a course, however, is only a starting point for strategies: experience always reshapes them as they evolve. Bush has been rethinking his strategy for some time now, despite his reluctance during the campaign to admit mistakes. With a renewed and strengthened electoral mandate, he will find it easier to make midcourse corrections. The best way to predict their extent is to compare what his administration intended with what it has so far accomplished. The differences suggest where changes will—or at least should—take place.

PRE-EMPTION AND PREVENTION

THE NARROWEST GAP between Bush's intentions and his accomplishments has to do with preventing another major attack on the United States. Of course, one could occur at any moment, even between the completion of this article and its publication. But the fact that more than three years have passed without such an attack is significant. Few Americans would have thought it likely in the immediate aftermath of September 11. The prevailing view then was that a terrorist offensive was underway, and that the nation would be fortunate to get through the next three months without a similar or more serious blow being struck.

Connecting causes with consequences is always difficult—all the more so when we know so little of Osama bin Laden's intentions or those of his followers. Perhaps al Qaeda planned no further attacks. Perhaps it anticipated that the United States would retaliate by invading Afghanistan and deposing the Taliban. Perhaps it foresaw U.S. military redeployments from Saudi Arabia to Afghanistan, Uzbekistan, Kyrgyzstan, and Iraq. Perhaps it expected a worldwide counterterrorist campaign to roll up substantial portions of its network. Perhaps it predicted that the Bush administration would abandon its aversion to nation building and set out to democratize the Middle East. Perhaps bin Laden's strategy allowed for all of this, but that seems unlikely. If it did not, then the first and most fundamental feature of the Bush strategy—taking the offensive against the terrorists and thereby surprising them—has so far accomplished its purposes.

A less obvious point follows concerning pre-emption and prevention, a distinction that arose from hypothetical hot-war planning during the Cold War. "Pre-emption" meant taking military action against a state that was about to launch an attack; international law and practice had long allowed such actions to forestall clear and immediately present dangers. "Prevention" meant starting a war against a state that might, at some future point, pose such risks. In mounting its post–September 11 offensive, the Bush administration conflated these terms, using the word "pre-emption" to justify what turned out to be a preventive" war against Saddam Hussein's Iraq.

It did so on the grounds that, in a post–September 11 world, both terrorists and tyrants threatened the security of the United States. Al Qaeda could not have acted without the support and sanctuary the Taliban provided. But the traditional warnings governments had used to justify pre-emption—the massing of armed forces in such a way as to confirm aggressive intent—would not have detected the September 11 attacks before they took place. Decisions made, or at least circumstances tolerated, by a shadowy regime in a remote country halfway around the world produced an act of war that killed more Americans than the one committed six decades earlier by Japan, a state known at the time to pose the clearest and most present of dangers.

Pre-emption in its older and narrower sense might have worked against the Japanese fleet as it approached Pearl Harbor—had it been detected in time. Pre-emptive arrests would have stopped Mohammed Atta and his 18 co-conspirators as they approached their respective airports if it had been possible to read their minds. No nation's safety, however, can depend on such improbable intelligence breakthroughs: as the Pearl Harbor historian Roberta Wohlstetter pointed out years ago and as the *9/11 Commission Report* has now confirmed, detecting telltale signals in a world full of noise requires not just skill, but also extraordinary luck.

That is why the Bush administration's strategists broadened "preemption" to include the Cold War meaning of "prevention." To wait for terrorist threats to become clear and present was to leave the nation vulnerable to surprise attacks. Instead, the United States would go after states that had harbored, or that might be harboring, terrorist gangs. It would at first seek to contain or deter such regimes the familiar means by which the Cold War had been fought—but if those methods failed, it reserved the right to pre-empt perceived dangers by starting a preventive war.

The old distinction between pre-emption and prevention, therefore, was one of the many casualties of September 11. That event revealed a category of threats so difficult to detect and yet so devastating if carried out that the United States had little choice but to use preemptive means to prevent their emergence. John Kerry made it clear during the 2004 campaign that he would not have relinquished that option had he won the presidency. His successful opponent certainly will not do so, nor are his successors likely to. This feature of the Bush grand strategy is here to stay.

SPEAKING MORE SOFTLY—AND MORE CLEARLY

PRE-EMPTION DEFINED as prevention, however, runs the risk amply demonstrated over the past two years—

that the United States itself will appear to much of the world as a clear and present danger. Sovereignty has long been a sacrosanct principle in the international system. For the world's most powerful state suddenly to announce that its security requires violating the sovereignty of certain other states whenever it chooses cannot help but make all other states nervous. As the political scientist G. John Ikenberry has pointed out, Washington's policy of pre-emption has created the image of a global policeman who reports to no higher authority and no longer allows locks on citizens' doors. However shocking the September 11 attacks may have been, the international community has not found it easy to endorse the Bush administration's plan for regaining security.

Bush and his advisers anticipated this problem. After brushing aside offers of help in Afghanistan from NATO allies, the administration worked hard to win multilateral support for its first act of pre-emption for preventive purposes: the invasion of Iraq. It expected success. After all, who, apart from the United States, could organize the overthrow of Saddam Hussein, a dictator who had abused his people, started wars, flouted UN resolutions, supported terrorists, and, in the view of intelligence agencies everywhere, probably possessed weapons of mass destruction (WMD)? The use of U.S. power to depose such a monster, Bush's strategists assumed, would be welcomed, not feared.

They were wrong. The war in Iraq gained far less international support than the administration had anticipated. One can debate at length the reasons why: the outdated structure of the UN Security Council, which better reflected the power balance of 1945 than 2003; the appearance Bush gave of having decided to go to war with or without that body's consent; the difficulty of establishing a credible connection between Saddam Hussein and al Qaeda; the absence of incontrovertible evidence that the Iraqi dictator really did have WMD; the distrust that lingered from Bush's unnecessarily harsh rejections of the Kyoto Protocol, the International Criminal Court, and the Anti-Ballistic Missile Treaty. Whatever the explanation, his strategy of pre-emption by consent did not get consent, and this was a major failure.

President Bush's decision to invade Iraq anyway provoked complaints that great power was being wielded without great responsibility, followed by an unprecedented collapse of support for the United States abroad. From nearly universal sympathy in the weeks after September 11, Americans within a year and a half found their country widely regarded as an international pariah.

It is easy to say that this does not matter—that a nation as strong as the United States need not worry about what others think of it. But that simply is not true. To see why, compare the American and Soviet spheres of influence in Europe during the Cold War. The first operated with the consent of those within it. The second did not, and that made an enormous difference quite unrelated to the military strength each side could bring to bear in the region.

The lesson here is clear: influence, to be sustained, requires not just power but also the absence of resistance, or, to use Clausewitz's term, "friction." Anyone who has ever operated a vehicle knows the need for lubrication, without which the vehicle will sooner or later grind to a halt. This is what was missing during the first Bush administration: a proper amount of attention to the equivalent of lubrication in strategy, which is persuasion.

The American claim of a broadly conceived right to pre-empt danger is not going to disappear, because no other nation or international organization will be prepared anytime soon to assume that responsibility. But the need to legitimize that strategy is not going to go away, either; otherwise, the friction it generates will ultimately defeat it, even if its enemies do not. What this means is that the second Bush administration will have to try again to gain multilateral support for the pre-emptive use of U.S. military power.

Doing so will not involve giving anyone else a veto over what the United States does to ensure its security and to advance its interests. It will, however, require persuading as large a group of states as possible that these actions will also enhance, or at least not degrade, their own interests. The United States did that regularly—and highly successfully—during World War II and the Cold War. It also obtained international consent for the use of predominantly American military force in the 1991 Persian Gulf War, in Bosnia in 1995, in Kosovo in 1999, and in Afghanistan in 2001. Iraq has been the exception, not the rule, and there are lessons to be learned from the anomaly.

One is the need for better manners. It is always a bad idea to confuse power with wisdom: muscles are not brains. It is never a good idea to insult potential allies, however outrageous their behavior may have been. Nor is it wise to regard consultation as the endorsement of a course already set. The Bush administration was hardly the first to commit these errors. It was the first, however, to commit so many so often in a situation in which help from friends could have been so useful.

Another lesson relates to language. The president and his advisers preferred flaunting U.S. power to explaining its purpose. To boast that one possesses and plans to maintain "strengths beyond challenge" may well be accurate, but it mixes arrogance with vagueness, an unsettling combination. Strengths for what purpose? Challenges from what source? Cold War presidents were careful to answer such questions. Bush, during his first term, too often left it to others to guess the answers. In his second, he will have to provide them.

A final and related lesson concerns vision. The terrorists of September 11 exposed vulnerabilities in the defenses of all states. Unless these are repaired, and unless those who would exploit them are killed, captured, or dissuaded, the survival of the state system itself could be at stake. Here lies common ground, for unless that multinational interest is secured, few other national interests—

convergent or divergent can be. Securing the state will not be possible without the option of pre-emptive military action to prevent terrorism from taking root. It is a failure of both language and vision that the United States has yet to make its case for pre-emption in these terms.

IRAQ IS NOT VIETNAM

THE BUSH ADMINISTRATION believed that it could invade Iraq without widespread consent because it expected a replay of the Afghanistan experience: military resistance would quickly evaporate, Iraqis would welcome the Americans and their allies, and the victorious coalition would quickly install an Iraqi regime capable of controlling and rebuilding the country. Success on the ground, together with confirmation that Saddam Hussein did indeed have WMD, would yield the consensus that diplomacy had failed to produce. The occupation of Iraq would become a broadly supported international effort, even if the invasion had not been.

The military campaign proceeded as anticipated, but nothing else did. Enough troops were deployed to defeat the Iraqi army, but not to restore order, suppress looting, and protect critical infrastructure. Iraqis did not step forward to form a new government, however grateful they may have been to have their old one removed. Pentagon planners misjudged how quickly many Iraqis would begin to see their liberators as oppressors. They even hastened that process through a laissez-faire attitude toward the rights of prisoners that produced sickening abuses. WMD were not found. And the expanded multilateral assistance Bush had hoped for in running the occupation never arrived. To note gaps between intentions and accomplishments in Iraq is to understate: they littered the landscape.

The Bush administration has been scrambling ever since to close those gaps. It has done so with an indecisiveness that is quite at odds with its normal method of operation: it has seemed, far too often, simply not to know what to do. As a consequence, it has come close, more than once, to losing the initiative in Iraq. Visions of a Vietnam-like quagmire have begun to loom.

Such visions are, however, premature. After a year and a half of fighting, U.S. casualties in Iraq have yet to exceed what the monthly total in the Vietnam War frequently was. Iraqi losses, although much greater, are nowhere near what the Vietnamese suffered. The insurgents receive far less external aid than the Soviet Union and China provided to the North Vietnamese and the Viet Cong. There is no Iraqi equivalent to Ho Chi Minh: Iraq's division among Sunnis, Shia, and Kurds has created a balance of antagonisms, not a unified resistance.

It is also the case that the U.S. military tends to learn from its mistakes. Historians now acknowledge that American counterinsurgency operations in Vietnam were succeeding during the final years of that conflict; the problem was that support for the war had long since crumbled at home. Military learning is also taking place in Iraq, but the domestic opposition is not even approaching Vietnam-era proportions: 2004 was nothing like 1968. There is still time, then, to defeat the insurgency—even though the insurgents are no doubt also learning from their own mistakes.

Victory, in the end, will go to the side that can rally the "silent majority" of Iraqis who have so far not taken sides. Here an advantage lies with the Americans and their allies, for they can offer elections. The insurgents cannot. Opportunities to vote in equally dangerous circumstances—in El Salvador, Cambodia, and most recently Afghanistan—have punctured the pretensions of terrorists by diminishing the fears on which they depend. There are, to be sure, no guarantees. Elections could produce governments that are weak, incompetent, unrepresentative, brutal, or even fanatically opposed to the occupiers themselves. The risks of holding them, however, are preferable to the alternatives of swamping Iraq with U.S. troops or abandoning it altogether.

And what if the United States, despite its best efforts, ultimately fails in Iraq? It is only prudent to have plans in place in case that happens. The best one will be to keep Iraq in perspective. It seems to be the issue on which everything depends right now, just as Vietnam was in 1968. Over the next several years, however, President Richard Nixon and National Security Adviser Henry Kissinger showed that it was possible to "lose" Vietnam while "gaining" China. What takes place during the second Bush term in Afghanistan, Egypt, Iran, Libya, Morocco, Pakistan, Saudi Arabia, Syria, Turkey, and especially the Israeli-Palestinian relationship may well be as significant for the future of the Middle East as what occurs in Iraq. And what happens in China, India, Russia, Europe, and Africa may well be as important for the future of the international system as what transpires in the Middle East. All of which is only to say that Iraq must not become, as Vietnam once was, the single lens through which the United States views the region or the world.

WINNING THE WAR ON TERRORISM

GRAND STRATEGY is as much about psychology as it is facts on the ground. The Bush administration intended that a demonstrated capacity for retaliation, pre-emption, and/or prevention in Afghanistan and Iraq would convince al Qaeda that the United States could not be run out of the Middle East. "Shock and awe" would dry up recruiting for that organization. And it would deter other states in the region and elsewhere from supporting terrorism in the future. The record of accomplishments here is mixed.

Not even bin Laden can now expect a diminished U.S. presence in the Middle East: in political, economic, and certainly military terms, the United States is more firmly entrenched there than it was prior to September 11. It is less clear, though, that the Bush strategy has impeded al Qaeda's

recruiting. The toppling of Saddam Hussein humiliated at least as many Arabs as it pleased. The occupation of Iraq revealed irresolution and inefficiency as often as the firmness it was meant to convey. The Israeli-Palestinian conflict remains a festering grievance: military victory in Iraq removed a threat to Israel, but it has yet to speed a settlement. On balance, U.S. power has become more respected in the Middle East. But respect for U.S. culture, institutions, and leadership has significantly declined.

Efforts to deter dangerous states have also produced mixed results. Whatever Colonel Muammar al-Qaddafi's reasons for abandoning Libya's quest for WMD, his decision was just what the Bush strategists hoped would happen on a wider scale. They can also claim, as a success, Pakistan's dismantling of Abdul Qadeer Khan's network for marketing nuclear weapons components. In Iran and North Korea, however, the picture is bleaker: the invasion of Iraq appears to have convinced leaders in those countries that they must have a nuclear capability of their own. Far from deterring them, the United States may have pushed them into finding ways to deter it.

Grand strategies always have multiple audiences: actions aimed at particular adversaries can (and usually do) make unintended impressions on others. A major priority for the second Bush administration, then, will be to determine the extent to which its aggressive use of U.S. military power in Afghanistan and Iraq has produced results it did not want elsewhere, and to adjust strategy accordingly.

It will be necessary, in doing this, to avoid extremes of pessimism and optimism. The Bush team made the worst of Saddam Hussein's alleged WMD, while making the best of the more credible capabilities Iran and North Korea have been developing. Whatever the reasons behind this disparity, it is not sustainable. For even if the United States should succeed in Iraq, its larger strategy will have failed if it produces a nuclear-capable Iran or North Korea, and those countries behave in an irresponsible way.

This is not to predict that they will. States that have acquired nuclear weapons have so far handled them carefully. To take comfort in this pattern, however, is like trying to find reassurance in an extended game of Russian roulette: sooner or later the odds will turn against you. The same is true of the risk that nuclear, chemical, and biological weapons could make the leap, like some lethal virus, from potentially deterrable states to undeterrable terrorists. It may take the use of such weapons to awaken the world to this danger. That too, however, is a Russian roulette solution, which makes it not worth waiting for.

There are opportunities, then, for a renewed U.S. commitment to the task of keeping WMD out of the hands of tyrants and terrorists by multilateral means. The prospects for such an effort, like those for the Iraqi occupation, are better than they might at first seem. UN sanctions do appear to have prevented the rebuilding of Saddam Hussein's WMD after the Gulf War. That organization has shown itself effective as well in publicizing, if not resolving, the crisis over Iran's nuclear program.

Cooperative initiatives elsewhere have also shown promise: examples include the Nunn-Lugar program to dismantle nuclear stockpiles, the Proliferation Security Initiative to intercept illegal weapons shipments, and the tacit agreement North Korea's neighbors have reached that none has an interest in seeing Pyongyang develop the capacity for mass destruction.

The Bush administration has been proceeding in this direction. Its multilateralism outside of Afghanistan and Iraq is insufficiently acknowledged—probably because it has been inadequately explained. What is needed now is a clear and comprehensive statement of which international organizations and initiatives the United States can cooperate with, which it cannot, and why. It is as bad to promise too much, as the Clinton administration did, as to propose too little, as happened during Bush's first term. But with tact, flexibility, and a willingness to listen—as well as the power to pre-empt if such strategies fail—Americans could by these means regain what they have recently lost: the ability to inspire others to want to follow them.

SOWING THE SEEDS OF CHANGE

PRESIDENT BUSH has insisted that the world will not be safe from terrorists until the Middle East is safe for democracy. It should be clear by now that he is serious about this claim: it is neither rhetorical nor a cloak for hidden motives. Democratization, however, is a long-term objective, so it is too early to assess accomplishments. What one can evaluate is the extent to which the Bush strategists have succeeded in a more immediate task they set for themselves: to clear the way for democratization by shattering a status quo in the Middle East that they believed had victimized the people of the region and had become a threat to the rest of the world.

The regimes responsible for this situation had three characteristics. They were authoritarian: liberation from colonialism and its equivalents had left the region in a new kind of bondage to tyrannical or at least unrepresentative rule. Most of them benefited from the geological accident of where oil lay beneath the surface of the earth, so that the need to remain competitive within a global economy did not produce the political liberalization that it did almost everywhere else. And several of these regimes had cut deals with an Islamist religious establishment that had its own reasons for resisting change, thereby reinforcing a long-standing trend toward literal readings of the Koran that left little room for alternative interpretations. This unhealthy combination of authoritarianism, wealth, and religious literalism, the Bush administration maintained, fed frustrations for many and fueled rage in a few: that was enough to bring about September 11. Breaking this status quo would make the world safer in the short run and facilitate democratization in the long run.

The shock and awe that accompanied the invasions of Afghanistan and Iraq were meant to begin this process,

but Bush and his advisers did not rely solely on military means to sustain its momentum. They expected that September 11 and other terrorist excesses would cause a majority of Muslims to recoil from the extremists among them. They anticipated that the United States would be able to plant the seeds of democracy in the countries where it had deposed dictators, and that these would spread. They also assumed that the Middle East could not indefinitely insulate itself from the democratization that had already taken hold in much of the rest of the world.

Divisions have indeed surfaced among Muslims over the morality and effectiveness of terrorism. Saudis have seen the terrorists they financed strike back at them. Well before Yasir Arafat's death, Palestinians were questioning what suicide bombing and a perpetual intifada had accomplished; now there is even more room for second thoughts. Iraqis have begun to speak out, if cautiously, against the hostage-taking and televised beheadings that have afflicted their country. And the Beslan massacre—the taking of a school in southern Russia, with the subsequent slaughter of more than 300 children and teachers has raised doubts throughout the Middle East that terror directed against innocents can ever be justified when decoupled from any apparent political objective.

Whether democracy can be "planted" through military occupation in that part of the world is not yet clear, however, and may not be for some time. Three years after the invasion of Afghanistan, that country still is not secure. Taliban and al Qaeda elements remain, economic recovery is spotty, warlords rule, opium cultivation thrives, and Westerners cannot travel safely much beyond Kabul. And yet, on October 9, 2004, millions of Afghans lined up to vote in an election that had no precedent in their nation's long history. Had anyone predicted this three years ago, the response would have been incredulity—if not doubts about sanity.

What this suggests is that forces of disruption and construction coexist in Afghanistan: their shifting balance is beyond precise measurement. If that is true there, then it is all the more so in Iraq, where the contradictions are greater, the stakes are higher, and the standards for making optimistic or pessimistic judgments are even more opaque. The best one can say at the moment, of both countries, is that they defy generalization. That is less than the Bush administration hoped for. It is far more, however, than any previous American administration has achieved in the Middle East. For better or for worse, the status quo exists no longer.

And what of the region's insulation from the wave of democratization that has swept the globe? According to Freedom House statistics, no countries allowed universal suffrage in 1900. By 1950, 22 did, and by 2000, the number had reached 120, a figure that encompassed 62.5 percent of the world's population. Nor, as the examples of Bangladesh, India, Indonesia, and Turkey suggest, is there reason to think that representative government and Islam are incompatible. Democratization has indeed been delayed in the Arab world, as Arabs themselves have begun to acknowledge. To conclude that it can never take hold there, however, is to neglect the direction in which the historical winds have been blowing. And the best grand strategies, like the most efficient navigators, keep the winds behind them.

The second Bush administration will now have the opportunity to reinforce the movement—the shift in the status quo—that the first Bush administration started in the Middle East. A Kerry administration would probably have done the same. What September 11 showed was that the United States can no longer insulate itself from what happens in that part of the world: to do so would be to ignore clear and present danger. A conservative Republican administration responded by embracing a liberal Democratic ideal—making the world safe for democracy—as a national security imperative. If that does not provide the basis for a renewed grand strategic bipartisanship, similar to the one that followed Pearl Harbor so long ago, then one has to wonder what ever would.

WHAT WOULD BISMARCK DO?

FINALLY, one apparent assumption that runs through the Bush grand strategy deserves careful scrutiny. It has to do with what follows shock and awe. The president and his advisers seem to have concluded that the shock the United States suffered on September n required that shocks be administered in return, not just to the part of the world from which the attack came, but to the international system as a whole. Old ways of doing things no longer worked. The status quo everywhere needed shaking up. Once that had happened, the pieces would realign themselves in patterns favorable to U.S. interests.

It was free-market thinking applied to geopolitics: that just as the removal of economic constraints allows the pursuit of self-interest automatically to advance a collective interest, so the breaking up of an old international order would encourage a new one to emerge, more or less spontaneously, based on a universal desire for security, prosperity, and liberty. Shock therapy would produce a safer, saner world.

Some such therapy was probably necessary in the aftermath of September 11, but the assumption that things would fall neatly into place after the shock was administered was the single greatest misjudgment of the first Bush administration. It explains the failure to anticipate multilateral resistance to pre-emption. It accounts for the absence of planning for the occupation of Iraq. It has produced an overstretched military for which no "revolution in military affairs" can compensate. It has left official obligations dangerously unfunded. And it has allowed an inexcusable laxity about legal procedures—at Guantánamo, Abu Ghraib, and elsewhere—to squander the moral advantage the United States possessed after September 11 and should have retained.

The most skillful practitioner ever of shock and awe, Otto von Bismarck, shattered the post-1815 European settlement in order to unify Germany in 1871. Having done so, however, he did not assume that the pieces would simply fall into place as he wished them to: he made sure that they did through the careful, patient construction of a new European order that offered benefits to all who were included within it. Bismarck's system survived for almost half a century.

The most important question George W. Bush will face in his second term is whether he can follow Bismarck's example. If he can shift from shock and awe to the reassurance—and the attention to detail—that is necessary to sustain any new system, then the prospects for his post–September 11 grand strategy could compare favorably m Bismarck's accomplishments, as well as to those of U.S. presidents from Roosevelt through Clinton. For their post–Pearl Harbor grand strategy, over more than half a century, persuaded the world that it was better off with the United States as its dominant power than with anyone else. Bush must now do the same.

JOHN LEWIS GADDIS is Robert A. Lovett Professor of History at Yale.

Hegemony on the Cheap

Liberal Internationalism from Wilson to Bush

Colin Dueck

One of the conventional criticisms of the Bush administration's foreign policy is that it is excessively and even disastrously unilateralist in approach. According to the critics, the administration has turned its back on a long-standing and admirable American tradition of liberal internationalism in foreign affairs, and in doing so has provoked resentment worldwide.[1] But these criticisms misinterpret both the foreign policy of George W. Bush, as well as America's liberal internationalist tradition. In reality, Bush's foreign policy since 9/11 has been heavily influenced by traditional liberal internationalist assumptions—assumptions that all along have had a troubling impact on U.S. foreign policy behavior and fed into the current situation in Iraq.

The conduct of America's foreign relations has—for more than a hundred years, going back at least to the days of John Hay's "Open Door" Notes and McKinley's hand wringing over the annexation of the Philip-pines—been shaped, to a greater or lesser extent, by a set of beliefs that can only be called liberal. These assumptions specify that the United States should promote, wherever practical and possible, an international system characterized by democratic governments and open markets.[2] President Bush reiterated these classical liberal assumptions recently, in his speech last November to the National Endowment for Democracy, when he outlined what he called "a forward strategy of freedom in the Middle East." In that speech, Bush argued that "as long as the Middle East remains a place where freedom does not flourish, it will remain a place of stagnation, resentment, and violence ready for export." In this sense, he suggested, the United States has a vital strategic interest in the democratization of the region. But Bush also added that "the advance of freedom leads to peace," and that democracy is "the only path to national success and dignity," providing as it does certain "essential principles common to every successful society, in every culture."[3] These words could just as easily have been spoken by Woodrow Wilson, Franklin Roosevelt—or

Bill Clinton. They are well within the mainstream American tradition of liberal internationalism. Of course, U.S. foreign policy officials have never promoted a liberal world order simply out of altruism. They have done so out of the belief that such a system would serve American interests, by making the United States more prosperous, influential, and secure. Americans have also frequently disagreed over how to best promote liberal goals overseas.[4] Nevertheless, it is fair to say that liberal goals and assumptions, broadly conceived, have had a powerful impact on American foreign policy, especially since the presidency of Woodrow Wilson.

The problem with the liberal or Wilsonian approach, however, has been that it tends to encourage very ambitious foreign policy goals and commitments, while assuming that these goals can be met without commensurate cost or expenditure on the part of the United States. Liberal internationalists, that is, tend to define American interests in broad, expansive, and idealistic terms, without always admitting the necessary costs and risks of such an expansive vision. The result is that sweeping and ambitious goals are announced, but then pursued by disproportionately limited means, thus creating an outright invitation to failure. Indeed, this disjuncture between ends and means has been so common in the history of American diplomacy over the past century that it seems to be a direct consequence of the nation's distinctly liberal approach to international relations.

The Bush administration's current difficulties in Iraq are therefore not an isolated event. Nor are they really the result of the president's supposed preference for unilateralism. On the contrary, the administration's difficulties in Iraq are actually the result of an excessive reliance on classically liberal or Wilsonian assumptions regarding foreign affairs. The administration has willed the end in Iraq—and a very ambitious end—but it has not fully willed the means. In this sense, the Bush administration is heir to a long liberal internationalist tradition that runs from Woodrow Wilson, through FDR and Harry Truman, to Bill Clinton. And Bush inherits not only the strengths of that tradition, but also its weaknesses and flaws.

The Lost Alliance

The liberal internationalist pattern of disjuncture between ends and means really begins in earnest with Woodrow Wilson. Wilson, of course, traveled to Europe at the end of 1918, in the wake of the First World War, intending to "make the world safe for democracy" while insisting that a universal League of Nations serve as the linchpin for a new international order. Wilson intended the League to function as a promoter of collective security arrangements, by guaranteeing the territorial integrity and political independence of all member states. But Wilson also intended the League to function, more broadly, as the embodiment of a nascent liberal international order where war would be outlawed and self-determination would remain supreme. The other great powers were to be asked to abandon their imperialistic spheres of influence, their protectionist tariff barriers, their secretive military alliances, and their swollen armories.[5]

Needless to say, in practice, such concessions were hard to extract. The actual outcome at the Paris Peace Conference, contrary to Wilson's desire, was a series of compromises: Japan maintained its sphere of influence in the Chinese province of Shantung; Britain maintained its great navy, as well as its colonial conquests from Germany and Turkey; many of the arrangements negotiated in secret by the Allied powers during the war were in fact observed, though running contrary to Wilson's own pronouncements (including the famous Fourteen Points); and in blatant disregard of Wilson's alleged aversion to "old diplomacy" horse trading, France and Britain had their way vis-à-vis the peace terms imposed on Germany at Versailles while obtaining an explicit security guarantee from the United States.[6] To be sure, Wilson did succeed in winning the assent of the other victorious powers toward common membership in a new League of Nations. Furthermore, it is clear that he took the League's collective security obligations quite seriously. He certainly hoped that future acts of territorial aggression could be prevented through such peaceful means as deterrence, arbitration, and the use of economic sanctions. But in the final analysis, he understood perfectly well that collective security would at times have to be enforced militarily, through the use of armed force on the part of member states. Indeed, Wilson said quite explicitly that the League was meant to function as "a single overwhelming, powerful group of nations who shall be the trustee of the peace of the world."[7] And the United States was to be the leading member of this group.

Still, at the same time that Wilson laid out this extremely ambitious vision, he refused to draw the logical implications for the United States. Obviously, under any sort of meaningful commitment to a worldwide collective security system, the United States would henceforth be obliged to help enforce the peace in areas outside its traditional sphere of influence as proclaimed in the Monroe Doctrine (and subsequent "corollaries")—that is to say, in Europe and Asia. This would necessarily require maintaining a large standing army. Yet Wilson refused to admit that any such requirement existed, just as he disingenuously maintained that the League's covenant would not impinge on America's sovereignty, by insisting that said article carried only a "moral" obligation. In fact, he argued that the League would render a large standing army unnecessary.

Some of Wilson's Republican critics, especially in Congress, far from being isolationist know-nothings, saw through the contradictions in the president's vision, and advocated a pragmatic alternative. Led by Sen. Henry Cabot Lodge, these conservative internationalists called for a straightforward security pact with France and Great Britain as the key to their and America's own postwar security. Lodge and his supporters were willing to enter into the new League of Nations, but not into any global collective security arrangement. These Republican internationalists favored clear but restricted U.S. strategic commitments within Western Europe as the best guarantee of future peace.[8]

Lodge's alternative of a limited, Western alliance actually made perfect sense, strategically speaking. It avoided the impossible implication that America would come to the aid of any state, worldwide, whose territory or integrity was threatened. At the same time, it specified that the United States would defend France from any future attack by Germany while encouraging Britain to do the same. In this way, America's strategic commitments would be based upon concrete, vital national interests, rather than upon vague universalities; and upon real military capabilities, rather than utopian aspirations. The one problem with this alternative vision is that it seems to have been incompatible with domestic liberal pieties. Even Lodge admitted in 1919—at the time of the battle in the Senate over the League—that the idea of a League of Nations was quite popular in America. As Wilson himself suggested, the only way to preserve America's sense of moral superiority, while at the same time bringing its weight to bear in favor of international stability, was through membership in a universal organization, rather than through any particular and "entangling alliances."[9] Lodge and his supporters managed to defeat Wilson's League in the Senate, but they did not succeed in replacing it with a more realistic alternative.

Containment

During the Second World War, Franklin Roosevelt attempted to learn from Wilson's mistakes by carefully building domestic support for American membership in a postwar United Nations. Roosevelt was much more flexible in his approach than Wilson had been. But in terms of his substantive vision for the postwar order,

Roosevelt was hardly any less idealistic than Wilson. Roosevelt's "grand design" was that the five major powers fighting the Axis would cooperate in policing the postwar system, each power (more or less) within its own regional sphere of influence. At the same time, however, each great power was to respect such liberal norms as nonaggression, democratic institutions, and free trade within its own sphere.[10] FDR was strikingly successful in nudging the American public toward a new internationalist consensus. His administration laid the groundwork for U.S. postwar leadership of a more liberal international political and economic order. The one great stumbling block to Roosevelt's plans was the Soviet Union. Roosevelt recognized that Moscow would end the war with disproportionate influence over Eastern Europe, but he insisted that such influence be exercised in a benign, democratic, and non-coercive fashion. Stalin, of course, would not accept such conditions, whatever his rhetorical commitments to the contrary. Once this basic clash of interests between Washington and Moscow became visible for all to see, by the end of 1945, American officials were faced with the inevitable dilemma of how to respond to Soviet behavior. To allow the Soviet Union to construct, with impunity, an autarchic, militarized sphere of influence within Eastern Europe—and beyond—would have flown in the face of America's wartime objectives. The United States, under Truman, therefore settled on a strategy of containment in order to curb Soviet power and at the same time preserve FDR's hope for a more liberal world order.

Containment was a pragmatic strategy, but it was also very much influenced by Wilsonian assumptions regarding the nature of international relations. The purpose of containment, after all, was not simply to check or balance the Soviet Union, but also to nurture the long-term vitality and interdependence of an American-led, liberal international order outside of the Communist bloc.[11] The strategists of containment refused to accept permanent Soviet control over Eastern Europe, or to negotiate in earnest with Moscow over the outlines of a general postwar settlement that did not accord with Wilsonian principles. Instead, they hoped to achieve an eventual geopolitical, economic, and ideological victory over the Soviet Union by using every means short of war.[12] The goal was not to learn to coexist with the enemy, but gradually to convert and/or help him destroy himself. It was precisely this ideological, uncompromising tone that gave containment its political viability at home.

During the late 1940s, under the strategy of containment, the United States embarked upon a series of dramatic and unprecedented commitments abroad. Military and economic aid was extended to friendly governments worldwide; anticommunist alliances were formed around the globe; and U.S. troops were deployed in large numbers to Europe and Asia. The Truman Doctrine, the Marshall Plan, and NATO all embodied this new commitment to a forward strategic presence overseas. The prob-

lem, however, was that the Truman administration hoped to implement this very ambitious strategy without sacrificing the traditional American preference for limited liability abroad. Defense expenditures, in particular, were at first kept at a level that was exceedingly low, given the diverse and worldwide military commitments the United States had actually undertaken. In effect, the administration gambled that the Soviet Union and its clients would not test America's willingness or ability to contain military aggression by conventional means.[13] With the outbreak of the Korean War in 1950, this gamble proved to be a failure. As a result, in the early 1950s, the United States finally raised defense expenditures to a level commensurate with its strategic commitments overseas. Inevitably, the Wilsonian preference for low-cost internationalism reasserted itself: high levels of defense spending turned out to be politically unsustainable at home, leading the Eisenhower administration to return to a potentially risky reliance on nuclear deterrence. Americans wanted to contain the Soviet Union—an ambitious and in many ways a remarkably idealistic strategy—but they did not necessarily want to bear the full costs of such a strategy. In this sense, even at the height of the Cold War, U.S. foreign policy operated very much within the Wilsonian tradition.

The implementation of containment continued to be characterized by a persistent gap between ambitious liberal ends, and somewhat limited capabilities. In the early 1960s, John F. Kennedy made a concerted effort to close this gap through a strategy of "flexible response," emphasizing conventional and counterinsurgent, as well as nuclear, capabilities. Yet at the same time, Kennedy escalated America's military involvement in Vietnam, without providing any clear idea of how that conflict could be won. The decision to stand by Saigon, on the part of both Kennedy and, later, Lyndon Johnson, was driven primarily by concerns over the credibility of America's worldwide alliance commitments. But this decision was also very much informed by the Wilsonian belief that developing countries such as Vietnam could be reformed, liberalized, and won over to America's side through a vigorous, U.S.-assisted program of nation building.[14] In the words of Walt Rostow, one of Kennedy's leading foreign policy advisors, "Modern societies must be built, and we are prepared to help build them."

In Vietnam, America's willingness to sustain serious costs on behalf of a liberal strategy of containment and nation building was tested to the breaking point. Within the United States, domestic political support for a protracted, expensive, and bloody engagement in Southeast Asia proved to have definite limits. The Johnson administration itself was unwilling to call for maximum effort on behalf of its goals in the region; instead, it tried to achieve them through a process of limited and gradual escalation. The Nixon administration, having inherited this immense commitment, attempted to square the circle through a policy of "Vietnamization." The United States would slowly withdraw its forces from the conflict, relying upon air power and increased military aid to bolster the regime in Saigon. But Nixon's approach was no more able to achieve its stated aims than Johnson's. If Communist forces in Vietnam could not be defeated by half a million American troops, a lower level of American engagement was not going to do the trick. In the end, the United States proved neither willing nor able to bear the costs of meeting its commitments to Saigon—commitments that had been deeply informed by liberal internationalist assumptions.

Even as they experimented with Vietnamization, the Nixon-Kissinger team attempted to place the United States in a more sustainable strategic position by toning down the Wilsonian rhetoric. The new emphasis was on great power relations, rather than on ideological crusades to liberalize or reform the internal politics of other states. As Henry Kissinger put it in 1969, "We will judge other countries, including Communist countries, on the basis of their actions and not on the basis of their domestic ideologies."[15] This more pragmatic approach bore considerable fruit through a relaxation of tensions with the Soviet Union, as well as a dramatic improvement in relations with China. Despite these successes, Nixon and Kissinger were attacked from both left and right for abandoning America's Wilsonian mission overseas. Both Jimmy Carter, who took office in 1977, and Ronald Reagan, who succeeded him in 1981, criticized the policy of détente from a Wilsonian perspective. Both Carter and Reagan, despite their many differences, insisted that U.S. foreign relations should be rebuilt upon the premise that the United States had a vital practical as well as moral interest in the promotion of a liberal world order. The collapse of the Soviet Union in 1989 seemed to many to have vindicated the Wilsonian approach. But it was the combined economic and military power of the United States and its allies, not Wilsonian idealism, that finally brought the Soviet Union to its knees. In the euphoria over the collapse of communism, the fact that for over 40 years the United States had often pursued a sweeping and ambitious foreign policy with inadequate means was forgotten. The United States had been forced to pay for this strategic mismanagement in both Korea and Vietnam. In the end, the relative weakness of the Soviet Union gave U.S. policy makers considerable room for error. However, the upshot was that Americans misattributed their victory in the Cold War to the unique virtues of the Wilsonian tradition, which only led to a continuing gap between ends and means in the conduct of American foreign policy.

Democratic Enlargement

Following the end of the Cold War, the United States was faced with the choice of either expanding its military and political presence abroad, or retrenching strategically. The Clinton administration decided to do both. Thus it pursued a very ambitious strategy of "democratic enlargement," designed to promote the spread of market democracies worldwide. This included, notably, a new emphasis on humanitarian intervention in civil conflicts of seemingly peripheral interest to the United States. But it also tried to carry out this strategy at an extremely low cost in terms of blood and treasure. Defense expenditures, for example, were kept at a level that was unrealistically low, given the global range of America's military commitments. Just as significantly, Clinton also proved remarkably reluctant to use force in support of his Wilsonian agenda.

Clinton came into office having criticized the foreign policy of George H. W. Bush for being insufficiently true to America's democratic ideals. The new president promised to be more consistent than his immediate predecessor in promoting democracy and human rights in countries such as China, the former Yugoslavia, and Haiti. A leading test of the Clinton administration's rhetorical commitment to the liberal internationalist credo was on the question of humanitarian intervention. Clinton and his advisors repeatedly stated that the United States had a vital humanitarian interest in cases of civil war and disorder. The administration therefore placed a new emphasis on American-led peacekeeping, peacemaking, and nation-building operations.[16] More broadly, foreign policy officials articulated a doctrine of "enlargement," by which they meant that the United States would press for the expansion of free trade, open markets, democratic governments, and human rights worldwide.[17] Their assumption— building on the old Wilsonian gospel—was that such an expansion would encourage an upward cycle of global peace and prosperity, serving American interests and allowing the United States to de-emphasize its own military strength.

Under the Clinton administration, the liberal internationalist assumptions of democratic enlargement informed U.S. policy in virtually every region of the globe. In Central Europe, three new members were brought into NATO. In Russia, democratic market reforms were the price demanded for improved bilateral relations with the United States. In China, U.S. diplomats pressed Beijing on human rights issues while working to bring the People's Republic into the international economic system. And in Bosnia, Haiti, Somalia, and Kosovo, Washington undertook to help create or recreate stable, democratic polities, through military intervention, amidst generally unfavorable conditions.[18]

Nevertheless, even as President Clinton laid out his extremely ambitious foreign policy goals, he proved unwilling to support them with the necessary means. In particular, he proved reluctant to support these initiatives with the requisite amount of military force. In one case after another of humanitarian intervention, a pattern emerged: the Clinton administration would stake out an assertive and idealistic public position, then refuse to act on its rhetoric in a meaningful way. Yet in every such case, whether in Somalia, Haiti, Bosnia, or Kosovo, the president was ultimately forced to act, if only to protect the credibility of the United States.[19] The result was a series of remarkably halfhearted, initially low-risk interventions, which only reinforced the impression that the United States was unwilling to suffer costs or casualties on behalf of its stated interests overseas.[20]

It might be argued that the nature of U.S. interventions during the Clinton years was a function of the low geopolitical stakes involved, rather than a reflection of the administration's naiveté. Certainly, the stakes were relatively low. But from a classical realist perspective, the answer would have been to avoid putting America's reputation on the line in the first place—to avoid defining American interests in such an expansive manner as to then call the nation's credibility into question. The fact is that the Clinton administration said, in each case, that the United States had a vital national interest in the pursuit of liberal or humanitarian goals. Then it refused to protect this stated interest with requisite seriousness until American credibility had already been undermined. This may have been partially the result of a presidency characterized by unusual fecklessness on matters of national security. But it was also a pattern of behavior very much in the liberal internationalist tradition: sweeping commitments, too often supported by inadequate means.

Wilson Redux

At first, the inauguration of George W. Bush seemed to indicate, if nothing else, that America's national security capabilities would be brought into line with the nation's strategic commitments. As a candidate for president, Governor Bush had called for significant increases in defense spending. At the same time, he criticized what he termed the "open-ended deployments and unclear military missions" of the Clinton era.[21] Bush was especially critical of employing armed force in nation-building operations overseas; indeed, he suggested that he would not have intervened in either Haiti or Somalia. As Bush phrased it during a debate with Al Gore in October 2000, while referring to the question of intervention, "I would be very guarded in my approach. I don't think we can be all things to all people in the world. I think we've got to be very careful when we commit our troops."[22]

To be sure, neoconservative visions of American primacy always had a certain influence on Bush's thinking, but for the most part, the dominant tone of Bush's foreign policy pre-9/11 was one of "realism." The new administration was determined to be more selective on questions of nation building and humanitarian intervention than its predecessor. American foreign policy was to be refocused on considerations of great power politics and more immediate national interests, and the United States was to play down its pretensions as an international social engineer. Key figures such as Colin Powell and Richard Haass in the State Department and Condoleezza Rice at the National Security Council were well within the tradition of Republican pragmatism on foreign affairs, and hawks such as Vice President Dick Cheney and Secretary of Defense Donald Rumsfeld were either unwilling or unable to press for a comprehensive strategy of primacy across the board.[23] Above all, Bush seemed uninterested in any new, sweepingly ambitious—i.e., Wilsonian—foreign policy departures.

The terrorist attacks of September 11, 2001, changed all of that, coming as a severe shock to the president, his advisors, and the American public at large. These attacks stimulated the search for a new national security strategy. Key advocates of a different approach—at first within the administration, and then including the president himself—took advantage of the opportunity to build support for a new foreign policy agenda. This new national security strategy would be considerably more assertive than before and, in important ways, considerably more idealistic.[24]

Within days of the September 11 attacks, and over the following months, the Bush administration began to outline and articulate a remarkable departure in American foreign policy. The clearest and most elaborate explanation of the new approach came in the National Security Strategy of September 2002. In that document, best known for its embrace of preventive military action against rogue states, the administration began by pointing out that "the United States possesses unprecedented—and unequaled—strength and influence in the world." It renounced any purely realpolitik approach to foreign policy, arguing instead that "the great strength of this nation must be used to promote a balance of power that favors freedom." The promotion of free trade and democratic institutions was held up as a central American interest. Democracy and human rights were described as "nonnegotiable demands." And, interestingly, the possibility of traditional great power competition was played down. Instead, other powers were urged to join with the United States in affirming the global trend toward democracy and open markets.[25]

Of course, this broad affirmation of classical liberal assumptions was no doubt employed, in part, for reasons of domestic political consumption. Liberal arguments have historically been used to bolster strategic arguments of any kind. But the United States had been no less liberal—broadly speaking—in the year 2000, when the nascent Bush team was stressing the need for realism in foreign affairs. So the new rhetoric does seem to have reflected a real shift on the part of the administration toward a more aggressive and, at the same time, more Wilsonian approach.

The implications of this new Wilsonianism were most visible in the decision for war against Iraq. The argument made by the pro-war camp was that a defeated Iraq could be democratized and would subsequently act as a kind of trigger for democratic change throughout the Middle East. As Bush put it in an address last February to members of the American Enterprise Institute, "a new regime in Iraq would serve as a dramatic and inspiring example of freedom for other nations in the region.... Success in Iraq could also begin a new stage for Middle Eastern peace, and set in motion progress toward a truly democratic Palestinian state."[26] From the perspective of many leading officials inside the Bush administration, this argument was probably secondary to more basic geopolitical and security concerns. But it did seem to have an effect on the president. And again, 9/11 was the crucial catalyst, since it appeared to demonstrate that U.S. support for authoritarian regimes in the region had only encouraged Islamic fundamentalism, along with such terrorist organizations as al-Qaeda.[27]

Here was a remarkably bold vision for American foreign policy, combining the argument for preventive war with Wilsonian visions of a liberalized or Americanized international system. The goals outlined were so ambitious as to invite intense domestic as well as international criticism. The most common objections to the Bush Doctrine, at least among foreign policy experts, were that the new national security strategy would lead America into "imperial overstretch"; that it would trigger antagonism and hostility toward the United States abroad; that it would set a precedent for aggression on the part of other countries; and that it would undermine sympathy and support for the United States overseas. These were the most frequently articulated criticisms, but in fact an even more likely danger was the opposite one: that the Bush team would fail to make good on its promise of a serious commitment to achieving peace, stability, and democratization in Iraq, let alone in the Middle East as a whole.

Certainly the precedent in Afghanistan was not encouraging. There, the United States relied upon proxy forces, supported by airstrikes, special forces operations, and financial aid, in order to overthrow the Taliban. The failure to send in American ground troops early on meant that many members of al-Qaeda were able to escape and reconstitute their terrorist camps along the Afghan-Pakistani border. Worse yet, the Bush administration proved unwilling to contribute substantially to the postwar political, military, or economic reconstruction of Afghanistan, leaving its central government without effective control over the countryside outside Kabul.[28]

Iraq's postwar reconstruction was even less well considered than Afghanistan's. Certainly, the Bush foreign policy team understood that Saddam Hussein would not be overthrown without a major commitment of American ground troops. But in terms of planning for a post-Saddam Iraq, the administration seems to have based its initial actions upon the most optimistic assumptions: ordinary Iraqis would rise up in support of U.S. forces; these same forces would rapidly transfer authority toward a friendly interim government; the oil would flow, paying for reconstruction efforts; and the great majority of American troops would come home quickly. These were never very likely prospects, and with all of the warnings that it received, the administration should have

known better. As Bush himself said during the 2000 presidential campaign, nation building is difficult and expensive. The administration's preference has been to avoid nation-building operations—an understandable predilection in itself. But once the administration made the decision to go to war against Saddam Hussein, it was also obliged to prepare for the foreseeable likelihood of major, postwar nation-building operations—not only for humanitarian reasons, but in order to secure the political objectives for which it had gone to war in the first place.

The Bush administration's early reluctance to plan for Iraq's postwar reconstruction has had serious and deadly consequences. Once Saddam's government was overthrown, a power vacuum was created, and the United States did not initially step in to fill the void. Widespread looting, disorder, and insecurity were the inevitable result. This set the tone for the immediate postwar era. Moreover, because of these insecure conditions, many of Saddam's former loyalists were given the opportunity to develop and pursue a dangerous, low-level insurgency against American forces. The subsequent learning curve within the Bush administration has been steep. By necessity, the president has come a considerable distance toward recognizing how expensive this particular process of nation building is going to be. The approval by Congress of $87 billion for continuing operations in Iraq and Afghanistan is clearly a step in the right direction. Bush has indicated repeatedly that the United States cannot cut and run from its commitments. At the same time, there are disconcerting signs, with American casualties mounting, and the president's reelection looming, that the White House may in fact decide to withdraw American forces from Iraq. Indeed, the administration's latest adjustment seems to be toward a version of Vietnamization: handing over authority to a transitional government in Baghdad, while encouraging Iraq's own police and security forces to take up the greater burden with respect to counterinsurgency operations. In itself, this approach has certain virtues, but if it indicates a comprehensive withdrawal of U.S. resources and personnel from Iraq, then the results will not be benign, either for the United States, or for the Iraqi people. Nation-building operations sometimes fail, even under favorable conditions. But without robust involvement on the part of outside powers, such operations simply cannot succeed. It is an illusion to think that a stable, secure, and democratic Iraq can arise without a significant long-term U.S. investment of both blood and treasure.[29]

The administration responded to the challenge of 9/11 by devising a more assertive, Wilsonian foreign policy. The stated goals of this policy have been not only to initiate "rogue state rollback" but to promote a more open and democratic world order. By all accounts, Bush and his advisors really do believe that 9/11 has offered the United States, in the words of Secretary of Defense Donald Rumsfeld, an "opportunity to refashion the world."[30] The problem is not that the president is departing from a long tradition of liberal internationalism; it is that he is continuing some of the worst features of that tradition. Specifically, in Iraq, he is continuing the tradition of articulating and pursuing a set of extremely ambitious and idealistic foreign policy goals, without providing the full or proportionate means to achieve those goals. In this sense, it must be said, George W. Bush is very much a Wilsonian.

Whatever the immediate outcome in Iraq, America's foreign policy elites are not likely to abandon their long-standing ambition to create a liberal world order. What is more likely, and also more dangerous, is that they will continue to oscillate between various forms of liberal internationalism, and to press for a more open and democratic international system, without willing the means to sustain it.

Under the circumstances, the choice between unilateralism and multilateralism, which currently characterizes public debate over U.S. foreign policy, is almost beside the point. Neither a unilateral nor a multilateral foreign policy will succeed if Americans are unwilling to incur the full costs and risks that are implied in either case. It is impossible to promote the kind of international system that America's foreign policy elites say that they want without paying a heavy price for it. Iraq is simply the latest case in point. Americans can either take up the burden of acting on their liberal internationalist rhetoric and convictions, or they can keep costs and risks to a minimum by abandoning this ambitious interventionist agenda. They cannot do both. They cannot have hegemony on the cheap.

Notes

1. For representative criticisms in this vein, see David C. Hendrickson, "Toward Universal Empire: The Dangerous Quest for Absolute Security," *World Policy Journal,* vol. 19 (fall 2002), pp. 1-10; G. John Ikenberry, "America's Imperial Ambition," *Foreign Affairs,* vol. 81 (September/October 2002), pp. 44- 60; Robert S. Litwak, "The New Calculus of Preemption," *Survival,* vol. 44 (winter 2002), pp. 53-79; and Joseph S. Nye, Jr., *The Paradox of American Power: Why the World's Only Superpower Can't Go It Alone* (New York: Oxford University Press, 2002), pp. 15, 39, 141-63.
2. See Michael H. Hunt, *Ideology and US Foreign Policy* (New Haven: Yale University Press, 1988), pp. 17-18.
3. "Remarks by the President at the 20th Anniversary of the National Endowment for Democracy," Washington, D.C., November 6, 2003, available at www.whitehouse.gov/news/releases/2003/11/iraq/20031106-2.html.
4. For a discussion of various schools of thought in the American foreign policy tradition, see Henry R. Nau, *At Home Abroad: Identity and Power in American Foreign Policy* (Ithaca: Cornell University Press, 2002), pp. 43-59; and Walter Russell Mead, *Special Providence: American Foreign Policy and How It Changed the World* (New York: Knopf, 2001).
5. See Arthur S. Link, *Woodrow Wilson: Revolution, War and Peace* (Wheeling, Ill.: Harlan Davidson, 1979), pp. 72-103.
6. In the former Ottoman Empire, for example, Wilson's initial pronouncements in favor of self-determination had raised hopes for postwar national independence among Arabs, Armenians, Jews, and Turks. At Paris, Wilson even promised a U.S. protectorate over an independent Armenia. Yet the eventual settlement in the region, disguised through the creation of League "mandates," closely resembled a classic sphere-of-influence bargain among Europe's great powers. The one major exception was in Turkey itself, where Kemal Atatürk rallied nationalist forces and ejected foreign troops from the Anatolian heartland. In this way, American promises with regard to Armenia were rendered completely irrelevant, even before the Senate's rejection of the Versailles Treaty. For a lively discussion of the postwar settlement within the Middle East, see Margaret MacMillan, *Paris 1919: Six Months That Changed the World* (New York: Random House, 2002), pp. 347-455.
7. Ray Stannard Baker and William Dodd, eds., *Public Papers of Woodrow Wilson,* (New York: Harper and Brothers, 1925-1927), vol. 5, pp. 341-44.
8. William C. Widenor, *Henry Cabot Lodge and the Search for an American Foreign Policy* (Berkeley: University of California Press, 1980), pp. 298, 331.
9. Baker and Dodd, eds., *Public Papers of Woodrow Wilson,* vol. 5, pp. 352-56.
10. See Warren F. Kimball, *The Juggler: Franklin Roosevelt as Wartime Statesman* (Princeton: Princeton University Press, 1991), pp. 63-81, 107-57.
11. See Melvyn P. Leffler, *A Preponderance of Power: National Security, the Truman Administration, and the Cold War* (Stanford: Stanford University Press, 1992), pp. 8-9, 15-18.
12. As George Kennan put it, "Our first aim with respect to Russia in time of peace is to encourage and promote by means short of war the gradual retraction of undue Russian influence from the present satellite area." See George Kennan, NSC 20/1, "US Objectives with Respect to Russia," August 18, 1948, in Thomas H. Etzold and John Lewis Gaddis, eds., *Containment: Documents on American Policy and Strategy, 1945-1950* (New York: Columbia University Press, 1978), p. 184.
13. See Steven L. Rearden, *History of the Office of the Secretary of Defense: The Formative Years, 1947- 1950* (Washington, D.C.: United States Government Printing Office, 1984), pp. 532-36.
14. See John Lewis Gaddis, *Strategies of Containment* (New York: Oxford University Press, 1982), pp. 202-03, 217-18, 223-25.
15. Ibid., p. 284.
16. Stephen John Stedman, "The New Interventionists," *Foreign Affairs,* vol. 72 (spring 1993), pp. 4-5.
17. Anthony Lake, Assistant to the President for National Security Affairs, at Johns Hopkins University, September 21, 1993, in *Vital Speeches of the Day, 1993,* vol. 60, p. 15.
18. See Karin von Hippel, *Democracy by Force: U.S. Military Intervention in the Post-Cold War World* (New York: Cambridge University Press, 2000).
19. See, for example, in the case of Bosnia, James Gow, *Triumph of the Lack of Will: International Diplomacy and the Yugoslav War* (New York: Columbia University Press, 1997), pp. 208, 218.
20. Daniel L. Byman and Matthew C. Waxman, *The Dynamics of Coercion: American Foreign Policy and the Limits of Military Might* (New York: Cambridge University Press, 2002), p. 143.
21. Governor George W. Bush, "A Period of Consequences," September 23, 1999, The Citadel, South Carolina, available at www.citadel.edu/pao/addresses/pres_bush.html.
22. Presidential debates, October 3, 2000, at Boston, Massachussetts, and October 11, 2000, at Winston-Salem, North Carolina, available at www.foreignpolicy2000.org/debate/candidate/candidate.html and

www.foreignpolicy2000.org/debate/candidate/candidate2.html.

23. For a good exposition of the initially "realist" bent of one of Bush's leading foreign policy advisors, see Condoleezza Rice, "Campaign 2000: Promoting the National Interest," *Foreign Affairs,* vol. 79 (January/February 2000), pp. 45-62.

24. Nicholas Lemann, "Without a Doubt," *The New Yorker,* October 14 and 21, 2002, p. 177.

25. The National Security Strategy of the United States of America (Washington, D.C.: The White House, September 2002), pp. 1, 3-4, 26-28.

26. George W. Bush, "President Discusses the Future of Iraq," February 26, 2003, Washington Hilton Hotel, Washington, D.C., available at www.whitehouse.gov/news/releases/2003/02/iraq/20030226-11.html.

27. George Packer, "Dreaming of Democracy," *New York Times Magazine,* March 2, 2003, pp. 46-49.

28. Anja Manuel and Peter W. Singer, "A New Model Afghan Army," *Foreign Affairs,* vol. 81 (July/August 2002), pp. 44-59.

29. Frederick Kagan, "War and Aftermath," *Policy Review,* no. 120 (August/September 2003), pp. 3-27.

30. "Secretary Rumsfeld Interview," *New York Times,* October 12, 2001.

Colin Dueck is assistant professor of political science at the University of Colorado, Boulder.

From *World Policy Journal,* Winter 2003/2004, pp. 1–11. © 2003 by the World Policy Institute. Reprinted by permission.

Reaganism v. Neo-Reaganism

Richard Lowry

SINCE THE end of the Cold War, conservatives have been at odds over the way forward for America in the world. September 11 and the new American orientation toward preventive defense have united most conservatives in strong support of President Bush, but have not clarified what it is exactly that conservatives believe about American grand strategy. Indeed, the picture has gotten muddier. The *New York Times* and other inartful observers characterize the conservative foreign policy choice as between the unmitigated crusading of a William Kristol or the rejectionist nativism of a Patrick Buchanan. This is a false dichotomy. It elevates flawed splinter schools of thought above the broad conservative foreign policy tradition.

The messianic vision of the neoconservatives and the rejectionist attitude of the paleoconservatives represent dueling fantasies. Neither is truly conservative. Both are impractical, bound to be unsuccessful in protecting America and unlikely to maintain public support. In fact, none of the three major foreign policy schools identified with the right—neo-, paleo-, or realist—fully captures a true conservative foreign policy. That foreign policy, and its major premises and practices, are hidden in plain view in the practical policy of the Bush Administration.

Too Hot, Too Cold and Just Right

THE TERM "neoconservative" has dominated discussion of conservative foreign policy over the last few years primarily because of Iraq. Any supporter of the war has been lumped in with the neocons, a slippery label that is most reliably applied to the sort of idealistic crusading associated with the *Weekly Standard.* It is important to recall that prior neoconservative causes, whether braying against China in the 1990s or supporting John McCain's presidential bid in 2000, were rejected by the conservative mainstream. Iraq was different. Most un-hyphenated conservatives supported the invasion. They did so for a host of strategic and moral reasons, and not just because it was thought Saddam possessed WMD. But neither they nor the broader American public would have supported the war on purely humanitarian grounds, as many of the neoconservatives would have done—something they made clear after WMD weren't found in Iraq. For neocons, digging up mass graves was enough to justify the war.

Herein lies an important difference between neocons and conservatives. Almost all conservatives believe that American power can be a force for good, and they are unashamed about the aggressive use of that power in defense of national interests. The difference is over limits. Neoconservatives appear to believe U.S. military power can be wielded in almost any situation to produce exactly the results they desire, and that it is appropriate to wield it even in interventions with only an attenuated connection to U.S. national interest. As Bill Kristol and Robert Kagan wrote in *Foreign Affairs* in 1996, since "America has the capacity to contain or destroy many of the world's monsters", failing to do so is to endorse "a policy of cowardice and dishonor."

Conservatives are more discriminating. As Charles Krauthammer has noted, an agenda of expanding the zone of open systems must be "targeted, focused and limited"—not a worldwide crusade, but one concentrated "in those regions where the defense or advance of freedom is critical" to vital U.S. interests.[1] Discrimination is the essence of pursuing this project—discrimination about how, where, why and when America is to use its power, especially its military power.

Much of the intra-conservative debate turns on this key question: the malleability of much of the world, and the suitability of the U.S. government as an agent for fundamentally changing it. Conservatives have a strong dose of Reaganite optimism but are also clear-eyed in their view both of human progress and of America's ability to promote liberal values around the world. Since Burke, conservatives have sought just this balance between respect for reality as it exists and the possibilities for change.

Neoconservatism displays impatience at any reminder that the world is not infinitely plastic and that not all problems will break down under the solvent of American power. It assumes a universal admiration for America that does not exist, and it tends to dismiss the desire of local actors to have a say in how a project is carried out. For neoconservatives, liberal democracy can be achieved simply by an American invasion, or a set of sanctions, or a ritual invocation of the policy of "regime change." The government of China will fall as long as the United States doesn't grant it "most favored" trading privileges. Proponents of such free trade are latter-day Neville Chamberlains (never mind that the rest of the world will keep trading with Beijing). Russian President Vladimir Putin will see the advantages of liberalism if

President Bush just scolds enough. And regime change—as much a wish as a policy—is promulgated as the U.S. strategy for every nasty government in the world. Those who are skeptical of this strategy might, according to their rhetorical barbs, have a "casual animus" about U.S. power.

Responding to such skepticism, neoconservatives routinely invoke the experience of Germany and Japan for the proposition that societies can be remade by American power. But those were exceptional cases where the countries were smashed by the United States in total war. Neoconservatives never cite the Philippines at the turn of the century, a host of Latin American countries (where the United States repeatedly intervened with Wilsonian aims in the early 20th century), and the subjects of the humanitarian ventures of the 1990s—Haiti, Somalia and the Balkans. All of them disappointed to varying degrees the ability of the United States to remake them.

Iraq may well avoid joining this litany of frustrations. Despite the success of the January 30 elections, however, Iraq is still a testament to the difficulties of nation-building in a tribal society ravaged by three decades of tyranny. No credible discussion of conservative foreign policy can take place without a serious and honest accounting of post-invasion Iraq, which the neocons have assiduously avoided, except for complaints about insufficient troop levels.

As John Nagl argues in his book, *Counterinsurgency Lessons from Malaya and Vietnam,* the British were quite successful at imperial policing because they were conditioned to accept less than 100 percent victories, had no illusions about the human timber with which they were working, and were always attuned to the idiosyncrasies and practical requirements of the cultures in which they were operating. It was an approach suffused with British empiricism, prudence and realism. These are the exact qualities for which neoconservatives often have a sneering contempt, preferring instead ideological grandiosity and sweeping moral universals.

Linked with this is a tendency to view foreign policy as a domestic political, philosophical and cultural project. Kristol and Kagan have maintained that the

> remoralization of America at home ultimately requires the remoralization of American foreign policy. For both follow from Americans' belief that the principles of the Declaration of Independence are not merely the choices of a particular culture but are universal, enduring, "self evident" truths.

But conservatives have always maintained that young American men should be sent abroad to die and be maimed only if it serves an important national interest, not to remoralize ourselves at home. Nor do they believe that if democracy should fail to take root in Iraq—because of a host of cultural, religious and economic factors—this invalidates the Founding Principles of America's democracy.

SOME OF these points are echoed by the most bitter ideological enemies of the neocons—the so-called paleoconservatives associated with Patrick Buchanan. Yet the paleocons are more flawed. The libertarian-isolationist tradition that the paleocon-

servatives and a few liberals seek to revive was marginalized in post-World War II conservatism from the start and soon died out as a political force. Indeed, the "paleo" in paleoconservatism is designed to obscure the fact that it is a recent ideological creation of post-Cold War politics.

If the "paleo" prefix is bogus, so in many ways is the "conservatism." The Buchananites' hostility to free trade violates the conservative faith in markets. Their belief that if the United States curls up in a defensive crouch, the world will leave it alone is naive, ahistorical and, especially after September 11, discredited. The United States never enjoyed any period of splendid isolation. The list of U.S. interventions prior to the Civil War is extensive; indeed, after the War of 1812, the United States pursued a unilateral policy of pre-emption and hegemony in the Western Hemisphere. Throughout the 20th century, America's responsibilities in the world inevitably grew with its power, and the conservative isolationism of figures such as Senator Robert A. Taft disappeared in the face of the imperative—deeply felt by virtually all conservatives—to confront the Soviet empire.

Finally, the arguments of the paleoconservatives are often tinged with anti-Americanism, or at least with a hostility to American power of the sort associated with the post-Vietnam Left. Some paleocons essentially blamed America and its support for Israel for 9/11. The *American Conservative*—to pick one example at random—ran an article comparing the U.S. intervention in Afghanistan to the Soviet occupation of that country, something that could have been ripped straight from the pages of the left-wing *Nation* (perhaps without the harsh words for the Soviets).

If neither neoconservatism nor paleoconservatism really represents American conservative views on foreign policy, neither does traditional realism. A policy rooted in amoral calculations of power and interest—grand strategies associated with Richelieu, Metternich, Kissinger and others—will never sit comfortably with Americans. The falsity of the core belief of the academic realists, that the internal nature of regimes doesn't matter, is demonstrated before our eyes daily.

Nor, as Burke argued, is clinging mindlessly to the status quo in an ever-changing world true conservatism. George Will, for instance, lodges powerful criticisms against Wilsonianism. But he sometimes seems to take it as a given that undemocratic political cultures are fated to stay undemocratic. This view cannot account for the liberalization of Europe, Latin America and Asia, or indeed for the entire "third wave" of democratization that swept the Second and Third Worlds from the 1980s onwards.

There is no longer any need to have a stale debate on the role of values in American foreign policy. It was settled long ago: They have a central one. That has been the case since Woodrow Wilson, as even Henry Kissinger acknowledges, and has become even more pronounced as the Christian Right—a vital member of the GOP coalition—has taken a greater interest in the world from an idealistic perspective. The question is whether vital distinctions and limits will be ignored as unnecessary, amoral accretions on our national strategy. A foreign policy can be prudent and moral at the same time. Indeed, insofar as prudence creates the conditions for increased success, it will be more moral than an unrealistic but self-consciously moral foreign policy that costs the nation dearly.

As numerous authors have outlined in these pages, this necessarily ties conservative strategy to a kind of realist thinking. The term realism is routinely rendered in sneer quotes in neoconservative commentary, as if nothing could be more contemptible. Neoconservatives maintain that realists are in fact unrealistic, that they systematically underestimate the power of idealism and the possibility of change in the world. There is something to this, but a conservative foreign policy begins with a keen sense of the contours of international reality, of the limits it places upon and the opportunities it holds for American power, and of the local conditions that must guide our actions in any part of the world. Prudence may never make for a rallying cry, but it is indispensable to a successful foreign policy.

A truly realistic foreign policy—and thus a truly conservative one—would be aware of the power of ideals and the necessity of expressing U.S. foreign policy in idealistic terms. It should have imagination and seek to shape the world to our advantage. But it should be prudent, flexible, aware of power relationships and immune to juvenile excess. It might be called "neorealism", or what Krauthammer has termed "democratic realism."

Conservatives and Foreign Policy

SEVERAL BASIC principles guide a conservative foreign policy, grounded in realism and conservative understandings of liberty and the American character. The first is that the best defense is a good offense. Conservatives are realistic about the world and its disappointments and dangers. They know war has always been with us and always will be, and that there are foreign actors who are so evil, intransigent or ambitious that only force will stop them. They are comfortable with wielding power and realize its importance. The Bush Doctrine—of pursuing threats where they originate rather than waiting for an attack—is a sound one for the post-9/11 world and accords with this vein in conservatism.

The second, related to their realism about the world, is a healthy skepticism about government action. If conservatives are believers in the law of unintended consequences at home, they should be believers in it abroad as well. A bombing raid may not bear much relation to a welfare program, but foreign interventions—especially ones more ambitious than simply punishing or defeating a given enemy—will have the same dismaying tendency to go astray and so can never be undertaken lightly as prospective "cakewalks."

This leads to the third bedrock principle: a healthy appreciation for all the instruments by which national power is projected. Conservatives have slipped—partly under the influence of the bullyboy rhetoric of the neocons—into a lazy contempt for diplomacy, allies and multilateral institutions. All are necessary tools in a foreign policy oriented toward the correct goals. All these tools can be grossly inefficient (such as unconditional foreign aid) or maddeningly corrupt (as evident in the UN Oil

for Food scandal), or they can prompt unintended consequences worse than the problems they were created to solve. But the power of these tools and others cannot be dismissed out of hand.

Conversely, many neoconservatives place far too much reliance on the U.S. military—an inspiring faith that stems from admiration of the institution. While American military power is indubitably a force for good, it is important to understand its true strengths and its fundamental purpose—to smash enemies of the United States. To throw combat units into nation-building projects with little or no preparation, as has happened in Iraq, serves neither the end of successfully achieving our policy goals nor the interests of the military as an institution.

The fourth principle is a proper appreciation for the role of democracy in fostering liberty. Democratic elections in Afghanistan and Iraq have been useful—even inspiring—exercises. The Afghan elections provided a boost of legitimacy to the U.S.-favored leader there and served to further isolate Taliban and Al-Qaeda remnants. The January 30 vote in Iraq gave Iraqis a jolt of confidence as they undertook a national project for which they had the chief responsibility—namely, showing up and voting—for the first time in decades. It satisfied the demands of the most powerful player in the country, Ayatollah Ali Sistani, and may have been the only way to create a government with enough legitimacy to navigate the country's religious and ethnic tensions. But, as a general matter, elections by no means guarantee a liberal society.

Liberty is a creature of institutions and culture that must be built slowly over time. Economic liberty is often the precursor of political liberty. Some neoconservatives dismiss this as economic determinism. It is really a core belief of Anglo-American liberalism from Locke onward. Elections without a proper institutional and cultural grounding will not necessarily produce liberty—and in some cases they can be the least important ingredient in it. The rule of law and institutions bolstering nonelectoral facets of constitutional liberalism have as much to do with liberty, prosperity and freedom as electoral democracy, a fact that should increase our patience for reforming authoritarian governments.

Indeed, if a U.S. intervention in a threat-producing region of the world can inspire the creation of unthreatening governments with political and economic systems that are benign versions of the region's norms, that is a perfectly reasonable goal. If the minimal conditions of pluralism can be attained, along with enduring stability (another value neoconservatives blithely dismiss), then we should be satisfied. This is certainly more attainable than a strategy implicitly based on the singular and exclusive legitimacy of American-style democracy.

Finally, any conservative foreign policy must be grounded in American traditions, built on the four schools identified by Walter Russell Mead: the Wilsonians (the crusading idealists), Jacksonians (the bloody-minded nationalists), Hamiltonians (the capitalists) and Jeffersonians (the lead-by-example-only idealists). Jacksonians are ignored at conservatives' peril, since they are such an important part of the conservative coalition, even if one without much in the way of intellectual expression. Their support is crucial for any sustained and difficult military intervention, and they will never support one for purely humanitarian reasons. This is why many of the humanitarian interventions of the 1990s were undertaken without formal congressional support, and why—absent the WMD case—it would have been difficult for Bush to muster support for an invasion of Iraq. It is also why Kristol and Kagan complained in the 1990s that the American public wasn't willing enough to go slay monsters willy-nilly, blaming "[w]eak political leadership and a poor job of educating the citizenry to the responsibilities of global hegemony."

Moreover, in these days of the all-volunteer force, it is the Jacksonians who are wearing the nation's uniform—especially in the combat branches. As military sociologists have noted, with an all-volunteer force, the combat branches of the military are increasingly the NASCAR warriors. These traditional members of America's fighting class do not shrink from sacrifice but want their losses incurred in pursuit of something enduring, important, practically attainable and related to American interests. Conservatives recognize that U.S. strategy is unsustainable if it is based on a Wilsonian elite's interventions that a Jacksonian citizenry will not sustain.

The Reagan Synthesis

So A CONSERVATIVE foreign policy has a sober framework of power, appreciates the imperatives of geopolitics and harbors a guarded optimism about the power of change. It integrates into its fiber conservative notions of political liberty, economic freedom, the role of the state, the power of culture and a realistic appraisal of human nature, as well as sheer pragmatism. It is aggressive in conducting a proactive defense against today's threats and is colored by American exceptionalism, but its application is framed by realism's appreciation for power and its limits.

What would such a foreign policy look like in practice? Ronald Reagan provides a model. His foreign policy was enunciated with a ringing idealism. It was not, however, idealism for its own sake or one applied indiscriminately, but one with a specific purpose and grounded in power politics. It aimed at eroding and defeating a hostile world empire. His means were not mere words, but the sheer weight of U.S. power, augmented in a massive arms build-up designed to spend the Soviets into the ground. All the "tear down this wall" speeches in the world wouldn't have won the Cold War without this exercise in cold-blooded power politics.

If Reagan was willing to give a corrupt authoritarian a shove when the opportunity presented itself (for example, Marcos in the Philippines), he also depended on authoritarian regimes as crucial allies in the Cold War. He was willing to work with the material the international order presented him; he would not allow an unrestrained idealism to get in the way of prudence and necessity; and he understood how progress toward liberalization often occurs. It usually happens gradually, as less-than-savory regimes change over time in reaction to a variety of forces, from the growth of a middle class to the development of a free market to American diplomatic pressure. This practical policy, which had its theoretical foundation in Jeane Kirkpatrick's

"Dictatorships and Double Standards", was condemned at the time by liberals who talked in the same sweepingly idealistic terms used by today's neoconservatives.

Reagan unapologetically called the Soviet Union evil. During the Cold War's endgame, however, he worked diplomatically with its leader—circumstances changed and his policy changed with them. Indeed, Reagan's embrace of Gorbachev in the face of traditional conservative opposition to dealings with communists was a lesson in the entrepreneurial nature of modern conservative thinking. Conservatives do take chances—but not without a cold-eyed appreciation of all the dynamics at hand. If Reagan had a black-and-white worldview, its implementation came in shades of gray.

It is precisely this approach that needs to animate a conservative foreign policy today. A conservative grand strategy will support simple but durable steps towards order and security in many of the world's poorly governed places. It will not resist change and indeed will support policies to quicken it, as Reagan did in Central America and Eastern Europe in the 1980s. But wise conservatives also know that the U.S. military is an imperfect instrument for openly forcing such change on alien populations. They are willing to put American energy behind the effort to promote the emergence of roughly harmonious political and economic systems—rather than asking the U.S. military to create American-style democracies and judging success or failure by that exacting and unrealistic standard.

With a few exceptions, Bush is pursuing this kind of conservative policy. Consider his handling of Russia, which has been prudent and mindful of the limits of U.S. influence over Moscow—although not by any means mindlessly wedded to the status quo. The administration supported the Orange Revolution in Ukraine over Putin's objections. The central organizing theme of Bush's foreign policy—the Bush Doctrine, emphasizing the expansion of liberty abroad and preventive war as a last resort—is correct. The Bush Doctrine reflects a fundamental belief in the goodness of American power and the necessity of its robust assertion around the world. The United States should be proactive in seeking to reshape an international order, especially in the Middle East, that produced the mass murder of 9/11. The expansion of liberty, constitutional liberalism and market-based economic systems will tend, although not inevitably or perfectly, to shape nations that respect the norms of civilized behavior and pose less of a threat to the United States. But the policy of achieving this goal will prudently reflect differing realities in countries from Pakistan to Iran and not one universal moral standard.

In the neocon over-interpretation, however, the Bush Doctrine becomes problematic. Yes, Bush's rhetoric—especially in his second inaugural address—suggests that the American model of democracy has universal validity and applicability. But in its grand sweep, the Bush rhetoric is just that—rhetoric, which he has not allowed to trump pragmatic considerations, whether with regard to Russia, China, the Central Asian republics or Saudi Arabia. Immediately after the inaugural, administration officials were out explaining the obvious—the administration's policy in the real world would remain largely unchanged. But the neocons often seem to take the rhetoric literally, as if the crooked timber of humanity can be straightened and emblazoned with the U.S. Bill of Rights.

It is crucial that the Bush Doctrine succeed. When it has indulged in neoconservative excess, as it has occasionally in its over-optimistic post-invasion approach to Iraq, it has teetered on the edge of failure. It is through Reaganite realism that Bush will navigate the world in a way that protects our interests, expands the zone of decency and makes us safer. For conservatives, this is the way forward for America in the world.

Notes

31. "In Defense of Democratic Realism", *The National Interest* (Fall 2004).

Richard Lowry is editor of *National Review*. He would like to acknowledge the contribution of a co-author who wishes to remain anonymous.

THE EAGLE HAS CRASH LANDED

Pax Americana is over. Challenges from Vietnam and the Balkans to the Middle East and September 11 have revealed the limits of American supremacy. Will the United States learn to fade quietly, or will U.S. conservatives resist and thereby transform a gradual decline into a rapid and dangerous fall?

By Immanuel Wallerstein

The United States in decline? Few people today would believe this assertion. The only ones who do are the U.S. hawks, who argue vociferously for policies to reverse the decline. This belief that the end of U.S. hegemony has already begun does not follow from the vulnerability that became apparent to all on September 11, 2001. In fact, the United States has been fading as a global power since the 1970s, and the U.S. response to the terrorist attacks has merely accelerated this decline. To understand why the so-called Pax Americana is on the wane requires examining the geopolitics of the 20th century, particularly of the century's final three decades. This exercise uncovers a simple and inescapable conclusion: The economic, political, and military factors that contributed to U.S. hegemony are the same factors that will inexorably produce the coming U.S. decline.

INTRO TO HEGEMONY

The rise of the United States to global hegemony was a long process that began in earnest with the world recession of 1873. At that time, the United States and Germany began to acquire an increasing share of global markets, mainly at the expense of the steadily receding British economy. Both nations had recently acquired a stable political base—the United States by successfully terminating the Civil War and Germany by achieving unification and defeating France in the Franco-Prussian War. From 1873 to 1914, the United States and Germany became the principal producers in certain leading sectors: steel and later automobiles for the United States and industrial chemicals for Germany.

The history books record that World War I broke out in 1914 and ended in 1918 and that World War II lasted from 1939 to 1945. However, it makes more sense to consider the two as a single, continuous "30 years' war" between the United States and Germany, with truces and local conflicts scattered in between. The competition for hegemonic succession took an ideological turn in 1933, when the Nazis came to power in Germany and began their quest to transcend the global system altogether,

seeking not hegemony within the current system but rather a form of global empire. Recall the Nazi slogan *ein tausendjähriges Reich* (a thousand-year empire). In turn, the United States assumed the role of advocate of centrist world liberalism—recall former U.S. President Franklin D. Roosevelt's "four freedoms" (freedom of speech, of worship, from want, and from fear)—and entered into a strategic alliance with the Soviet Union, making possible the defeat of Germany and its allies.

World War II resulted in enormous destruction of infrastructure and populations throughout Eurasia, from the Atlantic to the Pacific oceans, with almost no country left unscathed. The only major industrial power in the world to emerge intact—and even greatly strengthened from an economic perspective—was the United States, which moved swiftly to consolidate its position.

But the aspiring hegemon faced some practical political obstacles. During the war, the Allied powers had agreed on the establishment of the United Nations, composed primarily of countries that had been in the coalition against the Axis powers. The organization's critical feature was the Security Council, the only structure that could authorize the use of force. Since the U.N. Charter gave the right of veto to five powers—including the United States and the Soviet Union—the council was rendered largely toothless in practice. So it was not the founding of the United Nations in April 1945 that determined the geopolitical constraints of the second half of the 20th century but rather the Yalta meeting between Roosevelt, British Prime Minister Winston Churchill, and Soviet leader Joseph Stalin two months earlier.

The formal accords at Yalta were less important than the informal, unspoken agreements, which one can only assess by observing the behavior of the United States and the Soviet Union in the years that followed. When the war ended in Europe on May 8, 1945, Soviet and Western (that is, U.S., British, and French) troops were located in particular places—essentially, along a line in the center of Europe that came to be called the Oder-Neisse Line. Aside from a few minor adjustments, they stayed there. In hindsight, Yalta signified the agreement of both sides that they could stay there and that neither side would use force to push the other out. This tacit accord applied to Asia as well, as evinced by U.S. occupation of Japan and the division of Korea. Politically, therefore, Yalta was an agreement on the status quo in which the Soviet Union controlled about one third of the world and the United States the rest.

Washington also faced more serious military challenges. The Soviet Union had the world's largest land forces, while the U.S. government was under domestic pressure to downsize its army, particularly by ending the draft. The United States therefore decided to assert its military strength not via land forces but through a monopoly of nuclear weapons (plus an air force capable of deploying them). This monopoly soon disappeared: By 1949, the Soviet Union had developed nuclear weapons as well. Ever since, the United States has been reduced to trying to prevent the acquisition of nuclear weapons (and chemical and biological weapons) by additional powers, an effort that, in the 21st century, does not seem terribly successful.

Until 1991, the United States and the Soviet Union coexisted in the "balance of terror" of the Cold War. This status quo was tested seriously only three times: the Berlin blockade of 1948–49, the Korean War in 1950–53, and the Cuban missile crisis of 1962. The result in each case was restoration of the status quo. Moreover, note how each time the Soviet Union faced a political crisis among its satellite regimes—East Germany in 1953, Hungary in 1956, Czechoslovakia in 1968, and Poland in 1981—the United States engaged in little more than propaganda exercises, allowing the Soviet Union to proceed largely as it deemed fit.

Of course, this passivity did not extend to the economic arena. The United States capitalized on the Cold War ambiance to launch massive economic reconstruction efforts, first in Western Europe and then in Japan (as well as in South Korea and Taiwan). The rationale was obvious: What was the point of having such overwhelming productive superiority if the rest of the world could not muster effective demand? Furthermore, economic reconstruction helped create clientelistic obligations on the part of the nations receiving U.S. aid; this sense of obligation fostered willingness to enter into military alliances and, even more important, into political subservience.

Finally, one should not underestimate the ideological and cultural component of U.S. hegemony. The immediate post-1945 period may have been the historical high point for the popularity of communist ideology. We easily forget today the large votes for Communist parties in free elections in countries such as Belgium, France, Italy, Czechoslovakia, and Finland, not to mention the support Communist parties gathered in Asia—in Vietnam, India, and Japan—and throughout Latin America. And that still leaves out areas such as China, Greece, and Iran, where free elections remained absent or constrained but where Communist parties enjoyed widespread appeal. In response, the United States sustained a massive anticommunist ideological offensive. In retrospect, this initiative appears largely successful: Washington brandished its role as the leader of the "free world" at least as effectively as the Soviet Union brandished its position as the leader of the "progressive" and "anti-imperialist" camp.

ONE, TWO, MANY VIETNAMS

The United States' success as a hegemonic power in the postwar period created the conditions of the nation's hegemonic demise. This process is captured in four symbols: the war in Vietnam, the revolutions of 1968, the fall of the Berlin Wall in 1989, and the terrorist attacks of September 2001. Each symbol built upon the prior one, culminating in the situation in which the United States currently finds itself—a lone superpower that lacks true power, a world leader nobody follows and few respect, and a nation drifting dangerously amidst a global chaos it cannot control.

What was the Vietnam War? First and foremost, it was the effort of the Vietnamese people to end colonial rule and establish their own state. The Vietnamese fought the French, the Japanese, and the Americans, and in the end the Vietnamese won—quite an achievement, actually. Geopolitically, however, the war represented a rejection of the Yalta status quo by populations then labeled as Third World. Vietnam became such a powerful symbol because Washington was foolish enough to invest its full military might in the struggle, but the United States still lost. True, the United States didn't deploy nuclear weapons (a decision certain myopic groups on the right have long reproached), but such use would have shattered the Yalta accords and might have produced a nuclear holocaust—an outcome the United States simply could not risk.

But Vietnam was not merely a military defeat or a blight on U.S. prestige. The war dealt a major blow to the United States' ability to remain the world's dominant economic power. The conflict was extremely expensive and more or less used up the U.S. gold reserves that had been so plentiful since 1945. Moreover, the United States incurred these costs just as Western Europe and Japan experienced major economic upswings. These conditions ended U.S. preeminence in the global economy. Since the late 1960s, members of this triad have been nearly economic equals, each doing better than the others for certain periods but none moving far ahead.

When the revolutions of 1968 broke out around the world, support for the Vietnamese became a major rhetorical component. "One, two, many Vietnams" and "Ho, Ho, Ho Chi Minh" were chanted in many a street, not least in the United States. But the 1968ers did not merely condemn U.S. hegemony. They condemned Soviet collusion with the United States, they condemned Yalta, and they used or adapted the language of the Chinese cultural revolutionaries who divided the world into two camps—the two superpowers and the rest of the world.

The denunciation of Soviet collusion led logically to the denunciation of those national forces closely allied with the Soviet Union, which meant in most cases the traditional Communist parties. But the 1968 revolutionaries also lashed out against other components of the Old Left—national liberation movements in the Third World, social-democratic movements in Western Europe, and New Deal Democrats in the United States—accusing them, too, of collusion with what the revolutionaries generically termed "U.S. imperialism."

The attack on Soviet collusion with Washington plus the attack on the Old Left further weakened the legitimacy of the Yalta arrangements on which the United States had fashioned the world order. It also undermined the position of centrist liberalism as the lone, legitimate global ideology. The direct political consequences of the world revolutions of 1968 were minimal, but the geopolitical and intellectual repercussions were enormous and irrevocable. Centrist liberalism tumbled from the throne it had occupied since the European revolutions of 1848 and that had enabled it to co-opt conservatives and radicals alike. These ideologies returned and once again represented a real gamut of choices. Conservatives would again become conservatives, and radicals, radicals. The centrist liberals did not disappear, but they were cut down to size. And in the process, the official U.S. ideological position—antifascist, anticommunist, anticolonialist—seemed thin and unconvincing to a growing portion of the world's populations.

THE POWERLESS SUPERPOWER

The onset of international economic stagnation in the 1970s had two important consequences for U.S. power. First, stagnation resulted in the collapse of "developmentalism"—the notion that every nation could catch up economically if the state took appropriate action—which was the principal ideological claim of the Old Left movements then in power. One after another, these regimes faced internal disorder, declining standards of living, increasing debt dependency on international financial institutions, and eroding credibility. What had seemed in the 1960s to be the successful navigation of Third World decolonization by the United States—minimizing disruption and maximizing the smooth transfer of power to regimes that were developmentalist but scarcely revolutionary—gave way to disintegrating order, simmering discontents, and unchanneled radical temperaments. When the United States tried to intervene, it failed. In 1983, U.S. President Ronald Reagan sent troops to Lebanon to restore order. The troops were in effect forced out. He compensated by invading Grenada, a country without troops. President George H.W. Bush invaded Panama, another country without troops. But after he intervened in Somalia to restore order, the United States was in effect forced out, somewhat ignominiously. Since there was little the U.S. government could actually do to reverse the trend of declining hegemony, it chose simply to ignore this trend—a policy that prevailed from the withdrawal from Vietnam until September 11, 2001.

Meanwhile, true conservatives began to assume control of key states and interstate institutions. The neoliberal offensive of the 1980s was marked by the Thatcher and Reagan regimes and the emergence of the International Monetary Fund (IMF) as a key actor on the world scene. Where once (for more than a century) conservative forces had attempted to portray themselves as wiser liberals, now centrist liberals were compelled to argue that they were more effective conservatives. The conservative programs were clear. Domestically, conservatives tried to enact policies that would reduce the cost of labor, minimize environmental Constraints on producers, and cut back on state welfare benefits. Actual successes were modest, so conservatives then moved vigorously into the international arena. The gatherings of the World Economic Forum in Davos provided a meeting ground for elites and the media. The IMF provided a club for finance ministers and central bankers. And the United States pushed for the creation of the World Trade Organization to enforce free commercial flows across the world's frontiers.

While the United States wasn't watching, the Soviet Union was collapsing. Yes, Ronald Reagan had dubbed the Soviet Union an "evil empire" and had used the rhetorical bombast of calling for the destruction of the Berlin Wall, but the United States didn't really mean it and certainly was not responsible for the Soviet Union's downfall. In truth, the Soviet Union and its East European imperial zone collapsed because of popular disillusionment with the Old Left in combination with Soviet leader Mikhail Gorbachev's efforts to save his regime by liquidating Yalta and instituting internal liberalization (perestroika plus glasnost). Gorbachev succeeded in liquidating Yalta but not in saving the Soviet Union (although he almost did, be it said).

The United States was stunned and puzzled by the sudden collapse, uncertain how to handle the consequences. The collapse of communism in effect signified the collapse of liberalism, removing the only ideological justification behind U.S. hegemony, a justification tacitly supported by liberalism's ostensible ideological opponent. This loss of legitimacy led directly to the Iraqi invasion of Kuwait, which Iraqi leader Saddam Hussein would never have dared had the Yalta arrangements remained in place. In retrospect, U.S. efforts in the Gulf War accomplished a truce at basically the same line of departure. But can a hegemonic power be satisfied with a tie in a war with a middling regional power? Saddam demonstrated that one could pick a fight with the United States and get away with it. Even more than the defeat in Vietnam, Saddam's brash challenge has eaten at the innards of the U.S. right, in particular those known as the hawks, which explains the fervor of their current desire to invade Iraq and destroy its regime.

Between the Gulf War and September 11, 2001, the two major arenas of world conflict were the Balkans and the Middle East. The United States has played a major diplomatic role in both regions. Looking back, how different would the results have been had the United States assumed a completely isolationist position? In the Balkans, an economically successful multinational state (Yugoslavia) broke down, essentially into its component parts. Over 10 years, most of the resulting states have engaged in a process of ethnification, experiencing fairly brutal violence, widespread human rights violations, and outright wars. Outside intervention—in which the United States figured most prominently—brought about a truce and ended the most egregious violence, but this intervention in no way reversed the ethnification, which is now consolidated and somewhat legitimated. Would these conflicts have ended differently without U.S. involvement? The violence might have continued longer, but the basic results would probably not h ave been too different. The picture is even grimmer in the Middle East, where, if anything, U.S. engagement has been deeper and its failures more spectacular. In the Balkans and the Middle East alike, the United States has failed to exert its hegemonic clout effectively, not for want of will or effort but for want of real power.

THE HAWKS UNDONE

Then came September 11—the shock and the reaction. Under fire from U.S. legislators, the Central Intelligence Agency (CIA) now claims it had warned the Bush administration of possible threats. But despite the CIA's focus on al Qaeda and the agency's intelligence expertise, it could not foresee (and therefore, prevent) the execution of the terrorist strikes. Or so would argue CIA Director George Tenet. This testimony can hardly comfort the U.S. government or the American people. Whatever else historians may decide, the attacks of September 11, 2001, posed a major challenge to U.S. power. The persons responsible did not represent a major military power. They were members of a nonstate force, with a high degree of determination, some money, a band of dedicated followers, and a strong base in one weak state. In short, militarily, they were nothing. Yet they succeeded in a bold attack on U.S. soil.

George W Bush came to power very critical of the Clinton administration's handling of world affairs. Bush and his advisors did not admit—but were undoubtedly aware—that Clinton's path had been the path of every U.S. president since Gerald Ford, including that of Ronald Reagan and George H.W. Bush. It had even been the path of the current Bush administration before September 11. One only needs to look at how Bush handled the downing of the U.S. plane off China in April 2001 to see that prudence had been the name of the game.

Following the terrorist attacks, Bush changed course, declaring war on terrorism, assuring the American people that "the outcome is certain" and informing the world that "you are either with us or against us." Long frustrated by even the most conservative U.S. administrations, the hawks finally came to dominate American policy. Their position is clear: The United States wields overwhelming military power, and even though countless foreign leaders consider it unwise for Washington to flex its military muscles, these same leaders cannot and will not do anything if the United States simply imposes its will on the rest. The hawks believe the United States should act as an imperial power for two reasons: First, the United States can get away with it. And second, if Washington doesn't exert its force, the United States will become increasingly marginalized.

Today, this hawkish position has three expressions: the military assault in Afghanistan, the de facto support for the Israeli attempt to liquidate the Palestinian Authority, and the invasion of Iraq, which is reportedly in the military preparation stage. Less than one year after the September 2001 terrorist attacks, it is perhaps too early to assess what such strategies will accomplish. Thus far, these schemes have led to the overthrow of the Taliban in Afghanistan (without the complete dismantling of al Qaeda or the capture of its top leadership); enormous destruction in Palestine (without rendering Palestinian leader Yasir Arafat "irrelevant," as Israeli Prime Minister Ariel Sharon said he is); and heavy opposition from U.S. allies in Europe and the Middle East to plans for an invasion of Iraq.

The hawks' reading of recent events emphasizes that opposition to U.S. actions, while serious, has remained largely verbal. Neither Western Europe nor Russia nor China nor Saudi Arabia has seemed ready to break ties in serious ways with the United States. In other words, hawks believe, Washington has indeed gotten away with it. The hawks assume a similar outcome will occur when the U.S. military actually invades Iraq and after that, when the United States exercises its authority elsewhere in the world, be it in Iran, North Korea, Colombia, or perhaps Indonesia. Ironically, the hawk reading has largely become the reading of the international left, which has been screaming about U.S. policies—mainly because they fear that the chances of U.S. success are high.

But hawk interpretations are wrong and will only contribute to the United States' decline, transforming a gradual descent into a much more rapid and turbulent fall. Specifically, hawk approaches will fail for military, economic, and ideological reasons.

Undoubtedly, the military remains the United States' strongest card; in fact, it is the only card. Today, the United States wields the most formidable military apparatus in the world. And if claims of new, unmatched military technologies are to be believed, the U.S. military edge over the rest of the world is considerably greater today than it was just a decade ago. But does that mean, then, that the United States can invade Iraq, conquer it rapidly, and install a friendly and stable regime? Unlikely. Bear in mind that of the three serious wars the U.S. military has fought since 1945 (Korea, Vietnam, and the Gulf War), one ended in defeat and two in draws—not exactly a glorious record.

Saddam Hussein's army is not that of the Taliban, and his internal military control is far more coherent. A U.S. invasion would necessarily involve a serious land force, one that would have to fight its way to Baghdad and would likely suffer significant casualties. Such a force would also need staging grounds, and Saudi Arabia has made clear that it will not serve in this capacity. Would Kuwait or Turkey help out? Perhaps, if Washington calls in all its chips. Meanwhile, Saddam can be expected to deploy all weapons at his disposal, and it is precisely the U.S. government that keeps fretting over how nasty those weapons might be. The United States may twist the arms of regimes in the region, but popular sentiment clearly views the whole affair as reflecting a deep anti-Arab bias in the United States. Can such a conflict be won? The British General Staff has apparently already informed Prime Minister Tony Blair that it does not believe so.

And there is always the matter of "second fronts." Following the Gulf War, U.S. armed forces sought to prepare for the possibility of two simultaneous regional wars. After a while, the Pentagon quietly abandoned the idea as impractical and costly. But who can be sure that no potential U.S. enemies would strike when the United States appears bogged down in Iraq?

Consider, too, the question of U.S. popular tolerance of non-victories. Americans hover between a patriotic fervor that lends support to all wartime presidents and a deep isolationist urge. Since 1945, patriotism has hit a wall whenever the death toll has risen. Why should today's reaction differ? And even if the hawks (who are almost all civilians) feel impervious to public opinion, U.S. Army generals, burnt by Vietnam, do not.

And what about the economic front? In the 1980s, countless American analysts became hysterical over the Japanese economic miracle. They calmed down in the 1990s, given Japan's well-publicized financial difficulties. Yet after overstating how quickly Japan was moving forward, U.S. authorities now seem to be complacent, confident that Japan lags far behind. These days, Washington seems more inclined to lecture Japanese policymakers about what they are doing wrong.

Such triumphalism hardly appears warranted. Consider the following April 20, 2002, *New York Times* report: "A Japanese laboratory has built the world's fastest computer, a machine so powerful that it matches the raw processing power of the 20 fastest American computers combined and far outstrips the previous leader, an I.B.M.-built machine. The achievement… is evidence that a technology race that most American engineers thought they were winning handily is far from over." The analysis goes on to note that there are "contrasting scientific and technological priorities" in the two countries. The Japanese machine is built to analyze climatic change, but U.S. machines are designed to simulate weapons. This contrast embodies the oldest story in the history of hegemonic powers. The dominant power concentrates (to its detriment) on the military; the candidate for successor concentrates on the economy. The latter has always paid off, handsomely. It did for the United States. Why should it not pay off for Japan as well, perhaps in alliance with China?

Finally, there is the ideological sphere. Right now, the U.S. economy seems relatively weak, even more so considering the exorbitant military expenses associated with hawk strategies. Moreover, Washington remains politically isolated; virtually no one (save Israel) thinks the hawk position makes sense or is worth encouraging. Other nations are afraid or unwilling to stand up to Washington directly, but even their foot-dragging is hurting the United States.

Yet the U.S. response amounts to little more than arrogant arm-twisting. Arrogance has its own negatives. Calling in chips means leaving fewer chips for next time, and surly acquiescence breeds increasing resentment. Over the last 200 years, the United States acquired a considerable amount of ideological credit. But these days, the United States is running through this credit even faster than it ran through its gold surplus in the 1960s.

The United States faces two possibilities during the next 10 years: It can follow the hawks' path, with negative consequences for all but especially for itself. Or it can realize that the negatives are too great. Simon Tisdall of the *Guardian* recently argued that even disregarding international public opinion, "the U.S. is not able to fight a successful Iraqi war by itself without incurring immense damage, not least in terms of its economic interests and its energy supply. Mr. Bush is reduced to talking tough and looking ineffectual." And if the United States still invades Iraq and is then forced to withdraw it will look even more ineffectual.

President Bush's options appear extremely limited, and there is little doubt that the United States will continue to decline as a decisive force in world affairs over the next decade. The real question is not whether U.S. hegemony is waning but whether the United States can devise a way to descend gracefully, with minimum damage to the world, and to itself.

Want to Know More?

This article draws from the research reported in Terence K. Hopkins and Immanuel Wallerstein's, eds., *The Age of Transition: Trajectory of the World-System, 1945–2025* (London: Zed Books, 1996). In his new book, *The Paradox of American Power: Why the World's Only Superpower Can't Go It Alone* (New York: Oxford University Press, 2002), Joseph S. Nye Jr. argues that the United States can remain on top, provided it emphasizes multilateralism. For a less optimistic view, see Thomas J. McCormick's *America's Half-Century: United States Foreign Policy in the Cold War and After*, 2nd ed. (Baltimore: Johns Hopkins University Press, 1995). David Calleo's latest book, *Rethinking Europe's Future* (Princeton: Princeton University Press, 2001), cogently analyzes the ins and outs of the European Union and its potential impact on U.S. power in the world.

In 1993, the Norwegian Nobel Committee convened a meeting of leading international analysts to discuss the role and influence of superpowers throughout history. Their analyses can be found in Geir Lundestad's, ed., *The Fall of Great Powers: Stability, Peace and Legitimacy* (Oslo: Scandinavian University Press, 1994), which includes essays by William H. McNeill, Istvan Deak, Alec Nove, Wolfgang J. Mommsen, Robert Gilpin, Wang Gungwu, John Lewis Gaddis, and Paul Kennedy, among others. Eric Hobsbawm offers a splendid geopolitical analysis of the 20th century in *The Age of Extremes: A History of the World, 1914–1991* (New York: Pantheon, 1994). Giovanni Arrighi, Beverly J. Silver, and their collaborators take a longer view of hegemonic transitions over the centuries—from Dutch to British, from British to American, from American to some uncertain future hegemon—in *Chaos and Governance in the Modern World System* (Minneapolis: University of Minnesota Press, 1999). Finally, it is always useful to return to Andre Fontaine's classic *History of the Cold War* (New York: Pantheon, 1968).

FOREIGN POLICY's extensive coverage of American hegemony and the U.S. role in the world includes, most recently, **"In Praise of Cultural Imperialism?"** (Summer 1997) by David Rothkopf, **"The Benevolent Empire"** (Summer 1998) by Robert Kagan, **"The Perils of (and for) an Imperial America"** (Summer 1998) by Charles William Maynes, **"Americans and the World: A Survey at the Century's End"** (Spring 1999) by John E. Rielly, **"Vox Americani"** (September/October 2001) by Steven Kull, and **"The Dependent Colossus"** (March/April 2002) by Joseph S. Nye Jr.

For links to relevant Web sites, access to the *FP* Archive, and a comprehensive index of related FOREIGN POLICY articles, go to **www.foreignpolicy.com**.

Immanuel Wallerstein is a senior research scholar at Yale University and author of, most recently, The End of the World As We Know It: Social Science for the Twenty-First Century *(Minneapolis: University of Minnesota Press, 1999).*

Some Hard Truths about Multilateralism

Jonathan D. Tepperman

Throughout this year's presidential campaign, Democrats, when discussing foreign policy, have inevitably focused on a single theme: the value and benefits of multilateralism. The argument usually surfaced in one of two ways: when the candidates criticized President George W. Bush for acting (in Iraq and elsewhere) as though he didn't care what the rest of the world thought, and when they described how they themselves would conduct U.S. foreign policy if elected.

Retired general Wesley Clark, for example, liked to promise that if he were president, he would use something he called "efficient multilateralism," to "link diplomacy, law, and force [to] achieve decisive results without using decisive force." Former Vermont governor Howard Dean argued that the United States should "set a positive example and work together [that is, multilaterally] to meet the challenges facing the global community in this new century." Sen. John Edwards pledged "[to] lead in a way that brings others to us, not that drives them away." And Sen. John Kerry, the candidate with the most foreign policy experience and ultimately the nominee, told supporters that he would "replace the Bush years of isolation with a new era of alliances," would "work with allies across the world to defend and extend the frontiers of freedom," and would "rally democratic countries to join in a lasting coalition to address the common ills of a new century."

Coalitions, cooperation, alliances—in other words, multilateralism—were very much in the air. And since securing the nomination, Kerry has relentlessly pursued the theme. In April, in his first full-length television interview since winning the nomination, Kerry slammed Bush's "arrogant and ineffective" diplomacy and swore that, if elected, the United States would "formally rejoin the community of nations."

There is something blithe and simplistic about such language, however. Of course, pledging to cooperate with other countries for the greater good of humanity always sounds nice—especially when compared to the way George W. Bush has behaved as president, alienating more friends and allies with less cause than any other American leader in living memory.

The problem with these sorts of vague promises, however, is that they are notoriously hard for presidents to make good on. Multilateralism—which can be loosely defined as acting through alliances and international organizations and obeying the constraints they set—is much harder for presidents to practice than to praise. This has been true even for internationalist-minded Democrats, as Bill Clinton learned the hard way during his own term in office. No matter what a candidate pledges to do during a campaign, once in office, he inevitably finds that there are powerful obstacles—some of them domestic, some of them international, all of them hard to overcome—that make it impossible to pursue a consistently multilateral foreign policy. For, at the end of the day, the United States is not Sweden or even Canada, and although it has often led the internationalist charge—spurring the creation of the League of Nations, the United Nations, NATO, and the Bretton Woods network of international financial bodies— the United States also has powerful isolationist and exceptionalist streaks that reveal themselves at inconvenient moments. Moreover, there are sometimes good reasons why the world's sole superpower has to go it alone—even if Democrats may not like to admit this truth. And that's the case no matter who occupies the Oval Office.

Which is not to say that the United States is destined always to act without regard for the wishes or concerns of its friends and allies; or that American policymakers shouldn't at least *try* to cooperate with friends and allies as much as possible. For one thing, the Bush administration has of late amply demonstrated the costs of aggressive unilateralism. For another, past Democratic presidents have shown that America's unilateralist inclinations can sometimes be overcome, and John Kerry's pledge to "formally rejoin the community of nations" would certainly be a big step in the right direction (even if the details of his promise remain somewhat hazy).

But it's also important to recognize that acting multilaterally is far from easy for the United States; on the contrary, often presidents can do so only through enormous effort.

And even then, the White House is not always successful in convincing the rest of the country to hew to a multilateral path. Fighting for a multilateral foreign policy may therefore not always be worth the struggle. Admitting as much will not make for satisfying campaign rhetoric, but it is a truth Kerry would nonetheless do well to keep in mind.

Domestic Obstacles

The obstacles that make it so difficult for an American president to pursue a consistently multilateral foreign policy fall into two general categories: domestic and foreign. On the home front, the first hurdle to consider is popular opinion—or, to use the historian John Lukacs's more precise term, popular sentiment.[1] At first, this factor might not seem like an obstacle at all since, as supporters of international institutions like the United Nations often point out, a majority of Americans when polled appear to favor such bodies. Indeed, U.S. public support for the United Nations virtually matches that found in far more internationalist-minded countries such as Germany or France. When asked what kind of influence they think the United Nations has on world affairs, a full 72 percent of Americans say "very good" or "somewhat good." This is compared to 79 percent in Germany and 75 percent in France, a negligible difference.[2]

Such polling data, however, paint only part of the picture. For one thing, they fail to show that although Americans feel generally good about the United Nations, they—unlike many Europeans—continue to put greater faith in their own national institutions. Europeans remain traumatized by the memory of the Second World War and the rise of extreme nationalism that preceded it. Reactions to these nightmarish memories linger throughout Europe today, finding expression not only in the Germans' muchdiscussed pacifism but also in a more generalized distrust of "nationalistic" (read also "unilateral") initiatives on the global scene. In terms of international politics, Europeans tend to see legitimacy residing on the supranational level, be it in the European Union or the United Nations.[3]

Americans, on the other hand, are generally proud of their national heritage and far more likely to place their faith in their own country and its institutions. Indeed, a fierce exceptionalist streak runs through many American conservatives and liberals alike; after all, it was a Democrat, Secretary of State Madeleine Albright, who called the United States "the indispensable nation." As the foreign policy theorist Francis Fukuyama puts it, "Americans tend not to see any source of democratic legitimacy higher than the . . . nation-state."[4] Although this difference in transatlantic attitudes may sound academic, the results are anything but. According to a recent poll conducted by the German Marshall Fund, less than half of Europeans surveyed (47 percent) thought it ever justifiable to bypass the U.N. Security Council—even when their nation's vital interests were at stake. By contrast, a majority of Americans (57 percent) approved of bypass-ing the council in a similar situation.[5] Similarly, as Tufts international law professor Michael Glennon has written, "it is hard to imagine any circumstance in which [Americans] would permit an international regime to limit the size of the U.S. budget deficit, control its currency and coinage, or settle the issue of gays in the military. Yet these and a host of other similar questions are now regularly decided for European states by the supranational institutions (such as the European Union and the European Court of Human Rights) of which they are members."[6]

Moreover, while it is true that, in general, most Americans favor the United Nations, they do so only in a vague sort of way. Popular support for the United Nations and other international bodies is quite shallow, and there is no evidence that it affects the way the majority of Americans actually vote in congressional or presidential elections. The same cannot be said for opponents of multilateralism, however, who, though fewer in number, tend to express their bias— for example, by sending that champion of isolationism, Jesse Helms, to the Senate for five terms. As Harvard's Andrew Moravscik points out, the fierce core of U.S. opposition to the United Nations dates from the 1950s, when American conservatives feared that the world body would be used as a wedge to undermine such cherished local institutions as segregation.[7] Although the hot-button issues may have changed since then (conservatives today are much more likely to focus on U.N. support for abortion rights or opposition to the death penalty), the strong distrust among American conservatives for the United Nations, and all it represents, lingers still.

Further complicating the domestic picture, the United States is home to a number of broad interest groups that, while favoring multilateralism in principle, oppose it strongly in one specific area: namely, trade. The most obvious such group is organized labor, whose influence and popular support outweighs the small conservative core that opposes multilateralism across the board. Although the labor lobby is agnostic on many issues relating to multilateralism, it fiercely opposes the expansion of free trade through multilateral bodies such as the World Trade Organization (WTO). Two recent examples of such opposition were big labor's fight against the passage of the North American Free Trade Agreement (NAFTA) in the early 1990s, and its attempts to prevent Presidents Bill Clinton and George W. Bush from lowering textile tariffs through the WTO. Both of these efforts were ultimately unsuccessful. But even in defeat, labor proved too powerful to ignore, as both Clinton and Bush learned. In 2002, according to a study by the Center for Responsive Politics, organized labor contributed $90 million to political candidates (only big business spent more). And money is only part of the picture; according to the Rutgers economist Leo Troy, the value of big labor's in-kind assistance (which includes volunteers' time, favorable press in union newsletters and journals, and organizational help) to candidates for the White House and Congress this year could exceed $300 million.[8]

The protectionist labor movement is especially hard for Democrats to ignore, since it gives money disproportionately to Democratic politicians: in 2002, Democrats received 94 percent of labor's campaign contributions. Democratic presidents have on occasion managed to face down big labor—as Clinton did when he got the Senate to ratify NAFTA. But such bruising victories can be Pyrrhic. After Clinton signed NAFTA in 1993, for example, organized labor refused to campaign enthusiastically for the Democrats in the following year's congressional elections. Labor union voters dropped from 19 percent of the electorate in 1992 to 14 percent two years later.[9] This drop contributed to the sweeping Republican upset that made Newt Gingrich speaker of the House of Representatives.

Institutional Obstacles

In addition to opposition from the general public and special interest groups, any president who tries to pursue an unabashedly multilateralist foreign policy will quickly discover that the particular structure of the U.S. government—and of entrenched opposition to multilateralism in certain sectors of it—makes such an agenda even more difficult.

Consider, first, the military. Perhaps no other American institution has proved so unified in its opposition to key aspects of multilateralism in recent years—or so effective in influencing Washington in this regard. Although the uniformed brass tolerate certain forms of multilateral cooperation, such as NATO (perhaps because that organization is always led by an American general), it is dead set against others, as shown by two recent examples: the battles over the 1997 Landmine Convention and, the following year, over the International Criminal Court (ICC). The Clinton administration started out enthusiastically supporting both ventures; indeed, the ICC was in large part an American initiative. In both cases, however, the Pentagon soon made its opposition clear, arguing that both treaties failed to take into account America's unique role and position in the world. Landmines, the Pentagon insisted, were essential to protecting American peacekeepers in places such as the Korean Peninsula. And the ICC, the generals warned, was dangerously vague and exposed American military personnel serving abroad to the constant risk of politically motivated prosecutions. Clinton ultimately caved in to military pressure on both counts, refusing to sign the landmines ban and making no effort to get the ICC Treaty ratified by the Senate. Even if the next Democratic president proves more willing (or able) to stand up to pressure from his military advisers, much of the military's leadership is likely to remain implacably opposed to multilateral initiatives and missions that other countries more readily participate in—be it nation building or peacekeeping operations under U.N. command.

Moreover, no matter how many combat medals the next president may have won, they will do him little good in battling a U.S. Senate expected to remain in Republican hands. Under either party, the Senate is an institution that can prove unpredictable and uncooperative when it comes to foreign policy initiatives that appear to constrain U.S. sovereignty—not least because a simple majority isn't enough to get a treaty ratified (the constitution stipulates a two-thirds majority). This provision allows a minority of senators (just 34) to block any treaty, and it has spelled the death of major multilateral initiatives before (most famously, the ratification of the Versailles Treaty and the League of Nations Covenant in 1920). In fact, according to Andrew Moravscik, this two-thirds requirement "is a threshold higher than in nearly all other advanced industrial democracies, which generally ratify international treaties by a legislative majority.[10]

Furthermore, given that representation in the Senate is not based proportionally on population figures, the minority of senators who can block passage of a particular treaty often represent only a tiny percentage of the American public. According to Norman Solomon, a fellow of the media watchdog group Fairness and Accuracy in Reporting, "the 2000 Census found that 10 states—California, Texas, New York, Florida, Illinois, Pennsylvania, Ohio, Michigan, New Jersey, and Georgia—had an aggregate population of 152 million people. [Yet] they get the same representation in the U.S. Senate"—and hence exercise the same influence—"as the 8.3 million people who live in the 10 least-populated states."[11] Making matters worse, the clubbish rules of the Senate allow an individual senator (especially the powerful chairman of the Senate Foreign Relations Committee) to keep a bill from ever coming to a vote in the first place. Even once a bill is released from committee, it can still be blocked by a single senator, anonymously, or stalled by means of a filibuster. As a result, getting most American voters to support a multilateral measure is never enough. According to Moravscik, during the 1950s, more than 100 million Americans endorsed the passage of the Genocide Convention, yet this groundswell was insufficient to secure the measure's approval until 1986.[12] What all this means for the next Democratic president is that without control of the Senate, it will be difficult to reverse the course set by the Bush administration and all but impossible to ratify any major new multilateral treaties or conventions. In fact, as Moravscik notes, "the Senate has never ratified an international human rights treaty (even with reservations) when Democrats held fewer than 55 seats."[13]

Friends and Allies

As if the domestic obstacles weren't enough, America's foreign friends and allies often behave in ways that make multilateralism difficult to sell, even by a president well disposed to the idea. Part of the problem grows from the enormous power disparity between the United States and all other countries. Washington's unprecedented preponderance (at least in terms of hard power) has been so widely noted as to have become something of a truism. Nonetheless, it is worth pointing out yet again just a few of the vital statistics. Not only does the United States have, by a wide margin, the world's largest economy; its military budget also surpasses those of its nearest seven competitors combined (the amount allotted for research and development alone exceeds the entire military budget of any of its European allies). As is also well known, the United States boasts the largest army and air force in the world. But as *Newsweek*'s Fareed Zakaria has pointed out, it also has the second largest air force—the U.S. Navy's. In fact, America's control of the skies is now literally absolute and unchallenged. Not even the famed Royal Navy at the height of British power enjoyed such absolute supremacy.

Perhaps inevitably, other countries—including some of Washington's old friends—have grown progressively more nervous about this enormous imbalance. Thus France's former foreign minister, Hubert Védrine, famously announced in 1998 that France could not "accept . . . a politically unipolar world," and went on to explain, "that is why we are fighting for a multipolar one." His successor, Dominique de Villepin, publicly declared his preference for something he called "cooperative multipolarity," and his boss, Jacques Chirac, has opined that "any community with only one dominant power is always a dangerous one and provokes reactions." Moreover, such wariness toward American power seems to be shared by the European public as a whole. According to a 2003 poll, only 5 percent of French citizens and 10 percent of Europeans overall thought "the United States should remain the only superpower."[14]

This kind of nervousness (and resentment) all but guarantees that European countries will more than occasionally refuse to cooperate with, or take orders from, Washington—no matter who sits in the White House, and regardless of the intrinsic merit of particular U.S. policies. What makes true multilateral cooperation even less likely in the near term is the fact that, as recent polls suggest, Europeans no longer view the world and its problems the same way Americans do. Here another truism bears repeating: ever since September 11, most U.S. citizens have viewed the planet through the lens of the war on terror and their own national security concerns. Even after the Madrid bombings, many Europeans remain less focused on security, and those who are focused on security still tend to favor a less confrontational approach. Add to this major differences of opinion on such issues as regime change in pursuit of democratization, the Arab-Israeli conflict, and the question of Islamic fundamentalism, and it becomes more and more evident how hard a multilateralist U.S. foreign policy will be to achieve.

To add to an already messy situation, some of the United States' best friends sometimes seem to act without regard for America's peculiar sensitivities and responsibilities as the world's sole superpower and, for over 50 years, its global peacekeeper. Countries like Canada, the Netherlands, and others have at times pushed the internationalist agenda too far, too fast. The United States,

with 37,000 soldiers stationed on the firing line in the Korean Demilitarized Zone (DMZ), could be forgiven for continuing to favor the use of landmines, at least in some specific situations. Similarly, with a total of 350,000 troops posted abroad, Washington's squeamishness about the ICC was not entirely surprising. Foreign advocates of both treaties should have worked harder to satisfy legitimate American concerns: in the case of the ICC, by defining more specifically the crime of "aggression" and by building in special safeguards for U.S. peacekeepers; and, in the case of the landmines ban, by carving out an exception for the Korean DMZ. These examples suggest that even an American president who *wants* to pursue a multilateralist foreign policy won't always find cooperative partners abroad.[15]

Consider one final example: Belgium's passage of a universal jurisdiction law in 1993. This legislation allowed the prosecution in Belgian courts of crimes committed outside the country, even if neither the perpetrators nor the victims were Belgian. Such a measure, if carefully constructed, could have become a powerful tool for stamping out offenses, such as war crimes, that are otherwise hard to prosecute. Indeed, in 2001, the Belgian law led to the conviction of four Rwandans complicit in the 1994 genocide. But the Belgian measure was written so loosely that it also allowed for complaints to be filed against former president George H. W. Bush, Vice President (and former secretary of defense) Dick Cheney, Secretary of State (and former chairman of the Joint Chiefs of Staff) Colin Powell, and retired general Norman Schwarzkopf—all for their roles in the first Gulf war. Such frivolous, politically motivated complaints played directly into the fear that expanding the reach of international justice too quickly would expose American nationals to special risks. Washington responded by pressuring Brussels to repeal the law, even threatening at one point to relocate NATO headquarters. Belgium eventually buckled, repealing the statute on August 1, 2003. The only parties who profited from this fiasco were those guilty of real human rights violations, since it will now be easier for them to evade prosecution.

A Recipe for Success

All of these obstacles may make it seem unlikely that whoever becomes president in 2005 will be able to steer the country down a more cooperative path. Indeed, it's important to acknowledge that the sort of foreign policy that John Kerry is currently promoting—one relying heavily on the United Nations and other forms of international cooperation—will be hard to follow at times. However, the hurdles are not impossible to overcome—if a president decides it is truly worth the effort.

Were Kerry to become president next January, he could improve his chances of securing international cooperation by simply avoiding some of the worst mistakes Bush has made as president, mistakes Bush himself seems not to have learned from. In an act of unintended prophesying during the 2000 presidential debates, Bush warned Al Gore that "if we're an arrogant nation, they'll resent us," and told him that the United States should therefore act as a "humble partner in coalitions" instead of "go[ing] around the world and say[ing], 'This is the way it's got to be.'" Of course, after winning the election, Bush went on to do exactly what he warned against, thereby eloquently proving his point. Long before the war in Iraq, in his first days in office, Bush worried foreign friends, competitors, and allies alike by appointing fire-breathing isolationists to key diplomatic posts. With such officials in place, Bush then began to turn his back on the cooperative politics pursued by all of his postwar predecessors. His administration immediately embarked on a process of rejecting or withdrawing from a panoply of treaties it found inconvenient, such as the Comprehensive Test Ban Treaty, the Kyoto Protocol on climate change, the Biological Weapons Convention, and the ICC charter (which the Bush administration publicly "unsigned"—a heretofore unknown gesture of contempt).

Building on its unilateralist momentum, the White House then publicly announced a strategy of preemptive war and wide-ranging regime change in its 2002 National Security Strategy—thereby needlessly making explicit a power all American presidents have held implicitly. In that document, the Bush administration also declared that it would act to prevent the emergence of any powerful competitor—another needlessly provocative statement.

Since then, the White House has at times publicly humiliated its allies, as it did when it waved off NATO's initial offer of support in the days after 9/11, or subsequently, when it banned Canada, France, Germany, and Russia from postwar reconstruction contracts in Iraq due to their opposition to the war (the Canadian ban was subsequently reversed).

Publicly renouncing such policies could be very helpful. Symbolism is enormously important in foreign policy, and John Kerry—a fluent French-speaker, schooled in Switzerland, whose father was a diplomat and whose African-born (of Portuguese parentage) wife speaks five languages—has a good chance of improving on Bush's often abrasive style.

On substance, switching course will not mean sacrificing U.S. interests; for example, rather than rejecting problematic treaties, President Kerry could try to renegotiate them. Of course, this would require reengaging in the kind of patient diplomacy Bush has scorned but that both Republicans and Democrats have practiced in the past; and here again, with his pledge to work through the United Nations and with allies, Kerry would have a good chance of succeeding. To ensure he does, if elected he should immediately start sending U.S. officials abroad to make America's case to other countries and their publics directly, rather than trying to do so from Washington, as his predecessor has. He should return to hosting state dinners and observing other diplomatic niceties that the Bush administration dropped. The post of U.N. ambassa-

dor should be restored to cabinet rank (Bush downgraded it in 2001), which would show the world that Washington takes the United Nations—whatever its flaws—seriously.

The United States should also push to improve cooperation on matters of real concern to its European and other partners. Technical fixes could be found to secure U.S. participation in the ICC and the Landmine Convention (indeed, the Bush administration recently announced that it will begin modifying its landmines to make them less dangerous to civilians). Similarly, welcoming international participation in the reconstruction of Iraq (as Bush has belatedly been forced to do) could start to heal some of the wounds left by Washington's unilateral decision to go to war there. Having flubbed the diplomacy leading up to the war (and lest we think that a true coalition was impossible, one should remember that Bush's father managed to get over 30 countries, including France and Syria, on board for *his* Iraq war), Washington should have early on offered Europe and the United Nations a real role there. This would have allowed the United States to share the burden for reconstruction and mollified continental egos that had been badly bruised by the Security Council debate.

Such measures, however, might not be sufficient to build a truly multilateral foreign policy since the next president will still have to overcome the internal obstacles discussed above. Here too, however, there is room for improvement over the current administration. Past presidents—notably Franklin D. Roosevelt, Harry Truman, and Bill Clinton—have shown that major multilateral initiatives can sometimes be successfully accomplished, despite domestic skepticism, if the White House tries hard enough.

Probably the most famous example of a Democratic president managing to secure the passage of a big new multilateral measure is Truman's campaign for ratification of the U.N. Charter, an effort New York University's Thomas Franck has described as "one of the most dramatic examples of hard-sell hucksteering in twentieth-century politics."[16] In order to ensure that the United Nations avoided the fate of the League of Nations 25 years before, Truman launched a massive, multipronged blitz. To secure bipartisan congressional support, the White House involved key senators from both parties—including the Republican Arthur Vandenberg, an influential former isolationist—in the U.S. delegation that was sent to San Francisco to hammer out the charter. To get the public on board, Washington funded a major advertising campaign. The administration also enlisted everyone it could to stump for the treaty, and when it was finally ready for ratification, Truman presented it to the Senate personally—just the sixth time a president had ever done so. When the Senate finally voted three weeks later, the treaty was approved overwhelmingly, 89 to 2.

More recently, Bill Clinton used a similarly multipronged strategy to secure passage of NAFTA in November 1993 and the payment of past U.N. dues by the United States in December 2000. In both instances, Clinton faced stiff opposition: in the case of NAFTA, from the labor movement and protectionists in both parties, and in the case of U.N. dues, from Sen. Jesse Helms and other isolationist Republicans in Congress.

The deal worked out on U.N. dues was particularly audacious, since it forced Clinton to secure the agreement both of hostile Republicans and of the leery United Nations itself. As a condition for payment, the White House and its U.N. ambassador, Richard Holbrooke, had first to get the United Nations to agree to lower the annual U.S. contribution—a condition that had been set the year before by Congress. Amazingly, despite the strong anti-Americanism that had spread throughout the international body in previous years, Holbrooke and Clinton succeeded, a feat that, according to one former staffer on the U.S. delegation, was analogous to "Bill Gates, in response to an IRS enforcement action on back taxes owed, agree[ing] to pay up only if the IRS agreed to lower his tax bracket . . . regardless of what he earned."[17]

Washington managed this trick by using a complex combination of tactics. Like Truman in 1945, Clinton brought key Republicans (in this case Helms) into the negotiations. Holbrooke also lobbied Helms and other key congressmen tirelessly, traveling from New York to Washington at least once a week for over a year. This charm offensive eventually paid off; as another American staffer reported, many of the Republican members of Congress were intensely flattered by the attention, "having never before had a foreign policy discussion with a cabinet member."[18] Holbrooke even invited the Senate Foreign Relations Committee to New York, where Helms met with members of the U.N. Security Council. Meanwhile, the Clinton administration tried hard to meet some of the conservatives' demands, such as regaining a U.S. seat on the U.N. budget committee and getting Israel included for the first time in one of the organization's regional caucuses. And to ensure that the United Nations finally agreed to lower U.S. dues by more than $170 million a year, the U.S. mission embarked on a campaign of relentless "retail diplomacy": individually lobbying the representatives of virtually every member state.

The result was a historic compromise, and one that stands in stark opposition to other, more anemic, initiatives such as over the ICC Treaty, which Clinton claimed to support but never lobbied for, and which he quietly signed (but did not submit to the Senate for ratification) as he was about to leave office on New Year's Eve 2000. When Clinton and Truman staked their personal prestige on a bipartisan campaign and used their bully pulpit to support it, they often succeeded; when their efforts were halfhearted, as were Clinton's with the ICC, they failed.

This last point should serve as a caution. It highlights just how much effort is required for a president to convince the American people and the chaotic U.S. government to support multilateral cooperation. Yes, Herculean efforts sometimes do succeed. But such battles must be chosen wisely, for no administration will have the capital

necessary to win every foreign policy fight it picks. Although much can be done to improve on the record of the current administration, multilateralism can never be taken as a given, no matter what party or president occupies the White House. Cooperation can and should improve, but it will not always be possible, even for a well-disposed Democratic president. The sooner John Kerry recognizes this truth, the better will be his chances of governing effectively if he is elected in November.

Notes

1. John Lukacs, *Outgrowing Democracy: A History of the United States in the Twentieth Century* (Lanham, Md: University Press of America, 1984), p. 263. Lukacs, borrowing from Walter Bagehot, distinguishes between "public opinion" and "popular sentiment." The former term refers to "the opinion of the more-or-less educated classes," i.e., the opinion makers, whose thinking is disseminated by newspapers (and now television). "Popular sentiment," meanwhile, refers to the thinking of the masses, or what Bagehot called "the opinion of bald-headed men at the back of the omnibus." My thanks to Nicholas X. Rizopoulos for directing me to this work.
2. "Global Attitudes: 44-Nation Major Survey (2002)," Pew Center for People and the Press.
3. Of course, Europeans are not monolithic in their support for multilateralism, as the German scholar Joachim Krause points out. See his "Multilateralism: Behind European Views," *Washington Quarterly*, vol. 27 (spring 2004), pp. 48-50.
4. Francis Fukuyama, "The West May Be Cracking," *International Herald Tribune*, August 9, 2002.
5. "Transatlantic Trends 2003," Project of the German Marshall Fund and the Compagnia di San Paolo, p. 15.
6. Michael J. Glennon, "Why the Security Council Failed," *Foreign Affairs*, vol. 82 (May/June 2003), p. 21.
7. Andrew Moravscik, "The Paradox of U.S. Human Rights Policy," in *American Exceptionalism and Human Rights*, ed. Michael Ignatieff (Princeton: Princeton University Press, forthcoming), p. 38.
8. Author's conversation with Troy, May 10, 2004.
9. Sean Paige, "How Powerful Are Visions in Politics?" *Insight on the News*, November 9, 1998, p. 36.
10. Moravscik, "Paradox of U.S. Human Rights Policy," p. 31.
11. Norman Solomon, "No Media Interest in a Basic Matter of Democracy," Media Beat (www. fair.org/media-beat/), May 9, 2002.
12. Moravscik, "Paradox of U.S. Human Rights Policy," p. 25.
13. Ibid., p. 29.
14. "Transatlantic Trends," p. 9.
15. As Joachim Krause and others have pointed out, such disagreements between the United States and its allies can be self-perpetuating: "The more that European governments, particularly France and Germany, continue to use international organizations such as the Security Council and international law to check alleged U.S. hyperpower, the more Washington will circumvent international organizations, disregard international law, and look for unilateral ways or for

'coalitions of the willing,' no matter which party controls the White House and Congress" ("Multilateralism: Behind European Views," pp. 54-55).

16. Thomas M. Franck, *Nation Against Nation: What Happened to the U.N. Dream and What the U.S. Can Do About It* (Oxford: Oxford University Press, 1985), p. 7.

17. Suzanne Nossel, "Retail Diplomacy: The Edifying Story of UN Dues Reform," *The National Interest,* no. 66 (winter 2001/02), p. 96.

18. Derek Chollet and Robert Orr, "Carpe Diem: Reclaiming Success at the United Nations," *Washington Quarterly,* vol. 24 (autumn 2001), p. 11.

Jonathan D. Tepperman is senior editor at Foreign Affairs *magazine.*

UNIT 2

The United States and the World: Regional and Bilateral Relations

Unit Selections

Key Points to Consider

- Construct a list of the top five regional or bilateral problems facing the United States. Justify your selections. How does this list compare to one that you might have composed 5 or 10 years ago?

- What is the most underappreciated regional or bilateral foreign policy problem facing the United States? How should the United States go about addressing it?

- How much weight should the United States give to the concerns of other states in making foreign policy decisions? Should we listen to some states more than others? If so, who should we listen to?

- What should the United States expect from other states in making foreign policy decisions?

- Looking 5 years into the future, what do you expect to be the most important regional or bilateral issue facing the United States?

- What is the major complaint other states have about U.S. foreign policy today? How should the United States respond to this complaint?

Student Website

www.mhcls.com/online

Internet References

Further information regarding these websites may be found in this book's preface or online.

Inter-American Dialogue (IAD)
   http://www.iadialog.org

Political Science RESOURCES
   http://www.psr.keele.ac.uk/psr.htm

Russian and East European Network Information Center
   http://reenic.utexas.edu/reenic/index.html

World Wide Web Virtual Library: International Affairs Resources
   http://www.etown.edu/vl/

Possession of a clear strategic vision of world politics is only one requirement for a successful foreign policy. Another is the ability to translate that vision into coherent bilateral and regional foreign policies. What looks clear-cut and simple from the perspective of grand strategy, however, begins to take on various shades of gray as policymakers grapple with the domestic and international realities of formulating specific foreign policy. This will be particularly true in seeking the support of others in pursuing one's foreign policy goals. Cooperation will often come at a price. That price may be as simple as increased access to U.S. officials or it may carry very real military and economic price tags. It may take the form of demands for American acquiescence to the foreign or domestic policies of others.

No single formula exists to guide the Bush administration in constructing a successful foreign policy for dealing with other states and organizations. Still, it is possible to identify three questions that should be asked in formulating a foreign policy. First, what are the primary problems that the United States needs to be aware of in constructing its foreign policy toward a given country or region? Second, what does the United States

want from this relationship? That is, what priorities should guide the formulation of that policy? Third, what type of "architecture" should be set up to deal with these problems and realize these goals? Should the United States act unilaterally with selected allies or by joining a regional organization?

Each succeeding question is more difficult to answer. Problems are easily cataloged. The challenge is to distinguish between the real and imagined ones. Prioritizing goals is more difficult because it forces us to examine critically what we want to achieve with our foreign policy and what price we are willing to pay. Constructing an architecture is even more difficult because of the range of choices available and the inherent uncertainty that the chosen plan will work.

The readings in this section direct our attention to some of the most pressing bilateral and regional problem areas in American foreign policy today. The first readings in this unit examine U.S. relations with Russia. "Exploiting Rivalries: Putin's Foreign Policy," asserts that the core element of Russia's foreign policy toward other countries is that of playing rivals off against one another in order to maximize Russian influence. The next essay,

"The United States and Russia in Central Asia," argues that cooperation between Russia and the United States is needed if stability in this region is to be realized. The third reading examines U.S. relations with Europe. In "America as European Hegemon," Christopher Layne sees U.S.-European security relations as being competitive rather than complementary in nature. Now as in the past, the U.S. wants to be the dominant European power. The next section examines U.S. foreign policy toward Asia. "China's Response to the Bush Doctrine" chronicles China's recent foreign policy toward the United States and what it may mean for other Asian states and the United States. The last essay in this section, "Japan: America's New South Korea?" looks at the issue of how much can and should Japan do to provide for its own security. It also looks at the consequences of various answers for the United States.

The final set of readings examines the complex issues of dealing with the South. "The U.S. and Latin America through the Lens of Empire," feels that the window of opportunity for a true hemispheric partnership has passed and that relations have reverted back to a more conflictual pattern. In "Libya: Who Blinked and Why," George Joffe looks at the factors that led Libya to renounce its weapons of mass destruction program. He rejects the Bush administration's argument that it was linked to the new strategy of preemption. The concluding essay, "Darfur and the Genocide Debate," reviews the history of the conflict and the international and domestic politics of invoking the term "genocide" in fashioning a response to the tragic events taking place there.

Because of the central importance of Iraq and the Persian Gulf to American foreign policy today, essays on these topics can be found in their own section at the conclusion of this volume. They look at a complex array of issues including past U.S. foreign policy toward Iraq, current and future security concerns, the effectiveness of economic sanctions against Iraq, the future of Saudi Arabia, and Iran's nuclear ambitions.

Exploiting Rivalries: Putin's Foreign Policy

> "Russian foreign policy-makers seem convinced that playing both sides against the middle with other nations is a clever way to advance Moscow's interests. It may take many more foreign policy setbacks before they are persuaded otherwise."

MARK N. KATZ

Like previous Russian leaders—whether czarist, Soviet, or post-Soviet—President Vladimir Putin is determined to see Russia acknowledged as a great power. Indeed, many Russians across the country's political spectrum share this goal. There is, however, a serious obstacle in the path to achieving it: Russia's diminished military and economic strength. That strength underlay czarist and Soviet Russia's ability to act and be acknowledged as a great power. Today, Russia's ability to credibly threaten the use of force abroad has been undermined by its inability to defeat Chechen rebels within its own borders.

Of course, the fact that Russia no longer is regarded as a threat by most nations (except some of its neighbors) raises the possibility that Moscow can get what it wants through persuasion and cooperation. Moscow's post-Soviet experience, however, has taught it that good relations with Russia are not sufficiently important to most other states that they will alter their policies to accommodate Russian interests. Neither feared as a threat nor valued as a friend, Russia has often found itself simply ignored—much to the chagrin of both the Putin administration and the Russian public generally.

Putin appears to have found a solution to this problem. He has strived to exploit situations in which Moscow, despite its diminished circumstances, can affect the balance between opposing sides on a given issue, thus providing one side or even both an incentive to court Russia. Securing such a position can deliver not just tangible economic benefits for Moscow, but also the gratification that comes with being courted, as well as the self-image of Russia as a great power that this feeds. Of course, Russia is not the only country, nor is Putin the only Russian leader to attempt to exploit rivalries

between other states. Putin, however, has made this strategy the centerpiece of Russian foreign policy.

But how successful has the Russian leader been in pursuing this diplomacy? And what has Moscow actually gained by attempting to exploit rivalries between others? A look at the various areas in which Russia has tried this approach shows it has yielded far less than Moscow anticipated.

THE IRAQI OIL GAME

Well before Putin came to power, Moscow saw Iraqi-American hostility as a golden opportunity for Russia to exploit. With the cooperation of Soviet President Mikhail Gorbachev, stiff international economic sanctions were imposed on Iraq after its 1990 invasion of Kuwait. Although Iraqi President Saddam Hussein was undoubtedly displeased that Moscow, a once-staunch ally, had cooperated with Washington against him in the UN Security Council, his regime soon after the war over Kuwait began negotiating with several Russian firms lucrative oil development contracts that would come into effect once sanctions were lifted. Baghdad thereby provided Moscow with an incentive to seek repeal of the Security Council's sanctions while Saddam was still in power. Moscow, in fact, did repeatedly call for the lifting of the sanctions regime, albeit without success because the United States and Britain used their veto power in the Security Council to block the move. Even under sanctions, Baghdad managed to favor Russian firms when it came to signing oil development agreements under the Security Council imposed "oil for food" program that allowed Iraq to use oil sale revenues only for domestic "humanitarian" purposes.

This practice continued after Putin became president at the end of 1999. Beginning in late summer 2002, however, it became increasingly difficult for Moscow to exploit Iraqi-American hostility after the Bush administration made clear that it sought Saddam's ouster. At this point, the question that concerned Moscow was whether the oil development contracts Russian firms had signed (or initialed, negotiated, or just discussed) with Saddam's regime would be honored after his downfall. Moscow sought assurances both from Washington and American backed Iraqi opposition groups on this score, but they said that only a future Iraqi government could decide this. Further, Saddam became angry about Moscow's making these overtures. So he canceled the one major contract that a Russian oil firm—Lukoil—had actually signed to pump oil from Iraq's West Qurna field, which is believed to contain 15 billion barrels of oil.

Lukoil has insisted that Saddam's regime did not have a legitimate reason to cancel its contract, and that it remains valid. But neither the United States nor the Iraqi government has confirmed this. Lukoil, for its part, has threatened to sue any other company awarded a production contract for West Qurna. On March 9, 2004, the Iraqi oil ministry signed a contract allowing Lukoil to explore West Qurna, but not to extract oil from it. At the end of June 2004—when a new Iraqi interim government came into being—Lukoil's president said that his company would start producing oil in Iraq in 2005, but it is unclear whether the Iraqi government has reached an agreement to allow this to happen.

What Moscow had sought both from Saddam's regime and from Washington was certainty that Lukoil would retain the West Qurna contract even if regime change took place in Iraq. Having received no such certainty, it now faces the very task it had wanted to avoid: obtaining the new regime's permission for Lukoil to exploit West Qurna. Lukoil may yet succeed in operating the field, if only because neither the new Iraqi government nor other oil companies want to deal with the legal hassle Lukoil has threatened to create. But if Lukoil does get its way, Iraqi resentment over Lukoil's and Moscow's behavior in this matter may limit Baghdad's willingness to let Lukoil or other Russian firms develop Iraq's other proven but undeveloped oil fields.

GAMING THE IRAQ WAR

Russia was not alone in opposing a US-led intervention in Iraq. France, Germany, and many other countries did as well. French and German opposition offered Putin an opportunity to align Moscow with the impeccably democratic governments of two of the three most important West European states. However, while France opposed an American- led intervention against Iraq unless UN inspectors found incontrovertible evidence of an Iraqi weapons of mass destruction program, and Germany opposed war even if they did, Russia's opposition was far less categori-

cal. Beginning about six months prior to the intervention, Moscow signaled Washington that it would drop its opposition to a Security Council resolution authorizing the use of force against Iraq—for a price.

Accounts of what Moscow demanded included recognition of Russia's economic interests in Iraq (especially oil contracts and debt repayment). Some reports also said Moscow wanted Washington to drop its objections to Russian aid to the Iranian nuclear energy program and to grant Moscow a free hand to intervene in Georgia's Pankisi Gorge (a region where Moscow claimed many Chechen rebels had found refuge). At the same time, Moscow hoped that its alignment with France and Germany would lead those two countries to make certain concessions to Russia, including a halt to their criticism of Russian human rights violations in Chechnya and acceptance of visa-free travel for Russian citizens between Russia and its Kaliningrad exclave after Lithuania joined the European Union (and adopted its immigration policies regarding non-EU citizens). Some Russian commentators also hoped that the schism between Washington and "Old Europe" (as US Defense Secretary Donald Rumsfeld dubbed France and Germany) had become so deep that both sides would need Moscow to mediate between them.

> *Moscow has long recognized Iranian-American hostility as an opportunity for Russia to sell atomic energy technology and weaponry to Tehran.*

In the end Putin did not obtain any of the concessions he had hoped to gain, either from the United States or from France and Germany. Washington intervened in Iraq without conceding to any of Moscow's demands. And France and Germany declined to compensate Russia for siding with them against the United States. The EU and France have continued to criticize Russian policy in Chechnya. And the only concession made on the Kaliningrad issue was to call the papers that Russians must obtain an "expedited travel document" instead of a visa. Neither the Bush administration nor the governments of "Old Europe" called on Moscow to act as a mediator.

AIDING IRAN'S NUCLEAR PROGRAM

Another conflict that Putin has sought to exploit is between Iran and the United States. Moscow has long recognized Iranian-American hostility as an opportunity for Russia to sell atomic energy technology and weaponry to Tehran. During a more cooperative period of US-Russian relations in 1995, Washington and Moscow reached a secret agreement (signed by Vice President Al Gore and Prime Minister Viktor Chernomyrdin) whereby Russia agreed to limit its military and nuclear cooperation with Iran in exchange for US support for the Russian space program. But in late 2000, at a more acrimonious time in US-Russian relations, Putin renounced the Gore-Chernomyrdin agreement. Partly to assert Russia's independence from the United States and partly to earn money from Iran, the Putin administration indicated it would hasten the completion of the atomic energy reactor it was building for Iran, and expressed a willingness to sell additional reactors as well.

In response to Washington's concern that Tehran might divert spent fuel from its Russian-built nuclear reactors to fabricate nuclear weapons, Moscow publicly parroted Tehran's claims that the Iranian nuclear energy program was for peaceful purposes only and was in full compliance with International Atomic Energy Agency (IAEA) safeguards. Privately, the Putin administration indicated that it was willing to make a deal: Russia would end its assistance to the Iranian nuclear program in return for compensation.

Washington thought it had made just such a deal with the 1995 Gore-Chernomyrdin agreement, whereby the removal of US government obstacles to Russia's launch of communications satellites using American technology was seen as compensation to Russia for limiting its sales of nuclear and military technologies to Iran. Putin's abrogation of the Gore-Chernomyrdin agreement raised doubts that Moscow would honor any other compensation arrangement. Moreover, Putin seemed unwilling or unable to curb the ambitions of Russia's atomic energy agency to sell nuclear reactors to Iran—something the agency saw as vital to its very survival given the dearth of other customers for these products. Finally, as Iran appeared to be inching closer and closer toward being able to build a nuclear weapon, even an end to Russian atomic energy assistance to Iran seemed unlikely to prevent this from happening. Compensating Moscow to halt its nuclear assistance to Tehran appeared increasingly pointless to Washington.

While some Russian commentators have expressed concern about Iran's acquiring nuclear weapons, Putin administration officials insist that Iran cannot do this. Some have even claimed that Washington is not worried about this either, but wants Russia to stop selling nuclear reactors to Iran so that American firms can.

And yet, despite Iran's seeming dependence on Russia for the sale of nuclear reactors and conventional weaponry, Putin's government has been unable to get much of what it wants from Tehran. In an ongoing dispute over the delimitation of the oil-rich Caspian Sea, for example, Tehran has not accepted the "modified median line" proposed by Russia, Azerbaijan, and Kazakhstan that would give Iran 13 percent of the Caspian. Iran has insisted on a 20 percent share—even though it had only 11 percent of the Caspian Sea during the Soviet era.

In addition, as of mid-2004, Tehran had not signed an agreement to return spent fuel to Russia that Moscow says must occur if it is going to provide the uranium to operate the nuclear reactor it is building. Press reports indicate that such an agreement might be signed this fall. Although Russia hopes to build up to five more reactors in Iran, Tehran

insists that it will not sign contracts for further construction until the first reactor is completed (there have been numerous delays).

Instead of being able to exploit Tehran's dependence on Moscow to extract concessions from Iran, the Putin administration appears fearful that pressuring Iran on issues of concern to Moscow (not to mention Washington) could result in the Russian atomic energy industry's failure to secure contracts for the additional nuclear reactors it hopes to build for Iran.

KYOTO IN THE BALANCE

Putin also has sought international advantage in negotiations over the Kyoto climate treaty. The decision by the Bush administration and the Republican-controlled Senate not to ratify the agreement has provided Russia with extraordinary leverage over the treaty's fate. The Kyoto treaty will take effect only if the industrial nations that were responsible for 55 percent of greenhouse gas emissions in 1990 have ratified it by 2008. So far, the treaty has been ratified by nations—including Japan, Canada, and members of the EU—that produced 44 percent of the 1990 emissions levels. (The United States produced 21 percent.) Because Russia has an emissions share of 17 percent, its ratification alone could bring the treaty into effect. Aware of this, the Putin administration has sought to exploit Russia's position as the country that determines Kyoto's fate.

The treaty requires that the ratifying industrial nations reduce output of certain emissions to below the levels they were producing in 1990. But it allows states producing over their quota to purchase emissions credits from states producing under theirs. In addition, countries (or companies) producing over their quotas can invest in projects that cut greenhouse gases elsewhere, with the resulting reductions positively affecting the quota of the investing country. Because Russian greenhouse gas emissions have dropped by nearly a third since 1990 (as a result of economic decline—not greater environmental cleanup efforts), Russia would have a massive amount of spare emissions credits to sell and could be an attractive destination for foreign investors seeking credit from projects that cut Russian emissions.

The Putin administration was not satisfied with the potential for making money that ratifying the Kyoto treaty offered. Instead, it wanted guarantees from the EU, Japan, and Canada that they would purchase credits from—or make investments in—Russia in the amount of $3 billion annually. The three refused. Indeed, the EU in particular made clear that it was displeased by this form of bargaining. Putin, after first indicating that Russia would ratify the Kyoto treaty, now raised the possibility in September 2003 that Russia might not do so.

If these tactics were a ploy to pressure the Europeans into meeting Moscow's demands for fear of the treaty's not otherwise coming into effect, they backfired. Instead of giving in to Moscow's demands, the EU made its approval for Russian admission into the World Trade Organization conditional on a pledge that Russia would ratify the Kyoto treaty. Putin himself delivered the pledge at the EU-Russian summit in May 2004. The Russian Duma (the legislative body that must actually ratify the treaty) has not yet acted on it, and Moscow may still attempt to extract "guarantees" from the EU. But in this case it appears the EU has more leverage over Russia than vice versa. For if Moscow does not ratify the treaty by 2008 (when it will lapse if it has not yet gone into effect), the emissions credits and incentives to invest in the Russian energy sector created by Kyoto will not materialize.

OIL PIPELINE POLITICS

Russia's oil riches have created an opportunity to play off China and Japan against each other. Both China and Japan seek to reduce their dependence on oil imports from the volatile Middle East by purchasing oil from Siberia. Because Siberia does not appear to have enough oil to satisfy both China and Japan, a competition between them has emerged over which Siberian oil pipeline route Russia will build. Putin administration machinations and a dispute between two Russian oil companies have complicated the competition. Although there are numerous Russian oil companies, many of which have been privatized, the state-owned (and often slow and inefficient) Transneft exercises monopoly control over the construction and operation of oil pipelines in Russia. Privately owned Yukos, Russia's largest oil company, sought to break this monopoly by building a pipeline that would carry oil from fields it owned in eastern Siberia to Daqing, a city in China's northeastern interior.

> *While the cost of playing games with Beijing over Siberian oil export routes is not yet clear, it is certain that an annoyed China will impose some cost on Russia.*

As this deal was being finalized, the Japanese government proposed that Russia build a pipeline from eastern Siberia to Nakhodka on Russia's Pacific coast. This route would be twice as long (and two to four times more expensive) than Yukos's proposed pipeline to Daqing. But the Japanese argued that the Nakhodka route would benefit Russia more because oil piped there could be exported by sea to many different countries (including both Japan and China), whereas the Daqing route would make purchases of oil through that pipeline dependent on China alone.

Although Tokyo offered to buy all the oil from the Nakhodka route and to provide low-interest loans to cover the cost of its construction, Russian Prime Minister Mikhail Kasyanov indicated in April 2003 that it was the Daqing route that would be built. The following month, Yukos signed an agreement to sell oil to China from the Daqing route, which it expected to complete in 2005. But as the Putin administration turned against Yukos (both in retaliation for the political

challenge that its chief, Mikhail Khodorkovsky, posed to the president and possibly as a means for Putin supporters to seize Yukos's assets for themselves), completion of the Daqing route looked less and less likely.

In September 2003, the Russian Ministry of Natural Resources indicated that it would issue a negative assessment of the Daqing pipeline route on environmental grounds (it also had environmental objections to the Nakhodka pipeline route). On a visit to Beijing later that month, Prime Minister Kasyanov informed his Chinese hosts that construction of the Daqing pipeline would be "postponed." Shortly thereafter, Japan offered a beefed up package for the Nakhodka route, including $5 billion in financing to support pipeline construction and $2 billion for Siberian oil field development. Since then, press coverage indicates that Transneft will build the Nakhodka pipeline route, although Moscow will not make a final decision until the end of 2004.

A desire to exploit Sino-Japanese rivalry over export routes has not been the sole factor in the Putin administration's decision making on this issue; Transneft's interest in retaining its pipeline monopoly and Putin's vendetta against Yukos chairman Khodorkovsky also have played a role. Still, the existence of Sino-Japanese competition for Siberian oil certainly pushed Tokyo to provide very generous financial incentives in an attempt to induce Moscow to build the Nakhodka route.

On the other hand, the Putin administration irritated Beijing by derailing the deal for the Daqing pipeline route after it had been agreed to. And Beijing is in a position to impose some costs on Russia. China's decision in January 2004 to impose anti-dumping tariffs on Russian steel (announced as the Russian foreign minister was arriving in Beijing) was seen as clear retaliation for Moscow's back-tracking on the Daqing pipeline deal. Beijing has also revived its efforts to have an oil pipeline built from Kazakhstan to China's western Xinjiang region. Whatever oil China buys from Kazakhstan would represent lost sales for Russia.

THE SCORECARD

How well has Putin's policy of attempting to exploit rivalries between others worked? There have been some positive results. In Iraq Russia gained the promise of oil deals in the summer of 2002 just as the Iraqi-American crisis was heating up. Its international image may have been burnished as Germany and France and America and Britain courted Russia in the lead-up to the US-led invasion of Iraq. Moscow also appears to have prompted Japan to up the financial ante in the rivalry over where a Siberian oil pipeline should be built.

Often, however, Putin's attempts to exploit rivalries have produced negative results for Russia. Saddam canceled the Lukoil contract for the West Qurna field because Moscow was seeking commitments from Washington and the Iraqi opposition to honor the contract if Saddam was overthrown. The US-led Coalition Provisional Authority did not agree to restore it, nor has the Iraqi interim government done so yet. Despite Iran's dependence on Russia for completion of a nuclear reactor, Tehran has made no concessions to Moscow on the division of the Caspian Sea, and has not yet signed contracts for additional reactors or for the return to Russia of spent fuel from the one reactor Moscow is building. Not only did Moscow fail in its attempts to elicit guarantees that it would receive $3 billion annually from the EU in return for ratifying the Kyoto treaty, but the EU made its approval for Russian admission into the World Trade Organization conditional on a pledge from Putin that Russia would ratify Kyoto. And while the cost of playing games with Beijing over Siberian oil export routes is not yet clear, it is certain that an annoyed China will impose some cost on Russia.

A more general problem associated with attempting to exploit rivalries between other countries is that the other countries resent this approach. They may make some concessions to Moscow to get it to change its behavior. But if the Putin administration continues to play both sides off against each other, other governments may conclude that making concessions to Moscow does not buy them anything—hence concessions are not worth making. When one or both sides to an exploited rivalry decides there is nothing to be gained from acceding to Russia's wishes, then the Putin administration looks weak for setting forth demands that are rejected or ignored. And when this happens, Putin's ultimate goal of having Russia acknowledged by others as a great power becomes increasingly elusive.

Putin's efforts to seek advantage in international rivalries appear to have produced more losses than gains for Russian foreign policy. Yet it is doubtful that his administration will abandon this approach. Even though it has resulted in important setbacks, Russian foreign policy-makers seem convinced that playing both sides against the middle with other nations is a clever way to advance Moscow's interests. It may take many more foreign policy setbacks before they are persuaded otherwise.

MARK N. KATZ *is a professor of government and politics at George Mason University.*

Reprinted with permission from *Current History* Magazine (October 2004, pp. 337-341). © 2004 by Current History, Inc

The United States and Russia in Central Asia: Uzbekistan, Tajikistan, Afghanistan, Pakistan, and Iran

by Fiona Hill

I. Overview

Before 1991, the states of Central Asia were marginal backwaters, republics of the Soviet Union that played no major role in the Cold War relationship between the USSR and the United States, or in Soviet Union's relationship with the principal regional powers of Turkey, Iran, and China. But, in the 1990s, the dissolution of the Soviet Union coincided with the re-discovery of the energy resources of the Caspian Sea, attracting a range of international oil companies including American majors to the region. Eventually, the Caspian Basin became a point of tension in U.S.-Russian relations. In addition, Central Asia emerged as a zone of conflict. Violent clashes erupted between ethnic groups in the region's Ferghana Valley. Civil war in Tajikistan, in 1992–1997, became entangled with war in Afghanistan. Faltering political and economic reforms, and mounting social problems provided a fertile ground for the germination of radical groups, the infiltration of foreign Islamic networks, and the spawning of militant organizations like the Islamic Movement of Uzbekistan (IMU). The IMU first sought to overthrow the government of President Islam Karimov in Uzbekistan, later espoused greater ambitions for the creation of an Islamic caliphate (state) across Central Asia, and eventually joined forces with the Taliban in Afghanistan. With the events of September 11, 2001 and their roots in the terrorist groups operating in Afghanistan, Central Asia came to the forefront of U.S. attention.

II. Central Asia: Together but Divided

Central Asia now poses a particular set of challenges for American policy, not least because the U.S. had no history of engagement with the region until the 1990s and thus suffers from a serious lack of expertise in government as well as in academia. In addition, although the Central Asian states occupy a single, shared geographic sphere, they cannot now, in fact, be approached as a single entity. Over the last ten years of independence, the political divisions between and among the Central Asian states have hardened. The borders the states inherited from the USSR in 1991 were created on the principle of divide and rule from Moscow. Without Moscow to play the role of arbiter, these borders have become illogical, contested boundaries—fracturing ethnic groups, rupturing trade and communication routes, and breaking economic and political interdependencies. At the same time, the borders have remained porous to illicit trade, including weapons and drugs smuggling from Afghanistan, and the spread of infectious diseases like HIV/AIDS.

Central Asia's regional context has also become particularly complex since the collapse of the USSR. With the retreat of Russian influence, the states find themselves at the nexus of a number of interlocking regions: Russia and Eurasia, the Middle and Near East, South Asia, and Asia more broadly. Central Asia is simultaneously a buffer zone and a transit area among these regions. Ethno-linguistic and religious groups are spread across the regions, with Russia, Iran, China and Afghanistan sharing groups with Central Asian states, and Turkey representing the western extension of one of Central Asia's broader cultural spheres. Thus, in looking at Central Asia's external security, economic and political environment, *all* the neighboring states have to be factored in as an element in the region's future. In the context of the U.S. war on terrorism, Central Asia's linkages with Afghanistan, Iran, and Pakistan, as well as Russia, have been dramatically underscored.

Finally, the last ten years has also seen the economic, political and military involvement of new states in Central Asia. Northeast Asian countries—China, Japan, Korea—have now become engaged in the region. China has put a particular priority on relations with Central Asia to foster the development and stabilization of its vast western province, Xinjiang. Beijing also sees the region as a potential market, a source of energy and other natural resources, and as a communications bridge to Iran and the Middle East. Japan has become the largest donor country to Central Asia and, like China, sees the region—if it is stabilized and developed—as a potential market, source of raw materials, and bridge to the Middle East. And Korea has a more intimate relationship thanks to the distinct Korean populations deported there under Stalin, who have now become an influential social, political and economic component in Kazakhstan and Uzbekistan. Although China, Japan, and Korea, have only begun to make their presence felt, and their impact on trade and other regional issues has not yet been so substantial, in a sense Central Asia is rapidly becoming the heartland of Asia.

III. What are American Interests in These Countries Since September 11?

In spite of the construction in 2002 of bases in Central Asia to support the military campaign in Afghanistan, the primary U.S. interest in Central Asia is not *strategic*. Central Asia's importance to the United States is not as a bulwark against regional powers such as Russia, China, or even Iran. Nor is it to protect American commercial concerns in the exploitation of Caspian energy resources. The primary American interest is in *security*, in preventing the "Afghanicization" of Central Asia and the spawning of more terrorist groups with transnational reach that can threaten the stability of all the interlocking regions and strike the United States.

As a result, in Central Asia, America's focus is now on creating strong security ties with the states—building on military-military contacts established in the late 1990s—and on securing long-term access agreements to regional bases and military facilities, which can be used to respond to current and future security threats in Afghanistan. However, the primary goal for U.S. policy must also be to enhance Central Asia's *development* not just its military role. Like Afghanistan, if they are to transform themselves from potential breeding grounds for transnational terrorists into viable, stable states, the Central Asian countries must liberalize economically and democratize politically.

IV. What are Russian Interests?

Russia's interests in Central Asia are strikingly similar to those of the United States. Central Asia has lost its former importance to Russia as a military buffer zone—first between the Russian and British Empires, and then between the USSR and U.S. client states in Afghanistan and Pakistan, and between the USSR and China. After the Soviet Union's collapse, Russian troops were withdrawn from all the Central Asian states apart from Tajikistan and some token forces on the Kazakhstan and Kyrgyzstan borders with China.

Today, Russia's paramount concern is also one of security. Russia's own territory has been threatened by the spillover from Afghanistan through Central Asia of Islamic militancy, terrorism, and drug trafficking. Indeed, from the beginning of his presidency in January 2000, Russia's President, Vladimir Putin,

pushed the idea of a concerted campaign against terrorism with American as well as European leaders. He was one of the first to raise the alarm about terrorist training camps in Afghanistan, and to warn of linkages between these camps and well-financed terrorist networks operating in Europe and Eurasia. In addition, Russia actively supported the Northern Alliance in its struggle with the Taliban in Afghanistan. In December 2000, Moscow joined Washington in supporting United Nations sanctions against the Taliban, and later appealed for additional sanctions against Pakistan for aiding the Taliban—all a precursor to cooperation with the United States in the war against terrorism after September 11.

Russia's other major interest in the region is in Central Asian energy development, with a new focus on gas as markets expand in Europe and Asia. Together, Russia, Iran, and the Central Asian states hold more than half of world gas reserves. Gas is not as mobile as oil and is destined for regional rather than world markets. Retaining a major role in Central Asian gas production and export is a key issue for Russia's energy industry. Energy analysts doubt that Russia can both meet its domestic demand and growing ambitions for gas exports in the coming decades without having access to and influence over the flow of Central Asian gas.

In addition, Moscow seeks the restoration of Soviet-era communications and trade infrastructure between Russia and Central Asia, and some capacity for increasing Russian private sector investment in the region beyond the energy sector. In line with this interest, Russia has initiated a major project to revive and revitalize the former North-South transportation corridor from Russian Baltic ports down the Volga River, across the Caspian to Central Asia and Iran, and from there to Pakistan and India. In the Soviet period, this served as a major freight route and an alternative to the transportation of goods from Europe to Asia through the Mediterranean and Suez Canal.

All of this makes for a primary focus on economic rather than military and strategic issues for Russia in the region and, therefore, an increased interest in Central Asia's stability and development.

V. What are the Development Challenges in Central Asia?

American and Russian interests in the stability of Central Asia are challenged by the extreme domestic fragility of the states. Independence has not been kind to Central Asia. The transition from the Soviet command economy and authoritarian political system has been much more complex and difficult than anticipated. The Central Asian states were the poorest and least developed in the USSR and had to begin almost from scratch in their development in the 1990s. In losing Moscow as the center of gravity, the states lost crucial subsidies for budgets, enterprises and households, inputs for regional industries, markets for their products, transportation routes, and communications with the outside world—much of which was filtered through the Soviet capital.

The World Bank estimates that as a result of these losses, between 1990–1996, the Central Asian states saw their economies decline by 20–60% of GDP. Thanks to extensive borrowing from international financial institutions, reforms in the 1990s also saddled regional states with high and unsustainable debt burdens. Landlocked, resource-poor Tajikistan and Kyrgyzstan have fared particularly badly. A staggering 70–80% of their populations have now fallen beneath the poverty line, which puts them among the poorest of the developing countries. Soviet-era attainments in health, education, infrastructure, and industrial development have gradually eroded. As a result of this decline and deprivation, there has been a massive exodus of ethnic Russians and highly-skilled members of indigenous ethnic groups from Central Asia.

In addition, in the last decade, the Central Asian states have largely failed to develop effective post-Soviet state institutions. The legitimacy of their governments remains weak and has not been bolstered by democratic elections. As a result, governments have resorted to authoritarian, Soviet-era methods to retain control of the levers of the state—stifling opposition, clamping down on dissent, harshly cracking down on political manifestations of Islam, and frequently violating political freedoms and abusing human rights. In sum, the prospects for long-term economic and social stability in Central Asia are uncertain.

Before the events of September 11, 2001, there was a growing realization that the accumulation of challenges in Central Asia—especially given the escalating crisis in Afghanistan—demanded attention. But despite these concerns and ten years of development community involvement and engagement in the region, Central Asia was low down the priorities of the United States and other governments. Even for Japan, as the leading bilateral donor in Central Asia, its preeminence was largely the result of the disinterest of others rather than a major priority on the part of the government in Tokyo. In the 1990s, there was no real vision for the regions in world capitals, and no sense of their interaction with issues of global consequence. This changed with the terrorist attacks on the United States and the realization that civil war and acute state failure in Afghanistan had facilitated them.

Within the region, the fate of Uzbekistan is of particular concern. Uzbekistan is the most strategically located of the Central Asian states, with the largest population and the most significant military capabilities and resources, but it has also been a source of regional tension and a logjam for regional development. In the 1990s, a clamp-down on Islamic groups in response to acts of terrorism and militant activities led to the closure of mosques, a ban on political opposition movements, and arrests of practicing Muslims. This forced groups underground and increased support for insurgencies and extremists. In addition, Uzbekistan has had water and territorial disputes with all its neighbors and has used energy exports as a lever to pressure Tajikistan and Kyrgyzstan to make concessions. It has begun to mine its borders against militant incursions, further rupturing communication routes from Tajikistan and Kyrgyzstan. And, domestic economic crisis has become the *status quo*. Through a mixture of currency and exchange rate controls, state orders for its two main export commodities, cotton and wheat, and the good fortune of being self-sufficient in energy, Uzbekistan has muddled along for several years. It has stagnated economically

and politically, but defied expectations of collapse and refused to open up and deregulate its economy.

With pressure on Tashkent from the U.S. and other international donors in 2002, it seems that Uzbekistan is now contemplating renewed IMF and World Bank programs and a new phase of the macro-economic reforms. Progress in economic reform, an improvement in its economic performance, the removal of currency controls, and increased readiness to deal with regional issues in a cooperative manner would have major benefits for all of Central Asia. However, there is also a serious risk of increased domestic social dislocation, deprivation, and destabilization from new reforms, which could have disastrous implications for Uzbekistan's neighbors.

VI. What are the Prospects for Cooperation Between the United States and Russia in Central Asia?

The U.S. campaign in Afghanistan, its assault on Taliban forces including the IMU, and its military presence in regional bases, has vastly improved the security situation in Central Asia. President Putin and other Russian leaders, as well as the governments of Central Asia, have welcomed American action in Afghanistan, although some in Russian military circles are anxious about the prospects of long-term U.S. engagement on Russia's southern borders. The positive trajectory of overall U.S.-Russian relations fixed at the May 2002 summit meeting between Presidents Bush and Putin in Moscow, and consolidated in subsequent meetings and agreements during the May Russian-NATO summit, and the G8 summit in June 2002, has increased prospects for cooperation between the United States and Russia on a number of issues, including Central Asia.

Indeed, in spite of the decline of its own military influence in Central Asia, Russia remains indispensable to the region's future. Central Asian populations are dependent on Russia for temporary and migrant employment, remittances, and energy subsidies, while Russia is still the primary market for Central Asian goods. To tackle the roots of domestic fragility and prevent Central Asia from becoming a terrorist haven like Afghanistan, the United States will have to work with Russia. Although increased U.S. and international attention to Central Asia has brought additional resources for assistance, international aid will still remain limited and insufficient to cover all pressing development needs. Political interventions will be essential and several critical regional issues will require close cooperation between the United States and Russia, including tackling drug trafficking and HIV/AIDS, promoting energy development, and restoring trade and communications routes.

In the 1990s, Central Asia became the primary conduit for heroin trafficking from Afghanistan to Europe. This has now spawned a huge intravenous drug use problem in Russia, Ukraine, and Iran, and seen the rapid increase of HIV infection and AIDS extending back along the drug routes themselves into Central Asia. Efforts by regional governments to tackle the problem were stymied by the continuation of civil war in Afghanistan and direct linkages between militants and the drug trade. Programs to eradicate heroin production and trafficking, as part of long-term reconstruction efforts in Afghanistan, will require the full cooperation of Russia and all the neighboring states affected. For Russia, drug trafficking, drug use and HIV/AIDS have become a particular concern and security threat. A recent World Bank study of HIV, for example, notes that Russia has the fastest growing rate of new infection in the world, and estimates that by 2020, Russia will have more than 5 million people infected and face a 10.5 percent loss in GDP.

Energy development is seen as key to Central Asia's economic future and Kazakhstan, Turkmenistan, and Uzbekistan all have considerable oil and gas reserves. Gas is of increasing importance, but Central Asian fields are poorly situated for European and Asian markets and a lack of pipeline infrastructure has constrained the states' efforts to become independent producers and exporters. All existing export pipelines run through Russia, and international energy companies have failed to make the same inroads into regional gas production as they have in Caspian oil. In the 1990s, a series of ambitious international projects to transport Central Asian gas to world markets—from Kazakhstan to China, from Turkmenistan across the Caspian to Azerbaijan and Turkey, and, again, from Turkmenistan across Afghanistan to Pakistan and India—all eventually ran out of steam. In 2002, Russia promoted an Eurasian Gas Alliance to coordinate gas production, guarantee long-term purchases of Central Asian gas for Russia's domestic market, and continue to feed Central Asian gas through Russian export pipelines. Russia's energy industry plays the dominant role in Central Asian gas and Russia's participation is ultimately unavoidable and essential in any projects—U.S. or otherwise—to develop the region's energy potential.

Likewise, Russia is key to restoring trade and communications, and to transforming Central Asia into a route for licit rather than illicit trade between Europe and Afghanistan and South Asia. Projects for transporting gas from Turkmenistan and the broader Caspian Basin across Afghanistan to South Asia, which were precluded by the instability in Afghanistan, could one day be revived in the context of a broader effort to restore and improve road, rail and other transportation and communication links. The future restoration of Central Asia's links with India and Pakistan, which were also ruptured through war in Afghanistan opens up the possibility of access to Pakistani and Indian ports as well as markets for Central Asian goods.

Given Moscow's ongoing interest in reviving the North-South freight transportation corridor, Russia can play a particularly important role in developing infrastructure and bringing the landlocked Central Asian countries into the global marketplace. Here, the United States could also play a role by encouraging and assisting Russia in the development of this route as a complement to the East-West transportation routes from Central Asia across the Caspian, to the Caucasus and the Black Sea, promoted by the U.S in the 1990s. While the East-West route became a focus of early competition between America and Russia, the development of a North-South route that binds Central Asia to Europe and Asia could just as easily become a vehicle for cooperation.

Without cooperation between the U.S. and Russia, the prospects for stability in Central Asia are fairly slim. A renewal of competition will undermine both countries efforts to ensure their security in the region.

America as European Hegemon

Christopher Layne

As THE WISEST of all American philosophers, Yogi Berra, has insightfully observed, making predictions is hard, especially about the future. And he might have added—pointing to the predictions of an impending Euro-American rupture that have been a staple of debates about U.S.-European relations at least since the 1956 Suez crisis—prognosticating accurately about the future of Transatlantic relations is extra hard. Through all the ups and downs in U.S.-European relations over the years, those many Chicken Littles who have gone out on a limb to forecast an impending drifting apart of Europe and the United States never have had their predictions validated by events.

Until now, perhaps?

The Iraq War has produced a very different kind of rift. The damage inflicted on Washington's ties to Europe by the Bush Administration's policy is likely to prove real, lasting and, at the end of the day, irreparable. In other words, if the fat lady isn't singing already, she clearly can be heard warming up her voice.

To understand why this crisis is different, we must understand its causes. The rupture between the United States and Europe is not, as some have asserted, mainly about an alleged Transatlantic rift in the realm of culture, values and ideology.[1] It is not about the relative merits of unilateralism versus multilateralism. It is not even about the issues that framed the debate about Iraq during the run-up to war (Should the weapons inspections process have been allowed to play out? Was the United States wrong to go to war without a second resolution from the United Nations Security Council?). For sure, Iraq was a catalyst for Transatlantic dispute, but this crisis has been about American power—specifically about American hegemony.

Of Balance and Hegemony

When FUTURE historians write about how American hegemony ended, they may well point to January 22, 2003 as a watershed. On that day, commemorating the 40th anniversary of the FrancoGerman Treaty negotiated by Charles de Gaulle and Konrad Adenauer as a bulwark against American hegemony, French President Jacques Chirac and German Chancellor Gerhard Schröder jointly declared that Paris and Berlin would work together to oppose the Bush Administration's evident intent to resolve the Iraqi question by force of arms. Later that day, in a Pentagon briefing, Secretary of Defense Donald Rumsfeld responded to the Franco-German declaration by contemptuously dismissing those partners as representing the "Old Europe", thereby triggering a Transatlantic earthquake, the geopolitical after-shocks of which will be felt for a long time. And well they should, for these contretemps reflect what is already a very old issue.

The problem of hegemony has been a major issue in U.S.-European relations since the United States emerged as a great power at the end of the 19th century. The United States fought two big wars in Europe out of fear that if a single power (in those cases, Germany) attained hegemony in Europe, it would be able to mobilize the continent's resources and threaten America in its own backyard, the Western Hemisphere. The conventional wisdom holds that America's post-World War II initiatives—the Marshall Plan, the North Atlantic Treaty—were driven by similar fears of possible Soviet hegemony in Europe. Indeed, many American strategic thinkers define America's traditional European strategy as a text-book example of "offshore balancing."

As an offshore balancer, the United States supposedly remains on the sidelines with respect to European security affairs unless a single great power threatens to dominate the continent. America's European grand strategy, therefore, is said to be counter-hegemonic: the United States intervenes in Europe only when the continental balance of power appears unable to thwart the rise of a would-be hegemon without U.S. assistance. The most notable proponent of this view of America's European grand strategy toward Europe is University of Chicago political scientist John J. Mearsheimer.[2] He argues that the United States is not a global hegemon. Rather, because of what he describes as the "stopping power of water", the United States is a hegemon only in its own region (the Western hemisphere), and acts as an offshore balancer toward Europe. He predicts that the United States soon will end its "continental commitment" because there is no European hegemon looming on the geopolitical horizon. As an offshore balancer, Mearsheimer says, the United States will not remain in Europe merely to play the role of regional stabilizer or pacifier.

There is just one thing wrong with this view: it does not fit the facts.

If American strategy toward Europe is indeed one of counter-hegemonic off-shore balancing, it should have been over, over there, for the United States when the Soviet Union collapsed. By a different but not far-fetched reckoning, it should have been over in the early 1960s, when the Europeans were capable of deterring a Soviet military advance westward without the United States. With no hegemonic threat to contain, American military power should have been retracted from Europe after 1991, and NATO should have contracted into non-existence rather than undergoing two rounds of expansion. Of course, it may be that America will ultimately be ejected from the continent by the Europeans, but there are no signs that the United States will voluntarily pack up and go home any time soon.

It is not a "time lag", or mere inertia, that has kept American military power on the European continent more than a decade after the Soviet Union ceased to exist. There is a better explanation for why U.S. troops are still in Europe and NATO is still in business. It is because the Soviet Union's containment was never the driving force behind America's post-World War II commitment to Europe. There is a well-known quip that NATO was created to "keep the Russians out, the Germans down, and the Americans in." It would be more accurate to say that the Atlantic Alliance's primary *raison d'être*, from Washington's standpoint, was to keep America in—*and on top*—so that Germans could be kept down, Europe could be kept quiet militarily, and the Europeans would lack any pressing incentive to unite politically. The attainment of America's postwar grand strategic objectives on the continent required that the United States establish its own hegemony over Western Europe, something it would probably have done even in the absence of the Cold War. In other words, NATO is still in business to advance long-standing American objectives that existed independently of the Cold War and hence survived the Soviet Union's collapse.

American Aims

W E USUALLY look to history to help us understand the present and predict the future. But the reverse can be true, as well: sometimes recent events serve to shed light on what happened in the past, and why it happened. Many may react skeptically to the claim that America's postwar European grand strategy was driven at least as much—probably more—by non-Cold War factors as by the Soviet threat. But Washington's post-Cold War behavior provides a good deal of support for this thesis.

For starters, when the Berlin Wall fell and the Soviet Union began to unravel, the first Bush Administration did not feel in the least bit compelled to reconsider the relevance of, or need for, either the U.S. military commitment to Europe or NATO. As Philip Zelikow and Condoleezza Rice, both of whom served that administration as senior foreign policy officials, have observed:

[The] administration believed strongly that, even if the immediate military threat from the Soviet Union diminished, the United States should maintain a significant military presence in Europe for the foreseeable future....The American troop presence thus also served as the ante to ensure a central place for the United States as a player in European politics. The Bush administration placed a high value on retaining such influence, underscored by Bush's flat statement that the United States was and would remain 'a European power.'... *The Bush administration was determined to maintain crucial features of the NATO system for European security even if the Cold War ended.*[3]

The Clinton Administration took a similar view. As one former State Department official avers, NATO had to be revitalized after the Cold War because American interests in Europe "transcended" the Soviet threat.[4] And using phraseology reminiscent of Voltaire's comment about God, then-Secretary of State Madeleine Albright said, "Clearly if an institution such as NATO did not exist today, we would want to create one."[5]

The fact that American policymakers did not miss a beat when the Cold War ended with respect to reaffirming NATO's continuing importance reveals a great deal about the real nature of the interests that shaped America's European grand strategy after World War II, and that continue to do so today. The truth is that, from its inception, America's postwar European grand strategy reflected a complex set of interlocking "Open Door" interests.* These interests are at once economic, strategic and broadly political in nature.

The first of these is that U.S. postwar officials believed that America had crucial economic interests in Europe. Even if there was no communist threat to Western Europe, State Department Policy Planning Staff Director George F. Kennan argued in 1947, the United States had a vital interest in facilitating Western Europe's economic recovery: "The United States people have a very real economic interest in Europe. This stems from Europe's role in the past as a market and as a major source of supply for a variety of products and services."[6] These interests required that Europe's antiquated economic structure of small, national markets be fused into a large, integrated market that would facilitate efficiencies and economies of scale. ** As the U.S. Ambassador to France, Jefferson Caffery, argued in 1947, economic integration would "eliminate the small watertight compartment into which Europe's pre-war and present economy is divided."[7] Paul Hoffman, director of the Economic Cooperation Agency (which administered Marshall Plan aid to Europe), elaborated on the reasons why Washington favored Western Europe's economic integration: "Europe could not be self-supporting until it had made great progress towards unity and until there was a wide, free, competitive market to lower costs, increase efficiency, and raise the standard of living."[8]

To prevent far Left parties (especially the communists) from coming to power on the Continent's western half after World

War II, U.S. aims also required political and social stability there. Washington was not really so concerned that such governments would drift into Moscow's political orbit, but it was very concerned that they would embrace the kinds of nationalist, or autarkic, economic policies that were anathema to America's goal of an open international economy. As Averell Harriman, the U.S. Special Representative in Europe, put it, Washington was committed to multilateral trade and was "opposed to restrictive policies and especially to the creation of an autarkic Europe."[9]

Second, American strategists perceived that U.S. economic interests would be jeopardized if postwar Europe relapsed into its bad habits of nationalism, great power rivalries and realpolitik. To ensure stability in Europe after World War II, the United States sought to create a militarily de-nationalized and economically integrated—but *not* politically unified—Europe. Washington would assume primary responsibility for European security, thereby precluding the re-emergence of the security dilemmas (especially that between France and Germany) that had sparked the two world wars. In turn, Western Europe's economic integration and interdependence—under the umbrella of America's military protectorate—would contribute to building a peaceful and stable Western Europe. In this respect, U.S. economic and security objectives meshed nicely.

Postwar U.S. policymakers viewed Europe's traditional balance of power security architecture as a "fire trap" and, as Undersecretary of State Robert Lovett said following World War II, Washington wanted to make certain that this fire trap was not rebuilt.[10] Starting with those who were "present at the creation", successive generations of U.S. policymakers feared the continent's reversion to its (as Americans see it) dark past—a past defined by war, militarism, nationalism and an unstable multipolar balance of power. For American officials, Europe indeed has been a dark continent whose wars spilled over across the Atlantic, threatened American interests and invariably drew in the United States. Secretary Rumsfeld's disparaging remark about the "Old Europe" thus stands in a long and consistent line of American attitudes toward the Continent and its various historical crimes and misdemeanors.

After World War II, Rumsfeld's cabinet predecessors sought to maintain U.S. interests by breaking the Old Europe of its bad old geopolitical habits. As Secretary of State John Foster Dulles put it in 1953,

> Surely there is an urgent, positive duty on all of us to seek to end that danger which comes from within. It has been the cause of two world wars and it will be disastrous if it persists.[11]

Even during the Cold War, American policymakers acknowledged that, quite apart from the Soviet threat, the United States needed to be present militarily in Western Europe to create a political environment that permitted "a secure and easy relationship among our friends in Western Europe."[12] As Secretary of State Dean Rusk said in 1967, the U.S. military presence on the continent played a pivotal role in assuring stability *within* Western Europe: "Much progress has been made. But

without the visible assurance of a sizeable American contingent, old frictions may revive, and Europe could become unstable once more."[13] Former Secretary of State Acheson, too, observed in the mid-1960s that, as the vehicle for America's stabilizer role in Western Europe, "NATO is not merely a military structure to prepare a collective defense against military aggression, but also a political organization to preserve the peace of Europe."[14]

The U.S. goal of embedding a militarily de-nationalized, but economically integrated Western Europe within the structure of an American-dominated "Atlantic Community" dovetailed neatly with another of Washington's key post 1945 grand strategic objectives: preventing the emergence of new poles of power in the international system—in the form either of a resurgent Germany or a united Europe—that could challenge America's geopolitical pre-eminence. Since the 1940s, Washington has had to perform a delicate balancing act with respect to Europe. To be sure, for economic reasons, the United States encouraged Western Europe's integration into a single common market, but the United States sought to prevent that from leading to its political unification.

To prevent the emergence of a politically unified Western Europe, successive U.S. administrations sought to "denationalize" the region by establishing a military protectorate that integrated Western Europe's military forces under, and subordinated them to, American command. The goal was to neuter Western Europe geopolitically and thereby circumscribe its ability to act independently of the United States in the high political realms of foreign and security policy. Embedding West European integration in the American-dominated Atlantic community would prevent the Europeans from veering off in the wrong direction. "An increased measure of Continental European integration", Acheson and Lovett told President Truman,

> can be secured only within the broader framework of the North Atlantic Community. This is entirely consistent with *our own desire to see a power arrangement on the Continent which does not threaten us* and with which we can work in close harmony.[15]

Acheson stated American strategic concerns with crystal clarity when he spoke of the necessity of a "well-knit large grouping of Atlantic states within which a new EUR grouping can develop, thus ensuring unity of purpose within the entire group and precluding [the] possibility of [a] EUR Union becoming [a] third force or opposing force."[16]

Europe's military absorption into the Atlantic Community went hand in hand with its economic integration. By persuading the West Europeans to "pool" their military and economic sovereignty, Washington aimed to strip them of the capacity to take unilateral national action.[17] As Kennan observed, Western Europe should be unified on terms which "would automatically make it impossible or extremely difficult for any member, not only Germany, to embark upon a path of unilateral aggression." But it was the American diplomat Charles Bohlen who cut to the heart of the U.S. de-nationalization strategy when he said,

"Our maximum objective should be the general one of making common European interests more important than individual national interests."[18]

For the United States, therefore, institutions such as NATO, the aborted European Defense Community, the European Coal and Steel Community (ECSC) and the Common Market were the instruments it employed to contain the West Europeans.*† As the State Department said, the United States hoped that "cautious initial steps toward military, political, and economic cooperation will be followed by more radical departures from traditional concepts of sovereignty."[19] The American aim was to create "institutional machinery to ensure that separate national interests are subordinated to the best interests of the community", and achieving this subordination was deemed essential if the United States was to accomplish its grand strategic purposes in Europe.[20]

The Continental Response

JUST AS FEAR of a European hegemon led the United States to intervene in Europe's two great wars of the 20th century, the West Europeans after World War II understood that America had established its own hegemony over them. As realist international relations theory suggests, Western Europe tried to do something about it.

To be sure, West European balancing against the United States was constrained. On the one hand, although the West Europeans feared American power, they feared the Soviet Union even more during the Cold War. In a more positive sense, too, following World War II, Washington was able to use the carrot of economic assistance—notably, the Marshall Plan—to keep Western Europe aligned (albeit very tenuously at times) with the United States. Nevertheless, throughout the post-World War II era, West European inclinations to balance against American power were never far from the surface.

In the five years or so after the end of World War II, it was Britain that hoped to emerge as a "Third Force" in world politics to balance both the United States and the Soviet Union. As the British diplomat Gladwyn Jebb put it, London needed to prevent the geopolitical equilibrium from being undermined "by a 'bipolar' system centering around what Mr. Toynbee calls the two 'semi-barbarian states on the cultural periphery'."[21] The accelerating decline of Britain's relative power, of course, put paid to London's Third Force aspirations, but continental Europe's Third Force aspirations remained. In the late 1940s and 1950s, one of the hopes of the founding fathers of today's European Union was that the European Coal and Steel Community, and then the Common Market, would prove to be the embryo of a united Europe that could act as a geopolitical and economic counterweight to the United States. Commenting on the motives driving the West Europeans to integrate, the diplomatic historian Geir Lundestad observes:

Although they wanted the two sides of the Atlantic to cooperate more closely, in a more general sense it was probably also the desire of most European policymakers to strengthen Western Europe *vis-à-vis* the United States. This could be done economically by supporting the Common Market and politically by working more closely together on the European side.[22]

Even Jean Monnet, author of the Schuman Plan that led to the ECSC and the "father" of European integration, first toyed with the idea of an Anglo-French federation in the late 1940s because he saw this as the basis of a European bloc that could stand apart from both the United States and the Soviet Union.[23]

The 1956 Suez crisis gave fresh impetus to the arguments that Western Europe needed to counterbalance the United States. Britain's initial reaction to its humiliation by the Eisenhower Administration was to consider reviving the Third Force concept: "We should pool our resources with our European allies so that Western Europe as a whole might become a third nuclear power comparable with the United States and the Soviet Union."[24] Under Harold Macmillan, of course, Britain rejected becoming part of a West European Third Force, opting instead to curry favor—and maintain influence—with Washington through the "special relationship" ("playing Greece to America's Rome"). On the Continent, however, Suez focused French and West German attentions on the need for a West European counterweight to American power. As William I. Hitchcock recounts, Adenauer and French Premier Guy Mollet were meeting in Paris on November 6, 1956, at the height of the Suez crisis (and the simultaneous turmoil in Hungary). Shortly after Adenauer exclaimed that it was time for Europe to unite "against America", Mollet excused himself to take a phone call from the British Prime Minister, Anthony Eden, who informed Mollet that, under U.S. pressure, London had decided to call off the Anglo-French invasion of the Suez Canal Zone. When a crestfallen Mollet returned to the meeting room and conveyed the content of the telephone conversation to his guest, Adenauer consoled him by saying, "Now, it is time to create Europe."[25]

By the early 1960s, French President Charles de Gaulle believed that Western Europe had recovered sufficiently from World War II's dislocations and was poised to re-emerge as an independent pole of power in the international system. De Gaulle, clearly one of the 20th century's towering figures, was well versed in the realities of international politics. Following Washington's successful facing-down of the Soviet Union in the 1962 Cuban missile crisis, he concluded *then* that the world had become "unipolar"—dominated by a hegemonic America. To balance U.S. hegemony, de Gaulle pushed for France to acquire independent nuclear capabilities, and he sought to build a West European pole of power based on a Franco-German axis. That is what the 1963 treaty—the one Chirac and Schröder were commemorating on January 22—was all about, a fact that Washington apprehended clearly. U.S. policymakers were deeply concerned that Paris would lure West Germany out of the "Atlantic" (that is, U.S.) orbit, because such a Euro-centric strategic axis, as a 1966 State Department cable explicitly said, "would fragment Europe and divide the Atlantic world."[26] In plainer English, the foundations of America's European hegemony would be undermined.

Washington recognized the Gaullist challenge for what it was—a direct assault on U.S. preponderance in Western Europe—and reacted by re-asserting its own hegemonic prerogatives on the Continent. President Kennedy gave eloquent expression to the fear that Western Europe's emergence as an independent pole of power in the international system would be inimical to U.S. interests, and his doing so shows that U.S. concerns on this score were not limited to the immediate postwar period, as sketched out above. Kennedy voiced concern that U.S. leverage over Europe might be waning because the West Europeans, having staged a vigorous postwar recovery, were no longer dependent on the United States economically. Noting that "the European states are less subject to our influence", Kennedy expressed the fear that "if the French and other European powers acquire a nuclear capability they would be in a position to be entirely independent and we might be on the outside looking in."[27] By pushing for a Multilateral Nuclear Force for Western Europe (in reality, one that kept Washington's finger firmly on the trigger), the United States sought—unsuccessfully—to derail France's nuclear ambitions.

With considerably more success, however, the United States did manage to take the teeth out of the Franco-German Treaty. In so doing, Washington played the hardest kind of hegemonic hardball. Threatening to rescind the security guarantee that protected West Germany from the Soviets, the U.S. government insisted that the Bundestag insert a preamble to the treaty reaffirming that Bonn's Atlantic connection to the United States and NATO took supremacy over its ties with Paris.† This intervention by the United States hastened Adenauer's retirement and helped ensure that he would be succeeded by the more pliable Atlanticist, Ludwig Erhard.

What's New?

NOW, FORTY years later, the United States and Europe are still playing the same game. America still asserts its hegemony, and France and Germany still seek (so far without much success) to create a European counterweight. As has been the case in the past, too, Washington is employing a number of strategies to keep Europe apart.

First, the United States is still actively discouraging Europe from either collective, or national, efforts to acquire the full-spectrum of advanced military capabilities. Specifically, the United States has opposed the EU's Rapid Reaction Force (the nucleus of a future EU army), insisting that any European efforts must not duplicate NATO capabilities and must be part of an effort to strengthen the Alliance's "European pillar." The United States is also encouraging European NATO members to concentrate individually on carving-out "niche" capabilities that will complement U.S. power rather than potentially challenge it.

Second, Washington is engaged in a game of divide and rule in a bid to thwart the EU's political unification process. The United States is pushing hard for the enlargement of the EU—and especially the admission of Turkey—in the expectation that a bigger EU will prove unmanageable and hence unable to emerge as a politically unified actor in international politics. The United States also has encouraged NATO expansion in a similar vein, in the hope that the "New Europe" (Poland, Hungary, the Czech Republic and Romania)—which, with the exception of Romania, will join the EU in 2004—will side with Washington against France and Germany on most issues of significance. For the United States, a Europe that speaks with many voices is optimal, which is why the United States is trying to ensure that the EU's "state-building" process fails—thereby heading off the emergence of a united Europe that could become an independent pole of power in the international system.

Finally, the United States has continued to remind the rest of Europe, sometimes delicately, sometimes in a heavy-handed fashion, that they still need an American presence to "keep the Germans down." For example, at his speech in Prague during the November 2002 NATO summit, President George W. Bush—just before invoking the historically freighted memories of Verdun, Munich, Stalingrad and Nuremberg—alluded in a not-so-subtle fashion to the German threat from World War II to make the case for a U.S. role in Europe:

> U-boats could not divide us.… The commitment of my nation to Europe is found in the carefully tended graves of young Americans who died for this continent's freedom. That commitment is shown by the thousands in uniforms still serving here, from the Balkans to Bavaria, still willing to make the ultimate sacrifice for this continent's future.

Washington's aim of keeping Europe apart paid apparent dividends when, at the end of January, the leaders of Britain, Spain, Italy, Portugal, Denmark, Poland, Hungary and the Czech Republic signed a letter urging Europe and the international community to unite behind Washington's Iraq policy. This letter was notable especially because it illustrated that the United States is having some success in using the "New Europe" to balance against the "Old" Franco-German core. Clearly, Washington hopes that states such as Poland, Hungary, the Czech Republic and Romania will not only line up behind the United States within NATO, but will also represent Atlanticist interests over European ones within the EU itself.

In short, U.S. policy seeks to encourage an intra-European counterweight that will block French and German aspirations to create a united Europe counterweight to American hegemony. Indeed, in the wake of the Iraq War, Transatlantic relations are characterized by a kind of "double containment" in Europe: the hard core of Old Europe (centered around France and Germany, and possibly supported by Russia) seeks to brake America's aspirations for global hegemony, while the United States and its "New European" allies in central and eastern Europe seek to contain Franco-German power on the Continent. It is an old game, in a new form.

The Widening Atlantic

IN THE DECADE between the Soviet Union's collapse and 9/11, American hegemony (or as some U.S. policymakers called it during the Clinton Administration, America's "hegemony problem") was the central issue in American grand strategy debates. It still is. Although American policymakers have developed a number of (too) clever rationales to convince themselves that the United States will escape the fate that invariably befalls hegemons, the fallout of the Iraq crisis on the Transatlantic relationship illustrates that concern with America's hegemonic power—and the way it is exercised—is not confined to the Middle East and Persian Gulf.[28]

Why do France, Germany and much of the rest of the world, including other major powers such as Russia and China, worry about American hegemony? The simple answer is that international politics remains fundamentally what it has always been: a competitive arena in which states struggle to survive. States are always worried about their security. Thus when one state becomes overwhelmingly powerful—that is, hegemonic—others fear for their safety.

Doubtless the Bush Administration's fervent hegemonists will scoff at the idea that the United States will become the object of counter-hegemonic balancing. They clearly believe that the United States can do as it pleases because it is so far ahead in terms of hard power that no other state (or coalition of states) can possibly hope to balance against it.[29] They also know, and know that Europeans know, that the United States does not and will never literally threaten Europe with its military power. This confidence is misplaced, however, because it overlooks the effects of what can be called "the hegemon's temptation."

A hegemonic power like the United States today has overwhelming hard power—especially military power—and indeed there is no state or coalition with commensurate power capable of restraining the United States from exercising that power. For hegemons, the formula of overwhelming power and lack of opposition creates powerful incentives to expand the scope of its geopolitical interests. But over time, the cumulative effects of expansion for the United States—wars and subsequent occupations in the Balkans, the Persian Gulf, Afghanistan and the War on Terrorism; possible future wars against North Korea, Iran, Syria, or China over Taiwan—will have an enervating impact on U.S. power.

At the end of the day, hegemonic decline results from the interplay of over-extension abroad and domestic economic weakness.‡ Over time, the costs of America's hegemonic vocation will interact with its economic vulnerabilities— endless budget deficits fueled in part by burgeoning military spending, and the persistent balance of payments deficit—to erode America's relative power advantage over the rest of the world. As the relative power gap between the United States and potential new great powers begins to shrink, the costs and risks of challenging the

United States will decrease, and the pay-off for doing so will increase. As the British found out toward the end of the 19th century, a seemingly unassailable international power position can melt away with unexpected rapidity.

There are already today other potential poles of power in the international system waiting in the wings that could quickly emerge as counterweights to the United States. And with the Iraq crisis revealing the stark nature of American hegemony, these new power centers have increasingly greater incentive to do so. Here, by facilitating "soft" balancing against the United States, the Iraq crisis may have paved the way for "hard" balancing as well. Since the end of World War II, policymakers and analysts on both sides of the Atlantic have realized that Europe is a potential pole of power in the international system. Will France and Germany provide the motor to unite Europe in opposition to the United States? Time, of course, will tell.

But for sure, this is not 1963. The Cold War is over, and France and Germany are freer to challenge American hegemony. The EU is in the midst of an important constitutional convention that is laying the foundation for a politically unified Europe. And even as the Iraq War proceeded, there were straws in the wind pointing in the direction of hard balancing against the United States. Most notable are indications that France, Germany, Belgium and Luxemburg may act together to create Europe's own version of a coalition of the willing—by forming a "hard core" of enhanced defense cooperation among themselves.

In the short term, however, Paris and Berlin—supported by Russia—have lead the way in soft balancing to counter American hegemony. By using international organizations like the United Nations to marshal opposition to the United States, France and Germany—and similarly inclined powers such as Russia and China—are beginning to develop new habits of diplomatic cooperation to oppose Washington.

Similarly, it is likely that France and Germany (again, joined by Russia and China) will be more likely to cooperate in propping up key regional powers that might be the next targets in Washington's geopolitical gunsight. Iran is one such potential target. With Washington bidding for hegemony in the Persian Gulf region by establishing a protectorate over postwar Iraq, France and Germany—Russia and China, too— will have strong incentives for collaborating to ensure their own strategic and commercial interests in the region by building up, and supporting, Iran (and perhaps Syria) as a counter-weight to U.S. regional power. It was no coincidence, after all, that Dominique de Villepin showed up in Tehran within days after the fall of Baghdad.

AT THE END of the day, the most telling piece of evidence that the Iraq War marks a turning point in Transatlantic relations, and with respect to American hegemony, is this: Despite widespread predictions that they would fold diplomatically and acquiesce in a second UN resolution authorizing the United States and Great Britain to forcibly disarm Iraq, Paris and Berlin (and Moscow) held firm. Rather than being shocked and awed by America's power and strong-arm diplomacy, they stuck to their guns—just as Britain and France did *not* do at Suez—and refused to fall into line behind Washington. What this shows, at the very least, is that it is easier to be Number One when there is a Number Two that threatens Numbers Three, Four, Five and so on. It also suggests that a hegemon so clearly defied is a hegemon on a downward arc.

Many throughout the world now have the impression that the United States is acting as an aggressive hegemon engaged in the naked aggrandizement of its own power. The notion that the United States is a "benevolent" hegemon has been shredded. America is inviting the same fate as that which has overtaken previous contenders for hegemony. In the sweep of history, the Bush Administration will not be remembered for conquering Baghdad, but for a policy that galvanized both soft and hard balancing against American hegemony. At the end of the day, what the administration trumpets as "victory" in the Persian Gulf may prove, in reality, to have pushed NATO into terminal decline, given the decisive boost to the political unification of Europe (at least the most important parts of it), and marked the beginning of the end of America's era of global preponderance.

Christopher Lane is a visiting fellow in foreign policy studies at the Cato Institute. He is writing a book on America's hegemonic grand strategy for Cornell University Press.

Notes

* The seminal work of the "Open Door" school, of course, is William Appleman Williams' *The Tragedy of American Diplomacy* (New York: Delta, 1962). Williams' work has acted as a powerful stimulus that produced a broad body of historical scholarship that both built upon, and refined, the Open Door interpretation. When read as a whole, it encompasses economics, ideology, national interest and security as key factors in shaping U.S. grand strategy—and underscores their interconnectedness.

** In notes prepared for Secretary of State George Marshall, Kennan argued that the Marshall Plan was necessary for two reasons, the first of which was "so that they can buy from us." The second reason was "so that they will have enough self-confidence to withstand outside pressures." Memorandum Prepared by the Policy Planning Staff, July 21, 1947, FRUS 1947, III, p. 335.

*† Referring to NATO and the EGSC, Secretary of State Dulles observed, "These represent important unifying efforts, but it cannot be confidently affirmed that these organizations are clearly adequate to ensure against a tragic repetition of the past where the Atlantic community, and particularly Western Europe, has been torn apart by internecine struggles." He then underscored the need for even greater unity within the Atlantic Community, not simply to meet the Soviet threat, but "forms of unity and integration which would preserve the West from a continuance of internal struggles which have been characteristic of its past." U.S. Delegation at North Atlantic Council Ministerial Meeting to Dept. of State, May 5, 1956, *FRUS 1955–57*, IV, pp. 68–9.

† As Secretary of State Rusk said, "If Europe were ever to be organized so as to leave us outside, from the point of view of these great issues of policy and defense, it would become most difficult for us to sustain our present guarantee against Soviet aggression. We shall not hesitate to make this point to the Germans if they show signs of ac-

cepting any idea of a BonnParis axis." Rusk to the Embassy in France, May 18, 1963, *FRUS 1961–63*, XIII, p. 704.

‡ The two classic elaborations are Robert Gilpin, *War and Change in World Politics* (Cambridge: Cambridge University Press, 1981); and Paul Kennedy, *The Rise and Fall of the Great Powers: Economic Change and Military Conflict from 1500 to 2000* (New York: Random House, 1987).

References

1. Robert Kagan, *Of Paradise and Power: America and Europe in the New World Order* (New York: Alfred A. Knopf, 2003).
2. See Mearsheimer, *The Tragedy of Great Power Politics* (New York: W.W. Norton, 2001).
3. Zelikow and Rice, *Germany Unified and Europe Transformed: A Study in Statecraft* (Cambridge, MA: Harvard University Press, 1995), pp. 169–70 (emphasis added).
4. Ronald D. Asmus, *Opening NATO's Door: How the Alliance Remade Itself for a New Era* (New York: Columbia University Press, 2002), p. 290.
5. *Ibid.*, p. 261.
6. PPS/4, "Certain Aspects of the European Recovery Problem from the United States Standpoint", July 23, 1947, *PPSP*, I, p. 31.
7. Caffery to Marshall, July 10, 1947, *FRUS 1947*, III, p. 317.
8. Memorandum of Conversation, Prepared in the Department of State, September 15, 1949, *FRUS 1949*, IV, p.657
9. Harriman to Hoffman, March 12, 1949, *FRUS 1949*, IV, pp. 375–6.
10. See, Minutes of the First Meeting of the Washington Exploratory Talks on Security, July 6,1948, *FRUS 1948*, III, p. 151; Minutes of the Fourth Meeting of the Washington Exploratory Talks on Security, July 8,1948, *FRUS 1948*, III, pp. 167–8.
11. Statement by Dulles to the North Atlantic Council, December 14, 1953, *FRUS 1952–54*, V, p. 461.
12. Talking Paper prepared in the Department of Defense, undated, *FRUS 1964–68*, XIII, p. 728.
13. Letter from Rusk to Senator Mansfield, April 21, 1967, *FRUS 1964–68*, XIII, p. 562.
14. Memorandum by the Acheson Group, undated, *FRUS 1964–68*, XIII, pp. 406–7.
15. Acheson and Lovett to Truman, July 30, 1951, *FRUS 1951*, III, p. 850 (emphasis added).
16. Acheson to Bruce, September 19, 1952, *FRUS 1952–54*, V, p. 324.
17. Paper Prepared by Kennan, February 7, 1949, *FRUS 1949*, III, p. 92.
18. Minutes of the Seventh Meeting of the Policy Planning Staff, January 24, 1950, *FRUS 1950*, III, p. 622.
19. Policy Statement of Department of the State, September 20, 1948, *FRUS 1948*, III, pp. 652-3.
20. Paper Prepared in the Department of State, n.d., "Economic Benefits of European Integration", *FRUS 1949*, III, p. 133.
21. Jebb quoted in Michael Hogan, *The Marshall Plan: America, Britain, and the Reconstruction of Western Europe, 1947–52* (Cambridge: Cambridge University Press, 1987), p. 113.
22. Lundestad, *"Empire" by Integration* (New York: Oxford University Press, 1998), p. 135.
23. François Duchene, *Jean Monnet: The First Statesman of Interdependence* (New York: Norton, 1994), pp. 186–7.
24. Quoted in David Dimbleby and David Reynolds, *An Ocean Apart: The Relationship Between Britain and America in the Twentieth Century* (London: Hodder and Stoughton, 1988), p. 235.
25. Hitchcock, "Reversal of Fortune: Britain, France, and the Making of Europe, 1945–1956", in Paul Kennedy and Hitchcock, eds., *From War to Peace: Altered Strategic Landscapes in the Twentieth Century* (New Haven: Yale University Press, 2000), pp. 100–1.

26. Department of State to the Embassy in Germany, February 2, 1966, *FRUS 1964–68*, XIII, pp. 308-9.

27. Remarks of President Kennedy to the National Security Council, January 22, 1963, *FRUS 1961–63*, XIII, p.486.

28. See Josef Joffe, "Continental Divides", *The National Interest* (Spring 2003).

29. See Charles Krauthammer, "The Unipolar Moment Revisited", *The National Interest* (Winter 2002/03).

China's Response to the Bush Doctrine

Peter Van Ness

The American political scientist Mike Lampton has captured just the right image in Chinese for understanding America's relationship with China: *tong chuang yi meng* ("same bed, different dreams"). America and China are like two lovers in bed, with very different understandings about why they are there and what the future may hold.[1]

For more than 30 years, beginning with Richard Nixon's accommodation with Mao Zedong in 1971-72, capitalist America and communist China have cooperated with each other off and on, but always with very different agendas in mind. This is no less true today. After 9/11, the People's Republic of China (PRC) sided with the United States in Bush's "war on terror," but virtually every aspect of the Bush Doctrine (e.g., unilateralism, preemption, and missile defense) raises serious security problems for China. Faced with this series of strategic initiatives from Washington, Beijing is responding in an unexpected way, and has now begun to lay down an alternative strategic design to the Bush Doctrine. How relations between the United States and China evolve will probably be decisive in determining whether there is peace or war in the region.

In this essay, I first examine the strategic implications of the Bush Doctrine to date, then analyze the PRC's response, and, finally, highlight key issues for the next four years.

Understanding the Bush Doctrine

From the presidential election campaign of 2000 through George W. Bush's first months in office before the attacks of 9/11, there were strong indications of what was to come. Bush had staffed his administration with conservative Republicans, who, especially on defense and security issues, had articulated a hard-line, unilateralist position. Their strategic priorities included missile defense, withdrawal from the Anti-Ballistic Missile Treaty, the creation of a high-tech, rapid-reaction military of overwhelming scope and power, and the revitalization of the U.S. nuclear weapons industry. Their Manichean worldview led them to view U.S. security in terms of the development of such overwhelming capabilities (military, economic, and technological) that no other state or coalition of states would dare confront the United States.

To some people, it looked as though the Bush leadership did not understand what international relations theorists call the "security dilemma," the idea that when one country builds up its military capability to enhance its defense, an adversary may see that buildup as an offensive threat and increase its own military capabilities, thereby igniting an arms race in which both countries become less secure.

Other commentators thought that President Bush and his advisors understood the security dilemma only too well. The Chinese strategic analyst Yan Xuetong, in an interview in Beijing in April 2001, agreed that when the power capabilities of two states are roughly equal, the security dilemma is likely to have the expected outcome: namely, neither side benefits. But, he said, when one state is much stronger than other states it might deliberately create a security dilemma between itself and its perceived adversaries in order to intimidate and dominate them. That, Yan argued, is what the Bush administration was trying to do.

Writing in these pages after 9/11 but before the invasion of Iraq, the political scientist David Hendrickson explained the logic of the Bush Doctrine as a "quest for absolute security." Unilateralism and a strategic doctrine of preventive war were the key elements of this futile search. Hendrickson argued that these were "momentous steps," standing in "direct antagonism to fundamental values in our political tradition," which threaten "to wreck an international order that has been patiently built up for 50 years, inviting a fundamental delegitimation of American power."[2] Hendrickson concluded his essay with a quote from Henry Kissinger that sums up the basic flaw in a search for absolute security: "The desire of one power for absolute security means absolute insecurity for all the others."[3]

The invasion of Iraq, for the Bush leadership, became the prototype of this search for absolute security: "regime change" by military force to punish any adversary who dared to stand up to American power. The overthrow of Saddam Hussein in Iraq was intended to show the world that opposition to the Bush grand design was futile. Washington would have its way, through the use of overwhelming military force if necessary, even in the face of opposition by major allies. However, the deteriorating security situation in Iraq and Afghanistan and the continued bloodletting in the Israel-Palestine conflict have demonstrated that there are limits to what even the most powerful state in the world can do in imposing its will on other nations.[4]

President Bush, at his first press conference after his re-election, told the world: "I earned capital in the campaign, political capital, and now I intend to spend it. It is my style. That's what happened in the—after the 2000 election, I earned some capital. I've earned capital in this election—and I'm going to spend it for what I told the people I'd spend it on, which is—you've heard the agenda: Social Security and tax reform, moving this economy forward, education, fighting and winning the war on terror."[5] So, presumably, the Bush Doctrine will remain firmly in place.

The contrast between the preferences of the U.S. electorate and world opinion is sharp and potentially calamitous. While George Bush won reelection in 2004 with markedly improved margins of support over 2000, including clear control of both houses of Congress, world opinion has shifted sharply against his policies. The terrorist attacks of September 2001 on the World Trade Center and the Pentagon prompted almost universal sympathy for the victims and support for the United States, but President Bush has squandered that "capital" over the past three years by his contempt for international law and institutions, and his disdain for any who might dare to disagree with him. His administration has shown little concern for either legitimacy or the moral dimensions of the exercise of power.[6]

During the past two years, I have worked on a collaborative project with colleagues from around the Asia-Pacific on responses to the Bush Doctrine.[7] From our discussions, and informed by the insights of other colleagues like Yan Xuetong and David Hendrickson, we can infer four general propositions that are amply illustrated by the efforts of the Bush administration to date.

First, there is no such thing as absolute security, which is simply unattainable for any country, including the United States, the most powerful state the world has ever seen.

Second, the world is confounded by a unique and complex range of military, political, economic, environmental, and public health insecurities that we are only beginning to comprehend. For example, some scientists cogently argue that climate change, by itself, is the greatest threat to our existence. At the same time, specialists on Islam are convinced that if we do not treat the global problems of human security seriously, terrorism will be with us forever.

Third, no individual state, no matter how powerful, can adequately manage this range of insecurities alone. An effective response to the broad range of threats to national security presented by these problems requires a multilateral response. Obviously, the leaders of every independent state will attempt to advance their own interests as best they can, but the realist assumption that strategies based on narrow self-interest might be adequate to protect the security of a country are utopian in today's world.[8]

Fourth, the more the most powerful states seek to achieve absolute security by building up their economic and military power and operating with impunity to advance their perceived national interests, the more insecure the world—and they themselves—become.[9]

The Bush Doctrine is simply not sustainable in its current form.

It is often remarked that, since the collapse of the Soviet Union, there is no longer any state or group of states with the political will and material capabilities to balance U.S. power, and that following the delegitimation of socialism as a developmental alternative to capitalism, there is no longer any ideological alternative to market economics and representative democracy. Where does one stand intellectually in response to the Bush Doctrine, one is asked, other than to argue that the neoconservatives are not practicing what they preach when they say that what they are trying to do is to bring freedom and democracy to the world? On what basis can a systematic alternative to the Bush Doctrine be built?

The most substantive and promising international reaction to date has been Beijing's response. Rather than initiate an arms race to challenge U.S. hegemonic power directly, as one might expect, China reacted cautiously at first and then began to promote a fully elaborated response to the Bush Doctrine.

The Chinese Response

The Chinese leadership was aware of the hard-line political views of many of the people chosen for top positions in the new administration when George W. Bush was inaugurated in January 2001. Right-wing opinion in the United States had it that China was the most likely challenger to U.S. hegemony and that the "China threat" should be a priority for the new administration. When President Bush chose to identify certain "rogue states" as the main danger in his early speeches on national security, many analysts inferred that the main, unnamed rogue that the administration had in mind was China. When the classified Nuclear Posture Review of 2002 was leaked to the press, it identified China as one of seven possible targets for nuclear attack by the United States, and a PRC-Taiwan confrontation as one of three likely scenarios in which nuclear weapons might be used.[10] The administration's commitment to both missile defense and preemptive or preventive war further raised Chinese concerns.[11]

Official Chinese reaction to the Bush Doctrine has gone through three distinct stages: *avoidance, collaboration,* and *strategic response.* At first, Chinese policy seemed designed to avoid confrontation with the new president. As the administration set about putting its foreign and security policies in place, Beijing could see that many of the Bush initiatives clashed with China's interests. But rather than confront the new president directly, the Chinese leadership appeared determined to stand aside from the hard-line bulldozer, apparently hoping that Washington's enthusiasm for missile defense and preventive action against "rogue states" would wane over time.

However, September 11 changed all that. The terrorist attacks on the United States provided China with an opportunity to find common ground with the new administration—to collaborate with Washington in the new "war on terror." This second stage began almost immediately after the attacks, when Chinese president Jiang Zemin telephoned Bush to offer his sympathy and support. In effect, Beijing's message was: We have terrorists too (among China's 10 million Muslims), and we want to work with you in the struggle against terrorism.[12] When it came to invading Iraq, however, China joined France and Russia in opposition. If the United Nations Security Council had put a second resolution on Iraq to a vote, one that proposed to endorse a U.S.-led invasion, it was unclear whether China would have joined France and Russia in vetoing that resolution. But China clearly opposed the invasion. Nor did China join in other U.S. undertakings, such as the Proliferation Security Initiative, a multilateral effort to interdict shipments of weapons of mass destruction and missile delivery systems.

Meanwhile, Beijing began to implement a strategic response to the Bush Doctrine. In this third stage, the focus has been on Asia. The core of the Chinese alternative has been a cooperative security response to Bush's unilateralist, preventive war strategy. In response to America's determination to reshape the world by force, China now proposed to build cooperation among different groupings of states in creating new international institutions for achieving solutions to common problems.

For Beijing, these initiatives were unprecedented. From dynastic times to the present, China had adopted a largely realist view of the world, and, like the United States, it had preferred a bilateral approach to foreign relations. Moreover, neither in its dynastic past nor in its communist present had China been any more benevolent toward its neighbors, or more hesitant to use military force than most major powers.[13] For China now to adopt a multilateral, cooperative-security design was something new and important.

By the mid-1990s, some analysts had begun to identify China as a "responsible" power, pointing to Beijing's increasing participation in international institutions like APEC (Asia-Pacific Economic Cooperation), the Association of Southeast Asian Nations (ASEAN) Regional Forum, and the World Trade Organization. By seeking and winning the opportunity to host the Olympics in 2008, and in other ways, Beijing began to signal that it was aware of its growing stake in the status quo and was prepared to help in maintaining the strategic stability that is a prerequisite for the continued economic prosperity of East Asia.

From this beginning emerged the strategic response to the Bush Doctrine. Some called this "China's new diplomacy,"[14] but it was much more than that. Beijing followed the establishment of "ASEAN+3" (yearly meetings between the ten member countries of ASEAN with China, Japan, and South Korea) with the establishment of "ASEAN+1" (the ASEAN countries and China alone). China took the lead in creating the first multilateral institution in Central Asia, the six-member Shanghai Cooperation Organization (China, Russia, Kazakhstan, Tajikistan, Uzbekistan, and Kyrgyzstan),[15] and worked to demonstrate to its neighbors that both economic and strategic security could be based on a new design: cooperation for mutual benefit among potential adversaries rather than the building of military alliances against a perceived common threat.

In the name of "nontraditional" security cooperation to deal with terrorism and other transnational crime, Beijing even normalized its relations with its former adversary India,[16] and conducted unprecedented, joint naval exercises with both India and Pakistan in the East China Sea near Shanghai in late 2003. Chinese commentators emphasized the cooperative-security theoretical basis for these initiatives: "China has been a proponent of mutual understanding and trust through international security cooperation and opposed any military alliance directed at any other countries," and "China won't accept any military cooperation that is directed at other countries."[17]

In October 2003, China signed the ASEAN Treaty of Amity and Cooperation (the first non-ASEAN country to do so), and negotiated a "strategic partnership for peace and prosperity" with the ten ASEAN member countries. The objective is to build an East Asian Community founded on economic, social, and security cooperation.[18] Beijing also demonstrated its new approach by offering to host the six-party negotiations to find a peaceful solution to the North Korean nuclear crisis.

The key distinguishing features of the Bush administration's and Beijing's very different approaches to dealing with the post–Cold War world, stated schematically, are the following:

Bush	PRC
Absolute security for the United States	Cooperative security (seeking to work *with* potential adversaries, rather than to make war against them)
Unilateral	Multilateral
Preventive war and regime change	Rules-based collective action, and conflict resolution diplomacy
Zero-sum strategic games	Positive-sum strategic games, designed to achieve win-win outcomes
Disdain for international law, treaties, and institutions	International institution building

Beijing's approach is by no means a pacifist design. China is clearly seeking to modernize its military capability and giving very serious thought to exactly what kind of military would be most effective in dealing with the dangers of today's world, including a potential U.S. threat.[19] The military specialist Paul Godwin notes that "a primary objective of the PLA [People's Liberation Army] is to exploit perceived U.S. vulnerabilities."[20] For example, the PRC has made a careful study of so-called asymmetrical warfare and how weaker powers might successfully confront stronger powers. But it would be a mistake to understand the Chinese modernization project as predicated on launching an arms race with the United States—at least not yet.

To date, Chinese nuclear doctrine has focused on maintaining a "minimum nuclear deterrent" capable of launching a retaliatory strike after surviving an initial nuclear attack, rather than on building huge arsenals of more and more powerful nuclear weapons.[21] Beijing is well aware of the great disparity in military capabilities between China and the United States, as well as the disparity in financial and technological capacity. It is also aware of the argument that one of the key factors that finally broke the back of the former Soviet Union was its inability to sustain the arms race with the United States. It does not want to fall into that trap.

Chinese analysts have described their strategy as a design for *heping jueqi*, or "peaceful rise." Zheng Bijian, former vice president of the Central Chinese Communist Party School, says that this approach is prompted by the conviction that "China must seek a peaceful global environment to develop its economy even as it tries to safeguard world peace through development."[22] Building relations based on mutual benefit with all of its neighbors is a central objective of this strategy. Beijing wants to demonstrate that closer trade, investment, and even security relations with China can be beneficial to its neighbors.

Singapore commentator Eric Teo Chu Cheow has suggested that this new strategy resembles an old one: "China's Ming/Qing tributary system was based on three cardinal points: First, China considered itself the 'central heart' of the region; this tributary system assured China of its overall security environment. Second, to ensure its internal stability and prosperity, China needed a stable environment immediately surrounding the Middle Kingdom. Third, the Chinese emperor would in principle give more favors to tributary states or kingdoms than he received from them; for this generosity, the emperor obtained their respect and goodwill."[23]

Obviously, the international relations of the twenty-first century are very different from China's imperial relations during the Ming and Qing dynasties, but the idea of establishing mutually beneficial economic and security ties with neighboring states makes sense for everyone in Asia. Meanwhile, if successful, such a concert of power (in this case, among states that are formally equals rather than dependents of China) would help to maintain the strategic stability that China needs for its economic modernization. Critics, like activist Cao Siyuan, argue that to be successful, the "peaceful rise" strategy must be accompanied by substantial domestic political liberalization and greater transparency with respect to China's military posture: "Diplomacy is often the extension of domestic policy. A leadership's commitment to global fraternity and solidarity will be called into doubt if it is so reluctant to give its own people adequate human rights."[24] Can China practice at home what it has begun to preach abroad?

Beijing's new strategy has yet to be tested. How will Beijing's commitment to cooperative security hold up when disputes with neighbors over territory or political differences reemerge? Will it also apply to cross-strait relations with Taiwan? Yet when compared with Bush's record of making war to achieve peace in Afghanistan and Iraq, the Chinese response has substantial appeal, especially among the ASEAN countries, where cooperative security ideas have long been popular.

Clearly, China wants to avoid a conflict with the United States. The Japanese journalist Funabashi Yoichi quotes one Chinese think tank researcher as saying: "We are studying the origin of the U.S.-Soviet Cold War. Why did it happen? Was there no way to prevent it? Some see that a U.S.-China cold war is inevitable, but what can we do to prevent it?"[25] China's strategic response to the Bush Doctrine is not confrontational toward the United States and does not require China's Asian neighbors to choose between Beijing and Washington, something none of them wants to have to do.[26] Though it is not a design for what realists would call "balancing" against the United States, it challenges Washington to think and act in ways quite different from the policies prescribed by the Bush Doctrine when trying to resolve problems in international relations.

What Is to Come?

Leaders in both the United States and the PRC have recently consolidated their power: George W. Bush has been reelected, and Hu Jintao has finally moved former president Jiang Zemin into retirement from his Central Military Commission chairmanship and assumed the preeminent leadership of China's party, army, and state institutions. But there the similarities end.

While Beijing has been preoccupied with trying to cool down its burgeoning economy, which has been growing at the astonishing rate of some 9 percent a year, the United States appears stretched to the breaking point to meet its global commitments as the world's sole superpower. And despite the customary statements made by Secretary of State Colin Powell and his PRC counterpart about Sino-America cooperation and harmony, Qian Qichen, China's former vice premier and foreign minister, published an attack on the Bush Doctrine just before the U.S. presidential election that perhaps presented a more accurate picture of Chinese leadership thinking than the official Foreign Ministry statements.

Although it was immediately disowned by Beijing as in any sense reflecting official PRC views, Qian's article charged that the Bush Doctrine had opened a Pandora's box in advancing the notion that the United States "should rule over the whole world with overwhelming force, military force in particular." The Iraq war, Qian wrote, "has made the United States even more unpopular in the international community than its war in Vietnam." Washington, he said, was practicing "the same catastrophic strategy applied by former empires in history." But, he concluded, "it is incapable of realizing [its] goal." In his view, "the troubles and disasters the United States has met do not stem from threats by others, but from its own cocksureness and arrogance."[27]

China is not without its own problems, of course. A society of 1.3 billion people ruled by a Communist Party that insists on a monopoly of political power while trying to manage an increasingly open market economy is never going to be short of problems. Corruption, growing income inequality, and devastating environmental problems lead the list. Meanwhile, in terms of purchasing power parity, China is already the second-largest economy in the world. It is also second to the United States in energy consumption, having shifted over the past decade from being an oil exporter to an oil importer: China is now dependent on foreign sources for some 40 percent of its crude oil requirements, a number that is expected to rise to as much as 75 percent by 2025.[28]

But while China may be suffering from too much exuberance, the United States appears to be increasingly overextended. Nearly two decades ago, the historian Paul Kennedy sounded a warning about what he called "imperial overstretch," when a state's geopolitical ambitions exceed its material capabilities to sustain such ambitions.[29] In early 2001, when George W. Bush first took office, the Congressional Budget Office projected a federal budget surplus of $5 trillion over the next ten years; but following what the *Economist* has characterized as Bush's "binge of tax-cutting and spending," economists are now projecting instead a $5 trillion budget deficit.[30] Since Bush took office, the federal debt has increased by 40 percent, or $2.1 trillion, and Congress has been required to raise the federal debt ceiling several times already.[31] Meanwhile, the burden of U.S. military commitments in Afghanistan and Iraq, where tours of duty have been extended to keep sufficient troops on the ground, appears to preclude any new "preemptive" assaults on additional countries.

China, for its part, is concerned about Japanese participation in the U.S. missile defense system, new legislation to permit Japanese forces to play a larger supporting role in Bush initiatives, and the possible revision of Japan's constitution to facilitate a more substantial military modernization;[32] but except for possible miscalculation over the issue of Taiwan, there appears to be little likelihood of direct confrontation between the United States and China. Beijing and Washington understand each other much better today than they did in 1995-96 when China launched its "missile exercises" in a failed effort to influence the presidential elections in Taiwan, and since then,

they have established a variety of communication links in order to avoid misperception and miscommunication if tensions in the Taiwan Strait should reemerge.

Taiwan will continue to be an issue in Sino-American relations, but it is Iraq, Iran, and North Korea that should provide the best indicators of their strategic competition. China and the United States take very different positions with respect to each of the three states demonized by President Bush as an "axis of evil" in his 2002 State of the Union Address, and each one raises a separate kind of problem for the Bush Doctrine.

The most serious and immediate case is, of course, Iraq. China opposed the U.S. invasion and totally rejects the doctrine of preventive war. The PRC, like the other major powers, fears a disruption in petroleum imports from the Middle East if the U.S. intervention fails and Iraq descends into chaos, but Beijing clearly does not want the U.S. policy of unilateral military intervention to become the norm.

Iran's nuclear program raises a different issue, since it is unlikely that the United States will have the military capability in the near future to threaten an invasion of the country. It is possible that Bush might endorse at some point an Israeli air assault on the Iranian nuclear facilities, like the Israeli "surgical strike" on Iraq's plutonium-producing Osirak research reactor in 1981, but rather than a site for a new preventive war, Iran is currently a test case for Under Secretary of State John Bolton's policy of "counterproliferation," a coercive-diplomacy strategy designed to use international pressure to force Iran to give up its potential nuclear weapons capability.[33] China, like many of the European allies, rejects this approach in favor of a more conventional "arms control" or "nonproliferation" approach.[34]

Finally, by hosting the six-party talks on North Korea, China directly confronts the Bush Doctrine with its own cooperative security approach to conflict resolution.[35] China is no less concerned to stop nuclear weapons proliferation in Northeast Asia than the United States, fearing that a nuclear North Korea could prompt Japan, South Korea, and possibly even Taiwan to follow suit. But having rejected the coercive U.S. Proliferation Security Initiative, China is proposing instead a multilateral security mechanism for the region to engage and to incorporate the existing North Korean regime.

When Beijing and Washington come face to face, there are always a great many issues to discuss: Taiwan, the U.S. trade deficit with the PRC, and Beijing's concern about the falling U.S. dollar (China is heavily invested in U.S. Treasury bonds), as well as North Korea, Iraq, Iran, and other security problems. Beijing will wait to see who will hold the key foreign policy and security posts in the second Bush administration, and it will have to learn to work more closely with Condoleezza Rice as secretary of state after Colin Powell is gone.

China and the United States are still "in the same bed but dreaming different dreams," as Beijing and Washington each appeal to the world to support their distinctive approaches to resolving the problems of the twenty-first century. President Chen Sui-bian's failure to win a majority for his pro-independence position in Taiwan's legislature in the December 11 elections should help ease tensions over the Taiwan issue, but policies toward the "axis of evil" countries remain in dispute. For the next chapter in the Sino-American saga, it would be a good idea to keep a close watch on North Korea, Iran, and Iraq.

Notes

1. David M. Lampton, *Same Bed, Different Dreams: Managing U.S.-China Relations, 1989-2000* (Berkeley: University of California Press, 2001).

2. David C. Hendrickson, "Toward Universal Empire: The Dangerous Quest for Absolute Security," *World Policy Journal*, vol. 19 (fall 2002), pp. 1-2.

3. Ibid., p. 7.

4. See, for example, Ahmed Rashid, "The Mess in Afghanistan," *New York Review of Books*, February 12, 2004, pp. 24-27; Jamie Wilson, "Attacks Halt Rebuilding Work in Iraq," *Guardian Weekly*, April 29-May 5, 2004, p. 1; Scott Wilson, "US Abuse Worse Than Saddam's, Say Inmates," *Sydney Morning Herald*, May 4, 2004; and Sarah Boseley, "100,000 Iraq Civilians Have Died Since Invasion, Survey Finds," *Guardian Weekly*, November 5-11, 2004, p. 4.

5. "President Holds Press Conference," November 4, 2004, `www.whitehouse.gov`.

6. See Robert W. Tucker and David C. Hendrickson, "The Sources of American Legitimacy," *Foreign Affairs*, vol. 83 (November/December 2004), pp. 18-32. Regarding the issue of torture, which has so undermined the legitimacy of the U.S. role, see also Seymour M. Hersh, *Chain of Command: The Road from 9/11 to Abu Ghraib* (New York: HarperCollins, 2004); and Mark Danner, *Torture and Truth: America, Abu Ghraib, and the War on Terror* (New York: New York Review Books, 2004).

7. Melvin Gurtov and Peter Van Ness, eds., *Confronting the Bush Doctrine: Critical Views from the Asia-Pacific* (New York: RoutledgeCurzon, 2004).

8. See Peter Van Ness, "Hegemony, Not Anarchy: Why China and Japan Are Not Balancing US Unipolar Power," *International Relations of the Asia-Pacific*, vol. 2, no. 1 (2002), pp. 131-50.

9. For example, Richard Clarke, former head of counterterrorism in the White House during both the Clinton and George W. Bush administrations, found that for Bush and his neoconservative advisers "Iraq was portrayed as the most dangerous thing in national security. It was an idée fixe, a rigid belief, received wisdom, a decision already made and one that no fact or event could derail." Invading Iraq constituted "a rejection of analysis in favor of received wisdom. It has left us less secure. We will pay the price for a long time" (Richard A. Clarke, *Against All Enemies: Inside America's War on Terror* [New York: Free Press, 2004], pp. 265, 287).

10. See Timothy Savage, "Letting the Genie Out of the Bottle: The Bush Nuclear Doctrine in Asia," in Gurtov and Van Ness, eds., *Confronting the Bush Doctrine*; and David S. Mc-Donough, *The 2002 Nuclear Posture Review: The "New Triad," Counterproliferation, and U.S. Grand Strategy* (Vancouver, B.C.: Centre of International Relations, University of British Columbia, Working Paper No. 38, August 2003).

11. Li Bin, "China: Weighing the Costs," *Bulletin of the Atomic Scientists*, March/April, 2004, pp. 21-23. Paul Godwin argues that "assuring a reliable second-strike capability in the shadow of US ballistic missile defense programs is unquestionably China's highest priority" (Paul H. B. Godwin, "The PLA's Leap into the 21st Century: Implications for the US," Jamestown Foundation, *China Brief*, vol. 4, no. 9, April 29, 2004).

12. You Ji, "China's Post 9/11 Terrorism Strategy," Jamestown Foundation, *China Brief*, vol. 4, no. 8, April 15, 2004.

13. See, for example, Alastair Iain Johnston, *Cultural Realism: Strategic Culture and Grand Strategy in Chinese History* (Princeton, NJ: Princeton University Press, 1995); Allen S. Whiting, "The Use of Force in Foreign Policy by the People's Republic of China," *Annals of the American Academy of Political and Social Science*, no. 402 (July 1972), pp. 55-65; and Allen S. Whiting, *The Chinese Calculus of Deterrence: India and Indochina* (Ann Arbor: University of Michigan Press, 1975).

14. Evan S. Medeiros and M. Taylor Fravel, "China's New Diplomacy," *Foreign Affairs*, vol. 82 (November-December, 2003), pp. 22-35.

15. For the Shanghai Cooperation Organization statement on terrorism, see *Beijing Review*, January 17, 2002, p. 5.

16. For agreements signed and a chronology of Sino-Indian contacts, April-June 2003, see *China Report* (New Delhi), vol. 39 (October-December 2003).

17. Xiao Zhou, "China's Untraditional Thoughts on Security," *Beijing Review*, November 27, 2003, pp. 40-41.

18. "East Asian Community Now Possible," *Beijing Review*, October 30, 2003, pp. 40-41. *China: An International Journal*, published by the East Asia Institute, National University of Singapore, has taken a special interest in China's relations with ASEAN. This new journal publishes a chronology of events and documents on the relationship in each issue.

19. See David Shambaugh, *Modernizing China's Military: Progress, Problems, and Prospects* (Berkeley: University of California Press, 2002).

20. Godwin, "PLA's Leap into the 21st Century"; see also William S. Murray III and Robert Antonellis, "China's Space Program: The Dragon Eyes the Moon (and Us)," *Orbis*, vol. 47 (fall 2003), pp. 645-52.

21. Joseph Cirincione, with Jon B. Wolfsthal and Miriam Rajkumar, *Deadly Arsenals: Tracking Weapons of Mass Destruction* (Washington, D.C.: Carnegie Endowment for International Peace, 2002), pp. 141-64.

22. Willy Wo-Lap Lam, "China Aiming for 'Peaceful Rise,'" `www.cnn.com`, February 2, 2004.

23. Eric Teo Chu Cheow, "An Ancient Model for China's New Power: Paying Tribute to Beijing," *International Herald Tribune*, January 21, 2004.

24. Quoted in Lam, "China Aiming for 'Peaceful Rise.'"

25. Funabashi Yoichi, "China's 'Peaceful Ascendancy,'" December 2003, YaleGlobal Online, at `www.yaleglobal.yale.edu`.

26. Amitav Acharya, "Will Asia's Past Be Its Future?" *International Security*, vol. 28, (winter 2003/04), pp. 149-64.

27. Qian Qichen, "US Strategy Seriously Flawed," *China Daily Online*, November 1, 2004.

28. Pam Woodall, "The Dragon and the Eagle," *Economist*, October 2, 2004; and "Asia's Great Oil Hunt," *Business Week*, November 15, 2004.

29. Paul Kennedy, *The Rise and Fall of the Great Powers* (New York: Vintage, 1987), pp. 514-15.

30. *Economist*, October 9-15, 2004.

31. *International Herald Tribune*, October 16-17, 2004, p. 2.

32. Richard Tanter, "With Eyes Wide Shut: Japan, Heisei Militarization, and the Bush Doctrine," in Gurtov and Van Ness, eds., *Confronting the Bush Doctrine*.
33. John R. Bolton, "An All-Out War on Proliferation," *Financial Times*, September 7, 2004.
34. Li Bin, "China: Weighing the Costs."
35. Peter Van Ness, "The North Korean Nuclear Crisis: Four-Plus-Two—An Idea Whose Time Has Come," in Gurtov and Van Ness, eds., *Confronting the Bush Doctrine*.

Peter Van Ness is a visiting fellow in the Contemporary China Centre and lectures on security in the Department of International Relations at Australian National University. His new book, Confronting the Bush Doctrine: Critical Views from the Asia-Pacific, *edited with Melvin Gurtov and published by RoutledgeCurzon, is the basis for this essay.*

Japan:
America's New South Korea?

"There are signs that Japan will assume the geostrategic role of the 'new South Korea'—a leverage point against China. Missile defense in particular will transform the US-Japan relationship into a 'normal' alliance, taking it in directions not hitherto contemplated."

JAMES E. AUER AND ROBYN LIM

The key issue confronting US-Japan relations is how much Japan can and should do to ensure its own security. During the cold war, Japan was able to purchase its security at minimal cost; indeed, it was frequently criticized in the US Congress for free riding on America's anti-Soviet posture in the Pacific region. That is no longer possible. Now the United States has more strategic latitude than when it was tied down by countervailing Soviet power. And America is freer to give up on free-riding or feckless allies, as South Korea is discovering. Is Japan—which spends less than 1 percent of GDP on defense—willing to pay increased dues for an alliance that provides it with nuclear and long-range maritime security?

So far, the signs are positive that Tokyo will be able to make the required changes. Notably, the United States and Japan are cooperating in the development of missile defense, which is the primary issue that will help shape the alliance. Japan also has sent elements of its Self-Defense Force to Iraq (thus far in noncombat roles) in support of the US mission there.

All may not be smooth sailing, however. While a congruence of strategic interests still underpins the alliance, those interests are not quite as congruent as they were during the cold war. Moreover, Japan's security environment has become more volatile. This means Japan will have to make the kind of hard choices that it has hitherto been able to avoid.

JAPAN'S REDUCED LEVERAGE

Japan's strategic environment is now much less predictable, and thus potentially more dangerous, than during the cold war. That global strategic contest meant Japan had no reason to fear that it would be attacked by the Soviet Union in any circumstance short of general war. And general war was highly unlikely: both superpowers knew that the existence of nuclear weapons made a head-to-head collision far too dangerous.

During the cold war, the United States was willing, in the interests of its own security, to provide nuclear and maritime security for Japan. In return, Japan provided the United States with access to bases that could be used for regional purposes. Because the security connection was vital to the interests of both parties, they were able to insulate the security relationship from the frictions that began to develop as the Japanese economy started to boom in the 1960s.

Today's strategic environment in Asia is very different, not least because America has more strategic choices. Its vital interest, however, remains the same: maintenance of the balance of power on the opposite shore of the Pacific. Since 1952, one of America's main means of doing so has been the alliance with Japan. But that was not so before, and may not always be so in the future.

For Japan, the maritime basis of its security means that alliance with the dominant maritime power represents optimal security. That was so between 1902 and 1922, and has been so since 1952. But Japan today has less leverage on the alliance than it enjoyed during the cold war, and the United States has more strategic latitude. The United States is developing military technology that shrinks distance and helps reduce the need for allies who might defect in a crisis. And, at the same time, Japan has less weight in the alliance because its economy faltered just as the cold war was ending, and is only now beginning to recover. Moreover, while America still requires bases in Japan, it does not need them to the degree it did in the past.

The key long-term issue in the management of the US-Japan relationship is China. While China has strategic

61

ambition, Japan has growing strategic anxieties. But the immediate problem for peace and stability in the East Asia-Pacific region is North Korea.

THE "ORPHANED" NEIGHBOR

One of the reasons that Japan's security environment has turned for the worse is that North Korea, having been made an "orphan" by the end of the cold war, has become more dangerous. No longer able to play off Beijing against Moscow, North Korea has preserved its odious regime by developing missiles and weapons of mass destruction as instruments of blackmail and extortion.

In August 1998, North Korea's unannounced launch over the Japanese islands of a three-stage solid-fueled long-range missile, the Taepodong, signaled the end of the days when most Japanese thought they could pursue a head-in-the-sand approach to security. The Taepodong launch meant that the entire Japanese archipelago was now vulnerable to missile attack from a country that hated Japan (because of Japan's harsh occupation of the Korean peninsula from 1910 to 1945) and that also had a long history of state-sponsored terrorism. And by 2002, North Korea was boasting that it had an illegal uranium-enrichment facility.

Some observers claim that the North Korean missile threat to Japan has been exaggerated. They say the missiles represent less of a threat to Japan than when it was targeted by many more Soviet missiles, which were also far more accurate than the North Korean missiles. This is true, but irrelevant. During the cold war Japan had no reason to fear an attack on itself unless general war broke out.

But not long after the cold war ended, North Korea started to open up a gap between the United States and Japan on the vital issue of nuclear security. In fact, US Defense Secretary Donald Rumsfeld, when visiting Japan in late 2003, felt a need to confirm that the US "nuclear umbrella" would not leak. That was an indication that Japan was growing nervous lest America offer some kind of security guarantee to North Korea that might nullify US guarantees to Japan.

One of the consequences of North Korea's Taepodong launch was that Japan opted to build its own optical reconnaissance satellites. That was partly a victory for domestic Japanese industry, but it was also an indication that Japan might be starting to lose confidence in US nuclear protection.

Moreover, at the end of his tenure, President Bill Clinton was tempted to strike a deal with North Korea that would have seen Pyongyang freeze its long-range missile development, but would have left North Korea's existing missiles in place. This North Korean attempt at alliance busting ended only when prominent Republican voices, such as that of former Defense Department official Richard Armitage, indicated to the Clinton administration that if the party's candidate won the election, the new Republican administration would not honor any deal.

KOIZUMI'S UNILATERALISM

The Bush administration from the start indicated it was not willing to play such games, notably when President Bush included North Korea in the "axis of evil" in his State of the Union address in January 2002. So North Korean leader Kim Jong-il turned his attention to other ways of trying to drive wedges into the US-Japan alliance. This time, he came even closer to success when Japan's prime minister, Junichiro Koizumi, announced in August 2002 that he would visit Pyongyang.

Koizumi, in announcing his impending visit, presented Washington with a fait accompli. He was looking for a distraction from Japan's flagging economy, and wanted a political boost in order to reshuffle his cabinet. To this end, Koizumi saw his opening to Pyongyang as a means of achieving the return of Japanese kidnapped by North Korea in the 1970s and 1980s.

Koizumi went ahead with his plans even though he was told by Washington that North Korea had a clandestine highly enriched uranium program. On September 17, 2002, Koizumi held his "historic summit" with Kim. Koizumi also dangled before Pyongyang the prospect of largescale Japanese aid, in the form of so-called disguised reparations for Japan's occupation of the Korean peninsula from 1910.

The key long-term issue in the management of the US-Japan relationship is China.

It soon became apparent that the "Dear Leader" had miscalculated when he failed to keep alive enough of the kidnapped Japanese to use as future pawns. When the news reached Japan that most of the abductees were dead, attitudes hardened.

But Kim did not give up, and May 2004 saw Koizumi back in Pyongyang. With Upper House elections looming in July, Koizumi was looking again for a political boost, hoping to secure the release of relatives of the abductees who had been released in 2002.

When Koizumi reached Pyongyang in May, he did secure the return of five adult children of the Japanese hostages previously released. But he also promised to give North Korea 250,000 tons of rice and $10 million in medical aid. And he was willing to put up with rude treatment by Kim, including being filmed on North Korean television with the Dear Leader wagging his finger under Koizumi's nose. No doubt, this all played well in both Koreas.

THE SEOUL ALLIANCE UNRAVELS

While Koizumi unwittingly provided the North Koreans the opportunity to drive a wedge between Washington and Tokyo, the US alliance with South Korea has been unraveling as a consequence of the end of the cold war and China's turn to the market. South Korea has been unable to translate its economic supremacy over the north into political leverage. To the contrary, it is bent on appeasement of North Korea. This is out of a mixture of naïveté and fear—fear of the costs of reunification, and fear of North Korea's weapons of mass destruction and conventional arms.

As a consequence of growing interdependence between the Chinese and South Korean economies, South Korea has become a de facto ally of China. Thus its value to the United States as an ally has been undermined, and the congruence of strategic interest that underpinned this alliance during the cold war is rapidly eroding.

In early June 2004, the Pentagon told Seoul that it intends, by the end of 2005, to withdraw 12,500 troops from units stationed in South Korea. That decision followed the US decision in May to reassign to Iraq a combat brigade. The Pentagon made no promise that these ground troops would ever return to South Korea.

These moves were triggered in part by operational needs in Iraq. They are also part of global changes in US force structure designed to reduce permanent forward deployments, increase access to overseas facilities, and produce a more mobile and flexible military capable of more rapid deployment operations.

In relation to the Korean peninsula, the Pentagon wants its ground forces removed from their forward-deployed positions across the main invasion routes from North Korea. In these positions, they have become too vulnerable to North Korean rockets and artillery.

But there is more to it than that. Recent US moves in South Korea came also in response to the actions and interests of China and both Koreas. South Korea's increasing criticisms of the US presence, its decision to look to China for strategic security, and its solicitous attitude toward North Korea make nonsense of the US ground presence in South Korea.

Fortunately for South Korea, the United States retains nuclear, maritime, and air power in the Western Pacific that can be used to devastating effect on the Korean peninsula. But the US force structure in South Korea will be increasingly geared to US strategic needs, rather than defense of the invasion corridors north of Seoul. Washington will expect that its reconfigured forces will be available for use in regional contingencies, including Taiwan. Will South Korea permit that? It seems unlikely.

A Foil To China

China is East Asia's "rising" power. When the Soviet Union collapsed, China no longer had to worry about Soviet strategic pressure on its northern and western frontiers. Thus China was soon pressing on its maritime frontiers in the East and South China Sea. The collapse of Soviet power also saw the collapse of the de facto alignment forged between Washington and Beijing in the early 1970s, when the rapid development of Soviet military power threatened them both.

Today, China and the United States are not enemies. Their economies are increasingly interdependent, and they have some shared strategic interests, including avoiding war and achieving the denuclearization of the Korean peninsula. But they are not friends, either. If China were to become dominant in East Asia, it would detract from US security by excluding US military power from the region (or by seeking to do so), and indirectly by its effects on Japan.

There are signs that Japan will assume the geostrategic role of the "new South Korea"—a leverage point against China. Missile defense in particular will transform the US-Japan relationship into a "normal" alliance, taking it in directions not hitherto contemplated.

Japan dithered for years on missile defense, even in the face of the growing missile threat from North Korea, mostly because it feared "offending" China. That was until late 2002, when the United States made it clear that it was going ahead with missile defense anyway, if necessary without Japan. The subtext was that the Americans were unwilling to leave their forces unprotected in Japan if the means to protect them were being developed and Japan was unwilling to participate.

The pace of US-Japan cooperation has been accelerating since Japan decided in December 2003 to acquire ballistic missile defenses by 2007. Programs to provide initial missile defense systems to Japan are under way, and a Memorandum of Understanding is about to be signed.

Collaboration in missile defense will do much to make the US-Japan alliance "normal" in terms of interoperability for bilateral warfighting—in this case, shooting down missiles that threaten both Japan and US forces stationed in Japan. Moreover, Japan will inevitably become part of the defense of the United States. That is because the systems required for the defense of Japan (such as satellites and space-based sensors that detect the heat plumes from missile launches) will be integrally linked to systems required for the defense of the continental United States.

Hard choices lie ahead. In particular, Japan will have to abandon the self-serving notion that, while it is entitled to participate in collective self-defense (the right of all members of the UN), it chooses not to do so. In the past, this was a device that helped Japan avoid entanglement in America's conflicts, or potential conflicts, in East Asia. Koizumi is currently foreshadowing moves to abandon this interpretation of the constitution. Another hurdle is Japan's arms export policy, which makes cooperation with the US difficult since it prevents the joint development and production of weapons with a foreign country; this ban will have to be lifted if the United States and Japan are to collaborate in missile defense. Japan will also have to amend or reinterpret a 1969 Diet resolution that bans the military use of space. Although Japan protects intelligence reasonably well, new legislation protecting intelligence will also be required.

THE PARTNERSHIP DEEPENS

The United States and Japan were never able to savor their combined efforts in winning the cold war in the Pacific, in part because Saddam Hussein invaded Kuwait in August 1990. The defense relationship had evolved from extremely humble beginnings in the early 1950s, when the United States ordered Japan to rearm and loaned it old military equipment, into a sophisticated high-technology anti-submarine, air-defense partnership in the 1980s. But the relationship suffered a serious setback when Japan opted out of even token participation in Operation Desert Storm. Although Japan raised taxes and did contribute $13 billion, its efforts were criticized as checkbook diplomacy in the United States, Europe, and friendly Persian Gulf countries. Stung by criticism, Japan sought closer consultations with the United States. New *Guidelines for Defense Cooperation,* which came about in the latter half of the 1990s, authorized "rear area support," that is, noncombat Japanese assistance in "safe" areas.

In a very nontypical Japanese "grassroots" campaign, Koizumi came out of nowhere to become prime minister in April 2001 with a promise to reform Japan's economy and end business as usual. Armed with the new *Guidelines,* Koizumi's administration acted quickly following September 11, 2001, and sent Japanese naval tankers and destroyers to the Indian Ocean to support US and British forces in Afghanistan. The dispatch of one of Japan's four Aegis-class destroyers was considered too sensitive initially, but one Aegis ship has now also served. The enabling legislation was extended for two more years in 2003 and Japan's maritime contribution was comple-mented by the deployment of military transport aircraft and 600-plus Japanese soldiers to Samawah, Iraq, declared to be "safe" enough to receive Japanese noncombat humanitarian assistance. Although these Japanese troops are supposed to be withdrawn if the area becomes dangerous, the presence of Japanese "boots on the ground" near a combat zone is a phenomenon not seen since 1945.

ENDURING INTERESTS

Strategic circumstances change, but interests tend to be enduring. Today, America's vital interest in East Asia is the same as it has been since 1905— to secure a balance of power that suits its interests. Since the Korean War, America's main means of doing so has been alliance with Japan. But that could change.

If Japan proves unwilling to play the role of the "new South Korea," America might be tempted to pursue its "Perfidious Albion" option—playing off China against Japan. Rising strategic tension between China and Japan, despite their growing economic interdependence, makes it unlikely that the two countries would work together against the United States.

Thus the onus is on Japan to say what it is willing to do if it wishes to continue to enjoy all the benefits of alliance. For Japan, the choice could well be a "normal" alliance— in which it must be willing to fight if necessary—or no alliance at all.

JAMES E. AUER *is director of the Center for US-Japan Studies and Cooperation at Vanderbilt University. ROBYN LIM is a professor of international relations at Nanzan University, Nagoya. Her research for this article was aided by a Nanzan University Pache grant.*

The US and Latin America Through the Lens of Empire

"An unvarnished sense of superiority, displayed proudly on the regional and global stage, has revived the resentment and distrust of Latin Americans toward the United States that had recently shown signs of receding."

MICHAEL SHIFTER

For many Latin Americans, President George W. Bush's November 6, 2003, speech before the National Endowment for Democracy touched on an all-too-familiar theme. Bush boldly called for a democratic revolution, led by the United States, in Iraq and the Middle East. Two decades earlier, President Ronald Reagan had delivered a similarly audacious address to the British Parliament, one that laid the groundwork for the creation of the endowment itself. Just as Bush has now targeted the "axis of evil," Reagan had assailed the Soviet Union's "evil empire." Then, however, the principal theater the US president had in mind for his democracy mission was not thousands of miles away, in the Middle East, but much closer to home, in Central America.

Not surprisingly, Latin Americans are perhaps peculiarly sensitive to the stunning projection of US power in Iraq in 2003. The terms that are increasingly fashionable in describing international affairs—"unilateralism," "hegemony," "empire"—have long been used in analyses of inter-American relations. The vast asymmetry of power between the United States and the countries to its south has been a fundamental feature of the region's historical landscape. The Manichaean "you're either with us or against us" formulation has been implicit, and long assimilated.

With the collapse of the Berlin Wall, the use of terms such as empire and hegemony, tailored over decades to cold war realities, was substantially attenuated. Starting with the administration of George H. W. Bush (1988-1992), a window of opportunity opened for referring, without irony, to the prospect of constructing political partnerships and striving to become "enterprises of the Americas." Fresh and original ideas for defending democracy and extending commerce in the Americas offered considerable promise for more productive hemispheric cooperation.

Today that promise has largely faded. Relations between the United States and Latin America have acquired a rawness and a level of indecorum that recall previous eras of inter-American strain and discord. In the past, the rough edges had occasionally been blunted and softened, not only during the post-cold war interlude of the 1990s, but also at various other moments, such as the 1930s and early 1960s. Although Latin Americans have always resisted and opposed US power, from time to time their demands have been at least partially addressed.

Yet, at the beginning of the twenty-first century, the quality of American "exceptionalism" that sociologist Seymour Martin Lipset called a "doubleedged sword"—characterized, on the one hand, by generosity and democratic openness and, on the other, by unbridled moralism, bordering on intolerance—has tilted decidedly toward the latter. An unvarnished sense of superiority, displayed proudly on the regional and global stage, has revived the resentment and distrust of Latin Americans toward the United States that had recently shown signs of receding. It is an attitude captured in a November 2003 survey by Zogby International among key opinion makers in six Latin American countries, which showed that a startling 87 percent of respondents had a negative opinion of President Bush.

HISTORICAL BAGGAGE, AND LESSONS LEARNED

The United States has rarely exhibited the characteristics of an empire or imperial power in a classical sense. Unlike Britain, France, or Spain in previous eras, the United States has shown little propensity to completely take over another territory and control its institutions. Instead, since the elaboration of the Monroe Doctrine in 1823, there has been a tendency to keep other great powers out of the Western Hemisphere and permit national, independent development—provided that it posed little threat to the region's stability and assured the primacy of US interests.

In the early part of the twentieth century especially, the US role in Central America and the Caribbean was marked by various occupations carried out by the US armed forces when it was deemed necessary to protect American economic and strategic interests and to spread American values. Nicaragua, Haiti, the Dominican Republic—all at one time were occupied, often for considerable stretches. The occupations, which generally came to an end by the 1930s, proved difficult, and had mixed results at best. These experiences account, in part, for the enormous skepticism in much of Latin America about the current US occupation of Afghanistan and Iraq.

The cold war saw the United States return to Latin America in an attempt to assert its ideological hegemony and maintain the hemisphere as its sphere of influence, if not control. Whatever Washington perceived as an extension of Soviet influence in the hemisphere was typically met with a swift and severe response. This was the case even before the 1959 Cuban revolution (for example, in Guatemala in 1954), but became especially pronounced after the installation of a Communist government just off the US mainland. It would be hard to overstate the effect of Fidel Castro's regime in shaping US Latin America policy through the cold war—and even since the cold war's end. The US intervention in the Dominican Republic in 1965, and the US pressure that helped result in the 1973 military coup against Chile's elected president, Salvador Allende, can best be understood against this cold war backdrop.

In the 1980s, the cold war's intense ideological battle became concentrated in Central America, where the Reagan administration backed an authoritarian government in El Salvador to prevent a powerful leftist insurgency from taking over. The United States also waged a proxy war through the "contras" in Nicaragua, then controlled by a Sandinista government with close ties to Cuba and the Soviet Union.

The US obsession with security questions in the 1980s rendered a productive relationship with Latin America virtually impossible. Sharp differences in priorities had always existed, but occasional US initiatives in response to Latin American concerns attempted to bridge them. Franklin Roosevelt's Good Neighbor Policy of the 1930s, a serious effort to engage constructively with the region, was one example. Another was John Kennedy's lofty Alliance for Progress. No doubt calculated to counter the appeal of Castro's regime, it nonetheless projected a commitment to Latin America's social reform agenda. Although these initiatives did not transform the hemisphere's power relations, they did display a concern for Latin America's acute social conditions and reflect an effort to identify common interests, thereby cushioning the negative effects of US hegemony.

THE BUSH I AND CLINTON ERA

In fundamental respects, the first Bush administration reflected continuity with the US policies toward Latin America whose antecedents were Roosevelt's Good Neighbor Policy and Kennedy's Alliance for Progress. Transformations on the world stage—most notably the fall of the Berlin Wall— coupled with important changes in Latin America's political landscape toward more democratic rule, created fertile and favorable conditions for a more serious engagement with the region.

This period saw new precedents set in the critical areas of democracy and trade. Roughly coinciding with the end of Chilean dictator Augusto Pinochet's extended military rule, member governments of the Organization of American States, meeting in Santiago, Chile, in June 1991, approved a resolution that marked a sharp departure in inter- American norms. For the first time, any interruption in democratic, constitutional rule would become a matter of regional concern and would trigger a hemispheric response. That resolution, which has been invoked four times since its adoption, formed the cornerstone of the widely touted Inter-American Democratic Charter that was approved a decade later at an OAS General Assembly in Lima, Peru. The charter codified or systematized all the democracy-related declarations and resolutions that had been adopted over the previous decade, essentially giving these declarations and resolutions greater force.

The notion of creating a hemisphere-wide free trade area can also be traced to the first Bush administration. The Enterprise of the Americas initiative, launched in 1990, recognized the concerns of Latin American leaders who had expressed keen interest in securing greater access to US markets for their countries' products. Such responsiveness and engagement were welcomed south of the Rio Grande, and especially in Mexico. It was during the first Bush administration that the final terms of the North American Free Trade Agreement (NAFTA), involving the United States, Canada, and Mexico, were negotiated and signed. The US Congress approved the treaty in 1993, under the Clinton administration. The first Bush administration was responsive to Latin American concerns about foreign debt as well, devising the Brady Plan—after Treasury Secretary Nicholas Brady—to reduce the region's $450 billion in foreign debt.

Other nods to Latin America did not go unnoticed in the region. With the end of the cold war, Washington became more committed to achieving a peaceful resolution to longstanding conflicts in Central America—in Nicaragua in 1990 and El Salvador in early 1992 under the first Bush administration, and then in Guatemala under Clinton in 1996. The US role helped overcome doubts about whether the United States was prepared to apply its power constructively in former cold war battlegrounds. The first Bush administration also participated in two anti-drug summits—in Cartagena, Colombia, and San Antonio, Texas—during which the US president met with his Andean counterparts in a multilateral framework.

The momentum toward greater cooperation continued into the two terms that Bill Clinton served between 1992 and 2000. This era saw not only the passage of NAFTA, but also the convening of the Summit of the Americas, featuring all the hemisphere's elected leaders, in December 1994 in Miami. The summit was the first meeting of its kind in a quarter of a century. It set the goal of negotiating a Free Trade Area of the Americas (FTAA) by January 2005.

Two months before the summit, the Clinton administration used the threat of force to return to office the democratically elected leader of Haiti, Jean-Bertrand Aristide. This was in striking contrast to historical images of the United States propping up authoritarian regimes. It offered further evidence that the US government could use its power to advance legitimate democratic rule in the hemisphere.

The momentum stalled, however, in the latter part of the 1990s. Economic and political conditions in many Latin American countries deteriorated. In Venezuela, which endured two successive lost decades, strongman Hugo Chávez was elected president in December 1998, while in Peru, President Alberto Fujimori further entrenched his authoritarian rule. In short, a malaise gripped much of the region, making it less attractive to Washington. In addition, the US Congress continually denied Clinton the "fast track" authority he sought to negotiate trade agreements without congressional amendment, reflecting a more inward-looking society and the growing salience of domestic politics—in this case, pressure from labor unions identified with the Democratic party—in shaping US hemispheric policy.

Relations between the United States and Latin America have acquired a rawness and a level of indecorum that recall previous eras of inter-American strain and discord.

Latin Americans were deeply suspicious of what they regarded as unilateral moves in Colombia that culminated in the July 2000 approval of some $1.3 billion in US security aid to fight the drug war in that country. To be sure, Washington was responding to a deeply troubling situation: a democracy under siege. But the elements of the final assistance package nonetheless centered chiefly on combating drugs, a narrow piece of the wider problem, and mostly through law enforcement efforts. A more comprehensive strategy, embracing key dimensions of social development and institutional reform, was lacking.

BUSH II AND 9-11

The election in November 2000 of George W. Bush generated varied expectations about how the United States would approach hemispheric relations. Two separate ten-dencies within the executive branch could be discerned. That Bush appeared comfortable with Latin America—he had served as governor of Texas—and had initially evinced great enthusiasm for a tightly knit inter-American community, seemed to bode well for hemispheric relations. At the same time, senior officials such as national security adviser Condoleezza Rice showed little sympathy for the kind of "nation-building" mission the Clinton administration had carried out in Haiti and instead signaled that the new administration would pursue hard-headed policies, emphasizing the defense of vital national interests.

The first nine months of the Bush administration provided evidence of both of these tendencies. Bush met with many of the region's leaders, attended the third Summit of the Americas in Quebec, and cultivated a particularly close relationship with Mexican President Vicente Fox. At the White House on September 5, 2001, Bush famously referred to Mexico as "our most important relationship." Unlike its predecessor, however, Bush's team at the Treasury Department eschewed anything resembling a bailout in dire financial situations like the rescue the Clinton administration had provided to Mexico during the 1995 peso crisis. Thus, the deepening Argentine predicament in 2001—marked by unsustainable deficits, which resulted in widespread social unrest and the forced resignation of the country's president—was treated as merely a fiscal problem and initially elicited indifference from Washington. Eventually, however, the United States voted in favor of an IMF loan of nearly $3 billion to Argentina in January 2003, and also participated in an IMF aid package to Brazil.

The United States has instruments and resources at its disposal to mollify the virulent anti-Americanism that has returned to Latin America.

The attacks on the World Trade Center and Pentagon on September 11, 2001, dramatically eclipsed the incipient Bush administration approach to Latin America. The traumatic events engendered a sense of vulnerability and fear in American society, and transformed Bush into a wartime president. The moralist side of American exceptionalism described by Lipset was activated with unprecedented force. Crystallizing the emerging foreign policy concept was a new doctrine of "preemption," developed in the Bush administration's September 2002 *National Security Strategy*. The strategy made it clear that America would not hesitate to use power preemptively to protect itself. For the United States, this marked a departure. As historian Arthur Schlesinger noted in the October 23, 2003, *New York Review of Books*, "Mr. Bush has replaced a policy aimed at peace through the prevention of war by a policy aimed at peace through preventive war."

Much of the rest of the world overwhelmingly rejected this formulation. The response in Latin America was similar, but it had a distinctive twist. For Latin Americans, the practice of preventive military action by the United States had a long history, especially in Central America and Caribbean countries. It can be plausibly argued that the use of US force in 1983 in Grenada, or in 1989 in Panama, were early examples of preventive military action. But making the practice a matter of doctrine touched a raw nerve in Latin America, since it showed a blatant disregard for the precepts of international law. It also raised the specter of future US military adventures in the region, employing the war on terror as a justification.

The region has been sensitive as well to the treatment of prisoners of America's "war on terror" that are being held at the detention center in Guantánamo, Cuba. In this US-controlled territory, secured as a result of what many Latin Americans see as an imperialist war, basic standards of due process have not been respected and followed. Although, at the end of 2003, US courts had begun to raise serious objections to such treatment, the reports from Guantánamo have not helped enhance US credibility as a guardian of human rights and constitutional protections. Some comments in the Latin American press have been unsparing (one Colombian columnist referred to Guantánamo as the US "gulag"). Guantánamo, and the specter of military tribunals for suspected terrorists, raised the perennial question of double standards, and supplied ammunition for Latin Americans subjected to US sermons on the importance of adhering to the rule of law.

As the war on terror became the overriding priority of US foreign policy, claims of interest in and concern for Latin America within the Bush administration rang increasingly hollow. Senior officials became more and more distracted from a region that was supposed to be high on Washington's agenda. It is true that in September 2003 the US Congress, for the first time in five years, confirmed an assistant secretary of state for Western Hemisphere affairs, Roger Noriega. But, given that US prestige and credibility were on the line in Iraq and the war on terror, it would take a superman to successfully engage interest in Latin America among the most senior-level decision makers in Congress and the administration. Latin Americans hoped not so much for increased attention—the demand, after all, has a paternalistic ring to it—but rather a strategy that sought to take better advantage of the many mutual interests shared by the United States and Latin America.

Washington's distraction, indifference, and failure to seriously consider Latin America's own concerns have exacted considerable costs. The Bush administration's initially mishandled response to the April 2002 military coup against Venezuelan President Hugo Chávez—failing to show any concern and instead expressing undisguised glee—eroded the administration's credibility on the democracy question. That blunder effectively sidelined any potential US leadership role in trying to assure a peaceful, constitutional resolution to Venezuela's political crisis.

From Latin America's perspective, Washington also bore some responsibility for the democratic setback that Bolivia suffered in October 2003. The government of President Gonzalo Sánchez de Lozada, which had faithfully implemented the various economic and drug policy recipes advocated by Washington, could not withstand the enormous social pressure brought by a variety of angry and frustrated sectors, particularly the well-organized indigenous groups and coca growers. As was widely reported after the collapse of his government, President Sánchez de Lozada had in 2002 requested some $150 million in development assistance from Washington to deal with growing strain and unrest. He was rebuffed by the Bush administration, which offered merely $10 million. The Bolivian president was prescient in anticipating that, without the requested aid, he would have trouble surviving in office.

The Bolivia case underscores the myopia of a longstanding US drug policy excessively focused on law enforcement objectives—a policy that gives scant attention to social development issues and fails to take into adequate account its effects on democratic governance. More important, what happened in Bolivia illustrates a deeper malaise throughout the troubled Andean region that also extends to other pockets of concern in Latin America. Bolivia conveys a sense of an already fragile region breaking further apart, devoid of a coherent framework for political and economic development.

In this regard, the Latinobarómetro's comparative surveys offer little to cheer about. As the October 30, 2003, *Economist* summed it up, "A bare majority of Latin Americans are convinced democrats, but they are deeply frustrated by the way their democratic institutions work in practice." In 10 of the 17 Latin American countries polled, support for democracy has dropped significantly, and steadily, since 1996. Notably, 52 percent of the sample agreed with the statement: "I wouldn't mind if a nondemocratic government came to power if it could solve economic problems." Levels of confidence and trust in the region's political leaders and institutions—political parties are particularly discredited— remain alarmingly low.

Such worrying results are impossible to separate from Latin America's stubbornly stagnant economies. Many of the region's citizens are profoundly disenchanted with market-oriented prescriptions that they see as having yielded only greater corruption, few tangible benefits, and deepening social inequalities. Whether one refers to the precepts of "neoliberalism" or, as shorthand, the "Washington consensus," there is clearly a major backlash in much of Latin America. Bolivia highlights the spreading angst about lack of national control in the context of globalization as indictments of privatization gain growing support.

Increasing social dislocations and rising tensions are understandably of primary concern for most Latin Americans. Yet, in Washington, the war on terror, perhaps also understandably, is of overriding concern. The result is a disturbing disconnect that, as Latin America's social disintegration and the US-led war continue, could become even wider. The common language of open democracies and free markets used in the past decade by reform-minded opinion leaders throughout the hemisphere has less and less resonance. And, as the Latinobarómetro poll reports, at least among Mexicans and South Americans, regard for the United States in the past two years has fallen sharply. True, the unilateral US military adventure in Iraq in large measure accounts for the drop. But the sense that the United States has mainly been unresponsive to and disengaged from Latin America's deepening concerns—while expecting unquestioning support and loyalty for its own specific agenda—also helps to explain the growing anti-American sentiment in the region.

THE TEST OF HEGEMONY: TRADE AND BRAZIL

Although the Bush administration has not strayed from Washington's traditional indifference to Latin America's social distress and political turmoil, it has been far more engaged and energetic in seeking to advance the trade agenda. President Bush managed to secure the "fast track" trade authority that President Clinton failed to obtain, and achieved a long-awaited bilateral trade agreement with Chile. In late 2003, the United States announced a free trade agreement with four Central American countries, and prospects for reaching deals with Colombia and Peru looked promising. US trade representative Robert Zoellick has, more than any other senior Bush administration official, engaged Latin America—responding to the region's interest in obtaining access for its products to US markets.

Although there has been undeniable progress in this area, trade issues also pose significant challenges to inter-American relations and represent a fundamental test of the relationship between the United States and Brazil. Agreement between these two large countries is essential if there is to be any possibility of moving toward the goal of a Free Trade Area of the Americas, which has been generally supported by the hemisphere's elected governments since 1994. And on a wide array of other critical issues affecting the hemisphere, it is difficult to imagine important advances without close cooperation between the United States and Brazil.

The election of Luiz Inácio Lula da Silva as Brazil's president in October 2002 left Washington palpably nervous; it did not know what to expect from the leftist leader of the Workers Party. Yet 2003 proved to be the year of Lula (as he is commonly known) in Latin America. Impressively, he has so far sustained what might ultimately prove an impossible balancing act: straddling the worlds of the financial establishment and its critics. No

---

A Current History Snapshot …
HISTORY IN THE MAKING
90 years
1914-2004

"Some regret was voiced that the United States could not have made a sweeping and clean-cut renunciation of intervention in every form in all circumstances. . . . Nevertheless, it was felt, and this feeling grew with a reconsideration of [Secretary of State Cordell] Hull's assertion that 'no government need fear any intervention on the part of the United States under the Roosevelt administration,' that here indeed was a new chapter in the history of relations between the United States and Latin America. . . ."

"Pan-Americanism Reborn"
Current History, February 1934
Ernest Gruening

---

other leader, for example, participated in both the World Economic Forum in Davos, Switzerland, and its counterpoint, the Social Forum in Porto Alegre, Brazil. Lula appears to be the quintessential pragmatist, displaying a penchant for fiscal discipline and other economic policies associated with the Washington consensus. At the same time, unless he can make progress in tackling Brazil's immense social agenda and particularly its glaring inequalities, Lula risks disappointing many of his supporters, in Brazil and throughout Latin America, who have high hopes and expectations for another "way" in a frustrated region searching for alternatives.

Lula has surprised many observers not only with his pragmatism in national policies, but also because of his assertive role in regional affairs. Building on Brazil's self-image as a regional power, with disproportionate significance in South America, Lula has taken initiative in dealing with difficult situations in Venezuela, where he launched a Group of Friends mechanism to deal with the clash between President Chávez and his opponents, and in Colombia, where he offered support to President Álvaro Uribe in his pursuit of democratic security. Lula has also sought to strengthen his relationship with Argentina, particularly the government of Néstor Kirchner, to further consolidate MERCOSUR, the Southern Cone trade group. Indeed, Lula has staked out a position on reaching an FTAA pact, consistent with his predecessors, that emphasizes the importance of US concessions in lifting agricultural subsidies as a precondition for corresponding concessions on the Brazilian side.

Questions related to a trade agreement aside, what is crucial in the coming period will be the capacity of both the United States and Brazil to reach an accommodation and tolerate what are bound to be inevitable differences on policy issues. From all indications, the US government is split on how to deal with Brazil's attempt to establish itself as a regional power. (The Brazilian government appears similarly divided regarding the United States.) Growing strains between the two countries were apparent during the World Trade Organization meeting in Cancún, Mexico, in September 2003, and the gathering of trade ministers in Miami in November 2003. But the question is: will the United States exercise its hegemonic presumption in this context and show little tolerance for Brazil's heightened activism, or will it pursue an understanding with another regional power in this hemisphere? Will accommodation or an adversarial posture prevail? Can the United States accept real policy differences for the sake of building a broader relationship? There is no better opportunity for Washington to forge a strategic partnership and restore the declining goodwill among many Latin Americans toward the United States.

BACK TO THE BACKYARD?

How the United States deals with Brazil's evolving role in the hemisphere in the coming years will largely determine America's ability to adjust its thinking to the region's new realities. Analysts have long used the image of the "backyard" to depict US conceptions of Latin America, especially Central America. But in the context of globalization—where national problems have worldwide ramifications— such conceptions are woefully inadequate.

The regional test for the United States also includes its relationship with Mexico, which is fundamental to constructing a vital hemispheric community. After the September 11 attacks, no country has experienced more friction with the United States at the highest political levels than Mexico. Perhaps expectations were unrealistically high, but President Bush, based on his previous foreign policy experience and friendship, initially looked south, toward President Fox. The strain that developed after the attacks—Washington felt that Mexico did not show sufficient solidarity—was exacerbated once the Iraq enterprise started, and Mexico, as a member of the United Nations Security Council, had to take a public stand on the US decision to go to war. Mexico's opposition to the US position did not sit well with Congress and, especially, the Bush administration.

Not surprisingly, toward the end of 2003 signs appeared that the bilateral relationship was on the road to repair. Summits held in Mexico in October 2003 and January 2004 should help re-engage Washington with the bilateral agenda. Electoral politics in advance of the US presidential election of 2004—Mexicans make up a growing share of the voting population in key states—have also prompted another glance south.

President Fox, for his part, dismissed Mexico's ambassador to the United Nations, Adolfo Aguilar Zinser, in November 2003 for suggesting in a speech that the United States treats Mexico like its "backyard." While one can question Aguilar Zinser's discretion and diplomacy for such a remark, a shrinking number of Mexicans—and Latin Americans generally—would probably take issue with his characterization. It is a measure of how sour feelings have become since NAFTA was signed a decade ago.

Relations between the United States and Latin America—like those between the United States and Mexico—have often suffered from unrealistic expectations. Unless vital national security interests have been perceived to be at stake, as was the case in Central America in the 1980s, Latin America has not been a top priority for Washington, and that is unlikely to change in the foreseeable future. Still, the unmitigated projection of US power in the world, combined with the assumption that Latin America will automatically go along with any policy put forward by Washington, creates an unnecessary rift and strain in the Western Hemisphere.

The United States has instruments and resources at its disposal—and there are ample historical precedents—to mollify the virulent anti-Americanism that has returned to Latin America. Higher levels of engagement and greater responsiveness from Washington to the region's agenda—to create jobs, stimulate growth, and reduce crime—could once again put the first Bush administration's vision of a productive partnership in the Americas within reach.

MICHAEL SHIFTER, a Current History *contributing editor, is vice president for policy at the Inter-American Dialogue and an adjunct professor at Georgetown University.*

Libya:
Who Blinked, and Why

"There was plenty of self-satisfied offical comment about the efficacy of strong-minded policy in the Middle East, particularly the war in Iraq, in concentrating Colonel Qaddafi's mind on essential reform. But is was nothing of the kind that led to the breakthrough."

GEORGE JOFFÉ

British Prime Minister Tony Blair's visit to Libya at the end of March 2004 was a triumph—for Libya's Colonel Muammar el-Qaddafi. After years in the political and diplomatic wilderness, Blair's four-hour visit confirmed that, for Libya, a new era is about to begin. International business and Europe are courting the former pariah state. Even the United States is confidently expected to follow the British example in the near future, ending its unilateral sanctions and renewing diplomatic relations. Although this dramatic recovery has been expensive for Libya, it has not threatened Qaddafi's political heritage, or the fundamental nature of the regime he heads.

The key to this sudden change in international attitudes lies in Qaddafi's agreement at the end of 2003 to renounce the research, manufacture, and possible use of weapons of mass destruction (WMD) and to accept unrestrained inspections to determine what his country has been doing in this field in recent years. The agreement was trumpeted as a triumph of neoconservative America's policies of zero tolerance for these weapons (except, of course, in the case of allies such as Israel, a point Qaddafi did not overlook) and of Britain's diplomatic skills in bringing the two sides together, despite Washington's distaste for the Libyan regime. In Britain, too, there was plenty of self-satisfied official comment about the efficacy of strong-minded policy in the Middle East, particularly the war in Iraq, in concentrating Colonel Qaddafi's mind on essential reform.

ENFORCED ISOLATION

But it was nothing of the kind that led to the breakthrough, a point that the communiqué announcing the 2003 agreement hinted at when it observed that negotiations over the renunciation of weapons of mass destruction and allowing inspections had been going on for the past nine months. Most news reports ignored the implications of the admission. In reality, the talks had been under way, through British good offices, for far longer and had run in parallel with negotiations over compensation to be paid to the families of the victims of the bombing of Pan Am Flight 103 over Lockerbie, Scotland, in December 1988. The talks reflected, as did the announced agreement, a longstanding theme of Libyan foreign policy, stretching back—with occasional lapses—to April 1986, when Tripoli and Benghazi were bombed by American aircraft with British help in retaliation for a terrorist attack in West Berlin for which Libya was held responsible.

In the wake of the 1986 bombings, the Libyan regime came to the conclusion that it could no longer ignore the reality of American power, nor could it afford to tweak America's nose with its policies of support for international terrorism, whether merely rhetorical, as it claimed, or substantive, as the West believed. The point was reinforced by Libya's humiliating defeat in 1987 in its war in Chad against a government buttressed with direct French and indirect American support. Over the next few years, Libya engaged in what British diplomats, with increasing alarm, described as a successful "charm offensive," persuading European governments to reinforce their diplomatic links and their involvement in Libyan oil. Nor was there much doubt about Qaddafi's own conversion to moderation and cooperation, rather than radicalism and confrontation. In the early 1990s, he remarked that he wanted to see Libya as the "Kuwait of the Mediterranean," by which he seems to have meant a state based on political moderation, economic well-being, and participation in the global community.

The real target of this Libyan maneuver on the diplomatic scene was the restoration of links with both Britain and the United States. America had suspended relations in 1980 (by an oversight they were never formally broken off) as a result of Libyan support for the new Islamic regime in Teheran and the sacking of the American embassy in Tripoli. Britain had angrily severed all contacts in 1984 after the killing of policewoman Yvonne Fletcher outside the Libyan embassy in London during a demonstration by Libyan dissidents. The breach with Britain was embarrassing, since the country had become an important vacation and medical center for Libya. The breach with the United States was far more serious because it had immediate economic implications.

As part of the break in relations, the Reagan administration had imposed unilateral sanctions on the export of Libyan oil to the United States, the operations of American oil companies in Libya, and the supply of all except humanitarian goods to Libya, thus interdicting the supply of US oil field equipment on which the Libyan oil industry was based. The sanctions banned travel to Libya and made Libyan access to the United States very difficult through a highly restrictive visa regime. These were not the first American sanctions against Libya; those had begun in the 1970s under the Carter administration in response to charges of Libyansponsored terrorism. The Reagan sanctions were, however, the most severe and reinforced the point that Libya was in no position to seriously challenge US power.

Libya's hopes of achieving a rapid solution to its diplomatic problems received a massive setback in 1991, when it was accused of responsibility for the bombing of Pan Am Flight 103 over Lockerbie in 1988 and a French UTA airliner over Niger in September 1989. The following year, United Nations sanctions killed off any chance of a quick change in the diplomatic scene. And four years later, in 1996, the US Congress passed the Iran-Libya Sanctions Act, reinforcing the unilateral American sanctions regime. New opportunities for Libya emerged only after Britain, with the arrival of a new Labor government under Tony Blair in May 1997, decided to find a way to resolve the Lockerbie crisis. The suspension of UN sanctions in April 1999, once the Libyan government turned over for trial two Libyan suspects in the Lockerbie bombing, provided Tripoli with its first real chance of ending its isolation as far as Europe and America were concerned.

The lengthy gestation of this policy—some 17 years—should not be surprising, nor should be the occasional self-destructive ambiguities of Libyan policy makers, for this is inherent in the process of Libyan foreign policy. One driver of the current search for improved relations reflects the need to develop the economy through foreign investment and thus avoid domestic dissent. The scholar Mary-Jane Deeb has described Libyan foreign policy as a pyramid with neighboring states at the peak, the Arab world next, followed by the Islamic world overall, then the developing world, and, as a substratum at the base, the industrialized countries. She adds that, the more remote an issue is from Libya's core interests—which are security-led in nature and dominated by North Africa—the more ideologically motivated policy will often be. Yet Libya's foreign strategies, she notes, can also be pragmatic rather than principled. Longtime Libya observer Ronald Bruce St. John argues that foreign policy under Qaddafi has been ideologically driven and aggressive, but has drawn on the principles established for Libya's foreign relations by his monarchical predecessor. Libyan foreign policy, he suggests, has made use of a strategic constancy and a tactical flexibility based on Arab unity and anti-imperialism, while being prepared to exploit Western technological superiority. These interpretations show why it is quite possible for there to have been a coherent project of renewal and reentry into the global system alongside the continuation of anti-Western radicalism that produced the contradictions and tragedies of Lockerbie and the UTA bombing.

THE TURNAROUND

Libyan willingness to compromise was not sufficient for full rehabilitation, however. The UN resolutions required additional Libyan moves before sanctions could be definitively removed, including a renunciation of support for terrorism, acceptance of responsibility for and help with definitively resolving the Lockerbie affair, and the abandonment of weapons of mass destruction. In addition, the United States had its own demands for removing its unilateral sanctions regime. Libya saw few difficulties in satisfying these demands, as long as it could find a form of words that would not directly incriminate its leadership in accepting responsibility. After all, its WMD programs—mainly chemical weapons, as far as anybody knew, although there had been occasional hints of unsuccessful interest in nuclear weapons—had been blocked in the early 1980s after American protests and threats over the Rabta chemical plant that German companies had helped to equip.

With the arrival of the Bush administration in 2001 the picture changed radically: the neoconservatives and Reaganites in the new administration were far more suspicious of Libya than their predecessors. The new administration evidently rebuffed Libyan help and sympathy in the wake of the September 11 attacks on New York and Washington (the Libyan government, apart from having been the first to issue an international arrest warrant for Osama bin Laden, immediately offered its condolences to the United States after the attacks and was the first to offer concrete information on Al Qaeda to the Bush administration). This reaching out from the Libyan side did nothing to break the link in the new administration's mind between Libya and the so-called axis of evil, even though it was not explicitly tied to the axis in President Bush's January 2002 State of the Union address. New accusations of Libyan weapons of mass destruction emerged, principally from John Bolton, the administration's undersecretary of state for arms control. He repeatedly alleged that Libya was initiating new programs, although evidence was singularly lacking.

The Libyan regime came to the conclusion that it could no longer ignore the reality of American power, nor could it afford to tweak America's nose with its policies of support for international terrorism.

Libya, desperate for international recognition and anxious to attract American investment, began detailed negotiations in London in 2002, both over the issue of compensation—carried on with the legal representatives of the victims' families—and, with representatives of the State Department, over other outstanding issues, including weapons of mass destruction. The talks took place under British government auspices: the British Foreign Office minister, Mike O'Brien, had broached the subject with Qaddafi during his visit to Libya in August 2002 and had received positive assurances of Libyan cooperation on the WMD question.

The Libyan negotiators were led by the Libyan ambassador to Britain, Mohamed Zwai, his counterpart in Italy, Abdellati Obaidi, and Musa Kusa, a prominent member of the revolutionary committee movement, head of external security, close confidant of the colonel, and one-time British bugbear who was expelled as head of the Libyan Peoples' Bureau in London in 1980. Once agreement had been reached in September 2003 on satisfying the terms of the UN sanctions resolutions, leading to their removal with reluctant American acquiescence, the scene was set for final resolution of the WMD issue. Libya had already made it clear, months before, that it had no objection to renouncing these weapons or to inspections, provided agreement was reached on the modalities and that the United States consent not to seek pretexts for further adverse action.

As a gesture of good faith, Libya agreed to allow British and US investigators to examine the various sites at which weapons programs were alleged to operate. The investigators found stocks of mustard gas from the 1980s and reported that Libya had indeed begun a program for uranium enrichment—there had long been rumors that Libya had acquired yellowcake (a form of partially refined uranium) from Niger, although there was no firm evidence—despite

the fact that its nuclear research program was based on a small and outdated Soviet reactor at Tarhuna. Qaddafi's decision to formally renounce the program may have been accelerated by the parallel discovery of a ship carrying centrifuge components, essential for enriching uranium, allegedly destined for Libya, but the decision's ultimate driver was the desire to encourage America to renew diplomatic relations.[1]

This point was emphasized by Qaddafi's prime minister, Shukri Ghanem, in an interview with the *New York Times* in early 2004, when he claimed that the decision had been made in the London negotiations to speed diplomatic recognition and the removal of unilateral American sanctions. These events, he emphasized, had to occur by May 2004; otherwise Libya would halve the $2.7 billion-worth of compensation it paid to the Lockerbie victims' families, as was provided for in the compensation agreement. Interestingly enough, there is no sign as yet that this might happen. Although the US State Department has pointed out that the agreement was not signed by the United States government and was therefore not binding on it, other domestic pressures, not least from American oil companies desperate to return to Libya, might well change the administration's mind. Some Arab commentators were enraged at what they saw as Libyan duplicity and cowardice in abandoning WMD, although others realized the rationale behind the move. Qaddafi himself used the event to call for Israel to follow Libya's lead in renouncing such weapons.

The final irony, however, came from Mohamed ElBaradei, the head of the International Atomic Energy Agency, who rushed with a team of six inspectors to Libya after the announcement of the weapons agreement to inspect the alleged nuclear sites. Libya was, he reported, in the very preliminary stages of an enrichment program, with no enriched uranium and no facility to produce it. Libya's centrifuges numbered in the dozens, not the thousands that industrial production would require, and they were not even set up. The incident was to mark the beginning of an unedifying struggle between the agency and US inspectors to claim ownership of the process of dismantling Libya's nuclear program, with a disgruntled ElBaradei consistently deflating American claims about the size of the Libyan nuclear program. By March, the issue had ceased to matter. Libya's modestly equipped nuclear program has been dismantled and shipped to the United States, despite the ruffled feathers in Vienna.

THE WEST REACTS

Perhaps the most surprising feature of this unique experience of peaceful and collaborative disarmament has been the enthusiasm with which it has been received in Washington and London. The British case is, perhaps, easier to appreciate since the Blair government has been increasingly desperate to point to some success from its Middle Eastern policies in recent years. Moreover, it was the British government that had broken the diplomatic deadlock in 1999, which in turn led to the end of the UN sanctions regime. There is also evidence that Britain would like to rebuild its status in Europe and sees Libya as a means by which it can demonstrate to its partners its influence in a region of vital importance to Europe, particularly over questions of energy supply. (Trade statistics demonstrate clearly Libya's dependence on access to the industrialized world, particularly the European Union, which takes 85 percent of Libya's exports. Eighty percent go to just three countries: Germany, Italy, and Spain. For its part, the EU generates 75 percent of Libya's imports.) And, of course, the British had specific interests over access to commercial opportunities in the oil sector—generally seen as the most attractive prospect for oil and gas production worldwide—and in the refurbishment of Libya's decaying infrastructure.

Nonetheless, Blair's apparent enthusiasm for his four-hour meeting in March with the Libyan leader—a man until recently considered by Western statesmen to be idiosyncratic, mercurial, and unstable—was a little surprising. After all, the colonel had not offered to visit Britain.[2] Libya's foreign minister, Abdulrahman al-Shalgam, had made a visit to Britain—his first official visit—some weeks before, so it might have been more appropriate for his British counterpart to have visited Libya instead. The fact that Blair decided to go himself underlines the significance the Anglo-American alliance attached to Libya's rehabilitation. And it is clear that the initiative is Anglo-American in nature, for the pace of change in Washington's attitudes toward Libya since the start of 2004 has been surprisingly fast.

No doubt the Bush administration has felt under considerable pressure from commercial and industrial lobbies, such as USA Engage, which have long demanded an end to the use of sanctions as a policy because they disadvantage US commercial interests abroad. There is also the well-known link between the administration and America's powerful oil sector, which saw itself being shut out from the rush for new concessions in the wake of the suspension of UN sanctions.[3] Yet the administration had resisted these pressures for three years with little difficulty. The decision in early 2004 to begin dismantling the unilateral sanctions regime seems to have been spurred by a quite different dynamic: sudden enthusiasm in Congress to speed an improvement in diplomatic relations.

This was particularly surprising since Congress had been united in its hostility to Libya ever since it had passed, to the dismay of the Clinton administration, the Iran-Libya Sanctions Act in 1996. There had, however, been signs of congressional concern over the implications of the continued sanctions regime in 2002, when news emerged of European pressure on Libya to revoke the concessions held in trust for American companies; concessions that, in any case, would end in 2005. (Had they already been revoked, of course, the American companies would have been unable to seek their renewal.) The turning point seems to have been a congressional visit to Libya in early 2004 by a delegation led by Tom Lantos (D, CAL.). The delegation re-

turned impressed and ready to welcome a fundamental change in relations.

The degree of this change in attitude was underscored in early March this year when the Libyan prime minister, who is not accustomed to handling the Western media, was goaded by the British Broadcasting Corporation into expressing reservations about Libyan responsibility for the violent incident in London in 1984, which had led to the breach in diplomatic relations with Britain, and about the Lockerbie issue, which he said required a pragmatic approach to the problem of restoring relations with the United States. In fact, he merely reiterated the basic elements of the official Libyan position on both issues. But his intervention, to say the least, was hardly diplomatic. Even worse, it occurred at a particularly delicate moment, when the United States was about to make its first conciliatory gesture by removing restrictions on travel to Libya.

Of course, what had been planned had to be delayed, but the truly surprising aspect was the lack of significance attributed to the prime minister's remarks by congressional representatives, particularly Congressman Lantos. Indeed, within days of the incident, the State Department reinstated its initiatives to ease relations, new conciliatory measures were proposed, and the four oil companies were allowed to return to prepare the recovery of their concessions. Veteran diplomats privately voiced surprise at the sudden and unexpected pressure from the White House to speed up the rehabilitation of Libya, despite still outstanding demands on the American agenda: that Libya introduce democratic governance and a liberal economy. Now it is expected that presidential sanctions will be removed in June and congressional sanctions in August.

OIL FOR OUR TIME?

Will the removal of sanctions put an end to 24 years of mutual irritation and misunderstanding? Yes and no. Were the Qaddafi regime to undergo the complete reformation at which it has hinted, with an end to its idiosyncratic and discriminatory "state of the masses" and a profound reform of its state-centered economy, the answer would undoubtedly be in the affirmative.

Colonel Qaddafi, however, has shown his tenacity in the past and is unlikely to retire into obscurity. Nor is the regime, despite pressure for reform, about to become a shining beacon of democracy, accountability, and the rule of law in the Middle East and North Africa. The real question is whether sufficient change will occur in Libya for Washington and its European allies to be able to tolerate a regime that both have disliked for many years, for the sake of access to its irresistible assets in oil and gas.

NOTES

1. It was rumored that Libya itself tipped off British and US investigators to the shipment as a means of earning goodwill. If so, it was an expensive gesture; American sources claim that

Libya had paid over $100 million to the semi-official Pakistani network, run by Abdul Qadir Khan, that has been subsequently unveiled as responsible for promoting nuclear proliferation in North Korea and Iran.

2. Perhaps because he had not enjoyed his previous visit. Just before the September 1969 coup that brought him to power, the future Libyan leader had attended a military communications course in Beaconsfield, just outside London. He had not enjoyed the experience and there is a famous photograph of him in London's Piccadilly Circus, where his distaste for the crowds (and, no doubt, corruption) of the city is clearly expressed.

3. Four US-based oil companies were forced to abandon their interests in Libya when the Reagan administration introduced its own presidential sanctions in 1986. The four—Marathon, Occidental, Amerada Hess, and Hunt—left behind assets worth $2 billion that were generating an income flow of $2.3 billion a year. (The assets of the four have been worked in trust for them by companies linked to and created by Libya's National Oil Company for this purpose.)

George Joffé is a specialist in contemporary MIddle Eastern and North African studies at Kings College, London University, and at the Center of International Studies, Cambridge University.

Reprinted by permission from *Current History* Magazine (May 2004, pp. 221–225). © 2004 by Current History, Inc.

Darfur and the Genocide Debate

Scott Straus

WHAT'S IN A NAME?

IN SUDAN'S western Darfur region, a massive campaign of ethnic violence has claimed the lives of more than 70,000 civilians and uprooted an estimated 1.8 million more since February 2003. The roots of the violence are complex and parts of the picture remain unclear. But several key facts are now well known. The primary perpetrators of the killings and expulsions are government-backed "Arab" militias. The main civilian victims are black "Africans" from three tribes. And the crisis is currently the worst humanitarian disaster on the planet.

The bloodshed in Darfur has by now received a great deal of attention. Much of the public debate in the United States and elsewhere, however, has focused not on how to stop the crisis, but on whether or not it should be called a "genocide" under the terms of the Genocide Convention. Such a designation, it was long thought, would inevitably trigger an international response.

In July 2004, the U.S. Congress passed a resolution labeling Darfur a genocide. Then, in early September, after reviewing the results of an innovative government-sponsored investigation, Secretary of State Colin Powell also used the term and President George W. Bush followed suit in a speech to the United Nations several weeks later—the first times such senior U.S. government officials had ever conclusively applied the term to a current crisis and invoked the convention. Darfur, therefore, provides a good test of whether the 56-year-old Genocide Convention, created in the aftermath of the Holocaust, can make good on its promise to "never again" allow the targeted destruction of a particular ethnic, racial, or religious group.

So far, the convention has proven weak. Having been invoked, it did not—contrary to expectations—electrify international efforts to intervene in Sudan. Instead, the UN Security Council commissioned further studies and vaguely threatened economic sanctions against Sudan's growing oil industry if Khartoum did not stop the violence; one council deadline has already passed without incident. Although some 670 African Union troops have been dispatched to the region with U.S. logistical assistance to monitor a nonexistent ceasefire, and humanitarian aid is pouring in, the death toll continues to rise. The lessons from Darfur, thus, are bleak. Despite a decade of hand-wringing over the failure to intervene in Rwanda in 1994 and despite Washington's decision to break its own taboo against the use of the word "genocide," the international community has once more proved slow and ineffective in responding to large-scale, state-supported killing. Darfur has shown that the energy spent fighting over whether to call the events there "genocide" was misplaced, overshadowing difficult but more important questions about how to craft an effective response to mass violence against civilians in Sudan. The task ahead is to do precisely that: to find a way to stop the killing, lest tens of thousands more die.

DEATH IN DARFUR

TO UNDERSTAND the Darfur story it helps to know something about the conflict itself. The crisis in western Sudan has grown out of several separate but intersecting conflicts. The first is a civil war between the Islamist, Khartoum-based national government and two rebel groups based in Darfur: the Sudan Liberation Army and the Justice and Equality Movement. The rebels, angered by Darfur's political and economic marginalization by Khartoum, first appeared in February 2003. The government, however, did not launch a major counteroffensive until April 2003, after the rebels pulled off a spectacular attack on a military airfield, destroying several aircraft and kidnapping an air force general in the process. Khartoum responded by arming irregular militia forces and directing them to eradicate the rebellion. The militias set out to do just that, but mass violence against civilians is what followed.

The Darfur crisis is also related to a second conflict. In southern Sudan, civil war has raged for decades between the northern, Arab-dominated government and Christian and animist black southerners; fighting, in one form or another, has afflicted Sudan for all but 11 years since the country's independence from the United Kingdom in 1956 and has cost an estimated two million lives since 1983 alone. In recent years, the government and the main southern rebel movement have entered into comprehensive peace negotiations named after the Intergovernmental Authority on Development (IGAD), which mediated the process. After numerous rounds of talks, the two sides appeared close to finalizing an agreement in June 2004, and many international observers hoped that Sudan's long-running war would finally end.

Darfur, however, was never represented in the IGAD discussions, and the Darfur rebels decided to strike partly to avoid being left out of any new political settlement. Many fear that the fighting may now unravel the IGAD agreements: the southern rebels are wary of signing any deal with a government that is massacring their fellow citizens, and hard-liners in Khartoum have seized on the violence to undermine the IGAD talks, which they see as too favorable toward the south.

The Darfur crisis also has a third, local lineage. Roughly the size of Texas, Darfur is home to some six million people and several dozen tribes. But the region is split between two main groups: those who claim black "African" descent and primarily practice sedentary agriculture, and those who claim "Arab" descent and are mostly seminomadic livestock herders. As in many ethnic conflicts, the divisions between these two groups are not always neat; many farmers also raise animals, and the African-Arab divide is far from clear. All Sudanese are technically African, Darfurians are uniformly Muslim, and years of intermarriage have narrowed obvious physical differences between "Arabs" and black "Africans."

Khartoum responded to the rebellion in Darfur the same way it had to the conflict in the south: by arming Arab militias.

Nonetheless, the cleavage is real, and recent conflicts over resources have only exacerbated it. In dry seasons, land disputes in Darfur between farmers and herders have historically been resolved peacefully. But an extended drought and the encroachment of the desert in the last two decades have made water and arable land much more scarce. Beginning in the mid-1980s, successive governments in Khartoum inflamed matters by supporting and arming the Arab tribes, in part to prevent the southern rebels from gaining a foothold in the region. The result was a series of deadly clashes in the late 1980s and 1990s. Arabs formed militias, burned African villages, and killed thousands. Africans in turn formed self-defense groups, members of which eventually became the first Darfur insurgents to appear in 2003.

The mass violence against civilians began in the middle of that year. Khartoum responded to the rebellion in Darfur the same way it had to the conflict in the south: by arming and equipping Arab militias. Thus the *janjaweed* were born. Their name, which translates roughly as "evil men on horseback," was chosen to inspire fear, and the *janjaweed*, who include convicted felons, quickly succeeded. Khartoum instructed the militias to "eliminate the rebellion," as Sudan's President Omar al-Bashir acknowledged in a December 2003 speech. What followed, however, was a campaign of violence that primarily targeted black African civilians, in particular those who came from the same tribes as the core rebel recruits.

Human rights groups, humanitarian agencies, and the U.S. State Department have all reached strikingly similar conclusions about the nature of the violence. Army forces and the militia often attack together, as *janjaweed* leaders readily admit. In some cases, government aircraft bomb areas before the militia attack, razing settlements and destroying villages; such tactics have become central to this war. In late September, a U.S. offi-

cial reported that 574 villages had been destroyed and another 157 damaged since mid-2003. Satellite images show many areas in Darfur burned out or abandoned. The majority of the attacks have occurred in villages where the rebels did not have an armed presence; Khartoum's strategy seems to be to punish the rebels' presumed base of support—civilians—so as to prevent future rebel recruitment.

Testimony recorded at different times and locations consistently shows that the attackers single out men to kill. Women, children, and the elderly are not spared, however. Eyewitnesses report that the attackers sometimes murder children. For women, the primary threat is rape; sexual violence has been widespread in this conflict. Looting and the destruction of property have also been common after the *janjaweed* and their army allies swoop down on civilian settlements.

This violence has produced what one team of medical researchers has termed a "demographic catastrophe" in Darfur. By mid-October 2004, an estimated 1.8 million people—or about a third of Darfur's population—had been uprooted, with an estimated 1.6 million Darfurians having fled to other parts of Sudan and another 200,000 having crossed the border to Chad. Exactly how many have died is difficult to determine; most press reports cite about 50,000, but the total number is probably much higher. In October 2004, a World Health Organization official estimated that 70,000 displaced persons had died in the previous six months from malnutrition and disease directly related to their displacement—a figure that did not include violent deaths. By now, the number has probably grown much larger. Despite a huge influx of humanitarian aid since mid-2004, the International Committee of the Red Cross warned in October of an "unprecedented" food crisis; several months earlier, a senior official with the U.S. Agency for International Development told journalists that the death toll could reach 350,000 by the end of the year.

WORD PLAY

MOST OF THESE FACTS are undisputed; the reports from Darfur by aid workers and reporters have been remarkably consistent (although too little attention has been paid to rebel atrocities). Khartoum has, predictably, denied direct involvement in the attacks against civilians, and both the Arab League and the African Union have downplayed the gross violations of human rights (focusing on the civil war instead). Still, not much controversy exists over what is actually happening in Darfur. Yet public debate in the United States and Europe has focused less on the violence itself than on what to call it—in particular, whether the term "genocide" applies.

The genocide debate took off in March 2004, after *New York Times* columnist Nicholas Kristof published a number of articles making the charge. His graphic depictions of events there soon stimulated similar calls for action from an unlikely combination of players—Jewish-American, African-American, liberal, and religious-conservative constituencies. In July 2004, the Holocaust Museum in Washington, D.C., issued its first-ever "genocide emergency." MoveOn.org called on Powell to use the "genocide" label for Darfur, as did the Congressional

Black Caucus, African-American civil rights groups, and some international human rights organizations (but not Amnesty International or Human Rights Watch). Editorialists from a number of major newspapers, including *The Philadelphia Inquirer* and *The Boston Globe,* made similar appeals. Long concerned with the persecution of black Christian populations in southern Sudan, American evangelicals also called for a formal recognition of genocide and for U.S. action—even though the victims in Darfur were Muslim.

Proponents of applying the "genocide" label emphasized two points. First, they argued that the events in Sudan met a general standard for genocide: the violence targeted an ethnic group for destruction, was systematic and intentional, and was state supported. Second, they claimed that under the Genocide Convention, using the term would trigger international intervention to halt the violence. Salih Booker and Ann-Louise Colgan from the advocacy group Africa Action wrote in *The Nation,* "We should have learned from Rwanda that to stop genocide, Washington must first say the word."

Colgan and Booker made a fair point. During the Rwandan genocide—exactly a decade before Darfur erupted—State Department spokespersons in Washington were instructed not to utter the "g-word," since, as one internal government memorandum put it, publicly acknowledging "genocide" might commit the U.S. government to do something at a time (a year after the Somalia debacle) when President Bill Clinton's White House was entirely unwilling. As a result, the United States and the rest of the world sat on the sidelines as an extermination campaign claimed at least half a million civilian lives in three months. In the aftermath, many pundits agreed that a critical first step toward a better response the next time would be to openly call a genocide "genocide."

Never before had Congress or such senior U.S. officials labeled an ongoing crisis "genocide."

The idea that states are obligated to do something in the face of genocide comes from two provisions in the Genocide Convention. First, the treaty holds that contracting parties are required to "undertake to prevent and to punish" genocide. Second, Article VIII of the convention stipulates that signatories may call on the UN to "take such action ... for the prevention and suppression" of genocide. Prior to the Darfur crisis, and in light of the way the genocide debate unfolded in Rwanda, the conventional wisdom was that signatories to the convention (including the United States, which finally ratified it in 1988) were obligated to act to prevent genocide if they recognized one to be occurring. The convention had never been tested, however, and the law is in fact ambiguous on what "undertaking to prevent" and "suppressing" genocide actually mean and who is to carry out such measures.

In July, the U.S. House of Representatives entered the rhetorical fray by unanimously passing a resolution labeling the violence in Sudan "genocide." The resolution called on the Bush administration to do the same and, citing the convention, to "se-

riously consider multilateral or even unilateral intervention to prevent genocide" if the UN Security Council failed to act. The Bush administration, however, interpreted its international obligations differently. Facing mounting appeals to call Darfur "genocide," Powell insisted that such a determination, even if it came, would not change U.S. policy toward Sudan. Powell argued that Washington was already pressuring Khartoum to stem abuses and was providing humanitarian relief; applying the "genocide" label would not require anything more from the United States. He did, however, commission an in-depth study of whether events in Darfur merited the "genocide" label.

Meanwhile, other world leaders and opinion makers continued to show reticence about calling Darfur "genocide." EU, Canadian, and British officials all avoided the term, as did UN Secretary-General Kofi Annan, who was pilloried in the media for limiting his description of Darfur to "massive violations of human rights." Human Rights Watch and the Pulitzer Prize-winning author Samantha Power favored the slightly less charged term "ethnic cleansing," arguing that Darfur involved the forced removal of an ethnic group, not its deliberate extermination, and that genocide is hard to prove in the midst of a crisis.

The debate took a surprising turn in early September when, testifying before the Senate Foreign Relations Committee, Powell acknowledged that "genocide" was in fact taking place in Sudan. Powell based his determination on the U.S. government-funded study, which had surveyed 1,136 Darfurian refugees in Chad. Their testimony demonstrated that violence against civilians was widespread, ethnically oriented, and strongly indicated government involvement in the attacks. Two weeks after Powell's speech, Bush repeated the genocide charge during an address to the UN General Assembly.

ONCE MORE, NEVER AGAIN

TAKEN TOGETHER, the congressional resolution and the two speeches were momentous: never before had Congress or such senior U.S. officials publicly and conclusively labeled an ongoing crisis "genocide," invoking the convention. Nor, for that matter, had a contracting party to the Genocide Convention ever called on the Security Council to take action under Article VIII (as the United States has done). But the critical question remained: Would the Genocide Convention really be any help in triggering international intervention to stem the violence?

So far, the answer seems to be no. In late July, before Bush or Powell ever spoke the word "genocide," the UN Security Council had passed a resolution condemning Sudan and giving the government a month to rein in the militias. That deadline passed without incident, however. After Powell spoke out in September, the council passed a second, tepid resolution, which merely called on Kofi Annan to set up a five-member commission to investigate the charge (which he did). The resolution also vaguely threatened economic sanctions against Sudan's oil industry (although it gave no concrete deadline for when sanctions would be imposed) and welcomed an African Union plan to send a token force to the region to monitor a cease-fire (to which neither side has since adhered). Despite its weak wording, the resolution almost failed to pass. China, which has commercial and oil interests in Sudan, nearly vetoed the measure, only agreeing to abstain—along with Algeria, Pakistan, and Russia—after Annan strongly endorsed the resolution.

In mid-November, the Security Council held an extraordinary meeting in Nairobi, Kenya, to discuss Sudan. The session won a pledge from Khartoum and the southern rebels to finalize a peace agreement by the end of the year. On Darfur, however, the Security Council managed only to pass another limp resolution voicing "serious concern." Conceivably, Annan's commission could still determine that genocide has occurred in Darfur—giving the Security Council yet another chance to take concrete action. Given recent history, however, such action is unlikely. So far, the immediate consequences of the U.S. genocide determination have been minimal, and despite the historic declarations by Bush, Powell, and the U.S. Congress, the international community has barely budged. Nor has the United States itself done much to stop the violence.

The genocide debate and the Darfur crisis are thus instructive for several reasons. First, they have made it clear that "genocide" is not a magic word that triggers intervention. The term grabs attention, and in this case allowed pundits and advocates to move Sudan to the center of the public and international agendas. The lack of any subsequent action, however, showed that the Genocide Convention does not provide nearly the impetus that many thought it would. The convention was intended to institutionalize the promise of "never again." In the past, governments avoided involvement in a crisis by scrupulously eschewing the word "genocide." Sudan—at least so far—shows that the definitional dance may not have mattered.

Second, the Darfur crisis points to other limitations of using a genocide framework to galvanize international intervention. Genocide is a contested concept: there is much disagreement about what qualifies for the term. The convention itself defines genocide as the "intent to destroy, in whole or in part, a national, ethnical, racial or religious group, as such." The document also lists several activities that constitute genocide, ranging from obvious acts such as killing to less obvious ones such as causing "mental harm." One often-cited problem with the convention's definition is how to determine a perpetrator's intent in the midst of a crisis. And how much "partial" group destruction does it take to reach the genocide threshold? In April 2004, an appeals chamber of the International Criminal Tribunal for the Former Yugoslavia addressed the definitional question, upholding a genocide conviction of the Bosnian Serb commander Radislav Krstic for his role in the 1995 massacre at Srebrenica. In that case, the tribunal concluded that "genocide" meant the destruction of a "substantial part" of a group, which the court defined as 7,000-8,000 Bosnian Muslim men from Srebrenica.

By this standard, the violence in Darfur does appear to be genocide: a substantial number of men from a particular ethnic group in a limited area have been killed. For many observers, however, genocide means something else: a campaign designed to physically eliminate a group under a government's control, as in Rwanda or Nazi Germany. The definitional debate is hard to resolve; both positions are defensible. And the indeterminacy makes genocide a difficult term around which to mobilize an international coalition for intervention.

Assuming that humanitarian intervention remains a common goal in the future, one way forward would be to revisit and strengthen the ambiguous provisions in the convention. The confusion associated with the word "genocide" is not likely to disappear, however, and the term, at least as currently defined, excludes economic, political, and other social groups from protection. A better strategy might therefore be to develop a specific humanitarian threshold for intervention—including, but not limited to, genocide—and to establish institutional mechanisms to move from recognition of a grave humanitarian crisis to international action.

Darfur also shows that a genocide debate can divert attention from the most difficult questions surrounding humanitarian intervention. Any potential international action faces serious logistical and political obstacles. Darfur is vast and would require a substantial deployment of troops to safeguard civilians. The area has poor roads, and although it is open to surveillance from the air, ground transportation of troops would be difficult. International action also would need to address the complicated but enduring problems that have given rise to the violence in the first place. Such a strategy would require pressure on both the Darfur rebels and Khartoum to make peace.

Already heavily committed in Iraq and having lost considerable international credibility over the last two years, the Bush administration is not well positioned to lead such an effort. The hardest question about humanitarian intervention thus remains, Who will initiate and lead it? The problem is not just theoretical: the killing continues in Darfur and is unlikely to end soon. Until a powerful international actor or coalition of actors emerges, many more thousands of civilians are likely to die in western Sudan. If the international community fails to act decisively, the brave language of the Genocide Convention and the UN Charter—not to mention the avowed principles of the U.S. government and other states—will once more ring false.

Scott Straus is an Assistant Professor of Political Science at the University of Wisconsin, Madison.

UNIT 3

The Domestic Side of American Foreign Policy

Unit Selections

14. **The Paradoxes of American Nationalism**, Minxin Pei
15. **Doctrinal Divisions: The Politics of U.S. Military Interventions**, Jon Western
16. **Missed Signals**, Sherry Ricchiardi

Key Points to Consider

- Should policymakers listen to the U.S. public in making foreign policy decisions? Defend your answer.

- What types of foreign policy issues is the American public most informed about?

- Construct a public opinion poll to measure the relative support for internationalism and isolationism among students. What do you expect to find? Were your expectations correct?

- In what ways is U.S. foreign policy true to traditional American values?

- What is the most effective way for Americans to express their views to policymakers on foreign policy?

- What should be the major foreign policy issue debated in the next presidential campaign?

- Does global involvement threaten to destroy American national values? If so, what steps might be taken to prevent this from happening?

Student Website

www.mhcls.com/online

Internet References

Further information regarding these websites may be found in this book's preface or online.

American Diplomacy
  http://www.unc.edu/depts/diplomat/

Carnegie Endowment for International Peace (CEIP)
  http://www.ceip.org

RAND
  http://www.rand.org

Conventional political wisdom holds that foreign policy and domestic policy are two very different policy arenas. Not only are the origins and gravity of the problems different, but the political rules for seeking solutions are dissimilar. Where partisan politics, lobbying, and the weight of public opinion are held to play legitimate roles in the formulation of health, education, or welfare policy, they are seen as corrupting influences in the making of foreign policy. An effective foreign policy demands a quiescent public, one that gives knowledgeable professionals the needed leeway to bring their expertise to bear on the problem. It demands a Congress that unites behind presidential foreign policy doctrines rather than one that investigates failures or pursues its own agenda. In brief, if American foreign policy is to succeed, politics must stop "at the water's edge."

This conventional wisdom has never been shared by all who write on American foreign policy. Two very different groups of scholars have dissented from this inclination to neglect the importance of domestic influences on American foreign policy. One group holds that the essence of democracy lies in the ability of the public to hold policymakers accountable for their decisions and therefore that elections, interest group lobbying, and other forms of political expression are just as central to the study of foreign policy as they are to the study of domestic policy. A second group of scholars sees domestic forces as important because they feel that the fundamental nature of a society determines a country's foreign policy. These scholars direct their attention to studying the influence of such forces as capitalism, American national style, and the structure of elite values.

The terrorist attack of September 11, 2001, altered the domestic politics of American foreign policy—at least for the short run. Unity replaced division in the aftermath of the attacks as the public rallied behind President Bush. This unity began to fray somewhat as the George W. Bush administration made its case for war with Iraq but overall it remained in place. Domestic political forces began to reassert themselves after President Bush declared that major fighting had ended. Now issues such as the cost of the war, the length of time American forces would remain in Iraq, the constant attacks on American occupying forces, and the handling of pre-war intelligence came under close scrutiny. By June 2004, for the first time, public opinion polls showed a majority of Americans (54.6 percent) saying sending troops to Iraq was a mistake and that the war had made the United States less safe from terrorism.

By the first year of George W. Bush's second term the influence of domestic politics on the conduct of American foreign policy was highly visible. His nomination of John Bolton to be ambassador to the United Nations produced a lengthy and highly charged debate in the Senate that focused as much on Bush's foreign policy as it did on Bolton's qualifications. The rising tide of imports from China brought forward complaints from domestic producers and workers and led the administration to file complaints against it with the World Trade Organization for illegal trade practices. And, allegations of the mistreatment of prisoners and the Koran at Guantanamo Bay brought forward vigorous defenses and condemnations of American foreign policy and the role of the media.

The readings in this section provide us with an overview of the ways in which U.S. domestic politics and foreign policy interact. The first reading in this unit focuses on the influence that American values have on U.S. foreign policy as well as the impact American foreign policy has on those values. In "The Paradoxes of American Nationalism," Minxin Pie argues that American nationalism is strong but that it takes a different form from nationalism found elsewhere and that Americans do not understand this. Jon Western, "Doctrinal Divisions: The Politics of U.S. Military Interventions," argues that because of how they are presented the public often develops unrealistic expectations about the nature, cost, and efficacy of military interventions. The last article, "Missed Signals," examines the state of the media with regard to foreign news coverage. It looks at media coverage of the Abu Ghraib prisoner abuse scandal and asks why it took so long for the news media to uncover the situation.

The Paradoxes of American Nationalism

As befits a nation of immigrants, American nationalism is defined not by notions of ethnic superiority, but by a belief in the supremacy of U.S. democratic ideals. This disdain for Old World nationalism creates a dual paradox in the American psyche: First, although the United States is highly nationalistic, it doesn't see itself as such. Second, despite this nationalistic fervor, U.S. policymakers generally fail to appreciate the power of nationalism abroad.

By Minxin Pei

Nearly two years after the horrific terrorist attacks on the United States, international public opinion has shifted from heartfelt sympathy for Americans and their country to undisguised antipathy The immediate catalyst for this shift is the United States hard-line policy toward and subsequent war with Iraq. Yet today's strident anti-Americanism represents much more than a wimpy reaction to U.S. resolve or generic fears of a hegemon running amok. Rather, the growing unease with the United States should be seen as a powerful global backlash against the spirit of American nationalism that shapes and animates U.S. foreign policy.

Any examination of the deeper sources of anti-Americanism should start with an introspective look at American nationalism. But in the United States, this exercise, which hints at serious flaws in the nation's character, generates little enthusiasm. Moreover, coming to terms with today's growing animosity toward the United States is intellectually contentious because of the two paradoxes of American nationalism: First, although the United States is a highly nationalistic country, it genuinely does not see itself as such. Second, despite the high level of nationalism in American society, U.S. policymakers have a remarkably poor appreciation of the power of nationalism in other societies and have demonstrated neither skill nor sensitivity in dealing with its manifestations abroad.

BLIND TO ONE'S VIRTUE

Nationalism is a dirty word in the United States, viewed with disdain and associated with Old World parochialism and imagined supremacy. Yet those who discount the idea of American nationalism may readily admit that Americans, as a whole, are extremely patriotic. When pushed to explain the difference between patriotism and nationalism, those same skeptics might concede, reluctantly, that there is a distinction, but no real difference. Political scientists have labored to prove such a difference, equating patriotism with allegiance to one's country and defining nationalism as sentiments of ethno-national superiority. In reality, however, the psychological and behavioral manifestations of nationalism and patriotism are indistinguishable, as is the impact of such sentiments on policy.

Polling organizations routinely find that Americans display the highest degree of national pride among Western democracies. Researchers at the University of Chicago reported that before the September 11, 2001, terrorist attacks, 90 percent of the Americans surveyed agreed with the statement "I would rather be a citizen of America than of any other country in the world"; 38 percent endorsed the view that "The world would be a better place if people from other countries were more like the Americans." (After the terrorist attacks, 97 and 49 percent, respectively, agreed with the same statements.) The World Values Survey reported similar results, with more than 70 percent of those surveyed declaring themselves "very proud" to be Americans. By comparison, the same survey revealed that less than half of the people in other Western democracies—including France, Italy, Denmark, Great Britain, and the Netherlands—felt "very proud" of their nationalities [see chart, National Pride].

National Pride

Percentage of people by country, who say
they are "very proud" of their nationality

Country	1990	1999–2000
Britain	53	49
Denmark	42	48
Egypt	N/A	81 *
France	35	40
India	75	71
Iran	N/A	92 *
Ireland	77	74
Italy	40	39
Mexico	56	80
Netherlands	23	20
Philippines	N/A	85 *
Poland	69	71
United States	75	72
Vietnam	N/A	78 *

* 2001 survey data

Source: World Values Survey

Americans not only take enormous pride in their values but also regard them as universally applicable. According to the Pew Global Attitudes survey, 79 percent of the Americans polled agreed that "It's good that American ideas and customs are spreading around the world"; 70 percent said they "like American ideas about democracy." These views, however, are not widely shared, even in Western Europe, another bastion of liberalism and democracy. Pew found that, among the Western European countries surveyed, less than 40 percent endorse the spread of American ideas and customs, and less than 50 percent like American ideas about democracy.

Such firmly held beliefs in the superiority of American political values and institutions readily find expression in American social, cultural, and political practices. It is almost impossible to miss them: the daily ritual of the Pledge of Allegiance in the nation's schools, the customary performance of the national anthem before sporting events, and the ubiquitous American flags. And in the United States, as in other countries, nationalist sentiments inevitably infuse politics. Candidates rely on hot-button issues such as flag burning and national security to attack their opponents as unpatriotic and worse.

Why does a highly nationalistic society consistently view itself as anything but? The source of this paradox lies in the forces that sustain nationalism in the United States. Achievements in science and technology, military strength, economic wealth, and unrivaled global political influence can no doubt generate strong national pride. But what makes American nationalism truly exceptional are the many ways in which it is naturally expressed in daily life.

One of the most powerful wellsprings of American nationalism is civic voluntarism—the willingness of ordinary citizens to contribute to the public good, either through individual initiatives or civic associations. Outside observers, starting with the French philosopher Alexis de Tocqueville in the early 19th century, have never ceased to be amazed by this font of American dynamism. "Americans of all ages, all stations in life, and all types of dispositions are forever forming associations," noted Tocqueville, who credited Americans for relying on themselves, instead of government, to solve society's problems.

The same grass-roots activism that animates the country's social life also makes American nationalism vibrant and alluring, for most of the institutions and practices that promote and sustain American nationalism are civic, not political; the rituals are voluntary rather than imposed; and the values inculcated are willingly embraced, not artificially indoctrinated. Elsewhere in the world, the state plays an indispensable role in promoting nationalism, which is frequently a product of political manipulation by elites and consequently has a manufactured quality to it. But in the United States, although individual politicians often try to exploit nationalism for political gains, the state is conspicuously absent. For instance, no U.S. federal laws mandate reciting the Pledge of Allegiance in public schools, require singing the national anthem at sporting events, or enforce flying the flag on private buildings.

In the United States, promoting nationalism is a private enterprise. In other societies, the state deploys its resources, from government-controlled media to the police, to propagate "patriotic values."

The history of the pledge is an exquisite example of the United States' unique take on nationalism. Francis Bellamy, a socialist Baptist minister, wrote the original text in 1892; three major American civic associations (the National Education Association, the American Legion, and the Daughters of the American Revolution) instituted, refined, and expanded the ceremony of reciting it. The federal government was late getting into the game. Congress didn't officially endorse the pledge until 1942, and it didn't tamper with the language until 1954, when Congress inserted the phrase "under God" after being pressured by a religious organization, the Knights of Columbus.

Indeed, any blunt attempt to use the power of the state to institutionalize U.S. nationalism has been met with strong resistance because of popular suspicion that the government may be encroaching on Americans' individual liberties. In the 1930s, the Jehovah's Witnesses mounted a legal challenge when some school boards tried to make the Pledge of Allegiance mandatory, arguing that the pledge compelled children to worship graven images. The flag-burning amendment has failed twice in the U.S. Congress during the last eight years.

In the United States, promoting nationalism is a private enterprise. In other societies, especially those ruled by authoritarian regimes, the state deploys its resources, from government-controlled media to the police, to propagate "patriotic values." The celebration of national days in such countries features huge government-orchestrated parades that showcase crack troops and the latest weaponry. (The huge military parade held in Beijing in 1999 to celebrate the 50th anniversary of China allegedly cost hundreds of millions of dollars.) Yet despite its awesome high-tech arsenal, such orgiastic displays of state-sponsored nationalism are notably absent on Independence Day in the United States. Of course, Americans hold parades and watch fireworks on the Fourth of July, but those events are largely organized by civic associations and partly paid for by local business groups.

Herein lies the secret of the vitality and durability of American nationalism: The dominance of civic voluntarism—and not state coercion—has made nationalist sentiments more genuine, attractive, and legitimate to the general public. These expressions of American nationalism have become so commonplace that they are virtually imperceptible, except to outsiders.

A POLITICAL CREED

American nationalism is hidden in plain sight. But even if Americans saw it, they wouldn't recognize it as nationalism. That's because American nationalism is a different breed from its foreign cousins and exhibits three unique characteristics.

First, American nationalism is based on political ideals, not those of cultural or ethnic superiority. That conception is entirely fitting for a society that still sees itself as a cultural and ethnic melting pot. As President George W. Bush said in his Fourth of July speech last year: "There is no American race; there's only an American creed." And in American eyes, the superiority of that creed is self-evident. American political institutions and ideals, coupled with the practical achievements attributed to them, have firmly convinced Americans that their values ought to be universal. Conversely, when Americans are threatened, they see attacks on them as primarily attacks on their values. Consider how American elites and the public interpreted the September 11 terrorist attacks. Most readily embraced the notion that the attacks embodied an assault on U.S. democratic freedoms and institutions.

Second, American nationalism is triumphant rather than aggrieved. In most societies, nationalism is fueled by past grievances caused by external powers. Countries once subjected to colonial rule, such as India and Egypt, are among the most nationalistic societies. But American nationalism is the polar opposite of such aggrieved nationalism. American nationalism derives its meaning from victories in peace and war since the country's founding. Triumphant nationalists celebrate the positive and have little empathy for the whining of aggrieved nationalists whose formative experience consisted of a succession of national humiliations and defeats.

Finally, American nationalism is forward looking, while nationalism in most other countries is the reverse. Those who believe in the superiority of American values and institutions do not dwell on their historical glories (though such glories constitute the core of American national identity). Instead, they look forward to even better times ahead, not just at home but also abroad. This dynamism imbues American nationalism with a missionary spirit and a short collective memory. Unavoidably, such forward-looking and universalistic perspectives clash with the backward-looking and particularistic perspectives of ethno-nationalism in other countries. Haunted by memories of Western military invasions since the time of the Crusades, the Middle East cannot help but look with suspicion upon U.S. plans to "liberate" the Iraqi people. In the case of China, U.S. support for Taiwan, which the Chinese government and people alike regard as a breakaway province, is the most contentious issue in bilateral relations. The loss of Taiwan—whether to the Japanese in 1895 or to the nationalists in 1949—has long symbolized national weakness and humiliation.

INNOCENTS ABROAD

The unique characteristics of American nationalism explain why one of the most nationalist countries in the world is so inept at dealing with nationalism abroad. The best example of this second paradox of American nationalism is the Vietnam War. The combination of the United States' universalistic political values (in this case, anticommunism), triumphalist beliefs in U.S. power and short national memory led to a disastrous policy that clashed with the nationalism of the Vietnamese, a people whose national experience was defined by resistance against foreign domination (the Chinese and the French) and whose overriding goal was independence and unity, not the spread of communism in Southeast Asia.

In its dealings with several other highly nationalistic societies, the United States has paid little attention to the role nationalism played in legitimizing and sustaining those regimes the country regarded as hostile. U.S. policy toward these nations has either disregarded strong nationalist sentiments (as in the Philippines and Mexico) or consistently allowed the ideological, free-market bias of American nationalism to exaggerate the antagonism of communist ideologies championed by rival governments (as in China and Cuba). Former Egyptian President Ga-

Different Visions

U.S. NATIONALISM	OTHER NATIONALISMS
Based on universalistic ideals (democracy, rule of law, free marketplace) and institutions (separation of powers)	Based on ethnicity, religion, language, and geography
Product of grass-roots voluntarism; values and rituals are willingly embraced not artificially indoctrinated	Fostered by government elites and promoted by the apparatus of the state (police, military, state-run media)
Triumphalist; derives its meaning from victories in peace and war	Aggrieved; often derives its meaning from national humiliations and defeats
Forward looking, with a short collective memory and missionary spirit	Backward looking, dwelling on ancient glories and historic grudges

mal Abdel Nasser's brand of postcolonial Arab nationalism, which rejected a strategic alliance with either the U.S.-led West or the Soviet camp, baffled Washington officials, who could not conceive of any country remaining neutral in the struggle against communist expansionism. Echoes of that mind-set are heard today in the United States' "you're either with us or against us" ultimatum in the war against terrorism.

This ongoing inability to deal with nationalism abroad has three immediate consequences. The first, and relatively minor, is the high level of resentment that U.S. insensitivity generates, both among foreign governments and their people. The second, and definitely more serious, is that such insensitive policies tend to backfire on the United States, especially when it tries to undermine hostile regimes abroad. After all, nationalism is one of the few crude ideologies that can rival the power of democratic liberalism. Look, for example, at the unfolding nuclear drama on the Korean peninsula. The rising nationalism of South Koreas younger generation—which sees its troublesome neighbor to the north as kin, not monsters—hasn't yet figured in Washington's calculations concerning Pyongyang's brinkmanship. In these cases, as in previous similar instances, U.S. policies frequently have the perverse effects of alienating people in allied countries and driving them to support the very regimes targeted by U.S. policy.

Finally, given the nationalism that animates U.S. policies, American behavior abroad inevitably appears hypocritical to others. This hypocrisy is especially glaring when the United States undermines global institutions in the name of defending American sovereignty (such as in the cases of the Kyoto Protocol, the International Criminal Court, and the Comprehensive Test Ban Treaty). The rejection of such multilateral agreements may score points

at home, but non-Americans have difficulty reconciling the universalistic rhetoric and ideals Americans espouse with the parochial national interests the U.S. government appears determined to pursue abroad. Over time, such behavior can erode the United States' international credibility and legitimacy.

If American society had been less insulated from the rest of the world by geography and distance, these conflicting perspectives on nationalism might be less severe. To be sure, physical insularity has not diminished Americans' belief in the universalistic appeals of their political ideas. The nation was founded on the principle that all people (not just Americans) are endowed with "certain inalienable rights." That sentiment has been passed down through successive generations—from former President Franklin D. Roosevelt's vision of a world based upon "four freedoms" to President George W Bush's "non-negotiable demands of human dignity."

But the United States' relative isolation, which unavoidably leads to inadequate knowledge about other countries, has created a huge communications barrier between Americans and other societies. According to a recent survey by the Pew Global Attitudes Project, only 22 percent of Americans have traveled to another country in the last five years, compared with 66 percent of Canadians, 73 percent of Britons, 60 percent of the French, and 77 percent of Germans. Lack of direct contact with foreign societies has not been offset by the information revolution. In the years leading up to September 11, 2001, only 30 percent of Americans claimed to be "very interested " in "news about other countries." Even after the September 11, 2001, terrorist attacks, average Americans did not sustain a strong interest in international affairs. According to polls conducted by the Pew Research Center in early 2002, only about 26 percent of the Americans surveyed said they were following foreign news "very closely," and 45 percent of Americans said that international events did not affect them.

An amalgam of political idealism, national pride, and relative insularity, American nationalism evokes mixed feelings abroad. Many admire its idealism, universalism, and optimism and recognize the indispensability of American power and leadership to peace and prosperity around the world. Others reject American nationalism as merely the expression of an overbearing, self-righteous, and misguided bully. In ordinary times, such international ambivalence produces little more than idle chatter. But when American nationalism drives the country's foreign policy, it galvanizes broad-based anti-Americanism. And at such times, it becomes impossible to ignore the inconsistencies and tensions within American nationalism—or the harm they inflict on the United States' legitimacy abroad.

Minxin Pei is a senior associate and codirector of the China Program at the Carnegie Endowment for International Peace.

Want to Know More?

For classic works on the evolution of nationalism, see Eric J. Hobsbawm's *Nations and Nationalism Since 1780: Programme, Myth, Reality* (New York: Cambridge University Press, 1990) and Benedict Anderson's *Imagined Communities: Reflections on the Origin and Spread of Nationalism* (New York: Verso, 1991). For insights into the political thought underlying nationalism in the United Stares, see Louis Hartz's *The Liberal Tradition in American Thought: An Interpretation of American Political Thought Since the Revolution* (New York: Harcourt Brace, 1955).

In their study **"National Pride: A Cross-National Analysis"** (Chicago: National Opinion Research Center, 1998), Tom W Smith and Lars Jarkko measure nationalism in 23 countries and find that the United States ranks number one. Steven Kull reveals what average Americans really think about their role in the world in his virtual interview **"Vox Americani"** (Foreign Policy, September/October 2001). For a survey of national pride in the United States since September 11,2001, see Tom W. Smith, Kenneth A. Rasinski, and Marianna Toce's **"America Rebounds: A National Study of Public Response to the September IIth Terrorist Attacks"** (Chicago: National Opinion Research Center, 2001). For a comprehensive survey comparing public opinion in the United States and Europe, see the **Worldviews 2002** Web site, a joint project of the Chicago Council on Foreign Relations and the German Marshall Fund. The Pew Global Attitudes Project charts the rise of anti-American sentiments worldwide in its report **"What the World Thinks in 2002"** (Wash ington: The Pew Research Center for the People & the Press, 2002).

David Rothkopf argues the United States should dominate the world's information flows as Great Britain once ruled the seas in **"In Praise of Cultural Imperialism?"** (Foreign Policy, Summer 1997). Robert Kagan argues in **"The Benevolent Empire"** (Foreign Policy, Summer 1998) that even as the world decries U.S. arrogance, it relies on America as a guarantor of stability and prosperity.

For links to relevant Web sites, access to the *FP* Archive, and a comprehensive index of related Foreign Policy articles, go to **www.foreignpolicy.com**

Doctrinal Divisions

The Politics of US Military Interventions

Jon Western

In recent times, the United States has entered a particularly active phase in its use of military force. Since 1989, the United States has intervened in Panama, Kuwait, northern Iraq, Somalia, Bosnia, Haiti, Kosovo, Afghanistan, and Iraq. And, with the promulgation of the Bush Doctrine in the aftermath of the events of September 11, 2001, it appears that the United States is poised to continue its active intervention in the future.

Much is new in the world that helps to explain this increased frequency. First, the United States now stands unrivaled in the international system. This concentration of power permits US decision makers to consider the use of force in almost any crisis. Second, since the end of the Cold War, there has been a spate of violent regional and civil wars which, in addition to new information technologies, have led human rights activists to collect evidence of gross violations of international humanitarian laws and to launch intense advocacy campaigns across the world. This has pressured the United States to use its massive military arsenal to alleviate the extreme abuses and a flurry of new norms of humanitarian intervention. Third, a new wave of interventions has occurred in response to the emerging threats associated with terrorism and the illicit proliferation of WMD.

Despite all that has changed since 1989 and, more recently, since September 11, 2001, much remains the same. US citizens have always been divided about when and where the United States should use military force. Except in rare occasions of extreme national emergency, US decisions concerning the use of force are almost always contested. Political elites, in particular, differ about the nature of threats and the costs and efficacy of the use of force. As a result, in almost every instance when a US President considers the use of US force in overseas combat missions, there are intense political debates among US foreign policy elites about whether or not force should be used. Ultimately, decisions to intervene are almost always based on tenuous coalitions—not consensus. Because rhetoric campaigns are such an integral part of the process to mobilize public and political support, the public frequently develops unrealistic expectations about the nature, likely cost, and efficacy of military intervention.

These unrealistic expectations ultimately have profound implications not only for the intervention, but also for the long-term commitment to post war reconstruction.

The Politics of Intervention

Famed Christian theologian Reinhold Niebuhr once noted that "every nation is caught in the moral paradox of refusing to go to war unless it can be proved that the national interest is imperiled, and of continuing in the war only by proving that something much more than national interest is at stake." For the United States, this acute moral paradox has had a peculiar political twist. The debates over Federalism and Republicanism between Alexander Hamilton and Thomas Jefferson that surfaced in the early days of the United States were never resolved. They only marked the beginning of the enduring tension and confluence between realism and idealism that is still today the distinctive essence of US foreign policy. Throughout the past two centuries, we have grown accustomed to the differences between realists and idealists, interventionists and anti-imperialists and isolationists, and hawks and doves, among others. Today, we hear common references to hardliners, selective engagers, liberal internationalists, humanitarianists, isolationists, and pacifists. Whatever labels scholars or journalists attach to these differences, however, they all reflect one enduring element of US foreign policy: there is no singular or monolithic conception of national interest or of American values and principles.

World War II is the only instance in history when the nature of the threat was so clear and unambiguous that it generated as close to a consensus as possible in US society. Following the attacks on Pearl Harbor, there was only one single dissenting vote in the US Senate to the declaration of war and the subsequent full mobilization of US military and domestic resources.

In all other instances, presidents face decisions on intervention when there are different perceptions of the threat or implications for US strategic interests or values. Despite widespread public and political support in three of the major US military interventions —the Spanish-American War of 1898, the Korean Conflict, and the Vietnam War—the support rested on *ad hoc* coalitions of those who might be labeled selective engagers, hardliners, and liberals. Each held different reasons for their support of military intervention.

In the case of the Spanish-American War, many US officials saw Cuba as a strategic interest, especially because it was the last holdout of the Spanish Empire in the western hemisphere and because of its proximity to the shipping lanes for the future Atlantic- Pacific canal. Despite the strength of these strategic reasons, war against Spain would have been unthinkable without the yellow journalism of William Randolph Hearst and Joseph Pulitzer and the horrific policies of Spanish Governor of Cuba, General Valeriano Weyler, who triggered intense outrage in the United States by forcing re-concentration camps on rural populations. Even after the sinking of the USS Maine in February 1898, it took US Senator Redfield Proctor's report on the brutalities of Spanish rule to sway conservative politicians, and ultimately, US President William McKinley, to support the move to war. Ultimately, it was the combination of strategic interests and US principles that mobilized a broad-based coalition of disparate groups to generate support for the intervention.

Conversely, when US interests and principles obviously conflict, US presidents have found it very difficult to mobilize support for the use of force. For example, US President Dwight Eisenhower's decision not to intervene on behalf of French forces at Dienbienphu in Indochina in 1954 was influenced in large part by overwhelmingly US public opposition to fighting and dying for French colonialism. Eisenhower initially expressed serious reservations about intervention, but as the crisis intensified throughout the spring of 1954 he and US Secretary of State John Foster Dulles scrambled for ways to prevent the French from collapsing. They believed that if the French lost Dienbienphu they would withdraw from Indochina in defeat and the entire region would fall to international communism. Despite the administration's best attempts to reframe the conflict as part of the global war on international communism—Eisenhower coined the term the "domino theory" in specific reference to the crisis—the prevailing analytical narrative of the Dienbienphu crisis was that French colonialism had inspired Vietnamese nationalism.

No doubt intervention in Indochina would have been costly and the crisis' geographic and temporal proximity to the Korean War also influenced the strong public and political opposition, and ultimately Eisenhower's decision. But any intervention would have had to contend with arguments that US citizens were being sent to fight and die for French colonialism—a tough sell under any circumstance.

Not all cases present such clear conflicts between interests and values. This is when political complications increase dramatically. Perhaps the most common strategy used by advocates of intervention is to develop a worst-case analysis in the face of inaction coupled with best-case scenarios of US intervention. We are constantly told that

intervention is necessary to defeat an evil enemy and to liberate populations from the grips of repression and tyranny. As a result, political elites often portray the enemy as a paper tiger—a strong, calculating and decisive adversary who if left unchecked will create irreparable harm, but when faced with the power and resolve of the US military will be easily cowed into submission. In wide range of interventions from Korea, Lebanon, Vietnam, the Dominican Republic, Grenada, Panama, Somalia, and most recently in Iraq, US presidents have used strikingly similar language to warn of the dire consequences of inaction. Yet, in each case, the message was also sent that with strong and resolute action, victory would be at hand.

"DESPITE THE IMPORTANCE AND NECESSITY OF FIGHTING IN SUPPORT OF US VALUES . . . THE UNITED STATES OFTEN REMAINS HIGHLY DIVIDED ON THE QUESTION OF NATION BUILDING."

US presidents also use the prestige of the presidency to frame the analytical narrative of a conflict—this often includes co-opting the language of potential critics or slanting or withholding information to strengthen the case intervention. Despite the obvious threat to Middle East oil production and distribution and subsequently to the stability of the US and global economy in 1991, US President George Bush presented the case for war in terms of Saddam Hussein's brutality and his violation of international law and in terms of restoring freedom to Kuwait. In fact, when he announced the beginning of the Persian Gulf War to the US public, Bush did not make a single reference to US national interests. Liberals who expressed reservations with the war were ultimately left to defend why they would oppose a war to free "tiny Kuwait" from its ruthless neighbor or to uphold international law. In the 1983 case of Grenada, US President Ronald Reagan restricted the flow of all information concerning the deliberations on intervention from the public, the press, and even from the US Congress. Although Reagan and his advisors cited the need for "operational security," they later acknowledged that the restriction on information was not just to maintain operational security, but also to prevent members of the US Congress from opposing or sidetracking the intervention. Reagan's principal political advisor, Michael Deaver, later summed up his assessment of the Grenada mission: "We got away with it by establishing special ground rules, by not letting the press in and justifying it later."

The Perils of Politics

These mobilization strategies are not a problem if the intervention leads to quick and decisive outcomes—such as in Lebanon in 1958 or Grenada in 1983 or Panama in 1989 or if there are no significant costs to the intervention in terms of US casualties—such as has been the case in Bosnia and Kosovo. In each of those cases, the US military was able to achieve its military objectives and maintain widespread support for its actions.

However, the cases of quick and decisive victory are frequently overshadowed by instances in which the realities on the ground do not measure up to the rhetoric used to sell the intervention. Despite the increasingly causal language used to describe US military actions around the world, interventions are not sport and they rarely go according to script. Because most interventions are the product of coalitions, and not consensus, or at times are based exaggerated rhetorical claims, the political support for interventions is always tenuous. There is always the well-established "rally around the flag effect," but this tends to have limited duration. The war in Vietnam, like in Korea a decade earlier, witnessed a fragmentation of support as US citizens began to question the motivations for the war. While US Presidents Lyndon Johnson and Richard Nixon spoke both in terms of helping to defend a small nation from the brutality of international communism and in terms of prioritizing national security imperatives, the nature of the conflict could not be reduced to simple platitudes, nor could such simple rhetorical devices sustain US support in the face of evidence that conduct by both US and South Vietnamese forces often contradicted US values. Liberals initially supported the war, by and large, because they hoped not only to forestall a communist advance, but also to help the South Vietnamese. The graphic images of US soldiers burning the village of Cam Ne, of a South Vietnamese general executing a prisoner on a busy Saigon street, and of a naked child fleeing a napalm attack on her village all vividly suggested that the war often contradicted or violated the very principles many thought the United States was fighting to defend. The gap between the events on the ground and the rhetorical claims made by Johnson and Nixon galvanized and mainstreamed the anti-war movement. It also contributed in great part to the breakdown of the coalition that had initially supported the war.

A similar breakdown occurred in the war in the Philippines. In August 1898, US Commodore George Dewey's fleet defeated the Spanish forces in less than half-a-day. The effort so endeared Dewey to the US public, according to historian H. W. Brands, that he was immediately catapulted to being the "most famous man in America." Yet, less than a year later, more than 60,000 US forces were called up to the Philippines to quell an insurgency against American rule. By early 1900, McKinley had imposed strict censorship on reports from the Philippines and with more than 3,000 US citizens dead and perhaps as many as 20,000 Filipinos killed, many US citizens who had initially supported the war turned against it. William Randolph Hearst, for example, became a vocal critic following reports of atrocities during the war in the Philippines. US citizens were angered by the forced resettlement of peasant populations in the Batangas Province— a policy eerily similar to Weyler's campaign in Cuba. The massacre at Balangiga in which 48 US soldiers were killed also out-

raged many in the United States, but it was the execution of all males over the age of ten on the island of Samar by US Army General Jacob Smith that generated an even greater firestorm against the war.

Implications For Post-intervention Commitments

The political nature of interventions also carries over to the post-war commitment. Post-intervention strategies and the political viability and sustainability of US efforts cannot be divorced from the politics used to generate that intervention. Despite the importance and necessity of fighting in support of US values—democracy and freedom—the United States often remains highly divided on the question of nation building. Post-war reconstruction and democracy in Germany and Japan are frequently touted as the United State's great success stories. However, World War II was a total war, and even here, much of the US post-war commitment to rebuilding Germany and Japan was fueled by the emergence of the Cold War.

In contrast, however, US efforts have been less committed and the results much more mixed. The reality of post-intervention reconstruction and rebuilding is that these processes are enormously complex and costly, and the coalitions that emerge to support intervention are rarely sustained beyond the end of the initial military phase. As a result, the United States' post-intervention strategy for the promotion of democracy has been simply to call for free elections and then withdraw—as in many of the cases of Latin America and the Caribbean—or to assist in the development of new constitution and some institutional reform—such as the case of the Philippines. While these strategies do set an initial marker for democratic development, neither has proved particularly effective in creating stable, liberal democracies. For example, the pervasive problem for the development of stable democracy in the Philippines has been the fundamental disparities in the concentration of wealth and access to state and societal resources. The US administration during the occupation of the Philippines established basic civil and political institutions—free-elections, an independent judiciary, civilian control over the military, and widespread bureaucratic and administrative reform. However, without any real strategic imperative involved, there was only a small advocacy community calling for a more ambitious plan to break the landowning oligarchy that dominated the vast majority of property and wealth in Filipino society. The result has been that throughout the US occupation of the Philippines, there was no discernable improvement in rural landless poverty. Since the Philippines gained its independence in 1946, the problem of landless poverty continues to be one of the prime sources of instability for the future of Filipino democracy.

This process in US intervention is not limited to historical examples. The situation in Afghanistan today reveals dwindling public and political support for the commit-

US TROOPS ABROAD

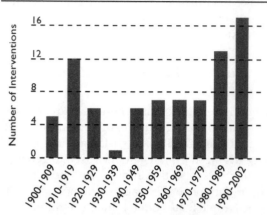

Recent years have seen a marked increase in the number of interventions in which US troops have taken part. In the graph above, each instance if intervention refers to the deployment of US military troops to a foreign state for engagement, protection of a US interest, execution of a military coup, or security stabilization of a region, not including US shows of strength. World War I and World War II were each counted as one combined intervention effort.

Congressional Research Service

ment of massive resources to rebuilding the war torn country. In the run-up to the military action in Afghanistan, the administration of US President George W. Bush pledged itself, at least rhetorically, to dramatically improve the quality of life in post-war Afghanistan. Yet, even before the major combat elements had concluded, conservatives who supported the war to remove the Taliban and disrupt Al Qaeda were already arguing that the United States could not and should not seek to fundamentally transform Afghan society. Henry Kissinger published an op-ed in the *Washington Post* calling on the Bush administration to move on to Iraq and to avoid getting trapped in some long-term commitment to re-make Afghanistan. For conservatives, the broad security problem in Afghanistan had been sufficiently addressed with the defeat of the Taliban and the dispersal of Al Qaeda. In sum, elements of the broad-based coalition that initially supported the intervention in Afghanistan are now moving on to other priorities. As a result, the US commitment in Afghanistan is limited to modest support for a rather weak NATO security presence and disjointed international financial assistance programs.

The Way Forward

One of the great myths of US foreign policy is that politics stop at the water's edge. Only in rare instances when the United States is directly attacked do politics seem to stop. Even then, they simply quiet down for a short time; they do not stop. Two things are certain. First, with the concentration of US power in the international system, there will be increased opportunities and demands for US-led military interventions in the future. Second, the political dimensions of the US decision making process will not go away.

Since interventions are inherently political decisions, contested within a highly political context, it is unlikely that any universal grand strategy or doctrine of intervention—such as the Bush Doctrine—is likely to prevail. Those who advocate a doctrine of pre-emption in anticipation of emerging threats are likely to find intense competition over assessing the nature of the threat and the costs of the war. Conversely, as was the case with the "Powell Doctrine," throughout the 1990s, those who rule out intervention from the outset may find themselves under intense and persistent pressure that will likely distract other foreign policy initiatives and ultimately lead to some form of intervention under less than desirable terms. This appeared to be the case in Somalia in 1992, Bosnia in 1995, and Kosovo in 1999.

Thus it will be difficult for any administration to sustain a high degree of consistency or adherence to a specific doctrine on intervention and the use of force. It also means that under these pressures, elites are likely to develop more sophisticated campaigns and strategies to sell intervention. Under such pressure, we would all do well [to] recall the concerns James Madison expressed to Thomas Jefferson at the beginning of the US republic. He warned: "The management of foreign relations appears to be the most susceptible to abuse of all the trusts committed to a Government, because they can be concealed or disclosed, or disclosed in such parts and at such times as will best suit particular views." With the prospect of more demands and opportunities for the use of force in the future, those words seem even more relevant today than they did in the late 18th century.

JON WESTERN *is Assistant Professor of International Relations at Mount Holyoke College. Previously he served as a Balkans and East Asian specialist in the US Department of State.*

Missed Signals

Sherry Ricchiardi

Donald H. Rumsfeld could not pass up a chance to gloat.

During a town hall-style meeting with Pentagon workers on May 11, the defense secretary smugly noted that it was "the military, not the media" that discovered and reported the prisoner abuse at Abu Ghraib, a hellhole 20 miles west of Baghdad.

Rumsfeld's remarks touched a nerve.

Because, for a variety of reasons, the media were awfully slow to unearth a scandal that ultimately caused international embarrassment for the United States and cast a shadow over the war in Iraq. Images of American prison guards using sexual humiliation and snarling guard dogs to terrify naked Arab prisoners may well have lasting repercussions for U.S. foreign policy.

What's worse, there was no shortage of signs that something was amiss. For two years, global monitors such as Amnesty International and Human Rights Watch repeatedly warned of mistreatment of detainees at the hands of Americans in the dark recesses of Afghanistan and at the holding tank for suspected terrorists in Guantanamo Bay, Cuba.

And there were prescient stories, stories that appeared and then vanished without a trace. On December 26, 2002, the Washington Post published a breakthrough piece on the CIA's "brass-knuckled quest for information" in Afghanistan. In March 2003, a cover story in The Nation said that torture was gaining acceptance in the Bush administration. In November, the Associated Press was among the first to raise alarms about abuse at Abu Ghraib—but few of the AP's clients showcased the story, if they ran it at all.

Then, on January 16 of this year, the U.S. Command in Baghdad issued a one-paragraph press release: "An investigation has been initiated into reported incidents of detainee abuse at a Coalition Forces detention facility. The release of specific information concerning the incidents could hinder the investigation, which is in its early stages. The investigation will be conducted in a thorough and professional manner."

The tantalizing but sketchy release didn't exactly set off a media firestorm. The New York Times published a 367-word report on page 7, noting that the inquiry was expected to "add fuel" to the burgeoning allegations of abuse. The Philadelphia Inquirer ran a 707-word story, also played on page 7, headlined, "U.S. probes report of abuse of Iraqi detainees." The Washington Post and USA Today did not run stories on the release, according to a Lexis-Nexis search. The Boston Globe had about 100 words on the investigation at the end of an 844-word Iraq story on A4. The Dallas Morning News ran a 20-word brief on 26A. Television largely ignored the announcement: CNN and Fox News Channel mentioned it briefly on January 16, NBC had a 41-word item the following morning, and that was about it.

Then the story largely disappeared. Few followed the misty clue.

Three-and-a-half months later, the degradation at Abu Ghraib finally became major international news after CBS' "60 Minutes II" on April 28 aired ghastly photographs of U.S. military police posing and grinning next to naked, hooded Iraqi prisoners. Two days later, The New Yorker posted Seymour M. Hersh's scorching account of prisoner mistreatment at the prison.

Why did it take so long for the news media to uncover the scandal? What went wrong?

Washington Post Executive Editor Leonard Downie Jr. wishes his newspaper had gone harder after the story at the outset. But, he asks, referring to the January press release, "Have you ever read that paragraph? They made it as innocent-sounding as possible, and it just wasn't noticed the way it should have been."

Journalists were not aggressive enough and were slow to grasp the significance of the military's announcement, says Philip Taubman, the New York Times' Washington bureau chief. "We didn't do our job with this until the photographs appeared on CBS" and Hersh's story hit the Internet.

"It was," says Taubman, "a failure of newsgathering."

After the televised images put the story into play, the relentless reporting of Sy Hersh helped build momentum. His first piece, "Torture at Abu Ghraib," which appeared in The New Yorker's May 10 issue after its late-April online debut, explored how far up the chain of command responsibility lay. Hersh provided details from a secret

Abu Ghraib Time Line

October 7, 2001
The war in Afghanistan begins.

December 26, 2002
The Washington Post runs a page-one story about prisoner abuse at secret CIA detention centers, including in the "forbidden zone" of the U.S. occupied Bagram air base in Afghanistan.

March 20, 2003
The war in Iraq begins.

March 31, 2003
The Nation's cover story, "In Torture We Trust?" asserts that torture is gaining mainstream acceptance in the age of 9/11.

May 17, 2003
The New York Times publishes a story out of Basra, Iraq, in which detainees claim they were abused by U.S. nd British soldiers. Amnesty International investigators say the patterns of mistreatment may constitute torture.

August 18, 2003
The Los Angeles Times spotlights four Army reservists from Pennsylvania, part of the 320th Reserve Military Police Battalion, charged with mistreating and beating Iraqi POWs.

October–December 2003
Many of the alleged abuses at Abu Ghraib take place.

October 5, 2003
The Associated Press reports on the closure of Camp Cropper, a notorious detention center at the Baghdad airport. Journalists had been barred from the camp, but reporter Charles J. Hanley interviews released detainees about abuses.

November 1, 2003
The AP distributes a major story by Hanley about alleged abuse at three Iraqi POW camps, including Abu Ghraib, based on interviews with former POWs.

January 13, 2004
Army Spc. Joseph M. Darby, an MP at Abu Ghraib, reports cases of abuse at the prison to military investigators.

January 16, 2004
The U.S. Command in Baghdad issues a one-paragraph press release about an investigation into prisoner abuse. A Lexis, Nexis search shows that most media outlets either ignored the announcement or ran brief stories.

January 19, 2004
Lt. Gen. Ricardo Sanchez orders a criminal investigation into the 800th Military Police Brigade.

January 21, 2004
CNN reports that U.S. male and female soldiers reportedly posed for photos with partially unclothed Iraqi prisoners and that the focus of the Army's investigation is Abu Ghraib.

January 31, 2004
Maj. Gen. Antonio M. Taguba is appointed to head an inquiry into allegations of abuse at Abu Ghraib. On March 3 he presents his report, citing widespread abuse of prisoners by military police and military intelligence officers, to Gen. David McKieman. On April 6 McKieman approves the findings, leading to the discharge of two soldiers from the 800th MP Unit and letters of reprimand to six others.

February 23, 2004
The U.S. military announces that 17 personnel have been relieved of duty during the abuse investigation.

March 3, 2004
Jen Benbury, a correspondent for the online magazine Salon, files a story out of Baghdad about allegations of beatings, sleep deprivation, sexual humiliation and neglect leading to deaths at Abu Ghraib.

March 20, 2004
Brig. Gen. Mark Kimmitt announces to the media that six military personnel have been charged with criminal offenses. On May 7, a seventh soldier is charged.

April 28, 2004
CBS' "60 Minutes II" airs graphic photographs of abuse at Abu Ghraib. The scandal quickly becomes major national and international news.

April 30, 2004
The New Yorker posts on its Web site a detailed report on Abu Ghraib by Seymour M. Hersh, fueling the media frenzy. The article is published in the magazine's May 10 issue. Hersh follows up on the burgeoning scandal in the next two issues.

---

report by Maj. Gen. Antonio M. Taguba documenting massive failures of the Army's prison system in Iraq. An accompanying photo, one that quickly became an iconic image, showed a hooded Iraqi prisoner balanced on a box, wires attached to his fingers, toes and penis.

Hersh followed up with articles in the magazine's next two issues, explaining how a covert Pentagon program, focused on the hunt for al Qaeda, had been expanded to the interrogation of Iraqi prisoners. He outlined how the Department of Defense mishandled "the disaster" at Abu Ghraib, and conducted a series of poorly conceived internal investigations. His third story tied the roots of the prison scandal to a decision approved last year by Rumsfeld to expand the highly secretive interrogation operation.

But it was the photographs that ignited a global firestorm. Top Arab networks Al Jazeera, based in Qatar, and

Al Arabiya, based in the United Arab Emirates, aired images around the clock of torture and the outraged reaction of the Islamic Middle East. Egypt's Akhbar el-Yom splashed the word "Scandal" across the front page above smiling U.S. soldiers posing by naked, hooded prisoners piled in a human pyramid. The Kuwaiti newspaper Al Watan warned that the "barbaric" treatment would rally Islamic fundamentalists.

American journalists were in a catch-up frenzy. News organizations quickly jumped on the story and began exploring whether Abu Ghraib was the work of a handful of proverbial "bad apples" or an officially sanctioned policy. The story dominated cable news and left conservative media personalities like Bill O'Reilly of Fox News Channel charging that the Abu Ghraib scandal was being used to destroy the Bush administration by news outlets with an agenda.

The Washington Post published a three-part series about the murky world of U.S. interrogation that could have been the script for a spy flick. Reporters described a clandestine "new universe...developed by military or CIA lawyers, vetted by the Justice Department's office of legal counsel and, depending on the particular issue, approved by the White House general counsel's office or the president himself." They told of a secret CIA interrogation center in Kabul nicknamed "The Pit," of "ghost detainees" held in secret prisons, of a covert airline used to transport prisoners.

The Post obtained some 1,000 photos documenting the abuse and disclosed previously secret sworn statements by Abu Ghraib prisoners alleging that they had been ridden like animals, sexually fondled by female soldiers and forced to retrieve their food from toilets.

The mushrooming scandal commanded the May 17 covers of Time, Newsweek and U.S. News & World Report. Abu Ghraib dominated the headlines for a month. Day after day top national newspapers brought to light new aspects of the debacle on their front pages.

"The whole tenor of the coverage definitely changed. It got much bolder" after the CBS and Hersh exposes, says Salon's Eric Boehlert, who writes about media issues. "Up to that point, the American news media seemed hesitant, almost dutiful" in reporting about prisoner mistreatment in Iraq, Afghanistan and Guantanamo Bay.

Why were the news media so slow to react? "There were multiple reasons why we fell off the mark," says Ken Auletta, The New Yorker's media reporter. "It can't be just one thing."

Media critics and newsroom professionals cite a wide array of factors: the Bush administration's penchant for secrecy and controlling the news agenda; extremely dangerous conditions that limited reporting by Western reporters in much of Iraq; the challenge of covering the multifaceted situation in the embattled country with a finite amount of reporting firepower. Some see a media

still intimidated by the post-9/11 orgy of patriotism. Yet there's little doubt that missed clues and ignored signals were part of the mix.

There's a strong consensus that the administration's skill at information management played a major role. The terse January 16 press release is Exhibit A. Then came the clampdown on information about Abu Ghraib immediately afterward. Prison camps in Afghanistan and Iraq tended to be forbidden zones.

"I have never seen greater news management in 30-plus years in this business," Loren Jenkins, foreign editor for National Public Radio, says of the administration's approach. "They are very skilled at it."

Journalists in pursuit of the Abu Ghraib story might have been thwarted by what Jenkins describes as an entrenched Pentagon strategy to obfuscate negative effects of the American occupation of Iraq. "But that's what the Fourth Estate is all about—poking holes in news management," says Jenkins, who covered the Vietnam War. "Our job is to find out whether we're being told the truth or not."

Yet, when it comes to Abu Ghraib, "basically we couldn't get at the story," he admits. "We all had people telling us about mistreatment, but it was hard to verify on our own. It took the pictures to say, 'This is undeniable.'"

New York Times Executive Editor Bill Keller agrees. "Any honest editor will give you the same answer. It's the pictures; that's what did it. But it shouldn't require visual drama to make us pay attention to something like this."

Safety concerns also could have played a role in the lack of coverage. There is little doubt that the high risk of being kidnapped, wounded or killed has quelled independent reporting efforts outside the safety zones of Baghdad over the past year. (See Letter from Baghdad, page 69.) The Committee to Protect Journalists lists Iraq as the most dangerous place in the world to cover the news. According to the CPJ, 27 media professionals have been killed since the war started in March 2003.

At the same time, suicide bombers, surprise attacks and oil-field sabotage have caused headaches for foreign desks juggling multiple assignments. Deciding where to expend reporter power often became a form of triage as resistance to the occupation ignited across the country and more foreigners were being targeted.

"We can't fault our reporters in Iraq for not dropping everything else they were doing, to get this story," says Los Angeles Times Washington Bureau Chief Doyle McManus.

"We can't fault our reporters in Iraq for not dropping everything else they were doing to get this story," says Doyle McManus, the Los Angeles Times' Washington bureau chief. "If one of those reporters had said, 'This is the tip of the iceberg,' which we now know it was, it's possible we would have put some more resources into it and done more digging. But I don't think they realized there was an iceberg underneath."

Asked if the L.A. Times had run a story after the January 16 press release about the abuse probe, McManus turned to his computer. He quickly found a 15-inch piece by a Times reporter that had run on page A6 titled "Coalition investigating prison abuse." "It was another red flag we didn't pick up on" in Washington, McManus said of the story. "I'm not happy about that."

Associated Press reporter Charles J. Hanley calls tracking evidence of the abuse a "needle in the haystack" venture that many news organizations, already stretched thin, did not have time to pursue. "We were all in a very pressure-filled, difficult situation, trying to cover a very sprawling story. Something like this was not readily available," says Hanley, who wrote an early but largely ignored story on prisoner mistreatment. "It took me weeks, on and off, to find the released detainees."

The Post's Downie offers a similar explanation: "There was a lot in Iraq to cover, and so it took a concerted effort to say, 'OK, we're going to spend a certain amount of our resources, time and attention on this particular story, in addition to all the others.'" In the case of the prisoner abuse, "We were nudged along by CBS, which did a very important journalistic act" when it aired the photographs, he says.

Several media experts hypothesize that since 9/11, the government has played on the patriotism of journalists, raising the terrorism banner to deflect press criticism. That could make a difference in how reporters pursue a story that might embarrass the U.S., particularly when soldiers are dying in a foreign land.

"There is an awareness on the part of the White House that this tendency exists, so they go for it, exploit it," says Marvin Kalb, a senior fellow at Harvard University's Joan Shorenstein Center on the Press, Politics and Public Policy. "It isn't that [the government] beats somebody over the head. They don't have to. That's what makes it so much more painful.

"Maybe the rush of patriotism we saw in spades after 9/11 has continued," he adds. "Maybe editors fell asleep and didn't ask reporters to pursue obvious lines of inquiry [about Abu Ghraib]. The news industry itself has not been glowingly successful in coverage of the war on terror."

On December 6, 2001, appearing before a Senate committee, Attorney General John Ashcroft chastised critics of the administration's terrorism policy, saying that they give "ammunition to America's enemies." Equating dissent with disloyalty and a lack of good citizenship can become deeply rooted, says Katrina vanden Heuvel, editor of The Nation.

She believes that could account for the media's failure to raise more probing questions in the run-up to the war in Iraq as well as over the allegations of prisoner abuse. "I really do think there has been a culture of intimidation," says vanden Heuvel. "Journalists are afraid not to be pa-

triotic." (See "Are the News Media Soft on Bush?" October/November 2003.)

Stephen Hess, a senior fellow emeritus at the Brookings Institution, doesn't see the patriotism card playing a role. "Of course, maybe right after 9/11, but by this time I don't think the press is so easily intimidated," he says. "It just might be that the story was too unbelievable."

Reporters may have found it difficult to fathom that the American military would carry out a policy of torture. That could have made it easier to dismiss abuse allegations by Iraqis or attribute them to an occasional lapse. Some correspondents may have problems reporting information that reflects badly on the U.S. military, says the AP's Hanley, especially when it comes from non-American sources.

The New Yorker's Auletta believes naïveté on the part of some correspondents could have played a role. "I am sure that a lot of reporters had a hard time imagining that we would be guilty of the kind of abuse we often associate with Third World dictators. We're often criticized for being too cynical; sometimes we're probably not cynical enough," he says. "Maybe [reporters] were afraid to look too negative; maybe they didn't have the information or couldn't get the sources in the military to pursue it. I don't think there is any one explanation."

Downie pays tribute to "60 Minutes II" for its "nudge" to the rest of the news media. But not everyone thought that nudge was such a good thing. Howls that the media were going overboard on the Abu Ghraib story were quick to emerge, particularly from the right.

One of the first to complain was talk radio's Rush Limbaugh, who accused the New York Times and others of using the scandal as a battering ram on the Bush administration. In May, Limbaugh told his 20 million weekly listeners that mainstream journalists felt threatened by talk radio, conservative bloggers and Fox News Channel. "Now they're feeling their oats again. They're all pumped up like Arnold Schwarzenegger was on steroids," he said. Limbaugh dismissed the behavior at Abu Ghraib as military personnel having a good time and blowing off some steam.

The host of Fox News' "The O'Reilly Factor" had a similar take. On May 27, Bill O'Reilly opened a show by asking, "Have the New York Times and the L.A. Times declared war on the Bush administration?" He noted that the Los Angeles Times had put Abu Ghraib on its front page "26 out of the past 28 days." "Does this story rate that kind of coverage? You decide," O'Reilly told his audience.

Around the same time, Jonah Goldberg, editor at large for National Review Online, wrote that "CBS should be ashamed for running those photos." Goldberg complained of a double standard in media coverage. "When shocking images might stir Americans to favor war, the Serious Journalists show great restraint. When those images have the opposite effect, the Ted Koppels let it fly," he wrote.

None of this surprised Mike King, public editor of the Atlanta Journal-Constitution. Immediately after the beheading of American businessman Nicholas Berg in May, King began receiving calls and e-mail messages from readers demanding coverage equal to Abu Ghraib. "It started before we even printed anything in the next morning's paper," King says. "It was like a mantra: 'We're watching to see how you treat it.' It was fascinating—like a challenge had been laid down. This was going to become the litmus test for fairness and war coverage in general."

King attempted to refute the idea that if the Berg execution didn't get the same level of coverage as the prison scandal, it would prove that left-leaning journalists care more about U.S. soldiers embarrassing Iraqi prisoners than they do about terrorists killing Americans. He argued in a column that the Berg murder was a different story and demanded a different level of coverage.

"It's getting increasingly rigid. Virtually every story gets filtered through some partisanship prism," he says. "This comes through loud and clear in e-mail and phone calls."

Los Angeles Times media writer David Shaw distilled the complaints he was hearing about media overreaction into four essential arguments. The coverage was an effort to damage the Bush White House; it provided material for propaganda to recruit more American-hating terrorists; Saddam Hussein was a far worse torturer; a few bad apples carried out the abuse.

Shaw debunked each one in a May 30 column, including the idea that the "liberal media" were in attack mode against the White House. Shaw maintained that the coverage did not represent "swarm journalism." He pointed out the substantial difference between giving massive attention to trivia like Janet Jackson's briefly bared breast and giving it to American soldiers abusing and humiliating prisoners.

Response from the public was roughly divided between those who agreed with him and those "who say we are making a big deal out of this to embarrass Bush," Shaw says.

It was the media's job, he says, "to deal with the news as it was and not attempt to prejudge what impact a given development was going to have on world opinion, on politics, on the administration."

Terence Smith, who covers the media for PBS' "The News-Hour with Jim Lehrer," rejects the notion that the Abu Ghraib coverage was politically motivated. It was the media's job, he says, "to deal with the news as it was and not attempt to prejudge what impact a given development was going to have on world opinion, on politics, on the administration." He points to the Washington Post, which obtained up to 1,000 of the prison photos in the wake of the CBS report, as a prime example of press

"responsibility and restraint" in covering the scandal. Says Smith, "They used only those [photos] that advanced the story, were newsworthy and in context."

While the American media were slow to discover the abuse at Abu Ghraib, a number of news organizations published stories on the mistreatment of American-held prisoners in Afghanistan and Guantanamo Bay as far back as 2002.

One of the first major pieces ran in the Washington Post on December 26, 2002. The page-one story by Dana Priest and Barton Gellman featured interviews with former intelligence officials and 10 current U.S. national security officials, including some who witnessed the handling of captured al Qaeda operatives and Taliban leaders. An official who supervised the transfer of prisoners told the Post, "If you don't violate someone's human rights some of the time, you probably aren't doing your job."

The story detailed torture allegations and told of captives being moved to secret detention centers in Jordan, Egypt and Morocco, all countries where security forces are known for their brutality. According to witnesses, MPs and U.S. Army Special Forces troops often "softened up" prisoners by covering their heads with hoods, beating them, throwing them against walls and depriving them of sleep.

Why didn't the Post continue to follow the trail? "In part, obviously, because information was not made readily available, and in part because we didn't always see the tip of the iceberg as clearly as we should have," Downie says.

The Nation's vanden Heuvel hails the Post piece as "a breakthrough in the U.S. press" and says it was one of the factors that inspired her to pursue a cover story on how torture was regaining mainstream acceptance in the age of 9/11. The piece ran on March 31, 2003, with the headline "In Torture We Trust?"

The story told of death certificates released for two al Qaeda suspects who died while in U.S. custody at the Bagram base in Afghanistan that showed both were killed by "blunt force injuries." Other detainees told of being hung from the ceiling by chains.

In the same issue, writer Eyal Press explored why there had been no outcry over such behavior. "There's been a painful silence about this," Human Rights Watch Executive Director Ken Roth told The Nation. "I haven't heard anyone in Congress call for hearings or even speak out publicly." The silence extends to the news media, wrote Press.

On November 1, 2003, the AP's Hanley filed a story out of Baghdad about alleged mistreatment at three detention centers, including Abu Ghraib. The others were Camp Cropper at the Baghdad airport and Camp Bocca in southern Iraq.

Hanley, a Pulitzer Prize winner, interviewed half a dozen former detainees who corroborated each other's stories about psychological abuse, beatings and other forms of severe punishment. Their information tended to dovetail with what Amnesty International had heard.

In mid-October 2003, Hanley submitted questions to the U.S. Command in Baghdad about the charges. Did the military tie people up and lay them out in the sun for hours? Did it deprive them of food for punishment? How many deaths have there been and what were the circumstances?

"They didn't respond," Hanley says. "They didn't even deny it."

In his November 1 piece, he also reported on two pending U.S. military legal cases in which four soldiers were accused of beating Iraqi prisoners and two Marines were charged with an Iraqi's death in detention.

It appears only a few newspapers picked up the story. Hanley says the AP does not do "exhaustive" play checks, "but we had the feeling from our experience and from the feedback, that it was relatively few" who published the piece. As for why more didn't use it, he says, "I'm a bit at a loss. It may have been a combination of factors ranging from a reluctance by some to publicize such charges coming from non-American sources to the length of the piece, which would be inconvenient to many papers."

In a March 3, 2004, story, Jen Banbury, a correspondent for the online magazine Salon, told of joining a crowd outside Abu Ghraib in search of former detainees or family members who could shed light on allegations of mistreatment coming from behind the walls. Suddenly, she heard an American voice shout, "What the hell is going on here?" Banbury was ordered to leave the area by U.S. Military Police. When she attempted to get permission to return to the area through U.S. Command channels, it was denied.

The reporter wrote a detailed account of the "obfuscation" by the military regarding Abu Ghraib prisoners and provided an overview of the charges from families and monitors like Human Rights Watch.

That was nearly two months before the harrowing images aired on CBS.

Psychiatrist and author Robert Jay Lifton believes that it's the news media's responsibility to educate the public on the true nature of war. "Wars are ugly and have grotesque dimensions people at home can hardly imagine," he says. "The role of the media is to bring them as close as possible to what is happening."

The photographs from Abu Ghraib burned into the American psyche, often sparking visceral reactions. Lifton believes that, ultimately, the photographs could lead more Americans to conclude "there is something tainted, dirty or wrong" about the war in Iraq. Lifton, who has written books about the Vietnam War and Nazi war crimes, says the reaction to Abu Ghraib was even stronger than the response to the My Lai massacre in the late 1960s.

Yet not everyone wants to see those horrific images.

When the Sacramento Bee ran only stories of the scandal, there was barely a ripple from the public. Then, on May 7, the paper published a front-page photo of U.S. Army Spc. Lynndie England holding a naked Iraqi man on a leash. Readers were outraged—not at the MP's behavior but at the Bee. They used words and phrases like "sensationalism," "Bush-bashing" and "pornographic" when they contacted the paper, according to Ombudsman Tony Marcano. A mere "handful" of readers commended the Bee for running the photograph.

Editors at the San Francisco Chronicle ran a front-page note explaining that the public's right to know outweighed the potentially disturbing nature of the images. Still there was a backlash. "What a disgusting bit of propaganda and deceit. Now that we know what side the Chronicle is on you can cancel my subscription posthaste," said one letter writer. The Chronicle's reader representative, Dick Rogers, made a stab at explaining the paper's decision in a column, writing that "it is not the newspaper's job to sanitize the war." The majority of readers who sent e-mails or letters to the editor supported the Chronicle's decision to publish the photos.

Some media outlets shied away from the photos at first. Though they were widely available on the wires, only a few of the major newspapers ran the images alongside front-page stories in the immediate aftermath. Among those who did: the Los Angeles Times, Chicago Tribune and Washington Post. The New York Times, Miami Herald and Baltimore Sun opted for inside pages.

For the New York Times, it was a matter of caution. Late on April 28, the CBS photos moved on the wire, but "our night crew was uncomfortable with their inability to independently verify that the pictures were legitimate," says Executive Editor Keller. "That held us up for a day." By then the photos weren't as "fresh," so the newspaper opted to run them inside. "I think we were a little slow to recognize what propulsive effect the pictures would have on this story," Keller adds.

Portland's Oregonian had an ethical debate about whether running the photos was the right thing to do. Public Editor Michael Arrieta-Walden attempted to help readers understand the newspaper's decision by posing key questions in a column: What is the journalistic mission? What about the privacy of the individual soldier or prisoner? What if that was my son in the photograph? Editors decided not to publish some of the more grisly photos, including one of a naked prisoner terrified by a growling German shepherd.

Some simply didn't display them at all. As the prison scandal reverberated, Fox News' O'Reilly interviewed conservative singer Pat Boone, who was furious at CBS and the media in general for igniting the global furor and exposing the U.S. military to criticism.

O'Reilly informed his guest: "I didn't use the photos at all. I didn't use any of them."

"God bless you," Boone replied.

Where is the story headed now? The AP's Hanley thinks he knows. On June 30, the New York Times published an editorial about the Bush administration's stonewalling on declassifying reports and documents that could help to unearth the truth about Abu Ghraib.

The next reporting frenzy, says Hanley, could come when these secrets finally are made public or are leaked to the media. The impending court proceedings for soldiers charged with abuse at Abu Ghraib also could be a treasure trove as defense lawyers attempt to answer the questions: How widespread was the policy? How high up did it go?

"So much of this still is being kept a secret," says Hanley. "That is the challenge."

UNIT 4

The Institutional Context of American Foreign Policy

Unit Selections

Key Points to Consider

- How relevant is the Constitution to the conduct of American foreign policy? Do courts have a legitimate role to play in determining the content of U.S. foreign policy?

- To what extent should the United States adjust its foreign policy and laws because of decisions made by international bodies such as the World Trade Organization or the International Criminal Court?

- What is the proper role of Congress in making foreign policy?

- How much power should the president be given in making foreign policy?

- Make a case for or against the creation of a Department of Globalization Affairs.

- Which of the foreign affairs bureaucracies, discussed in this unit, is most important? Which is the most in need of reform? Which is most incapable of being reformed?

Student Website

www.mhcls.com/online

Internet References

Further information regarding these websites may be found in this book's preface or online.

Central Intelligence Agency (CIA)
http://www.cia.gov

The NATO Integrated Data Service (NIDS)
http://www.nato.int/structur/nids/nids.htm

U.S. Department of State
http://www.state.gov/index.html

United States Institute of Peace (USIP)
http://www.usip.org

U.S. White House
http://www.whitehouse.gov

Central to any study of American foreign policy are the institutions responsible for its content and conduct. The relationship between these institutions often is filled with conflict, competition, and controversy. The reasons for this are fundamental. Edwin Corwin put it best: The Constitution is an "invitation to the president and Congress to struggle over the privilege of directing U.S. foreign policy." Today, this struggle is not limited to these two institutions. At the national level, the courts have emerged as a potentially important force in the making of American foreign policy. State and local governments have also become highly visible actors in world politics.

The power relationships that exist between the institutions that make American foreign policy are important for at least two reasons. First, different institutions represent different constituencies and thus advance different sets of values regarding the proper direction of American foreign policy. Second, decision makers in these institutions have different time frames when making judgments about what to do. The correct policy on conducting a war against terrorism looks different to someone coming up for election in a year or two than it does to a professional diplomat.

This close linkage between institutions and policies suggests that if American foreign policy is to successfully conduct a war against terrorism, policy-making institutions must also change their ways. Many commentators are not confident of their ability to respond to the challenges of the post–September 11 foreign policy agenda. Budgetary power bases and political predispositions that are rooted in the cold war are seen as unlikely to provide any more of a hospitable environment for a war against terrorism than they were for promoting human rights or engaging in peacekeeping operations. The creation of the Department of Homeland Security was a first institutional response to the terrorist attacks of September 11. The appointment of a Director of National Intelligence, a post advocated by investigative reports of why September 11 happened and how intelligence was handled in the lead up to the Iraq War, was a second.

We can organize the institutions that make American foreign policy into three broad categories. The first are those composed of elected officials and their staffs: the Presidency and Congress. One topic of enduring interest is the relationship between these bodies. Considerable variation has existed over time with such phrases as the "imperial presidency," "bipartisanship," and "divided government" being used to describe it. A more contemporary issue that has raised considerable concern is the ability of elected officials to manage and organize their appointed staffs effectively so as to retain control over, and responsibility for, making decisions.

Bureaucratic organizations constitute a second set of institutions that need to be studied when examining American foreign policy. The major foreign policy bureaucracies are the State Department, Defense Department, and the Central Intelligence Agency. Often agencies with more of a domestic focus such as the Commerce Department and Treasury Departments also play important foreign policy roles in highly specialized areas. The Department of Homeland Security might be described as the first foreign policy bureaucracy to have a domestic mandate. Bureaucracies play influential roles in making foreign policy by supplying policymakers with information, defining problems, and implementing the selected policies. The current international environment presents these bureaucracies with a special challenge. Old threats and enemies have declined in importance or disappeared entirely and new ones have arisen. To remain effective, these institutions must adjust their organizational structures and ways of thinking—or risk being seen by policymakers as irrelevant anachronisms.

The final institutional actor of importance, in making American foreign policy, is the courts. Their involvement tends to be sporadic and highly focused. Courts serve as arbitrators in the previously noted struggle for dominance between the president and Congress. A key issue today involves determining the jurisdictional boundary of the American legal system and international bodies such as an International Criminal Court and the World Trade Organization. Another involves determining the boundary of legitimate national security concerns and Constitutional rights and protections of those accused of/or suspected of engaging in terrorist activities.

The essays in this section survey recent developments in and controversies surrounding the key institutions that makeup American foreign policy. The first essay, "The Return of the Imperial Presidency?" looks at the relationship between Congress and the president. The author cautions against becoming overly enamored with the concept of an imperial presidency and urges that presidential power be examined in the context of congressional power and the influence of the public. The next essay looks at bureaucracy. "In Defense of Striped Pants" reviews the pattern of presidential relations with career foreign policy professionals—focusing on the common strategies presidents use to "fix" the bureaucracy problem. The final essay in this section "Checks, Balances, and Wartime Detainees," reviews the Supreme Court's ruling on the enemy combatant cases and the implications of Congress' lack of involvement in this policy dispute.

The Return of the
Imperial Presidency?

One lesson of American politics since September 11 is that some tensions between presidents and Congress spring from a deeper source than the partisan passions of the moment.

by Donald R. Wolfensberger

Moments after President George W. Bush finished his stirring antiterrorism speech before Congress last September, presidential historian Michael Beschloss enthusiastically declared on national television that "the imperial presidency is back. We just saw it."

As someone who began his career as a Republican congressional staff aide during the turbulence of Vietnam and Watergate in the late 1960s and early 1970s, I was startled by the buoyant tone of Beschloss's pronouncement. To me, "imperial presidency" carries a pejorative connotation closely tied to those twin nightmares. Indeed, *Webster's Unabridged Dictionary* bluntly defines *imperial presidency* as "a U.S. presidency that is characterized by greater power than the Constitution allows."

Was Beschloss suggesting that President Bush was already operating outside the Constitution in prosecuting the war against terrorism, or did he have a more benign definition in mind? Apparently it was the latter. As Beschloss went on to explain, during World War II and the Cold War, Congress deferred to presidents, not just on questions of foreign policy and defense, but on domestic issues as well. Whether it was President Dwight D. Eisenhower asking for an interstate highway system or President John F. Kennedy pledging to land a man on the moon, Congress said, "If you ask us, we will." Without such a galvanizing crisis, the president would not be able to define the national interest so completely. "Now," continued Beschloss, "George Bush is at the center of the American solar system; that was not true 10 days ago." In fact, just nine months earlier Beschloss had described Bush as "the first post-imperial president" because, for the first time since the Great Depression, "we were not electing a president under the shadow of an international emergency like the Cold War or World War II or an economic crisis." Then came September 11.

Still, it's hard to join in such a warm welcome for the return of an idea that was heavily burdened just a generation ago with negative associations and cautionary experiences. Presidential scholars understandably become admirers of strong presidents and their presidencies. But a focus on executive power can become so narrow as to cause one to lose sight of the larger governmental system, with its checks and balances. To invest the idea of the imperial presidency with an aura of legitimacy and approbation would be a serious blow to America's constitutional design and the intent of the Framers.

It was historian Arthur M. Schlesinger, Jr., who popularized the term *imperial presidency* in his 1973 book by that title. Schlesinger, who had earlier chronicled the strong presidencies of Andrew Jackson and Franklin D. Roosevelt in admiring terms, admits in *The Imperial Presidency* his own culpability in perpetuating over the years "an exalted conception of presidential power":

> American historians and political scientists, this writer among them, labored to give the expansive theory of the Presidency historical sanction. Overgeneralizing from the [pre-World War II] contrast between a President who was right and a Congress which was wrong, scholars developed an uncritical cult of the activist Presidency.

The view of the presidency as "the great engine of democracy" and the "American people's one authentic trumpet," writes Schlesinger, passed into the textbooks and helped shape the national outlook after 1945. This faith of the American people in the presidency, coupled with their doubts about the ability of democracy to respond adequately to the totalitarian challenge abroad, are what gave the postwar presidency its pretensions and powers.

"By the early 1970s," Schlesinger writes, "the American President had become on issues of war and peace the most absolute monarch (with the possible exception of Mao Tse Tung of China) among the great powers of the world." Moreover, "the claims of unilateral authority in foreign policy soon began to pervade and embolden the domestic presidency."

Uniforms redolent of imperial pomp briefly appeared on White House guards in the Nixon administration, only to vanish after a public outcry.

The growth of the imperial presidency was gradual, and occurred "usually under the demand or pretext of an emergency," Schlesinger observes. Further, "it was as much a matter of congressional abdication as of presidential usurpation." The seeds of the imperial presidency were sown early. Schlesinger cites as examples Abraham Lincoln's 1861 imposition of martial law and his suspension of habeas corpus, and William McKinley's decision to send 5,000 American troops to China to help suppress the Boxer Rebellion of 1900. It is a measure of how much things have changed that Theodore Roosevelt's 1907 decision to dispatch America's Great White Fleet on a tour around the world was controversial because he failed to seek congressional approval. Then came Woodrow Wilson's forays into revolutionary Mexico, FDR's unilateral declaration of an "unlimited national emergency" six months before Pearl Harbor, and Harry Truman's commitment of U.S. troops to the Korean War in 1950, without congressional authorization, and his 1952 seizure of strike-threatened steel mills.

In 1973, the year *The Imperial Presidency* was published, Congress moved to reassert its war-making prerogatives during non-declared wars by enacting the War Powers Resolution over President Nixon's veto. The following year, prior to Nixon's resignation under the imminent threat of impeachment, Congress enacted two more laws aimed at clipping the wings of the imperial presidency and restoring the balance of power between the two branches. The Congressional Budget and Impoundment Control Act of 1974 was designed to enable Congress to set its own spending priorities and prohibit the president from impounding funds it had appropriated. The Federal Election Campaign Act of 1974 was supposed to eliminate the taint of big money from presidential politics. Subsequent years witnessed a spate of other statutes designed to right the balance between the branches. The National Emergencies Act (1976) abolished scores of existing presidential emergency powers. The Ethics in Government Act (1978) authorized, among other things, the appointment of special prosecutors to investigate high-ranking executive branch officials. The Senate, in 1976, and the House, in 1977, established intelligence committees in the wake of hearings in 1975 revealing widespread abuses; and in 1980 the Intelligence Oversight Act increased Congress's monitoring demands on intelligence agencies and their covert operations.

Since those Watergate-era enactments, presidential scholars have decried the way Congress has emasculated the presidency. As recently as January of last year, political scientist Richard E. Neustadt, author of the classic *Presidential Power* (1964), lamented that "the U.S. presidency has been progressively weakened over the past three decades to the point where it is probably weaker today than at almost any time in the preceding century." Neustadt cited congressional actions as one of several causes of the decline.

As one who worked in the House of Representatives from 1969 to 1997, I have long been puzzled by such complaints. They have never rung true. What I witnessed during those years was the continuing decline of the legislative branch, not its ascendancy. Even Congress's post-Watergate efforts to reassert its authority look rather feeble in the harsh light of reality. The War Powers Resolution has been all but ignored by every president since Nixon as unconstitutional. They have abided by its reporting requirements, but presidential military forays abroad without explicit congressional authority continue unabated. Bosnia, Kosovo, Haiti, Somalia, and Serbia come readily to mind.

The congressional budget act has been used by every president since Ronald Reagan to leverage the administration's priorities by using budget summits with Congress to negotiate the terms of massive reconciliation bills on taxes and entitlements. The independent counsel act has been allowed to expire twice—though, in light of the unbridled power it gives counsels and the potential for abuse, this may have been wise. Federal funding of presidential campaigns has not stopped campaign finance abuses. And congressional oversight of perceived executive abuses has met with mixed results at best.

In the meantime, presidents have been relying more heavily than before on executive agreements to avoid the treaty ratification process, and on executive orders (or memorandums) of dubious statutory grounding in other areas. Administrations have defied Congress's requests for information with increasing frequency, dismissing the requests as politically motivated. And they have often invoked executive privilege in areas not previously sanctioned by judicial judgments.

The most recent example is Vice President Richard Cheney's refusal, on grounds of executive privilege, to turn over to the General Accounting Office (GAO), an arm of Congress, information about meetings between the president's energy task force and energy executives. The controversy took on added interest with the collapse of Enron, one of the energy companies that provided advice to the task force. Vice President Cheney, who served as President Gerald R. Ford's White House chief of staff, said his action was aimed at reversing "an erosion of the powers" of the presidency over the last 30 to 35 years resulting from "unwise compromises" made by past Administrations. President Bush backed Cheney's claim of executive privilege, citing the need to maintain confidentiality in the advice given to a president.

It is revealing in this case that the congressional requests for information came not through formal committee action or subpoenas but more indirectly from the GAO, at the prompting of two ranking minority committee Democrats in the House, even though their Senate party counterparts are committee chairmen with authority to force a vote on subpoenas. The committee system, which should be the bulwark of congressional policy-making and oversight of the executive branch, has been in steady decline since the mid-1970s. Not the least of the causes is the weakening of committee prerogatives and powers by Congress itself, as a response to members' demands for a more participatory policy process than the traditional committee system allowed. Party leaders eventually replaced committee leaders as the locus of power in the House, a shift that was not altered by the change in party control of Congress in 1995.

Another contributing factor has been the shift in the Republican Party's base of power to the South and West, which has given a more populist and propresidential cast to the GOP membership on Capitol Hill.

Even with recent promises by Speaker of the House Dennis Hastert (R-Ill.) and Senate Majority Leader Tom Daschle (D-S.D.) to "return to the regular order" by giving committees greater flexibility and discretion in agenda setting and bill drafting, Congress is hamstrung by self-inflicted staff cuts and three-day legislative workweeks that make deliberative lawmaking and careful oversight nearly impossible. The "permanent campaign" has spilled over into governing, diminishing the value members see in committee work and encouraging partisan position taking and posturing. (It also makes members eager to get back to their districts for the serious work of campaigning, which explains the three-day work week in Washington.) It is easier to take a popular campaign stand on an unresolved issue than make a painful policy choice and explain it to the voters.

Bill Clinton had the common touch— and an imperial taste for sending U.S. troops abroad without congressional approval.

Is it any wonder that even before the current emergency the executive was in a stronger position than Congress? Such power alone is not necessarily a sign of an imperial presidency. But testing the limits of power seems to be an inborn trait of political man, and presidents are no exception. Even presidential power proponent Richard Neustadt, who sees the presidency at the beginning of this 21st century as the weakest it's been in three decades, concedes that none of the formal limits on presidential powers by Congress or the courts have managed to eliminate those powers of greatest consequence, including the "plentitude of prerogative power" (a Lockean concept of acting outside the

constitutional box to save the nation) that Lincoln assumed during the Civil War.

Both presidents George H. W. Bush and George W. Bush, to their credit, sought authorization from Congress for the use of force against Iraq and international terrorists, respectively, before committing troops to combat. Yet both also claimed they bad inherent powers as president to do so to protect the national interest. (The younger Bush was on firmer ground since even the Framers explicitly agreed that the president has authority to repel foreign invasions and respond to direct attacks on the United States.)

The presidency is at its strongest at the outset of a national crisis or war. Just as President Franklin D. Roosevelt was encountering public and congressional wariness over his depression-era policies in the late 1930s, along came World War II and a whole new lease on the throne. Presidential power tends to increase at the expense of Congress. Alexander Hamilton put it succinctly in *The Federalist* 8: "It is of the nature of war to increase the executive at the expense of the legislative authority."

One way to gauge this balance of power is to look at the extent to which Congress deliberates over policy matters and the extent to which it gives the president most of what he requests with minimal resistance. Two weeks after Congress passed a $40 billion emergency spending bill and a resolution authorizing the president to use force against those behind the World Trade Center attacks, Senator Robert S. Byrd (D-W.Va.) rose in a nearly empty Senate chamber to remind his colleagues of their deliberative responsibilities. "In the heat of the moment, in the crush of recent events," Byrd observed, "I fear we may be losing sight of the larger obligations of the Senate."

> Our responsibility as Senators is to carefully consider and fully debate major policy matters, to air all sides of a given issue, and to act after full deliberation. Yes, we want to respond quickly to urgent needs, but a speedy response should not be used as an excuse to trample full and free debate.

Byrd was concerned in part about the way in which language relating to the controversy over adhering to the 1972 antiballistic missile treaty had been jettisoned from a pending defense authorization bill in the interest of "unity" after the terrorist attacks. But he was also disturbed by the haste with which the Senate had approved the use-of-force resolution "to avoid the specter of acrimonious debate at a time of national crisis." Byrd added that he was not advocating unlimited debate, but why, he asked, "do we have to put a zipper on our lips and have no debate at all?" Because of the "paucity of debate" in both houses, Byrd added, there was no discussion laying a foundation for the resolution, and in the future "it would be difficult to glean from the record the specific intent of Congress."

A review of the *Congressional Record* supports Byrd's complaint. Only Majority Leader Daschle and Minority Leader Trent Lott (R-Miss.) spoke briefly before the Senate passed the emergency spending bill and the use-of-force resolution. The discussion was truncated chiefly because buses were waiting to take senators and House members to a memorial service at the National Cathedral.

The House, to its credit, did return after the service for five hours of debate on the resolution, which it passed 420 to 1. Some 200 members spoke for about a minute each—hardly the stuff of a great debate. At no time did any member raise a question about the breadth, scope, or duration of the authority granted by the resolution. The closest some came were passing references to the way in which President Lyndon B. Johnson had used the language of the 1964 Gulf of Tonkin Resolution as authority to broaden U.S. involvement in Vietnam.

To the credit of Congress, a small, bipartisan leadership group had earlier negotiated a compromise with the White House to confine the resolution's scope to "those nations, organizations or persons" implicated in the September 11 attacks. The original White House proposal was much broader, extending the president's authority "to deter and pre-empt any future acts of terrorism or aggression against the United States." The language change is significant. If President Bush cannot demonstrate that Iraq was somehow involved in the September 11 attacks but decides to take military action against it, he will have to decide whether to seek additional authority from Congress or act without it, as President Bill Clinton did before him.

In times of war or national emergency, presidents have always acted in what they thought to be the national interest. That is not to say that Congress simply becomes a presidential lap dog. While it tends to defer to the commander in chief on military matters once troops have been committed to combat, it continues to exercise oversight and independence on matters not directly affecting the war's outcome. For example, President Bush was forced to make drastic alterations in his economic stimulus package by Senate Democrats who disagreed with his tax relief and spending priorities. And even in the midst of the war on terrorism, the House and Senate intelligence committees launched a joint inquiry into why our intelligence services were not able to detect or thwart the September 11 terrorist plot. In the coming months, moreover, Congress is sure to have its own ideas on how the federal budget can best be allocated to meet the competing demands for defense, homeland security, and domestic social-welfare programs.

Is the imperial presidency back? While at this writing the White House has not overtly exercised any extraconstitutional powers, the imperial presidency has been with us since World War II, and it is most likely to be re-energized during times of national crisis. Every president tends to test the limits of his power during such periods in order to do what he deems necessary to protect national security. To the extent that Congress does not push back and the public does not protest, the armor of the imperial presidency is further fortified by precedent and popular support against future attacks.

What is the danger in a set of powers that have, after all, evolved over several decades into a widely recognized reality without calamitous consequences for the Republic? As James Madison put in *The Federalist* 51, "The separate and distinct exercise of the different powers of government... is admitted on all hands to be essential to the preservation of liberty." The "great security against a gradual concentration of power in the same department," he went on, is to provide each department with the "necessary constitutional means and personal motives to resist.... Ambition must be made to counteract ambition."

The Constitution's system of separated powers and checks and balances is not a self-regulating machine. Arthur M. Schlesinger, Jr., observed in *The Imperial Presidency*, that what kept a strong presidency constitutional, in addition to the president's own appreciation of the Framers' wisdom, was the vigilance of the nation. "If the people had come to an unconscious acceptance of the imperial presidency," he wrote, "the Constitution could not hold the nation to ideals it was determined to betray." The only deterrent to the imperial presidency is for the great institutions of our society—Congress, the courts, the press, public opinion, the universities, "to reclaim their own dignity and meet their own responsibilities."

DONALD R. WOLFENSBERGER *is director of the Congress Project at the Wilson Center and the author of* Congress and the People: Deliberative Democracy on Trial *(2000). He retired as chief of staff of the House Rules Committee in 1997 after a 28-year career on the staff of the U.S. House of Representatives.*

From *The Wilson Quarterly*, Spring 2002, pp. 36-41. © 2002 by Donald R. Wolfensberger. Reprinted by permission of the author.

In Defense of Striped Pants

Morton Abramowitz & Leslie H. Gelb

FROM THE day after the United States toppled the regime of Saddam Hussein, it has run into one problem after another in Iraq. We failed to establish security. We steadily lost support from Arab Sunnis and Shi'a. We entered the war with limited international support and have even less today. However encouraging the January elections, Iraq is a work in progress, and it is straining our resources, roiling our military and complicating our diplomacy. How long public support will last is uncertain. So who is responsible for our current predicament, and what can we learn from a serious answer to that highly charged question?

Politics requires scapegoats, whether they bear guilt or not. And the media seem less interested in discovering who is responsible than in providing a megaphone for the accusations. But the questions need to be asked. We cannot begin to fix the policymaking process until we see who broke it—and even then, the damage may be beyond repair.

Cheered on by conservative think tanks and journals, the administration has focused on the sins of that easiest of targets, the career professionals. That requires bloodletting, and it has gushed at the top levels of the CIA. The State Department was expected to be next, but Secretary of State Condoleezza Rice thus far has selected very able foreign service officers for a number of top positions. It is, of course, unclear how she will want to use their advice—or whether she will be able to do so. The Pentagon had already experienced significant bloodletting in the ranks of the career military through Secretary of Defense Donald Rumsfeld's highly personal and unorthodox choices for top jobs.

The administration, and even more its vocal outside supporters, assert that Iraq, as well as democracy promotion and other important policies, have not gotten traction because career professionals are incompetent, unable to see the merit of these policies, unwilling to carry them out, or insufficiently aggressive in explaining their wisdom to a skeptical world. They blame the CIA for faulty information, and military leaders for not insisting on more troops. Some conservative critics even blame the State Department and the CIA for the occupation of Iraq, when it could have been avoided, they say, by just installing Ahmed Chalabi and withdrawing U.S. troops quickly thereafter. (Are George Bush, Dick Cheney and Donald Rumsfeld such pussy cats for State and the CIA?) Many career professionals were indeed skeptical of the Iraq enterprise as

conceived, publicly explained and carried out. These views were hardened by the persistent internal warfare between the Pentagon and other agencies, where battles were frequently denied publicly while Mr. Rumsfeld was mostly winning them.

Conservative critics also generally believe that the top bureaucratic ranks are essentially inhabited by cautious officials overly wed to international institutions and fearful of wholesale change or the pursuit of a foreign policy mission with big, politically difficult objectives. They also see many career officials as Democrats, disloyal or at least unsympathetic to the Bush Administration, who will often try to undermine policy by leaking secret information that casts doubt on the effectiveness of administration policies. They point to the CIA's allowing the publication before the November election of a book by a relatively senior official that was highly critical of the administration's Iraq and counter-terrorism policies. Indeed, some of the usually quasi-public statements of several CIA officials were surprising in their direct criticism of the Bush Administration, particularly in comments denying Iraq's ties to international terrorism. Unidentified officials in all agencies were also frequently quoted in the press, questioning what the U.S. government was publicly saying about Iraq.

A more detached view that partially supports this perspective comes from the 9/11 Commission (and more recently the CIA's inspector general). The commission found the federal bureaucracy under at least two administrations to have been mostly out of touch with the threat posed to the United States by Islamic jihadism. But the commission did not focus on the road to Iraq, the administration's role, or the interplay between political leaders and career professionals.

The opposite perspective—one shared by many Democrats, editorialists, academics and senior officials—regards these charges as little more than scapegoating of the bureaucracy by the administration and its supporters—a way to hide its own massive mistakes in Iraq. Vice President Cheney's visits to the CIA notwithstanding, the bureaucrats' defenders charge the administration with failure to seriously consult the bureaucracy, and with pushing aside uniformed officers in the Pentagon who were upset with the planning for war. As a matter of historical fact, this group does have a big truth on its side: The administration did little to encourage any serious internal debate or real consideration of alternate policy approaches.

Some holding this view consider the Iraq War a historic policy mistake based on profound ignorance and the arrogance of administration "ideologues." They also believe that the administration has been mendacious in shaping the limited public debate, and that the mainline agencies are being punished while the principal authors of Iraq policy and their cheerleaders are allowed to remain in office—another expression of the administration's inability to admit the slightest error. And they assert that the Bush foreign policy has been run without diplomacy, almost purposefully, in order to avoid the kind of compromises that presumably might have avoided armed conflict in Iraq.

When the debris of charges and counter-charges is set aside, two broad conclusions remain. First, even had the bureaucratic professionals had their full say on Iraq policy, it is far from clear that President Bush would have changed his basic decision and policy to remove Saddam Hussein from power by force of arms. It seems the odds are that he would have resorted to arms in any event. Second, even with war as a given, a strong case can be made that the president's Iraq policy would have been strengthened had he listened to the career professionals on three critical issues: better mobilizing international support by giving the UN inspections some additional time; better managing the postwar occupation; and the need for far more troops to establish and maintain security.

It is too soon to measure the ultimate impact of our Iraq effort. But with the war still underway and with other major problems between political masters and career professionals, it is none too soon to re-examine, and hopefully fix, the policymaking process.

TENSION BETWEEN presidential administrations and their foreign affairs, intelligence and career military bureaucracies is hardly a new phenomenon. Since the centralization of national security decision-making in the White House in the 1960s, most presidents and their national security advisors—Democratic and Republican— have been distrustful of the bureaucracies. They have often viewed them as disloyal competitors and as resistant to change. And often, the political masters have excluded them from high-level considerations of critical issues, relegating them to producing unneeded papers or busying them with planning trips and motorcades.

This now built-in tension becomes acute when there is a major foreign policy discontinuity or a radical change in course or style. We saw it in the Reagan Administration and in the first George W. Bush Administration in spades. From the very start of the current administration, internal tensions grew over what was immediately seen as an unnecessarily unilateralist and arrogant White House style. That seemed immediately "proven" when Mr. Bush publicly told South Korean President Kim Dae Jung that his policy toward North Korea was totally wrong (a view and an act held to be destructive by many career officials). Simmering feelings then exploded from many quarters over Iraq. Most professionals adjusted, but some found ways of going to war with the administration and its policy. Very few left, particularly those in the senior ranks.

But the administration does have legitimate gripes about the capabilities of two key agencies, the State Department and the CIA. (The serious limitations in the Defense Department are of a different character.) The State Department is not now, to put it charitably, at its zenith. Its policymaking capabilities and functions have declined, it has reduced its interest in field reporting, and its implementation of policy sometimes has been taken over by Defense or the CIA. State also has not exhibited much imagination. Nor has it honed its political skills. For example. State put its highly regarded study of postwar Iraq under the aegis of a very capable midlevel foreign service officer whose name was not known far beyond his own office. This valuable study was shunted aside, possibly by the senior officials surrounding Colin Powell in the officer's own building.

Nevertheless, the State Department remains a great source of talent, information and analytical skills. Its international experience is unrivaled and can be applied on numerous issues. It has a wealth of important and often unique associations, and it is filled with people dedicated to pursuing our national interests. And for all its complaining about political masters, it does try hard to satisfy them. State is almost Zelig-like in its capacity to adjust to political leadership, whatever the personal views of its professionals. Many administrations fail to take advantage of this trait and prefer to talk about the disloyalty of the State Department. But most political appointees to Foggy Bottom will tell you, correctly, that the department responds to anyone who takes the institution seriously. Taking the place seriously will not stop all the leaks—that's life. But it will reduce them.

The CIA's reputation, never very high, has significantly declined despite a huge infusion of resources. But its recent roguish behavior is not typical. Indeed, quite the opposite. When the U.S. government embarks on a major effort, its employees, including the CIA, usually salute. Top officials want very much to please their big bosses, and they usually find ways to match the intelligence to the policy proclivities. And when things go wrong, their political masters inevitably turn against the agency. None of this should obscure the general capability of CIA analysts and their dedication to preserving the integrity of the intelligence process.

The CIA's analytical product faces some serious hurdles. First, its importance is inflated in the public eye, even as its reports go mostly unread by top policymakers. And second, if there are intelligence errors on big issues, it casts a pall over the whole intelligence analysis effort. The agency's failure on Iraq's WMD, and its lack of understanding of the potemkin and dysfunctional nature of the Saddam regime, have had a serious impact on American credibility as well as attitudes toward the agency.

It is not the CIA's analytical directorate but the operations directorate— the field-agent effort and the one so important to dealing with terrorism— that has been getting most of the flak, and the one whose career senior leaders have been summarily fired by Mr. Goss. They have been variously accused of delinquencies ranging from gross incompetence to extreme caution—no "risktakers there." That may be one reason the Defense Department is taking over many of the CIA's activities. This part of the CIA has had trying times, from the Church Committee in the 1970s to their involvement in the Iran-Contra affair to their difficulties in the early Clinton years. They have gone up and down in manpower. In the last few years they have been the beneficiaries of a significant infusion of resources, but if the recent firings are any indication, the enhancements have not yet paid off.

It is difficult for the outsider to draw any conclusion about the effectiveness of the CIA's clandestine efforts. Congressional oversight cannot be given much credence. The agency claims that only its failures become public, that there are many unheralded and unknown achievements, particularly in preventing terrorist incidents. One thing is clear: Greater risk-taking and reorganization of the whole intelligence community does not necessarily produce more intelligence on extremely difficult targets like North Korea. The challenges in acquiring such information are enormous. The Clandestine Service is not likely to be "transformed" by simply changing the organization's wiring diagram and the top people.

THE FIXES to these "problems" within the professional bureaucracy and between it and the political masters have mainly taken three forms. First, there are times when the political masters have grown so exasperated or so eager to place blame elsewhere that they have fired senior career people. On many occasions, these firings are justified, as with some of the recent moves in the upper reaches of the CIA. But it is hard for senior professionals to swallow righteous firings when those whose mistakes are seen as even more egregious, like several high-level Pentagon officials, retain their positions and are praised for performance. While bloodletting is needed at times to get rid of particular problems, it does not solve systemic ones.

A second tried-and-true formula has been to reorganize the bureaucracy, redirect supporting lines, and move boxes for whole agencies from one place to another. Most times these reorganizations are a waste of time and money. Moving bureaucrats does not necessarily change the culture or the performance. And wherever they are moved. Congress is almost always unmoved. Organizational changes that occur within administrations are often negated by unchanged and parochial congressional relationships—as demonstrated by the utter disregard with which Congress has treated the reforms to its own operations that were recommended by the 9/11 Commission. It is argued that the recent attempts to improve counter-terrorism efforts have proven successful. But a serious evaluation will take several more years.

Third, the final fix resorted to by political masters has been to rail against or ignore the bureaucracy. That is the approach discussed in this article. It has proven very costly to the nation. As we have noted, it is clear in retrospect that U.S. policy in Iraq could have benefited at almost every turn from the advice and information of the professional bureaucracy. From the president on down, political appointees must realize that, yes, bureaucracy is sluggish and out of touch, resistant to change, lacking in imagination, and often wrong, but career professionals can save them from disastrous mistakes. By virtue of having worked seriously on these problems, countries and cultures for years, no one is better than they are at spotting obstacles and landmines. No policy can be successful that fails to anticipate these hurdles. Political masters ignore this expertise at their peril.

EVERY ADMINISTRATION must be zealous in the pursuit of important national security goals. Political appointees, however, must not confuse an absence of candor with loyalty in their career subordinates. Career professionals are being most loyal when they are being candid with their bosses about situations and when they press for a serious examination of policy. They have a sense of American national interests that tries to transcend an individual administration and should be fully and fairly examined before administrations change course.

This will not stop all leaking to the press. But the kind of draconian measures that would be needed to prevent all significant leaks would be bad for the policymaking process and, it could well be argued, worse for the democratic process. Sometimes the people know what's going on or what the choices are only because of these leaks. Ditto for Congress.

Thus, probably the most effective way to address the bureaucracy's weaknesses and take advantage of its strengths is not bloodletting, or reorganization, or ignoring and condemning the bureaucrats. It is having a sensible attitude at the top, starting with presidents and secretaries. Beneath them, the key to making the system work is to have appointees at the assistant secretary level who are responsive to the policy imperatives of the political leadership and willing to engage and draw on the skills of their career experts. The assistant secretary jobs are where the proverbial rubber meets the road.

At this time, the country has a particular need for preserving candor in the departments and a variety of viewpoints from different agencies, particularly in the intelligence world. The War on Terror has given the U.S. government enormous power to do what it thinks is necessary to protect this country. Today, everything done in the name of that effort seems to be acceptable to, even demanded by, the public. The mechanisms for self-examination or self-correction either do not work or are diminishing. Congress provides little serious oversight. The media, particularly on television, are disadvantaged by the secrecy of subject matter and often by their lack of interest. In this post-9/11 environment, the permanent bureaucracy is the last line of defense in possibly subjecting critical policy considerations to the most informed scrutiny. If the administration does not want to consult them seriously, they must themselves persist in trying to make their views known to their leaders in constructive ways that go beyond anonymous leaks to the *Washington Post*.

Morton Abramowitz *is senior fellow at the Century Foundation and former Assistant Secretary of State for Intelligence and Research. Leslie H. Gelb is president emeritus of the Council on Foreign Relations.*

Checks, Balances, and Wartime Detainees

BENJAMIN WITTES

THE DAY THE Supreme Court handed down what have collectively become known as the enemy combatant cases—June 28, 2004—was both widely anticipated and widely received as a legal moment of truth for the Bush administration's war on terrorism. The stakes could not have been higher. The three cases came down in the midst of election-year politics. They each involved challenges by detainees being held by the military without charge or trial or access to counsel. They each divided the Court. And they appeared to validate or reject core arguments that the administration had advanced—and had been slammed for advancing—since the fight against al Qaeda began in earnest after September 11, 2001.

The dominant view saw the cases as a major defeat for President George W. Bush—and with good reason. After all, his administration had urged the Court to refrain from asserting jurisdiction over the Guantanamo Bay naval base in Cuba, and it did just that in unambiguous terms: "Aliens held at the base, no less than American citizens, are entitled to invoke the federal courts' authority."[1] The administration fought tooth and nail for the proposition that an American citizen held domestically as an enemy combatant has no right to counsel and no right to respond to the factual assertions that justify his detention. The Court, however, held squarely that "a citizen-detainee seeking to challenge his classification as an enemy combatant must receive notice of the factual basis for his classification, and a fair opportunity to rebut the Government's factual assertions before a neutral decision-maker."[2] It held as well that "[h]e unquestionably has the right to access to counsel" in doing so. These holdings led the *New York Times* (June 29, 2003) to call the cases "a stinging rebuke" to the administration's policies, one that "made it clear that even during the war on terror, the government must adhere to the rule of law."

A dissident analysis of the cases, however, quickly emerged as well and saw them as a kind of victory for the administration dressed up in defeat's borrowed robes. As David B. Rivkin Jr. and Lee A. Casey put it in the *Washington Post* (August 4, 2004):

> In the context of these cases, the court accepted the following critical propositions: that the United States is engaged in a legally cognizable armed conflict with al

Qaeda and the Taliban, to which the laws of war apply; that "enemy combatants" captured in the context of that conflict can be held "indefinitely" without criminal trial while that conflict continues; that American citizens (at least those captured overseas) can be classified and detained as enemy combatants, confirming the authority of the court's 1942 decision in *Ex Parte Quirin* (the "Nazi saboteur" case [317 U.S. I (1942)]); and that the role of the courts in reviewing such designations is limited. All these points had been disputed by one or more of the detainees' lawyers, and all are now settled in the government's favor.

Even among those who celebrated the administration's defeat, this analysis had some resonance. Ronald Dworkin, for example, began his essay on the cases in the *New York Review of Books* ("What the Court Really Said," August 12, 2004) by triumphantly declaring, "The Supreme Court has finally and decisively rejected the Bush administration's outrageous claim that the President has the power to jail people he accuses of terrorist connections without access to lawyers or the outside world and without any possibility of significant review by courts or other judicial bodies." But he then went on to acknowledge that the Court had "suggested rules of procedure for any such review that omit important traditional protections for people accused of crimes" and that the government "may well be able to satisfy the Court's lenient procedural standards without actually altering its morally dubious detention policies." How big a rebuke could the cases really represent if they collectively entitle the president to stay the course he has chosen?

The court managed to leave all of the central questions unanswered.

In my view, both strains of initial thought have considerable merit. The administration clearly suffered a "stinging rebuke" in rhetorical terms. But Dworkin, Rivkin, and Casey (an unlikely meeting of the minds if ever there were one) were quite correct that, in the long run, the president's actual power to detain enemy combatants may not have been materially damaged either with respect to citizens domestically or with respect to enemy fighters captured and held abroad. In a profound sense, the Supreme Court, despite delivering itself of 178 pages of text on the subject of enemy combatant detentions, managed to leave all of the central questions unanswered. In fact, if a new front in the war on terrorism opened tomorrow and the military captured a new crop of captives, under the Court's rulings, the administration would face very nearly the same questions as it did in 2002. Can the military warehouse foreign citizens captured overseas at a military base abroad without intrusive interference by American courts keen to protect their rights under either American or international law? What process must the military grant to an American citizen it wishes to hold as an enemy combatant, and is that process different if the citizen is detained domestically by law enforcement, rather than overseas by the military? Must such a person be granted immediate access to a lawyer or can he be held incommunicado for intelligence-gathering purposes? And if he can be so detained, for how long? The answers to these questions are only a little clearer today than they were a few months ago. The Court has only begun to forge the regime that, in the absence of congressional intervention, will govern the detention of enemy combatants. Until that regime comes into clearer focus, it will be too early to determine the real winners and losers in this landmark struggle.

It is not, however, too early to begin assessing the performance of the responsible institutions of American government and civil society with respect to the forging of this regime—that is, to look seriously at the engagement so far among the courts, the administration, Congress, and the civil liberties and human rights groups that have opposed the administration's policies. The exercise, in my judgment, flatters none of the aforementioned institutions. Congress has simply abandoned the field, leaving a series of questions which obviously require legislative solutions to a dialogue between the executive and judicial branches. The administration has encouraged this abdication by, instead of seeking legislative input, consistently asserting the most needlessly extreme vision of executive power to resolve novel problems unilaterally. By doing so, it has all but guaranteed a skeptical reception for even its stronger arguments. The courts, meanwhile, have proven uneven in the extreme both at the lower court level and at the Supreme Court. For their part, the human rights and civil liberties communities have responded to the cases with an almost total lack of pragmatism, advancing a reading of federal and international law no less selective and convenient than the administration's own and consistently failing, over the three years since these cases arose, to offer a plausible alternative to the administration's proposed regime.

In the end, the enemy combatant cases—at least so far—stand as a kind of case study of the consequence of abandoning to the adversarial litigation system a sensitive policy debate in which powerful and legitimate constitutional concerns animate both sides. By nearly universal agreement, these cases were submitted to common-law decision making in the face of almost-as-universal agreement that the extant body of law did not fully address the novel conditions of the war on terrorism. As a result, as I shall attempt to show, nuance was lost, flexibility and imag-

ination in envisioning an appropriate regime were jettisoned, and the courts were left to split the difference between polar arguments to which few Americans would actually sign on and which should not have defined the terms of the discussion. It needn't have been this way. But until Congress assumes responsibility for crafting a system to handle enemy combatants, the regime necessarily will remain a crude, judge-made hybrid of the criminal and military law traditions that will, I suspect, satisfy nobody save the judges who—piece by piece, bit by bit, question by question—will decree it into existence.

What the Court ruled

$\mathcal{I}$T OVERSTATES THE matter to say that the enemy combatant cases were full of sound and fury and signifying nothing, but they certainly signified a great deal less than their sound and fury portended. It is worth, therefore, beginning by examining exactly what the Court did, what it didn't do, and what questions it left unaddressed.

To begin with the least consequential case, in *Padilla v. Rumsfeld,* the Court did virtually nothing at all—clarifying only that a habeas petitioner in military custody must bring suit in a court with jurisdiction over his immediate physical custodian.[3] While this holding was in considerable tension with the Court's ruling concerning Guantanamo—where it divined jurisdiction for seemingly any federal court in the country—it was neither especially surprising nor substantively important. It affects, after all, not one jot the procedural rights an accused enemy combatant will enjoy, nor does it alter at all the substantive standard the government must satisfy in order to justify the combatant's detention. It affects only the question of what court he must appear in to challenge that detention.

So far Padilla *stands for nothing but a perfectly pedestrian jurisdictional point.*

The only feature of *Padilla* that seems important at all is a footnote in the dissent, in which four members of the Court appear to address the case's merits head on and dismiss the government's substantive position that President Bush could, under current authorities, designate Jose Padilla—a citizen suspected of planning terrorist attacks on al Qaeda's behalf—as an enemy combatant and hold him as such. "Consistent with the judgment of the Court of Appeals," wrote Justice John Paul Stevens, "I believe that the Non-Detention Act, I 8 U.S.C. § 4 0 0 I (a), prohibits—and the Authorization for Use of Military Force Joint Resolution, 115 Stat. 224, adopted on September 18, 2001, does not authorize—the protracted, incommunicado detention of American citizens arrested in the United States." This language, though certainly dicta, suggests that a majority on the Court may exist for the proposition that someone in Padilla's position, a suspected al Qaeda operative arrested domestically, must either be charged criminally and prosecuted or else released—at least in the absence of a more explicit congressional authorization for enemy combatant detentions. Justice Antonin Scalia wrote in dissent in *Hamdi* that he did not believe a citizen could be detained as an enemy combatant at all, an opinion Justice Stevens joined. Combine the two opinions, and you may have a glimmering of the Court's future direction on this question. So far, however, *Padilla* stands for nothing but a perfectly pedestrian jurisdictional point: that an enemy combatant detained domestically has to go to his local federal court for relief. Which court should hear the claims of detainees was hardly the question that animated the spirited public discussion of enemy combatants over the past three years. So clearly, *Padilla* answers nothing.

The Court said a lot more in *Hamdi*, and in important respects, it did repudiate the military's position. The government, after all, had argued that the courts should show nearly total deference to the executive branch's determinations concerning citizens alleged to be enemy combatants: They should rely entirely on the government's factual allegations, as laid out in a hearsay affidavit by a midlevel Defense Department official. The detainee need not have any ability to contest these allegations or any assistance of counsel in challenging his detention. And the standard of review itself should be trivial, merely whether the material in the cursory, page-and-a-half affidavit would, if presumed true, support the designation. Eight members of the Court rejected each of these suggestions. The controlling plurality opinion insisted that Yaser Esam Hamdi had a right to contest his designation and to submit evidence to the court in doing so, that he had a right to the assistance of counsel, and, it insisted, that the government's designation be supported with "credible evidence." Rivkin's and Casey's contention that the decision was really a victory is belied by the fact that the plurality opinion in Hamdi tracks closely with—indeed, in critical respects, is less favorable to the government than—the district court's opinion in *Padilla*, an opinion the government aggressively appealed.

The plurality reaffirmed the power of the president to detain a citizen as an enemy combatant.

But if *Hamdi* establishes that the executive's hand is not entirely free, it by no means clarifies that judicial review—even in cases involving citizens—will function as a meaningful, as opposed to a symbolic, restraint on executive behavior. For starters, the government won on a truly fundamental point in the case: The plurality reaffirmed the power in principle of the president to detain a citizen as an enemy combatant—a power it articulated in *Ex parte Quirin*—writing that "[there is no bar to this Nation's holding one of its own citizens as an enemy combatant." In other words, the plurality allowed the military to exempt an individual from the full protections of criminal process on the basis of a finding that he has enlisted in a foreign military struggle against the United States in the context of a use of force authorized by Congress. The Court's acceptance of this basic premise of the government's argument is no small matter.

Moreover, Justice Sandra Day O'Connor was a bit cagey on the subject of Hamdi's access to counsel, and what she doesn't hold is as important as what she does. "Hamdi asks us to hold that the Fourth Circuit also erred by denying him immediate access to counsel upon his detention and by disposing of the case without permitting him to meet with an attorney," she noted at the end of the plurality opinion. "Since our grant of certiorari in this case, Hamdi has been appointed counsel, with whom he has met for consultation purposes on several occasions, and with whom he is now being granted unmonitored meetings. He unquestionably has the right to access to counsel *in connection with the proceedings on remand.* No further consideration of this issue is necessary at this stage of the case" (emphasis added). The language granting Hamdi access to counsel is ringing. It is framed in the language of constitutional rights, not—as the district courts in both *Hamdi* and *Padilla* envisioned it—as a discretionary grant of access for the purpose of airing all the issues in the case fully. But as the italicized language indicates, the "right" is only clear prospectively. Justice O'Connor did not address the question of whether Hamdi had this right from the outset of the litigation, when the right attached, or whether it was appropriate for the government—in the interests of interrogating him for intelligence—to have withheld it for two years.

What's more, Justice O'Connor left open the possibility that her due process concerns could be satisfied by tribunals within the military and that had such military process been available to Hamdi, judicial review would have been far more deferential as a consequence. "Plainly, the 'process' Hamdi has received is not that to which he is entitled under the Due Process Clause," she wrote. But "[t]here remains the possibility that the standards we have articulated could be met by an appropriately authorized and properly constituted military tribunal. Indeed, it is notable that military regulations already provide for such process in related instances, dictating that tribunals be made available to determine the status of enemy detainees who assert prisoner-of-war status under the Geneva Convention. … In the absence of such process, however, a court that receives a petition for a writ of habeas corpus from an alleged enemy combatant must itself ensure that the minimum requirements of due process are achieved." The tribunals to which she refers are, historically speaking, cursory affairs that do not involve a right to counsel or contemplate a great deal of factual development. If the import of *Hamdi* is that the military can, in the future, buy the total judicial deference it sought in this case by affording citizens alleged to be enemy combatants the limited process contemplated by Article 5 of the Third Geneva Convention, then the military has lost little and gained much in its apparent defeat this time around.

In short, although the government was rebuked by the Court, it is by no means clear that the next time an American citizen is captured abroad while apparently fighting for the other side, the military will not be able to behave very nearly as it behaved toward Hamdi—that is, hold him incommunicado for an extended period of time while interrogating him for intelligence. Nor are we likely to find out the answer to this question any time soon. The *Hamdi* case, after all, has been settled, and Hamdi himself released. While clarity could come as a consequence of future developments in *Padilla,* there is a substantial possibility that it too will become moot, not because of Padilla's release but because of his criminal indictment.[4] The question of whether enemy combatant detention is a legally tenable approach for the government toward citizens remains, despite the cases, very much an open one.

The high court's pronouncements with respect to the detainees at Guantanamo Bay, Cuba, were just as Delphic. The justices, by a 6–3 vote, declared that the federal courts had jurisdiction to consider habeas petitions filed on behalf of inmates at the facility. Indeed, the justices formulated the question posed by the case in language emphasizing the stakes for liberty and the rule of law: "What is presently at stake is only whether the federal courts have jurisdiction to determine the legality of the Executive's potentially indefinite detention of individuals who claim to be wholly innocent of wrongdoing," Justice Stevens wrote. The assertion of jurisdiction necessarily cast the Bush administration's conduct in a negative light, implying that there were substantial questions to litigate concerning the legality of the detentions—questions that rendered the Court's jurisdiction significant. And, to be sure, Justice Stevens's language did nothing to dispel this impression. He noted at one point in a footnote, for example, that "Petitioners' allegations—that, although they have engaged neither in combat nor in acts of terrorism against the United States, they have been held in Executive detention for more than two years in territory subject to the long-term, exclusive jurisdiction and control of the United States, without access to counsel and without being charged with any wrongdoing—unquestionably describe 'custody in violation of the Constitution or laws or treaties of the United States.'"

Heartless as it may sound, however, this apparently unobjectionable statement may not actually be true. That is to say, even if all of the Guantanamo inmates were completely innocent of any wrongdoing—which they most assuredly are not—and, more important, even were they all demonstrably not combatants, it would remain something of a puzzle what, if any, judicially enforceable law would be implicated by such reckless executive behavior. Indeed, the court has not generally held that the protections of the Bill of Rights apply to aliens overseas.[5] The Geneva Conventions have not traditionally been regarded as self-executing, and Congress has never explicitly given the courts power to enforce the terms of the conventions, which have been generally guaranteed by diplomatic pressures and reciprocity, not by litigation.[6] Exactly what does American law promise a suspected Taliban soldier—much less an al Qaeda operative—that a court in this country can ensure he gets?

Since only the jurisdictional question was before it, the Court avowedly declined to answer this question. "Whether and what further proceedings may become necessary after respondents make their response to the merits of petitioners' claims are matters that we need not address now," Justice Stevens wrote. And this coyness can, I suppose, be reasonably defended as judicial restraint—an unwillingness to address questions before they are fully presented and briefed. But the result is that nobody knows today what the great rebuke to the executive branch that the Court delivered in *Rasul* means in practice. Detainees have filed numerous claims since the decisions, alleging treaty, statutory, and constitutional deprivations. The great rebuke could be a giant nothing, If the Court has, in fact, asserted jurisdiction in order to determine later that no judicially cognizable rights have been violated, the executive will have lost nothing save a certain embarrassment and the inconvenience of having to brief and argue the subsequent legal questions.[7] Civil libertarians and human rights groups—not to mention the detainees—will have won nothing more than the satisfaction of having lost on the merits, rather than on a jurisdictional point. The litigation will have rendered the executive branch barely more accountable than had it won on the jurisdictional point—indeed, the administration will have had its legal position actively *affirmed*, not just deemed unreviewable. The detainees will certainly be no freer as a consequence of their victory. On the other hand, if the Court is truly prepared to act as the enforcer of legal rights toward alien detainees who have never set foot in this country, *Rasul* heralds a sea change in judicial power in wartime, an earthquake of untold magnitude and importance. The Court could also attempt some kind of intermediate step.

What does American law promise a Taliban soldier that a court can ensure he gets?

But the fog does not even end there. For the Court was less than clear about precisely what it was holding, even with respect to mere jurisdiction. At times, the majority opinion seemed to depend on the unique legal status of Guantanamo Bay, which is leased on an indefinite basis to the United States and subject during that time to the "exclusive jurisdiction and control" of the United States. At other times, however, the decision appears to rest on no such gimmick, relying instead only on the allegation of an illegal detention and the Court's proper jurisdiction over the Pentagon: "Petitioners contend that they are being held in federal custody in violation of the laws of the United States. No party questions the District Court's jurisdiction over petitioners' custodians. ... [The habeas statute], by its terms, requires nothing more." So while it is clear, after the court's decision, that the federal courts have the power to decide legal questions concerning the Guantanamo detainees, it is no clearer than before that decision whether the detentions at Guantanamo are in fact legally defective, nor is it clear whether the executive could still evade federal court oversight altogether by simply avoiding detention facilities abroad that happen to be formally leased to exclusive, indefinite American jurisdiction. Once again, the Court left all of the fundamental questions unanswered.

In short, while it is indisputable that the administration suffered a major atmospheric defeat at the hands of solid, though shifting, majorities of the Court, it remains premature to describe the true winners and losers in the cases. One cannot, at this stage, say—with Rivkin and Casey—that the administration has won the fight. But one has to acknowledge the possibility that the doctrinal seeds of its ultimate victory are germinating in the Court's decisions, and one cannot dismiss the possibility that in the long run, the true import of the decisions will lie more in what they permit than in what they forbid.

Article 2 fundamentalism

*E*VEN IN THIS moment of uncertainty as to the ultimate significance of the cases, however, one can attempt to assess the performance of the institutions, governmental and other, that have brought us to this point. The one that has attracted the most attention—criticism, controversy, and defense—is the executive branch. This is natural enough given the president's necessary leadership role in moments of national crisis, his control over the military, and, in this instance, his personal responsibility for many of the policies in question. Padilla was, after all, plucked out of the criminal justice system on the personal order of President Bush. It is right and proper that President Bush should be held accountable for the detention policies practiced by his administration. Still, in my judgment, the centrality of executive branch decisions in the public discussion of detention policies seems slightly too forgiving of the failures of other institutions. What's more, the criticism seems, in a fundamental sense, misdirected. For the president's original sin lay not simply—or even chiefly—in the substance of the positions he took with respect to captured enemy fighters. It lay, rather, in his utter unwillingness to seek legal sanction from Congress for those positions.

When you step back and examine the detention policies of the war on terrorism from the highest altitude, the administration's posture is not quite as outrageous as it seems from the ground. After all, countries at war detain the enemy. They interrogate those captured enemy fighters not entitled to privileged treatment. They don't usually provide foreign fighters with lawyers, except when those fighters are tried for war crimes. And they claim the right to hold those fighters until hostilities end. In the broadest sense, therefore, there is nothing exceptional about the Bush administration's position toward those it has detained. What's more, the civil liberties intrusion of these policies is quite constrained compared with past wars. The affected universe of detainees is limited to those the military believes to be fighters for the other side—neither large civilian populations (like the Japanese Americans interned during World War II) nor opponents of the war (like socialists during World War I). And in contrast to the Civil War, the writ of habeas corpus has not been suspended, so the courts remain at least formally open for business in judging any challenges to detentions. There is, quite simply, nothing intrinsically unreasonable about the administration's desire to use the traditional presidential wartime power to detain enemy combatants in this particular conflict.

What is unreasonable, however, is the pretense, almost since the beginning of the conflict, that the proper altitude for considering this problem is that of a jetliner. For zoom in only a little, and the differences between this conflict and those that have preceded it make the clean application of prior law and precedent nearly impossible. What does it mean to detain combatants for the duration of hostilities in a conflict that may never end? In a conflict with a shadowy, international, nonhierarchical, nonstate actor as enemy, what would victory look like if we achieved it? If we then released detainees, as international law requires, wouldn't that act merely restart the conflict? More immediately, given that al Qaeda does not fight along a front but seeks to infiltrate American society and destroy it from within, how can one reliably distinguish between combatants and mere sympathizers or even uninvolved parties caught in the wrong place at the wrong time? These differences are not mere oddities of the current conflict. They are fundamental challenges to the legal regime that governs traditional warfare, which presupposes clearly defined armies and a moment of negotiated peace, after which those captured will be repatriated as a consequence of diplomatic negotiation. The premise of detention in traditional warfare is that the warring parties have no issue with the individual soldier detained, who is presumed to be honorable. That premise is simply false in the current war, in which America's battle is very much with the individual jihadist. After all, unlike, say, Germany or Japan, al Qaeda is nothing more than the sum of its members.

Given the profound differences between the war on terror and past conflicts, there was no good reason for the administration to treat the resolution of questions as simple matters of executive discretion. They are essentially legislative in character—for notwithstanding the administration's pretenses, they go far beyond questions of how to apply old law to new circumstances. Rather, they represent the questions that will define the legal regime we, as a society, create in order to govern a situation never fully imagined, let alone encountered, in the past. As such, it was sheer folly for the Bush administration to attempt to answer them on its own—and that folly was as profoundly self-destructive as it was injurious to liberty and fairness.

The simple truth is that the administration could have gotten almost anything it wanted from Congress in the way of detention authority for enemy aliens abroad in the wake of September 11. If the debate over the USA Patriot Act proved anything, it was that Congress had little appetite for standing in the way of the most robust response the executive could muster. The administration would likely have had to stomach a certain amount of process for the detainees, particularly for citizens held domestically. One can imagine that Congress might have required some eventual provision of counsel for some detainees, perhaps even mandated a forum in which the evidence against them in some form could be tested. The administration may even have been forced to provide the process contemplated by Article 5 of the Third Geneva Convention for distinguishing between lawful and unlawful combatants—a process it certainly should have been granting in any event. In my estimation, however, it is simply inconceivable that Congress would have crafted a regime that did not amply accommodate the president's wartime needs, particularly if President Bush had been clear about what he needed, why he needed it, and what the stakes were if he didn't get it. Going to Congress would have required two things of President Bush: a willingness to accept certain minimal limits on executive conduct imposed from the outside and, more fundamentally, a recognition that the wartime powers of the president, while vast, are not plenary—an acceptance that the presidential power to wage war can be enhanced by acknowledging the legislature's role in legitimizing it. Had Bush proceeded thus—as presidents often have in past conflicts—he would have entered his court battles with clear statutory warrant for his positions. Had this happened, I believe the deference he sought from the Supreme Court would have been forthcoming and very nearly absolute.

But Bush did not take this approach. His administration's insistence on what might be termed Article II fundamentalism caused him to take maximalist positions that are genuinely troubling: The president's judgment that a person is an enemy combatant is essentially unreviewable. The courts should defer to the executive, even in the absence of an administrative record to which to defer. Long-term detentions without trials of hundreds of people are entirely outside the purview of the courts. They all amount to the same basic position: Trust us. Trust the executive branch, in a wholly new geopolitical environment, acting with the barest and most general approval from the other political branch, to generate an entirely new legal system with the power of freedom and liberty and life and death over anyone it says belongs in that system. The executive branch learned last spring that exactly one member of the Supreme Court—Clarence Thomas—trusts President Bush that much. The court's skepticism seems to me to have been an entirely foreseeable result that competent counsel advising the president ought to have hedged against. When the history of this period is written, I feel confident that Bush will be deemed exceedingly ill-served by his top legal advisers.

Congressional abdication

$\mathcal{B}$UT THE PRESIDENT'S responsibility, however heavy, is not exclusive. Congress, after all, has its own independent duty to legislate in response to problems that arise in the course of the nation's life. And in a system of separated powers. Congress is not meant to legislate simply for the executive's convenience or at its beck and call. Indeed, if the executive branch sought to shunt the legislature aside in this episode, the legislature certainly proved itself a most willing shuntee. Congress institutionally seemed more than content to sideline itself and let the executive branch and the courts sort out what the law should be.

This abandonment of the field is disturbing on several levels. At the most analytical, America's constitutional design presupposes that each branch of government will assert its powers, that those powers will clash, and that this clash will prevent the accumulation of power in any one branch. This is the famous premise of Federalist 5I: "[T]he great security against a gradual concentration of the several powers in the same department, consists in giving to those who administer each department the necessary constitutional means and personal motives to resist encroachments of the others. The provision for defense must in this, as in all other cases, be made commensurate to the danger of attack. Ambition must be made to counteract ambition." Yet in the war on terrorism. Congress has done very nearly the opposite of countering the executive's ambition. It has run from its own powers on questions on which its assertion of rightful au-

thority would be helpful, and it sloughed the difficult choices onto the two branches of government less capable than itself of designing new systems for novel problems.

The problem of congressional abdication of its responsibilities during wartime is not exactly new. It is most remarked upon in the context of the decision to go to war in the first place, which migrated in the twentieth century almost entirely to the executive branch. John Hart Ely noted, "It is common to style this shift a usurpation, but that oversimplifies to the point of misstatement. It's true our Cold War presidents generally wanted it that way, but Congress (and the courts) ceded the ground without a fight. In fact … the legislative surrender was a self-interested one: Accountability is pretty frightening stuff."[8] Ely's remedy for this problem—treating war powers as presenting jusiticiable questions with which the courts should be actively engaged—presents substantial difficulties on its own terms. Judges, after all, are not foreign policy experts, and decisions concerning war and peace are quintessentially political judgments, not principled legal ones. But even a robustly activist judiciary that was eager to explore such uncharted territories would have difficulty designing an appropriate regime for enemy combatants, because, to put it bluntly, the terms of any debate presented by litigation are destined to be too narrow.

Having no legislative involvement quite simply cuts off policy options. Once you consider the problem of enemy combatant detentions as a set of policy questions, a world of options opens. This world necessarily remains elusive to those who insist on finding in the doctrinal space between *Ex parte Milligan*[9] and *Ex parte Quirin* the answer to the question of how a Louisiana-born Saudi picked up in Afghanistan must be treated in a world in which a hegemonic United States has to consider nuclear terrorism a possibility. To cite only one conceivable example, the Constitution allows the civil commitment of mentally ill citizens who pose a danger to themselves or others. For a reasonably imaginative Congress, this might be a far better model for the alleged al Qaeda operative captured domestically than either the traditional laws of war or the criminal justice apparatus. A regime of civil commitment, after all, would recognize the preventive nature of the arrest, and it would coopt the use of a process that American society already tolerates as adequate for indefinite detentions in another context. Surely, al Qaeda operatives pose at least as great a threat to society as do schizophrenics.

One can imagine other models as well. Immigration law tolerates long detentions based almost entirely on executive branch process. Various forms of military tribunals might be attractive as well, as *Hamdi* intimates. The point is that the terms of the debate are today artificially constrained by the unwillingness of the one branch with the capacity to imagine a system from scratch to engage the problem at all. While individual members of Congress have raised the issue,[10] the congressional leadership—perhaps out of an unwillingness to publicly second-guess the Bush administration, perhaps out of sheer laziness, most likely out of a combination of the two—has shown no interest in actually legislating. Congress, in short, has concurred in the executive's unilateralism, offering neither legal support for its positions nor redirection of them. By the consent of both political branches, in other words, the design of the detention regime is being determined in a dialogue between the president and the courts.

Perhaps the most peculiar aspect of this decision is that it sparked so little controversy. The fact that few observers even comment upon Congress's absence from the discussion says a great deal about how Americans have come intuitively to weigh the responsibilities and contributions of the three branches of government. To be sure, many critics of the administration complain of the absence of specific congressional authority for detentions or military commissions by way of arguing against the legality of the administration's course. But the critics, by and large, are not urging congressional intervention, much less are they describing what a constructive intervention would look like. They have merely cited its absence as a bar to whatever action the administration proposes. Somehow, everyone seems to agree that the initial crack at writing the rules should be left to common-law jurisprudence.

NGOs for the defense

$\mathcal{T}$HIS AGREEMENT—which remains, frankly, inexplicable to me—has put a considerable premium on the performance of nongovernmental actors: the human rights and civil liberties groups that opposed the military in these litigations. While Padilla, Hamdi, and the Guantanamo plaintiffs all had counsel to argue their cases, these groups greatly magnified the arguments against the administration's course, both in amicus filings and in the broader realm of public debate. Consequently, they became, in some sense, the "other side" of the debate—the organized force whose arguments marked the major alternative to the direction the administration chose. Unfortunately, they did not provide the Court with a useful alternative to the administration's vision, for their arguments were marked at once by failures of pragmatism and weak and selective understanding of doctrine. This is forgivable in the case of defense lawyers, who are obliged to advance the arguments most likely to aid their individual clients. And in the human rights and civil liberties groups, the decision was undoubtedly as much strategic as it was driven by conviction. By staking out a hard line, the groups ensured that they had not conceded key points even before any compromises took place. But the result of their wholesale adoption of the defense arguments was to present the court with a strategy for preserving liberty that was as unembracable as the administration's strategy for ensuring security.

Doctrinally, the ground staked out by the human rights community made fetishes of certain components of the laws of war and American constitutional law, even while ignoring other countervailing components of the same bodies of law. The human rights groups generally elided the importance of *Ex parte Quirin,* for example, which quite unambiguously endorses the premise that the American citizen can be detained by the military as an unlawful combatant.[11] Though their briefs were usually more careful than to make this error, they often seemed to deny in public statements that a detainee could be held as an unlawful combatant at all—a position flatly at odds with long-standing traditions of warfare. They nearly uniformly denied that the congressional authorization for the use of force against al Qaeda and its state sponsors necessarily implied the lesser power to detain combatants.[12] And all regarded it as self-evident that federal courts should supervise the detentions of noncitizens abroad—something they have never done previously in American history.[13]

One doesn't have to be a raging enthusiast for executive power to worry that these positions, particularly cumulatively, are simply inconsistent with any serious attempt to wage war against al Qaeda—even an attempt that does not partake of the excesses in which the Bush administration so indulged. In the rather fanciful regime the human rights groups appear to contemplate (and I acknowledge here that I am blending different arguments into a melange that might reflect no single group's precise position), the citizen is entitled to criminal process even if caught on a battlefield. The courts are engaged in day-to-day monitoring of executive compliance with the Geneva Conventions—though those treaties are not self-executing and have not historically been enforced through judicial action. Even the unlawful combatant—that is, a combatant not entitled to the status of prisoner of war—is nonetheless entitled to the same criminal procedure, the court-martial, as both the lawful combatant and the American soldier accused of misconduct.

It is a beautiful vision, but it does not happen to be the vision encapsulated in either international law or American law. And it's hard even to imagine fighting a war within its constraints. Should someone like Khalid Sheikh Muhammad be entitled to immediate access to counsel upon capture in Pakistan? Should he be able immediately to file a habeas corpus action alleging deprivations of his constitutional and treaty rights? There is embedded in this vision a very deep discomfort with the premise that the war on terrorism is, legally speaking, a war at all.

The consequence of the human rights groups staking out such unflinching ground was that the courts were faced, in all three cases, with a choice between extremes. Instead of confronting a well-constructed—or even a badly constructed—statutory scheme that sought to balance the competing constitutional values at stake in these detentions, it confronted a choice between total deference to the executive, aided only by the most general support from Congress, or total rejection of its claims, including its legitimate claims. In other words, it faced a choice between throwing the baby out with the bathwater and drinking the bathwater. The unifying theme of the Supreme Court's action in the enemy combatant cases is the refusal to choose—that is, the insistence on splitting the difference, even where prior precedent gave it scant leeway to do so.

Splitting the baby

$\mathcal{T}$HE PERFORMANCE OF the courts in this endeavor was enormously uneven. Unlike the executive, which ultimately takes a unitary position on virtually all issues, and the Congress, which essentially took no position on the enemy combatant questions, the different courts, not to mention the different judges within individual courts, took several positions. And these ran the gamut in terms of quality and seriousness. For example, the district court that handled Padilla's case in New York produced—notwithstanding its ultimate reversal on the jurisdictional question on which the Supreme Court decided the case—the single most compelling judicial opinion yet written on the due process rights of citizens held as enemy combatants.[14] Chief Judge Michael Mukasey's handling of Padilla's case was a model of the combination of deference and skepticism that judges need to show in the war on terrorism, and it clearly became the model for Justice O'Connor's plurality opinion at the Supreme Court level. Judge Robert Doumar in Virginia, by contrast, was completely out of his depth in *Hamdi*. His rulings served to muddy, not clarify, the issues, as did his petulance toward government counsel.

More particularly for our purposes, in both appellate courts in the domestic cases—in the Fourth Circuit in *Hamdi* and in the Second Circuit in *Padilla*—the majority opinions simply adopted one or the other of the ultimately untenable hard-line positions, either the government's or that of the human rights groups and defense bar. In *Hamdi*, the Fourth Circuit declared the government's submission adequate to consign a citizen to his fate, at least where it is "undisputed" that he was captured in a "zone of active combat operations abroad."[15] To render beyond dispute the question of whether Hamdi was, in fact, captured in a zone of active combat abroad without hearing from Hamdi himself, the court found putative factual concessions in court filings, which the man had never seen or approved and which were written by lawyers with whom he had never been permitted to meet. The Second Circuit, meanwhile, declared Padilla's detention unlawful, buying in its entirety the notion that Congress's authorization to use force had not triggered the traditional war power of detaining the enemy until hostilities were at an end.[16] In both cases, dissenting judges showed considerably more sophistication, taking approaches that approximated the one the high court plurality ultimately adopted.[17] But because these were dissents in both courts of appeals, both *Padilla* and *Hamdi* came before the high court with stark stakes indeed: One court had held that the appropriate process was no process at all, while the other had held that—at least absent a neurotically specific act of Congress—nothing short of full criminal process could satisfy the Constitution.

The Guantanamo case approached the courts with the battle lines drawn similarly sharply, albeit for a different reason. The Supreme Court's own opinion in *Johnson v. Eisentrager* left little room for argument at the lower court level as to the jurisdiction of the federal courts over habeas petitions from the base. The Court wrote baldly at that time that "[w]e are cited to no instance where a court, in this or any other country where the writ [of habeas corpus] is known, has issued it on behalf of an alien enemy who, at no relevant time and in no stage of his captivity, has been within its territorial jurisdiction. Nothing in the text of the Constitution extends such a right, nor does anything in our statutes."[18] Any lower court tempted to assert jurisdiction over the base consequently had a high bar to clear in terms of binding precedent. In the *Rasul* litigation, no judge even attempted it.

The district court wrote, "Given that under Eisentrager, writs of habeas corpus are not available to aliens held outside the sovereign territory of the United States, this Court does not have jurisdiction to entertain the claims made by Petitioners."[19] The D.C. Circuit Court of Appeals unanimously affirmed, and not a single judge voted for en banc review.[20] In other words, when the Court considered the petition for certiorari, the justices were facing—as a consequence of the fidelity of the lower courts to what *Eisentrager* plainly said—the prospect of being wholly shut out of the discussion of enemy combatants held abroad. (It should be noted that an attempt was made by the Ninth Circuit to assert jurisdiaion over the base, but this was after certiorari had already been granted in *Rasul*.[21] Had the Court declined to consider *Rasul*, it would likely have had to jump to settle the conflict between the two circuits that developed as a result of this decision.)

As can probably be gleaned from the discussion so far, I am far more sympathetic to the high court's handling of *Hamdi* than to its resolution of *Rasul*. But critically, I believe the instinct behind both decisions was a similar one: the desire to split the baby between the claims of liberty and the claims of military necessity.

The plurality opinion in *Hamdi*, with all its vagueness and uncertainty, seems to me a creditable job of balancing constitutional values, and one that gets the big picture just about right. It acknowledges, first, the fact that the war on terrorism is not a metaphorical war like the war on drugs or the war on cancer—that is, it is not a statement of seriousness of purpose on a policy question but an actual state of military hostilities authorized by Congress and triggering traditional presidential war powers. Second, it acknowledges that implicit in Congress's authorization to use force is an authorization to detain those using force on the other side, even if they are American citizens. For different reasons, Justices Stevens, Scalia, Ginsburg, and Souter would have refused to recognize even this basic premise. Finally, the plurality recognizes that a citizen so detained is, by virtue of his citizenship, differently situated from a foreign national and entitled to a fair and impartial hearing should he choose to contest his status. These three basic premises seem to me all correct, whether they ultimately work to the government's advantage or to that of the detainees. In the absence of guidance from the legislature, I do not think American society could have expected more from the high court than finding this middle road and taking it.

Finding a middle course was naturally harder in *Rasul*. For jurisdiction, like pregnancy, is not a gray area; it either exists, or it doesn't exist. In this instance, the legal argument for jurisdiction was exceptionally weak. To get around *Eisentrager*, the Court had to argue that the famous holding had effectively been overruled in 1973—at least on the question of statutory jurisdiction in habeas cases—in a decision that does not even mention *Eisentrager*.[22] As noted above, the Court left unclear whether its assertion of jurisdiction applied only to Guantanamo or whether any detainee anywhere has access to American courts. For anyone with a sense of judicial restraint, *Rasul* should properly induce some embarrassment, for it is as dismissive of the Court's own precedent as it is disrespectful of the executive branch's reliance on that precedent in designing its detention policies. As Justice Antonin Scalia put it for the three dissenting justices.

> This is not only a novel holding; it contradicts a half-century-old precedent on which the military undoubtedly relied. The Court's contention that *Eisentrager* was somehow negated by *Braden v. 30th Judicial Circuit Court of Ky.*—a decision that dealt with a different issue and did not so much as mention *Eisentrager*—is implausible in the extreme. This is an irresponsible overturning of settled law in a matter of extreme importance to our forces currently in the field. I would leave it to Congress to change [the habeas statute], and dissent from the Court's unprecedented holding [internal citations omitted).

But if *Rasul* is an embarrassment, it is one that illuminates the same baby-splitting instinct as the plurality opinion in *Hamdi*. For while the court could not split the difference between the administration and its critics in this case—the substantive issues not being before it yet—it could preserve its ability to split the difference in the future. The result may be a cheap, cynical opinion, but it is one that keeps the justices in the discussion without promising anything tangible. Its vagueness, I believe, is part of its point—a shot across the executive's bow, warning that if it doesn't get its act together, the Court will force it to do so by divining some cognizable rights, just as it divined its own power to consider the detainees' fates in the first place. If the executive behaves responsibly, by contrast, my guess is that the plaintiffs will find that *Rasul* proves an empty vessel for pushing the military toward greater liberality for detainees. In other words, by finding jurisdiction in *Rasul*, however implausibly, the Court positioned itself to play exactly the role it played in *Hamdi*, though admittedly on what will inevitably prove thinner legal reeds.

The baby-splitting instinct evident in these cases is, I suspect, a vision of the future of the legal war on terrorism in the absence of congressional intervention. The courts have positioned themselves not to impose particular processes but, rather, like figure-skating judges at the Olympics, to hold up signs granting marks to the players as they struggle to carve their own way: This process gets a 5.6; this one is inadequate because it lacks a bit more of this value or has too much of that value at the expense of some other one. Because the court is allergic to simply letting one side win—an instinct which, in and of itself, deserves some sympathy given the exceedingly harsh choices posed by the parties—the result is likely to be ongoing uncertainty, the absence of a legal safe harbor for executive conduct, and a big legal question mark hanging over the fates of all detainees held by the military domestically or abroad.

There is, of course, an alternative: a serious and deliberative legislative process that would design a regime within the confines of the Court's dictates to date—a regime to which the courts could defer in the future and which could define the role they should play going forward. This alternative, however, would require two developments: The administration would have to assume a modicum of humility in its dealings with the other branches of government. The administration s foes, meanwhile, would have to accept that war is a reality, not a metaphor, and that, consequently, not everyone detained in the war on terrorism is going to be rushed in front of a magistrate and encouraged to hire Johnny Cochran or Ramsey Clark to handle an immediate habeas action. At this stage, it's hard to say which necessary precondition for a more constructive approach seems a remoter possibility.

Notes

1. *Rasul v. Bush,* 124 S. Ct. 2686 (2004).
2. *Hamdi v. Rumsfeld,* 124, S. Ct. 2633 (2004).
3. *Rumsfeld v. Padilla,* 124 S. Ct. 2711 (2004).
4. Padilla's habeas case was refiled in South Carolina in light of the Supreme Court's ruling and was argued in federal district court there early in 2005. U.S. District Judge Henry F. Floyd, on February 18, 2005, found in favor of Padilla and issued a writ of habeas corpus. The government immediately announced plans to appeal. Even as the habeas case has progressed, however, there has been some indication that Padilla is now a cooperating witness in a case unrelated to the circumstances of his arrest, a status that implies that a plea may be in the works. See Dan Christensen and Vanessa Blum, "Padilla Implicated in Florida Terror Case," *Legal Times* (September 20, 2004).
5. See e.g., *U.S. v. Verdugo-Urquidez,* 494 U.S. 2 5 9 (1990), and *Johnson v. Eisentrager,* 339 U.S. 7 6 3 at 784 (1950). While the latter decision has been called into question by *Rasul,* the former has not. And there still exists no authority for the proposition that the Bill of Rights limits government action against aliens operating in foreign theaters of warfare. The Court, however, has applied the Bill of Rights to some degree in American territories overseas. So, in the wake of *Rasul,* the Court will have to decide whether Guantanamo is truly foreign territory or whether it is analogous to such overseas possessions.
6. In the wake of *Rasul,* this premise has come into considerable doubt. In *Hamdan v. Rumsfeld* (D.D.C. 04-CV1519, November 8, 2004), U.S. District Judge James Robertson held that the Third Geneva Convention was self-executing: "Because the Geneva Conventions were written to protect individuals, because the Executive Branch of our government implemented the Geneva Conventions for fifty years without questioning the absence of implementing legislation, because Congress clearly understood that the Conventions did not require implementing legislation except in a few specific areas, and because nothing in the Third Geneva Convention itself manifests the contracting parties' intention that it become effective as domestic law without the enactment of implementing legislation, I conclude that, insofar as it is pertinent here, the Third Geneva Convention is a self-executing treaty." The opinion, under appeal as of this writing, can be found at http://www.dcd.uscourts.gov/o4-1 5 1 9.pdf. See also *In re Guantanamo Detainee Cases* (D.D.G. 02-CV-02.99, January 31 , 2005), which can be found at http://www.dcd. uscourts.gov/02299b.pdf.

7. The first of the rash of detainee suits to follow *Rasul* played out in exactly this fashion at the district court level. In *Khalid v. Bush* (D.D.C. CV 04-1142, January 19, 2005), U.S. District Judge Richard Leon held that notwithstanding *Rasul,* "no viable legal theory exists by which [a federal court] could issue a writ of habeas corpus under these circumstances." The decision can be found at http://www.dcd.uscourts.gov/o4-1142.pdf. On the other hand, less than two weeks later, Senior Judge Joyce Hens Green of the same court handed down *In re Guantanamo Detainee Cases,* in which she held precisely the opposite: The Fifth Amendment applies in Guantanamo and confers due process rights that are violated by the government's review procedures, and the Geneva Conventions are self-executing and confer individual litigable rights as well.

8. John Hart Ely, *War and Responsibility: Constitutional Lessons of Vietnam and Its Aftermath* (Princeton University Press, 1993), ix.

9. *Ex parte Milligan,* 71 U.S. 2 (1866).

10. See, e.g., H.R. 1029, the Detention of Enemy Combatants Act, introduced by Rep. Adam Schiff on February 23, 2003.

11. The briefs in *Hamdi* can be found at http://www.jenner.com/news/news_item.asp?id=12551224. Those in *Padilla* can be found at http://www.jenner.com/news/news_item.asp?id=12539624. The amicus filings of the American Civil Liberties Union, the Center for National Security Studies, Human Rights First, and other human rights and civil liberties groups, for example, all deny that current law authorizes enemy combatant detentions in at least one of the two cases, even if the detainee is granted a meaningful ability to contest his designation.

12. See, again, the amicus filings in both *Hamdi* and *Padilla*. Interestingly, the brief of the libertarian Cato Institute presents a notable exception.

13. The briefs in *Rasul* can be found at http://www.jenner.com/news/news_item.asp?id=12520724. The range of institutional support for the assertion of jurisdiction is dramatic.

14. *Padilla v. Rumsfeld,* 233 F. Supp. 2d 564 (2002).

15. *Hamdi v. Rumsfeld,* 316 F, 3d 450 (2003).

16. *Padilla v. Rumsfeld,* 352 F. 3d 695 (2003).

17. See Judge Motz's dissent from denial of rehearing en banc in *Hamdi,* reported at 337 F. 3d 335, 368 (2003). See also judge Wesley's dissent in *Padilla.* reported at 352 F. 3d 695, 726 (2003).

18. *Johnson v. Eisentrager,* 339 U.S. (1950).

19. *Rasul v. Bush,* 215 F. Supp. 2d 55 (2002).

20. *Al Odah v. United States,* 321 F. 3d 1134 (2003). The decision denying rehearing en banc is reported as *Al Odah v. United States,* 2003 U.S. App. LEXIS 11166.

21. *Gherebi v. Bush,* 374 F. 3d 727 (2003).

22. Justice Stevens's discussion in *Rasul* concerning *Braden v. 30th Judicial Circuit Court of Ky.,* 410 U.S. 484.

Benjamin Wittes *is an editorial writer for the* Washington Post *specializing in legal affairs, and the author of* Starr: A Reassessment (*Yale University Press, 2002*). *This essay is also forthcoming in Peter Berkowitz, ed.,* Terrorism, the Laws of War, and the Constitution (*Hoover Institution Press, 2005*).

UNIT 5

The Foreign Policy-Making Process

Unit Selections

Key Points to Consider

- Construct an ideal foreign policy-making process. How close does the United States come to this ideal? Is it possible for the United States to act in the ideal manner? If not, is the failing due to individuals who make foreign policy or to the institutions in which they work? Explain.

- What is the single largest failing of the foreign policy-making process? How can it be corrected? What is the single largest strength of the foreign policy-making process?

- What changes, if any, are necessary in the U.S. foreign policy-making process if the United States is to act effectively with other countries in multilateral efforts?

- What advice would you give to the president who is considering undertaking military action?

- How would you run a meeting that was organized to respond to a terrorist act? Whom would you invite? What would you expect of those you invited? How much dissent would you permit?

Student Website
www.mhcls.com/online

Internet References
Further information regarding these websites may be found in this book's preface or online.

Belfer Center for Science and International Affairs (BCSIA)
http://ksgwww.harvard.edu/csia/

The Heritage Foundation
http://www.heritage.org

National Archives and Records Administration (NARA)
http://www.nara.gov/nara/welcome.html

U.S. Department of State: The Network of Terrorism
http://usinfo.state.gov/products/pubs/

We easily slip into the habit of assuming that an underlying rationality is at work in the conduct of foreign policy. A situation is identified as unacceptable or needing change, goals are established, policy options are listed, the implications of competing courses of action are assessed, a conscious choice is made as to which policy to adopt, and then the policy is implemented correctly. This assumption is comforting because it implies that policymakers are in control of events and that solutions do exist. Moreover, it allows us to assign responsibility for policy decisions and hold policymakers accountable for the success or failure of their actions.

Comforting as this assumption is, it is also false. Driven by domestic, international, and institutional forces, as well as by chance and accident, perfect rationality is an elusive quality. This is true regardless of whether the decision is made in a small group setting or by large bureaucracies. Small groups are created when the scope of the foreign policy problem appears to lie beyond the expertise of any single individual. This is frequently the case in crisis situations. The essence of the decision-making problem here lies in the overriding desire of group members to get along. Determined to be a productive member of the team and not to rock the boat, individual group members suppress personal doubts about the wisdom of what is being considered and become less critical of the information before them—than they would be if they alone were responsible for the decision. They may stereotype the enemy, assume that the policy cannot fail, or believe that all members of the group are in agreement on what must be done.

The absence of rationality in decision making by large bureaucracies stems from their dual nature. On the one hand, bureaucracies are politically neutral institutions that exist to serve the president and other senior officials by providing them with information and implementing their policies. On the other hand, they have goals and interests of their own that may not only conflict with the positions taken by other bureaucracies but may also be inconsistent with the official position taken by policymakers.

Because not every bureaucracy sees a foreign policy problem in the same way, policies must be negotiated into existence, and implementation becomes anything but automatic. While essential for building a foreign policy consensus, this exercise in bureaucratic politics robs the policy process of much of the rationality that we look for in government decision making.

The problem of trying to organize the policy process to conduct a war against terrorism is an especially daunting task. In part this is because the enormity of the terrorist attacks and the language of war embraced by the Bush administration lead to expectations of an equally stunning countermove. Rationality is also strained by the offsetting pressures for secrecy and the need for a speedy response on the one hand and the need to harmonize large numbers of competing interests on the other. Finally, no matter how many resources are directed at the war against terrorism, there will continue to be the need to balance resources and goals. Priorities will need to be established and trade-offs accepted. There is no neutral equation or formula by which this can be accomplished. It will be made through a political process of bargaining and consensus building in which political rationality rather than any type of substantive rationality will triumph.

The readings in this unit provide insight into the process by which foreign policy decisions are made by highlighting activity at several different points in the policy process. The first essay, "Misunderestimating Terrorism," reviews the process by which key decisions have been made within the State Department in putting together the data for *Patterns of Global Terrorism*, one of the most widely read annual reports it has ever produced. The second essay, "Words vs. Deeds," looks at the central place that public opinion polling now holds in foreign policy decision making. The final essay by John Prados, "The Pros from Dover," casts a critical eye on decision-making processes and structures put into place by the George W. Bush administration. He asserts that either the system did not work or it worked to keep terrorism off of the foreign policy agenda in its first months in office.

"Misunderestimating" Terrorism

The State Department's Big Mistake

Alan B. Krueger and David D. Laitin

As the war on terrorism continues, statistics on terrorist attacks are becoming as important as the unemployment rate or the GDP. Yet the terrorism reports produced by the U.S. government do not have nearly as much credibility as its economic statistics, because there are no safeguards to ensure that the data are as accurate as possible and free from political manipulation. The flap over the error-ridden 2003 *Patterns of Global Terrorism* report, which Secretary of State Colin Powell called "a big mistake " and which had to be corrected and rereleased, recently brought these issues to the fore. But they still have not been adequately addressed.

Now-common practices used to collect and disseminate vital economic statistics could offer the State Department valuable guidance. Not long ago, economic statistics were also subject to manipulation. In 1971, President Richard Nixon attempted to spin unemployment data released by the Bureau of Labor Statistics (BLS) and transferred officials who defied him. This meddling prompted the establishment of a series of safeguards for collecting and disseminating economic statistics. Since 1971, the Joint Economic Committee of Congress has held regular hearings at which the commissioner of the BLS discusses the unemployment report. More important, in the 1980s, the Office of Management and Budget issued a directive that permits a statistical agency's staff to "provide technical explanations of the data" in the first hour after principal economic indicators are released and forbids "employees of the Executive Branch" from commenting publicly on the data during that time.

The State Department should adopt similar protections in the preparation and dissemination of its reports. In addition to the global terrorism report, the State Department is required by Congress to report annually on international bribery, human rights practices, narcotics control, and religious freedom. Gathering and reporting data for congressional oversight is presently a low-level function at the State Department. The department rarely relies on high-quality, objective data or on modern diagnostic tests to distinguish meaningful trends from chance

associations. Adopting safeguards against bias, both statistical and political, would enable Congress to better perform its constitutional role as the White House's overseer and allow the American public to assess the government's foreign policy achievements.

A PATTERN OF ERRORS

Congress requires that the State Department provide each year "a full and complete report "that includes "detailed assessments with respect to each foreign country ... in which acts of international terrorism occurred which were, in the opinion of the Secretary, of major significance." The global terrorism reports are intended to satisfy this requirement, but, over time, they have become glossy advertisements of Washington's achievements in combating terrorism, aimed as much at the public and the press as at congressional overseers.

The 2003 global terrorism report was launched at a celebratory news conference in April. Deputy Secretary of State Richard Armitage and Ambassador J. Cofer Black, the State Department coordinator for counterterrorism, outlined some remaining challenges, but principally they announced the Bush administration's success in turning the terrorist tide. Black called the report "good news," and Armitage introduced it by saying, "You will find in these pages clear evidence that we are prevailing in the fight." The document's first paragraph claimed that worldwide terrorism dropped by 45 percent between 2001 and 2003 and that the number of acts committed last year "represents the lowest annual total of international terrorist attacks since 1969. "The report was transmitted to Congress with a cover letter that interpreted the data as "an indication of the great progress that has been made in fighting terrorism" after the horrific events of September 11.

But we immediately spotted errors in the report and evidence contradicting the administration's claims. For example, the chronology in Appendix A, which lists each significant terrorist incident occurring in the year, stopped on November 11—an unusual end to the calendar year. Clearly, this was a mistake, as four terrorist attacks occurred in Turkey between November 12 and the end of 2003. Yet it was impossible to tell whether the post-November 11 incidents were inadvertently dropped off the chronology and included in figures in the body of the report or completely overlooked.

More important, even with the incomplete data, the number of significant incidents listed in the chronology was very high. It tallied a total of 169 significant events for 2003 alone, the highest annual count in 20 years; the annual average over the previous five years was 131. How could the number of significant attacks be at a record high, when the State Department was claiming the lowest total number of attacks since 1969? The answer is that the implied number of "nonsignificant "attacks has declined sharply in recent years. But because nonsignificant events were not listed in the chronology, the drop could not be verified. And if, by definition, they were not significant, it is unclear why their decrease should merit attention.

On June 10, after a critical op-ed we wrote in *The Washington Post,* a follow-up letter to Powell from Representative Henry Waxman (D-Calif.), and a call for review from the Congressional Research Service, the State Department acknowledged errors in the report. "We did not check and verify the data sufficiently," spokesman Richard Boucher said. "… [T]he figures for the number of attacks and casualties will be up sharply from what was published."

At first, Waxman accused the administration of manipulating the data to "serve the Administration's political interests." Powell denied the allegation, insisting that "there's nothing political about it. It was a data collection and reporting error." Although there is no reason to doubt Powell's explanation, if the errors had gone in the opposite direction—making the rise in terrorism on President George W. Bush's watch look even greater than it has been—it is a safe bet that the administration would have caught them before releasing the report. And such asymmetric vetting is a form of political manipulation.

Critical deficiencies in the way the report was prepared and presented compromised its accuracy and credibility. Chief among these were the opaque procedures used to assemble the report, the inconsistent application of definitions, insufficient review, and the partisan release of the report. These deficiencies resulted in a misleading and unverifiable report that appeared to be tainted by political manipulation.

It is unclear exactly how the report was assembled. The report notes that the U.S. government's Incident Review Panel (IRP) is responsible for determining which terrorist events are significant. It says little, however, about the panel's members: how many there are, whether they are career employees or political appointees, or what affiliations they have. Nor does it describe how they decide whether an event is significant. Do they work by consensus or majority rule? What universe of events do they consider?

The State Department announced a decline in total terrorist attacks, which resulted from a decline in nonsignif-

icant events. But without information about the nonsignificant events, readers were essentially asked to blindly trust the nameless experts who prepared it.

The report's broad definitions, moreover, are sometimes too blunt to help classification. Terrorism is defined as "premeditated, politically motivated violence perpetrated against noncombatant targets by subnational groups or clandestine agents, usually intended to influence an audience." The report specifies that an international terrorist attack is an act committed by substate actors from one nation against citizens or property of another. An incident "is judged significant if it results in loss of life or serious injury to persons, major property damage, and/or is an act or attempted act that could reasonably be expected to create the conditions noted."

But hardly any explanation was provided about how the IRP distinguishes significant from nonsignificant events. When is property damage too minor for an event to be significant? How are nonsignificant events identified? Is the IRP responsible for making these determinations too? Has the source and scope of their information changed over time? The corrected 2003 report, the first to list individual nonsignificant acts, defines as "major" property damage that exceeds $10,000. It does not indicate, however, whether that criterion applied to previous reports.

Admittedly, measuring international terrorism is no easy task. Even scholarly reckonings are not free from subjective judgment, and there are inevitably close calls to be made. The most one can hope for in many cases is consistent application of ambiguous definitions.

Unfortunately, in the global terrorism reports the rules have been applied inconsistently. Many cross-border attacks on civilians in Africa have not been included in the reports, for example, even though similar attacks in other regions have been. The report for 2002, moreover, counts as significant a suicide attack by Chechen *shaheeds* (Islamist martyrs) against a government building in Moscow that killed 72 people. Yet none of the numerous suicide attacks by the Chechen "black widows" that terrorized Russia and killed scores in 2003 was tallied as an international terrorist attack in the latest report. After one such attack, Russian President Vladimir Putin said, "Today, after a series of recent terrorist attacks, we can say that the bandits active in Chechnya are not just linked with international terrorism, they are an integral part of it." If the State Department considers such attacks domestic, rather than international, it should do so consistently from one year to the next.

Another problem is that the staff that prepared the 2003 global terrorism report did not participate in releasing it; in fact, they have yet to be identified. High-level Bush administration officials presented the report to the media, using it to support White House policies and take credit for the alleged decline in terrorism. Even after the report's flaws were recognized, they continued to spin the figures. When the corrected version was released, Black repeated that "we have made significant progress," despite being pressed to acknowledge that last year the number of significant attacks reached a 20-year high. Given the war on terrorism's central role in the upcoming presidential election, such presentation gives the appearance that the report is being manipulated for political gain.

The State Department has tried to explain the report's flaws using language eerily reminiscent of the Bush administration's justification of the failure to find weapons of mass destruction in Iraq. Spokesman Boucher told reporters that previous claims that the war on terrorism was succeeding had been based "on the facts as we had them at the time [and] the facts that we had were wrong." Even Powell partook in the spinning. On the one hand, he announced that "the [original] narrative is sound and we're not changing any of the narrative." On the other hand, he acknowledged, "We will change the narrative wherever the narrative relates to the data."

To his credit, Powell instructed those responsible for preparing the report to brief Waxman's staff on the procedures they had used and the origins of their mistakes. Based on a summary of the briefing by Waxman's staff, much has come to light. Authority for compiling the list of attacks was shifted from the CIA to the Terrorist Threat Integration Center (TTIC), an organization created in May 2003 to "merge and analyze all threat information in a single location." The TTIC provided information to the IRP, which, it was disclosed, consists of representatives from the CIA, the Defense Intelligence Agency, the National Security Agency, and the State Department's Bureau of Intelligence and Research. A TTIC representative chaired the meetings and could cast a vote to break ties on the classification of an event as significant or nonsignificant.

At least this year, chaos prevailed. The IRP's members changed from meeting to meeting—when they attended the meetings at all. The CIA employee responsible for the database left but was never replaced; in mid-process, an outside contractor who entered data was replaced by another contractor. Because of technical incompetence, the report relied on the wrong cutoff date.

Arithmetic errors were rampant. Larry Johnson, a retired CIA and State Department professional, discovered that the total number of fatalities in the chronology exceeded the number listed in the statistical review in Appendix G. According to Black, the errors resulted from "a combination of things: inattention, personnel shortages and database that is awkward and is antiquated and needs to have very proficient input be made in order for to be sure that the numbers will spill then to the different categories that are being captured [sic]." The debacle is more like an episode of the Keystone Kops than a chapter from Machiavelli, but even that analogy is not very comforting.

SETTING THE RECORD STRAIGHT

Despite the data's limitations, the chronology of significant events in the 2003 global terrorism report yields important information about terrorism's trends, its geographical characteristics, and its magnitude.

Time-series analysis, which seeks to discern trends in given phenomena over time, requires a consistent approach to collecting data. The State Department's terrorism report presents time-series analysis, but by focusing on the total number of attacks it misleadingly combines verifiable data on significant events with nonverifiable data on insignificant ones. And because, as TTIC director John Brennan admitted, "many nonsignificant events occur throughout the world that are not counted in the report, "one must also be concerned about consistency in the measurement of the total number of terrorist events. Even if the nonsignificant events were listed (and thus could be verified), trends in significant events are more relevant because they track events that, by definition, are more important. Accurately measuring these trends is a prerequisite for understanding the factors that underlie them and the policies that shape them. In fact, an analysis of the revised report reveals that the number of significant attacks increased from 124 to 175, or by 41 percent, from 2001 to 2003—a significant fact indeed.

The detailed chronology also allows analysts to cumulate terrorist events for each country and cross-classify them according to the country where they occurred and the perpetrators' country of origin. These figures can then be related to the countries' characteristics, yielding information that can help policymakers devise strategies to address terrorism's root causes. Using the global terrorism reports for the years 1997-2002, the authors of this article have previously found that terrorists tend to come from nondemocratic countries, both rich and poor, and generally target nationals from rich, democratic countries.

The State Department has rightly emphasized that the threat of terrorism remains serious, but a close examination of its data helps put the magnitude of the threat in perspective. In 2003, a total of 625 people—including 35 Americans—were killed in international terrorist incidents worldwide. Meanwhile, 43,220 died in automobile accidents in the United States alone, and three million died from AIDS around the world. Comparative figures, particularly when combined with forecasts of future terrorism trends, can help focus debate on the real costs people are willing to bear—in foregone civil liberties and treasure—to reduce the risk posed by terrorism.

CHANGING TRACKS

The State Department currently uses, and Congress accepts, nineteenth-century methods to analyze a twenty-first-century problem. To prevent errors of the type that riddled the 2003 global terrorism report, Congress has two alternatives. It could reassign the State Department's reporting responsibilities to a neutral research agency, such as the GAO (the General Accounting Office, recently renamed the Government Accountability Office) which routinely uses appropriate statistical practices. The problem is that the GAO has little foreign policy expertise and does not necessarily have access to the (sometimes classified) information that goes into the reports. Alternatively, Congress could keep the reports within the State Department's purview but demand that its practices for data collection and analysis be improved and that the reports be insulated from partisan manipulation.

If responsibility remains within the State Department, Congress should establish a statistical bureau in the department to ensure that scientific standards are respected in all reports, thereby elevating the status of data-gathering and statistics there. The bureau would promote consistency, statistical rigor, and transparency. When appropriate, it could seek input from the scientific community. And, while respecting classified sources, it could also insist that sufficient information be released to independent analysts for verification.

To overcome conflicts of interest facing political appointees who issue government reports, the State Department should adopt rules similar to those that govern the production and dissemination of key economic indicators. Career staff who prepare the reports should be given an hour to brief the media on technical aspects of the data, during which time political appointees would be precluded from making public comments. (After the hour elapses, it is expected that political appointees would offer their interpretations.) Career staff should be protected so they can prepare mandated reports without interference from political appointees and then present them for review by the statistics bureau. Once the reports are finalized, but before they are publicly released, they should be circulated to designated political appointees who need to prepare for their release. Disclosure dates should be announced long in advance to prevent opportunistic timing by political appointees.

Last October, in a candid memorandum to top aides that was leaked to the press, Secretary of Defense Donald Rumsfeld admitted, "Today, we lack metrics to know if we are winning or losing the global war on terror. Are we capturing, killing, or deterring and dissuading more terrorists every day than the *madrassas* [Islamic schools] and the radical clerics are recruiting, training, and deploying against us?" The statement was a stinging acknowledgment that the government lacks both classified and unclassified data to make critical policy decisions. It is also a reminder that only accurate information, presented without political spin, can help the public and decision-makers know where the United States stands in the war on terrorism and how best to fight it.

ALAN B. KRUEGER is Bendheim Professor of Economics and Public Policy at Princeton University. **DAVID D. LAITIN** is Watkins Professor of Political Science at Stanford University.

Words vs. Deeds: President George W. Bush and Polling

by Kathryn Dunn Tenpas

President George W. Bush pledged repeatedly throughout his presidential campaign that his administration would have no use for polls and focus groups: "I really don't care what polls and focus groups say. What I care about is doing what I think is right." Shackled by that promise, President Bush and his staff have shrouded his polling apparatus, minimizing the relevance of polls and denying their impact. But public records available from the Federal Election Commission, documents from presidential libraries, and interviews with key players paint a fairly clear picture of the Bush polling operation. The picture, which turns out to be a familiar one, calls into question the administration's purported "anti-polling" ethos and shows an administration closely in keeping with historical precedent.

President Bush in Historical Context

Every president since Richard Nixon has hired professional pollsters to take, periodically, the pulse of the electorate. Earlier presidents clearly had relationships with pollsters, who obligingly tacked questions onto their existing polls for the benefit of the administration. But polling was not under White House control. Nixon's use of pollsters marked a turning point in the history of presidential polling because it signaled the birth of White House-commissioned polls. No longer tethered to the timetables and agendas of pollsters like Lou Harris and George Gallup, presidents began to direct both the timing and the substance of their polls. Nor were polls limited to the campaign season; presidents and their staff could test the popularity of various programs and policy initiatives on their own schedule. Scholars, noting that the transfer of campaign tactics to governing was blurring the distinction between the two, began describing the result as the "permanent campaign."

Rapid advances in technology played a big part in the new ways presidents used polling. By the time Nixon took office, computers, though costly, had become sophisticated enough to process vast quantities of data. Not only were telephones ubiquitous enough to make their use in polling methodologically feasible, but the advent of random digit dialing increased the efficiency and validity of telephone polling. In short, the "science" of polling became more mature, enabling presidents not only to learn about their past performance but to gain "prospective" intelligence. Today, testing key phrases in a speech or catchphrases designed to sell a policy or program has become so commonplace that presidential speeches and public pronouncements endure many rounds of focus group testing before being judged ready for primetime. Innovative techniques like the mall intercept (interviewing shoppers at a mall storefront), tracking polls, overnight polling, dial meters, and focus groups are part of any professional pollster's repertoire. And new Internet focus groups are being used, by the Bush pollsters among others, as a more timely, less expensive way to conduct focus groups. Though still in its nascent stages, Internet polling is thought to be the next generation of survey research, significantly lowering costs while increasing the speed with which polls can be conducted.

The names of many past presidential pollsters are familiar, if not exactly household names. Robert Teeter did polling for Presidents Nixon, Ford, and George H.W. Bush; Patrick Caddell for President Carter; Richard Wirthlin for President Reagan; and Stanley Greenberg (1993-94) and Mark Penn (1995-2000) for President Clinton. Most began as pollsters for the campaign and were "promoted" to presidential pollsters, taking on a higher profile in the process. Indeed, the unprecedented visibility and perceived influence of Clinton's pollsters created much advance interest in President George W. Bush's prospective pollsters. But Bush's determination to be the "anti-Clinton" and his repeated campaign promises to give polls and focus groups no role in his administration led him to relegate his pollsters to near anonymity. Still, their low profile, particularly compared with that of Clinton's pollsters, has not kept them from performing essential polling for the White House.

By the Numbers

The Republican and Democratic National Committees subsidize presidential political expenses such as polling and political travel and routinely report those expenses to the Federal Election Commission. Table 1 sets out polling expenditures only for designated presidential pollsters during the first two years of the Reagan, Bush I, Clinton, and Bush II administrations. The pollsters for the second Bush administration come in well behind those of Presidents Reagan and Clinton and only slightly ahead of the first Bush administration. Though the parties spent extraordinary amounts on both Reagan and Clinton, Reagan's administration was popularly perceived as being driven by deeply rooted philosophical principles while Clinton's was seen as merely pandering—suggesting that polling does not always taint a president's reputation.

When the party of the president is in power, the national committee becomes a veritable White House annex staffed with loyalists eager to secure the president's re-election. Toward that end, no amount of polling is too much, particularly when the polling can also inform broader party strategy and statewide campaigns. A look at Republican National Committee spending on polling more generally (not just designated presidential pollsters) reveals that it spent roughly $3.1 million during the first two years of the current Bush administration. And even that figure understates the polling available to the White House because it does not include polling conducted on behalf of the National Republican Senatorial Committee and the National Republican Congressional Committee, which totals some $6.5 million—more than double what the RNC spent on polling. Though neither of those organizations is responsible for subsidizing White House polling, Bush's presidential pollsters, Jan van Lohuizen (Voter/Consumer Research) and Fred Steeper (Market Strategies), have done work for these committees totaling more than $800,000—a sum that if added to presidential polling would bump up the Bush total to $2.5 million, more than $1 million more than Bush I. And Karl Rove's extraordinary sway makes it unlikely that any request by him for statewide polls that might be of interest to the president would be denied either by the president's pollsters or by any pollsters doing work for the RNC. In addition, the RNC spent $2.7 million on "political consulting." And although the FEC reports do not detail the various projects, the reports include work by former White House adviser Karen Hughes and a broad range of Republican consulting firms.

As interesting as the total amount of RNC spending on polling is its timing (figure 1). Rather than being more or less consistent monthly, spending peaks in ways that seem hard to explain. Though noteworthy events—the September 11 attacks and the midterm elections—may account for two of the peaks, Matthew Dowd, senior adviser at the RNC, has indicated that events do not necessarily drive polling. And while pollsters may be interested in gauging the impact of unexpected events or

National Party Presidential Polling Expenditures
(In 2002 dollars)

ADMINISTRATION	FIRST YEAR	SECOND YEAR	TOTAL
Reagan –			
Richard Wirthlin	1,635,000	2,531,000	4.1 million
Bush I –			
Robert Teeter	831,683	470,811	1.3 million
Clinton –			
Stanley Greenberg	2,433,000	2,415,000	4.8 million
Bush II –			
Jan van Lohuizen			
and Fred Steeper	715,771	947,422	1.7 million

*Data for the current administration obtained on-line from fec.gov with the assistance of Elizabeth Redman and Larissa Davis of the Brookings Institution, April 2003. All other data obtained by author from the Federal Election Commission.

new developments, their billing is not systematic in a way that could support the event-driven explanation. Nevertheless, a statistical regression analysis reveals a general trend upward, roughly an average increase of $4,000 a month, suggesting that, over time, there are forces driving the RNC to spend more money on polling. Short of obtaining White House-commissioned polls, it is impossible to define the precise role that events play in polling. Regardless, the variation in spending reflects the idiosyncratic usage of polling within the Bush administration.

Why Poll?

Presidential documents and interviews with White House staff and pollsters from past administrations suggest that presidents use polling for two primary reasons. The first is tactical. Given the limited resources available to them, new presidents must determine the best way to sell their agenda, minimizing costs and maximizing their influence. Campaign professionals, armed with state-of-the-art public opinion technology and an "outside the Beltway" perspective on pressing issues and problems, provide a service that the modern White House is unequipped to offer. The second reason, rooted in democratic theory, is a president's desire to represent his constituents by acting in consonance with a majority of the public. Although the Bush administration is willing to admit it uses polls to help package and sell its policies to the public, it regards as heresy any suggestion that it follows the polls (even the Clinton administration denied that it used polls for this purpose).

Regardless, presidential pollsters from all administrations since Nixon's have been known to poll on foreign and domestic issues alike. Nixon polled about Vietnam and about admitting China to the United Nations. Carter surveyed American attitudes toward Israel and the Iran hostage crisis. Reagan tracked polls on the Iran-Contra affair and the Marine barracks bombing in Lebanon. During President George H.W. Bush's administration, pollsters Robert Teeter and Fred Steeper conducted polls

Republican National Committee Polling Costs, 2001–2002

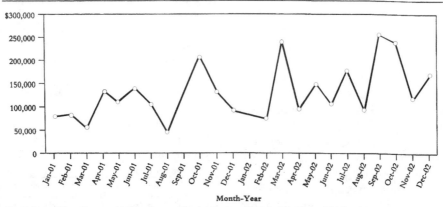

*Data obtained from fec.gov with the assistance of Larissa Davis and Elizabeth Redman of the Brookings Institution, April 2003.

and focus groups both before and during the Gulf War. Examples of polling on domestic policy—busing, agriculture, government regulation, bilingual education, health care policy, energy, and the budget—abound. Presidential pollsters provide additional data before midterm elections and become pivotal during the president's reelection campaign. Typically, the fourth year of the president's term generates the highest spending on polling. Speech content is another area where pollsters can provide useful advice. Finally, all presidential pollsters need to collect national tracking polls on a regular basis to provide an internal baseline to compare against other polls. In short, presidential polling is a staple of the modern presidency.

Consumer of Polls: The Bush Political Machine

The way one political insider explained President Bush's attitude toward polling reinforced the president's campaign mantra: "One of the worst arguments a White House adviser can make to the president is to say that 'the polls show X.'" But despite the president's disdain for public opinion polls, he has created a formidable White House political operation that focuses closely on them. The Office of Strategic Initiatives monitors and analyzes the results of numerous public surveys by major networks and news organizations as well as the findings of privately commissioned polls. And access to state surveys and other polls conducted by GOP pollsters informs their analyses. Why does the nature of the White House political operation matter? Because no amount of polling is worthwhile unless it is properly analyzed and incorporated into White House policy and political discussions.

President Bush's chief political confidant, Karl Rove, is considered by Republicans and Democrats alike to be an extraordinarily shrewd presidential adviser. On entering the White House in 2001, Bush established the first White House Office of Strategic Initiatives and appointed Rove its director—giving him a perch from which to survey the political landscape with the aim of expanding the president's electoral coalition in 2004. Unlike Bush's father, who placed his chief political adviser, Lee Atwater, at the helm of the RNC, George W. Bush understands the importance of proximity. Though the president deliberately distances himself from pollster Jan van Lohuizen (political insiders claim the two rarely meet), his close relationship with Rove virtually ensures a key role for polling in presidential policymaking.

Assisting Rove as chief political adviser is Matthew Dowd, the RNC senior adviser who coordinates the pollsters and analyzes the political pulse with the help of van Lohuizen, who conducts focus groups as well as national surveys. And Fred Steeper, 1992 campaign pollster for Bush's father, is assigned a variety of special projects that address specific research questions, some of which involve focus groups. Combining the less "scientific" focus groups with polling enables the political shop to determine what people are thinking and then test those attitudes rigorously through national surveys. Unlike survey research, the focus group allows researchers to present text from a speech or a segment of a television ad and gauge the intensity of emotions, observe body language, and probe more deeply on key issues. The focus group alone may not be especially helpful, but combined with survey research, it can create a more refined questionnaire that zeroes in on previously tested issues and preferences. Similarly, the focus group technique can be applied after a national survey to probe specific questions and issues. The Steeper-van Lohuizen team clearly enhances the value of survey research while the Rove–Dowd–van Lohuizen/Steeper chain of command ensures that the pollsters stay well outside the political circle—and away from the eyes of the White House press corps.

The final part of this well-oiled political machine is the White House Office of Political Affairs director and recipient of polling data, Ken Mehlman. Since the Reagan administration, this office has become a standard component of all White House political operations, but its influence depends largely on the president and his chief aides. The first President Bush downplayed the office, and it experienced high turnover during the first term of the Clinton administration. But in today's White House, Ken Mehlman's job is deemed an important one—though unlike Karl Rove's macropolitical strategy, Mehlman tends to the care and feeding of state and local partisans in hopes of paving the way for victory in 2004.

White House Polling in Perspective: Perception Is Everything

President Bush's use of polling is by no means pathbreaking, nor is the amount of polling particularly astounding. What is unusual about the Bush team's polling operation is the chasm between its words and actions. Never before has a White House engaged in such anti-polling rhetoric or built up such a buffer between the pollsters and the president. The placement of long-

time Bush loyalist Dowd at the RNC to coordinate the polling means that the pollsters do not have contact with the White House. Such unusual behavior reflects a broader tension between a determined attempt to avoid the mistakes of Bush the elder—especially the failure after the Persian Gulf War to consider the implications of a stagnant economy for the 1992 reelection campaign—and a continuous effort to shed the vestiges of the Clinton administration. The Bush team fully understands the value of polling, but the perceived overuse of polling within the Clinton administration has led to serious overcompensation, which in turn has bred secrecy and denial. All presidents are subjected to the pressures of the "permanent campaign." Information is integral to any successful presidency. Polling is part of a broader game of politics and policymaking. No one can dictate how presidents use polls, but denying the role of polls in the policy process is fruitless.

Kathryn Dunn Tenpas, a guest scholar in the Brookings Governance Studies program, is associate director of the University of Pennsylvania's Washington Semester Program.

The pros from Dover

By John Prados

President Bush surrounded himself with what should have been a crack team of national security experts. So what went wrong? Did their system just not work, or did they have the wrong agenda?

There is a hilarious scene in the movie *M*A*S*H* where two young doctors from a field hospital at the front in the Korean War travel to Japan and proceed to have their way with local commanders and the military bureaucracy. Arriving to carry out the heart operation for which they have been summoned, the doctors call themselves the "pros from Dover."

In the way life has of imitating art, the national security process of the Bush administration has been the province of its own fresh set of professionals. The result has not been hilarity but something else. With the Bush people having gotten the United States enmeshed in situations of grave concern throughout the globe, it is important to ask whether the American government is up to handling the job, not in terms of capabilities but of policy process.

In the American system of government, the top executive authority, the president, is assisted in areas of foreign affairs and military matters by the National Security Council (NSC). The council consists of the president, vice president, secretary of state, and defense secretary. The national security adviser to the president does not have a statutory role but is typically made a senior member of the council. The director of central intelligence and chairman of the Joint Chiefs of Staff sit as advisers to the group. The president is the king of policy hill, of course, and may arrange the NSC and its work at his whim, organizing and reorganizing whenever it suits him. NSC staff members under the na-

tional security adviser directly serve the president by coordinating the issues and providing the chief executive with their understanding of the options, pros, and cons.

Three years into the Bush administration, in spite of a host of developments in the national security realm, there has yet to be any serious inquiry into its methods of policymaking and their impact on American security. That inquiry is overdue.

The players

George W. Bush has certainly benefited from a dream team of senior advisers on his National Security Council. Bush chose carefully among people of conservative cast of mind to match his own, and while one may deplore the ideology of the crew, the president's right to be served by the officials he wants is unquestioned. Ideology notwithstanding, the Bush people have the right stuff—the credentials to actually be the pros from Dover—from the top people on the NSC to the second tier at the agencies and staff. On January 21, 2001, an observer could have said this administration was primed for success.

In terms of organization of the policy process, the Bush administration also started out on familiar ground. Presidents create their own policy machinery, and different presidents have approached the national security process in a variety of ways.[1]

The Carter administration designed a two-committee structure that has become almost the standard NSC organization for subsequent presidencies, including that of George W. Bush. In the current scheme, the president meeting with his senior advisers constitutes the National Security Council. Without the president, the rump NSC meets as the Principals Committee, chaired by the vice president or national security adviser. These groups focus on decisions. Below them is the Deputies Committee, a group chaired by the deputy national security adviser, which concentrates on implementing the president's decisions. Staff assistants attend as required. Teleconferencing and secure video links between various U.S. government centers have enabled greater flexibility in participation, but the essence of the system remains the same.

The most remarkable aspect of Bush's national security organization is the role of the vice president. Historically, vice presidents have had a relatively minor impact on national security decision making. Walter Mondale and Al Gore were more active under presidents Carter and Clinton, and Bush's father, George H. W. Bush, had an enhanced role under Ronald Reagan. In the current administration, however, Dick Cheney is of critical importance in virtually all aspects of national security policy. From the first moments of George W. Bush's presidency, Cheney functioned as the power behind the throne, privately advocating policies, then coming out in public with discourse designed to build constituencies for those same policies. He also became the official whom Bush tapped for the tough jobs—and the president's hatchet man. Cheney emerged as an assistant with an agenda more ample than that of his master. His role encouraging Bush to make war on Iraq has been so widely remarked it has virtually eclipsed his work early in the administration heading a presidential commission on energy policy, his views on military transformation, and the task force on federal-local antiterrorism cooperation that Bush appointed him to chair four months before the 9/11 attacks.

To match his policy role, the vice president has crafted a sort of mini-NSC staff among his White House retinue. Where Al Gore as vice president employed Leon Fuerth as his national security adviser (plus a couple of staff aides), and Bush's father, as vice president under Reagan, had a security staff of two professionals (plus aides), Cheney employs a national security staff of 15. The importance Cheney gives that staff is indicated by the fact that his own overall chief of staff, I. Lewis ("Scooter") Libby, serves simultaneously as the vice president's national security adviser. Early last year, at a key moment in the run-up to the Iraq war, Cheney's deputy national security adviser Eric Edelman was appointed U.S. ambassador to Turkey, another indication of the standing of the Cheney national security staff. Edelman was succeeded by Aaron Friedberg, a China expert and former director of policy planning on the Cheney staff. That the staff even had a policy-planning component demonstrates the quantum advance of the Cheney operation over the staff resources available to previous vice presidents.

Cheney himself is no stranger to national security issues, or to government for that matter. In his current incarnation he is mostly known for his role as chief executive of the Halliburton Corporation during the 1990s, but less noted is the extent to which Halliburton worked with and for the U.S. military. More to the point, Cheney was defense secretary—the job Donald Rumsfeld now has—during the first Bush administration, including the first Gulf War. Before that, Cheney served as White House chief of staff to President Gerald R. Ford from 1975 to early 1977 and deputy chief of staff 1974-1975. At the time, he was deputy to Donald Rumsfeld, whom President Ford subsequently sent to the Pentagon. In the Ford White House, Cheney worked on a number of national security issues, most notably advising Ford on how to handle the intelligence scandals of 1975. Cheney was an architect of the presidential commission on intelligence (the Rockefeller Commission) created by Ford in an effort to head off what became the Church and Pike Committee investigations. While the attempt proved unsuccessful, Cheney gained experience he put to work later as a member of Congress and then in his own Pentagon job.

Next to the vice president, the person closest to the Oval Office is the national security adviser. For George Bush this is Condoleezza Rice. Like Cheney—like a number of the pros from Dover—Rice is no stranger to the issues, or even to the national security staff. Retired Air Force Gen. Brent Scowcroft (who held the post of national security adviser for Gerald Ford, alongside Cheney and Rumsfeld) discovered Rice during the 1980s at the Aspen Institute. She was then a recently minted academic with a doctorate in international relations from the University of Denver. Her dissertation was on Soviet political control of the Czechoslovak armed forces. She taught at Stanford University. When Scowcroft did a second tour as national security adviser in the administration of President George H. W. Bush, he brought in "Condi," as she is familiarly known, as director for Soviet affairs. Rice was active on the NSC staff during the passing of the Cold War, when the Soviet Union collapsed, Germany reunified, and the old Yugoslavia disintegrated, leaving in its wake the Bosnian civil war.

Among the stories told about Rice that show her willingness to do whatever was necessary is one from the beginning of the first Gulf War, when the NSC staff person responsible for the Iraq-Kuwait region was Richard Haass. When the first President Bush needed a set of talking points for his initial public comment on the Iraqi invasion of Kuwait, Haass could not respond quickly enough because, unfamiliar with computers, he had to hunt and peck at the keyboard. Rice took over and typed out the paper even though Middle East matters were far from her own bailiwick. In 1991 Rice returned to Stanford as a teacher—but not for long. A month after receiving tenure in 1993 she was appointed provost of the university and held that key management position during difficult years. She quickly rallied to the presidential campaign of George W. Bush, however, and was its foreign policy director from early 1999. Rice not only coordinated Bush's issues papers but kept in line the "Vulcans"—the brain trust of national security experts who periodically assembled to give Bush the benefit of their accumulated wisdom. All the Vulcans (Richard Armitage, Robert Blackwill, Stephen J. Hadley, Richard Perle, Paul Wolfowitz, Dov Zakheim, Robert Zoellick) went on to important jobs or advisory posts in the Bush administration, and it was hardly surprising that Rice landed as national security adviser.

Stephen J. Hadley became Rice's deputy. The only other of the Vulcans to make the leap to work directly within the president's official family, Hadley regarded himself as a detail man. He too had a national security past, having served as assistant secretary of defense for policy under Dick Cheney in the first Bush administration. For those who worried about the influence of Cheney in the White House, Hadley's presence suggested that the vice president, in addition to having his own mini-NSC staff, simultaneously had a front man who was deputy director of the Rice staff itself.

As for the seniors, the members of the actual council of the NSC, they were pros from Dover, too. Donald Rumsfeld has already been mentioned. He is the only person to serve twice as defense secretary—in two different administrations, separated by more than two decades. Colin Powell, retired four-star army general, had been chairman of the Joint Chiefs of Staff during the first Gulf War, a deputy national security adviser to Ronald Reagan, and military assistant to Defense Secretary Caspar Weinberger. CIA Director George Tenet was held over from the Clinton administration and had worked on the Hill, at the White House, or at the CIA since the late 1980s. Their seconds, people like Wolfowitz and Armitage, had similar credentials.

The system

President George W. Bush enhanced the role of his national security adviser by endowing her with cabinet rank. But formal organization of the system remained in limbo until mid-February 2001, when Bush issued his National Security Presidential Directive (NSPD) 1. That document ended speculation as to Vice President Cheney's role—a number of observers had anticipated that Cheney's deep interest in these matters would be reflected by his being made chairman of the Principals Committee.[2] This did not happen. Instead Rice, as national security adviser, would chair the group. What did happen was more significant: By avoiding the chairmanship of the Principals Committee, Cheney left himself free to be an advocate at national security meetings rather than having any responsibility to ensure that all views be aired.

The other significant thing about NSPD 1 was its lateness in the cycle. Most new administrations enter office determined to hit the ground running and typically put out their directives on NSC machinery their first day in office. Bush did not get around to this business for almost a month. By then there had already been two meetings of the Principals Committee. Even the appointments of Condi Rice and the top NSC staffers date from January 22, not the day after the inauguration. The implication is that, at least at the outset, Bush did not consider the national security agenda his top priority.

In terms of size and depth, the Rice NSC staff diminished from the standard under the Clinton administration, but this had more to do with notions of streamlining than with some idea of reducing the importance of national security. Rice cut the staff as a whole by about a third while reducing the number of professional staff from 70 to about 60. She eliminated the legislative affairs and communications offices, limited the staff to a single speechwriter and press spokesperson, and recast some functions. Most importantly, the Russian office merged into a single new desk that included all of Europe, the Balkans, and the former Soviet republics. The Asian affairs office reabsorbed Southeast Asia, which had been assigned to another regional unit in the Clinton White House. North Africa and the Middle East were combined as well. Africa and the Western Hemisphere completed the list of regional offices on the NSC staff. There were also functional specializations, including offices for defense policy and arms control and for intelligence.

Clinton had had an NSC staff unit to supervise nonproliferation and export controls. Under Rice this was reconceptualized as "Nonproliferation Strategy, Counterproliferation, and Homeland Defense." This is instructive for it served as a device to take the ballistic missile defense issue out of the defense policy basket and put it in the much more ideological framework of "homeland defense." That in turn became awkward after the September 11, 2001, attacks, when an Office of Homeland Defense was created at the White House as a parallel to the NSC staff, but in which "homeland defense" held a very different meaning.

The Clinton NSC staff also had a unit covering "transnational threats" and put terrorism at the top of that list. Clinton appointed Richard Clarke, a hard-headed advocate for proactive measures against those threats, to head the unit. Clarke stayed over into the Bush presidency even though, as a press account put it several weeks into the new era, what to do with the transnational threats office was "still up in the air."[3] It is here that the real story begins.

Bush and terrorism

Bill Clinton's last national security adviser, Samuel ("Sandy") Berger, held a number of briefings for Condoleezza Rice and the incoming national security staff as part of the transition from the Clinton to Bush presidencies. Every NSC staff office had been directed to compile a report and present its view of America's strengths and weaknesses to the new crowd. According to an account that has been disputed, the only one of these sessions Sandy Berger personally attended was that which concerned terrorism (Rice has said through a spokesperson that she recalls no briefing at which Berger was present).[4] Berger had left by the time Richard Clarke made the main presentation, but there can be no doubt that the briefing highlighted the need to act on terrorism.

Berger clearly had terrorism on his plate. The question is, did Rice? Berger would tell the joint House-Senate committee investigating the September 11, 2001, attacks that he had convened the Principals Committee every day for a month in an effort to stave off terrorist attacks timed around the millennium celebrations.[5] He quoted himself as telling Rice, "You're going to spend more time during your four years on terrorism generally and Al Qaeda specifically than any [other] issue."[6] For her part, Rice had numerous questions for Clarke, who was asked to prepare a paper on steps against Al Qaeda. Clarke not only had the paper on Stephen J. Hadley's desk within days of the inauguration, he saw the opportunity to get the new president to sign on to an action plan against terrorism, and his paper amounted to an outline. So far, so good. But Clarke's plan then sat gathering dust for weeks.

In speeches, articles, and conversations during the 2000 campaign, Rice had written and spoken of the need in national security to separate the marginal issues from what was truly important.

What Rice and the Bush team made centrally important in the weeks and months after entering office was not terrorism but changing the U.S.-European relationship. The troubles with "Old Europe" that seem so intractable in the wake of the Iraqi war did not just happen coincidentally in 2002-2003. They were prefigured in the very stuff of the NSC staff reorganization, when the Russian and Western European offices were consolidated. Publicly the Bush administration sought to end any notion of a special relationship with Russia, the former Soviet Union, cutting back funding for special cooperative programs designed to help secure Russian nuclear weapons and expertise, abrogating the Anti-Ballistic Missile (ABM) Treaty, and in a variety of other ways. The move on the ABM Treaty also came as a shock to Old Europe, as did Bush's rejection of the Kyoto protocols on environmental action, and the equally sudden U.S. coyness on formation of an international criminal court. When President Bush made his first visit to Europe in June 2001, these issues were the main stuff of American diplomacy.

On the overarching front of defense policy, the maneuver on the ABM Treaty is itself indicative of the Bush administration's goals. Defense Secretary Rumsfeld used the word "transformation" so many times that it became enshrined as the descriptive term for Bush defense policy. Ballistic missile defenses were a key component, and indeed President Bush chose to deploy a technically immature defense system just to ensure that the United States had committed itself to this program. Rumsfeld's talk about space platforms,

his predilection for air force programs, and his fight with the army over its future were the stuff of the transformation.

While circumstances dictated that an action plan on terrorism needed to move to the top of policy hill, the government was preoccupied with anything but that issue. It was only after Bush intervened that anything happened at all. One spring morning, following the departure of CIA briefers who had just given him news in the President's Daily Brief (PDB) of a manhunt for one particular terrorist, Bush complained to Rice: "I'm tired of swatting at flies. . . . I want to play offense, I want to take the fight to the terrorists," Bush said.[7] Rice took the implication that President Bush wanted a plan to attack the terrorists. When she asked the NSC staff how they could put something together, Richard Clarke had his original plan ready.

By late April 2001 the NSC was ready for a policy review on terrorism. After, we are told, six weeks of preliminary sessions, the Deputies Committee met on April 30 to consider an outline plan that Clarke presented. Stephen J. Hadley chaired the meeting, which included Scooter Libby (for Cheney), Richard Armitage (for Powell), Paul Wolfowitz (for Rumsfeld), and John McLaughlin (for Tenet). Here was a case in which the State Department favored going ahead but the CIA proved more cautious. Rather than initiating action, the Deputies Committee called for not one but three policy reviews, one on Al Qaeda, a second on Pakistani internal politics, and a third on the India-Pakistan problem.[8] According to Deputy National Security Adviser Hadley, "the goal was to move beyond the policy of containment, criminal prosecution, and limited retaliation for specific attacks, toward attempting to 'roll back' Al Qaeda."[9] The device of adding extra policy reviews inevitably slowed action, however. As Hadley noted in his response to 9/11 congressional investigators quoted above, between May and July there would be four successive meetings of the NSC Deputies Committee "directly related to the regional issues that had to be resolved in order to adopt a more aggressive strategy."[10] The last one of these sessions discussed the text of a draft presidential directive on July 16.

Meanwhile, on May 8 President Bush created a new unit to focus on terrorism within the Federal Emergency Management Agency, and a new interagency board to consider terrorism issues. He put Cheney in charge of that operation. This was the only actual action President Bush took before September 11, 2001, and it was not about rollback. Cheney's mandate was merely to study preparedness for homeland defense and make recommendations by October.

A second group, the Counterterrorism Security Group (CSG), part of the NSC interagency machinery, was chaired by Richard Clarke. It would be the CSG, not the vice president, that acted, or more properly, reacted. Beginning in March, U.S. intelligence and military sources received a series of reports indicating possible terrorist attacks. First came a report that Al Qaeda operatives in Canada might attack the United States in April.

In April, one source made a rather suggestive speculation that Osama bin Laden was interested in commercial aircraft pilots as terrorists for "spectacular and traumatic" attacks. In May came a report that Al Qaeda supporters were planning to enter the United States to carry out some operation using high explosives. There was also a Pentagon report that seven key suspected terrorists had begun moving toward Canada, the United States, and Britain. Between May and July, the National Security Agency intercepted no fewer than 33 communications suggesting an attack, including one evaluated at the time as an order to execute the plan. In June, the CIA Counterterrorism Center received information that key operatives were disappearing from view. At the end of June, Clarke convened the CSG, and by July 5 there were sufficient alarms to warrant a meeting among Rice, Clarke, and presidential chief of staff Andrew Card.

By then the intelligence scene had shifted and threats seemed centered on the American embassies in Rome, Paris, or Ankara. The CSG met again on July 6, and from then through the end of August, Clarke kept up meetings two or three times a week.[11]

In short, numerous disturbing intelligence reports came in over a period of months *after* President Bush had declared he wanted to go after terrorists, a period of time during which nothing happened with the U.S. government's planning for a rollback of Al Qaeda. Such Bush administration actions that occurred consisted entirely of putting certain selected military forces on precautionary (and defensive) alerts, or issuing warnings to the airlines.

Bush left for Crawford, Texas, and summer vacation on August 4. Two days later, he was given a fresh intelligence report—the PDB again mentioned terrorist attack. As characterized by national security adviser Rice, this PDB "was an analytic report that talked about [Osama bin Laden's] methods of operation, talked about what he had done historically in 1997, in 1998. It mentioned hijacking, but hijacking in the traditional sense, and in a sense said that the most important and most likely thing was that he would take over an airliner holding passengers [and then make demands]."[12]

Much has been speculated about what Bush knew about the Al Qaeda terrorist threat, especially after the leak of the existence of the August 6, 2001 PDB and the report that it had mentioned aircraft hijacking. But the most important thing about the intelligence reports is something we already know: Neither the August 6 PDB, any of the other reports, nor the daily flurry of NSC staff activity on terrorist warnings moved Bush to demand the action plan he had supposedly called for in the spring, to ask that its preparation be accelerated, or to take any other action whatsoever. There is also no indication that Rice, whose job it was to be aware of these alarming reports, made any move to remind the president of his interest in the matter.

Absent presidential initiative, in fact, the plan to roll back Al Qaeda sat dormant six full weeks after mid-July 2001. The draft National Security Presidential Directive was finally considered by the NSC Principals Committee on September 4, and the group recommended that President Bush approve it. When Rice, or others, claim that an approved directive was on Bush's desk on 9/11, they exaggerate. The president had approved nothing. He had received a recommendation to sign a directive that had finally worked its way up through the bureaucracy.

The response of the Bush administration after 9/11 was rather different. When investigators raised questions regarding what Bush had done about intelligence he had received before the attacks, Vice President Cheney mounted a frontal assault on the 9/11 investigators, alleging they were responsible for the appearance in the press of reports of National Security Agency intercepts regarding the attacks, intercepts that White House spokesmen had themselves mentioned in press briefings in the days immediately after 9/11. Cheney demanded and got an FBI investigation of the investigators.

Ever since the 9/11 attacks the Bush White House has taken pains to avoid the revelation of any of the intelligence material provided to the president. The White House denied this material to the joint congressional committee investigating 9/11. It has also stonewalled the national commission inquiring into the attacks. The official rationale has been that no one should ever see the reports provided to a president.

That is not a legitimate declassification policy. A number of PDBs have been declassified and are in the public domain, including ones sent to President John F. Kennedy during the Cuban Missile Crisis and to President Lyndon Johnson during the Vietnam war. Excerpts of PDBs have been leaked on other occasions, not only the one to Bush for August 6, 2001, but one to his father before the Gulf War of 1990-1991. Our democracy has not been shaken by these revelations. And declassification is an ultimate step; the issue here is whether official inquiries operating under full security safeguards are entitled to view documents that are material to their investigations. The real reason to shield them is political: They would reveal the extent of warnings to George W. Bush in the face of which he stood immobile.

The November 2003 Bush compromise with the National Commission on Terrorist Attacks Upon the United States is designed to protect the president while appearing to cooperate. Under the arrangement, the White House will provide edited texts of some PDBs to a team of four (out of ten) commissioners, who will be permitted to take notes that can then be edited by the White House. Two commissioners will be permitted to review all the PDBs and ask that the White House make available additional ones. This formula will be cumbersome in practice and will not ensure public confidence in the 9/11 investigation.

Fast forward

The truth about 9/11 is one of two things. Either Rice's NSC machinery did not work, or else it worked perfectly to ensure that what Bush and his cohorts considered a marginal issue like terrorism did not clutter up the schedule of a president intent on another agenda—transforming America's relationships with traditional allies and former enemies. Either of these conclusions is disturbing. Once the Iraq war is factored into the equation the outlook is even more troubling. Again the NSC machinery operated in a fashion to prevent important objections or alternative policies from coming to the fore. U.S. policy going into the Iraq war was indifferent to alliance politics, to failures to attain needed U.N. approval, to U.S. military objections that the war plan was inadequate, to intelligence warnings that war would be succeeded by guerrilla resistance, to global public opinion, to international disarmament monitors who failed to turn up evidence supporting the Bush rationale for war, and more.[13] Dick Cheney served as an important driver of the policy that would be implemented. Condoleezza Rice became one of its most prominent public advocates; indeed Rice has served far more frequently as a public proponent than any of her national security adviser predecessors. Even Stephen J. Hadley, in the infamous manipulation of speech texts now encapsulated as the "Sixteen Words" controversy, made key contributions to a course of action that became an international and domestic political disaster.

The gang who produced all this were pros from Dover, using a tried and tested organizational structure for national security machinery. How could it be? Hubris, wishful thinking, incorrect assessment of the major issue facing the United States, wrongheaded notions of imposing change on the world—each played a role. Yet no heads have rolled. President George W. Bush promised to bring a new standard of accountability to Washington. In *that* he has succeeded. The picture is not a pretty one.

1. An overview of presidents' practices is in John Prados, *Keepers of the Keys: A History of the National Security Council from Truman to Bush* (New York: William Morrow, 1991). The Bush in the title is, however, George H. W. Bush, the current president's father. There is no good study of the NSC during the Clinton years.
2. Jane Perlez, "Directive Says Rice, Bush Aide, Won't Be Upstaged by Cheney," *New York Times,* Feb. 16, 2001, p. A10.
3. Karen DeYoung and Steven Mufson, "A Leaner and Less Visible NSC," *Washington Post,* Feb. 10, 2001, p. A6.
4. Massimo Calabresi et al., "They Had a Plan: Special Report: The Secret History," *Time,* August 12, 2002, p. 30.
5. Samuel R. Berger, "Joint Intelligence Committee Testimony," prepared text (copy in author's possession), September 19, 2002, pp. 4-5.
6. Daniel Benjamin and Steven Simon, *The Age of Sacred Terror,* p. 328.
7. Barton Gellman, "A Strategy's Cautious Evolution: Before September 11 the Bush Anti-Terror Effort Was Mostly Ambition," *Washington Post,* Jan. 20, 2002, p. A1.
8. The main sources for this account are the Barton Gellman story cited in note 7 and the study by a large team of *Time* correspondents cited in note 4.
9. United States Congress (107th Congress, 2nd Session). Senate Select Committee on Intelligence and House Permanent Select Committee on Intelligence, *Report: Joint Inquiry Into Intelligence Community Activities Before and After the Terrorist Attacks of September 11, 2001,* hereafter cited as 9/11 Congressional Report (Washington: Government Printing Office, 2003), p. 235. White House sources deny that Richard Clarke's original January memorandum had featured an actual "plan," Calabresi et al. (cited in footnote 4) note that Slide 14 of Clarke's presidential transition briefing on dealing with Al Qaeda included the words "rollback" and "breakup." Although dated December 2002, disputes with the Bush White House over secrecy of material on some of the very subjects under discussion here delayed the actual appearance of this report for many months, into the fall of 2003.
10. Ibid.
11. The data on intelligence indications is from the 9/11 Congressional Report, pp. 201-205; the material on Counterterrorism Security Group activities is from Condoleezza Rice at her news conference of May 16, 2002 as cited in "Excerpt From National Security Adviser's Statement," *New York Times,* May 17, 2002, p. A22.
12. Rice news conference, May 16, 2002.
13. This subject cannot be treated at length here, but see John Prados, *Hoodwinked* (forthcoming).

The early note text: Clinton-era NSC staffer Daniel Benjamin, who worked with Richard Clarke in the transnational threats office, confirms both the briefing session itself and the presence of Berger. See Daniel Benjamin and Steven Simon, *The Age of Sacred Terror* (New York: Random House, 2002), p. 328.

John Prados is an analyst with the National Security Archive in Washington, D.C. His current books are *Hoodwinked* (forthcoming), on America headed into the Iraq war, and *White House Tapes* (2003), a selection of recordings that show American presidents at work on key issues of their times.

UNIT 6

U.S. International Economic Strategy

Unit Selections

Key Points to Consider

- Which type of international system, global free trade or regional trading blocs, is in America's national interest? Explain.

- Which country is the more important trading partner for the United States—Japan, Europe, or Mexico? Defend your answer.

- Select a country in need of foreign aid. What type of foreign aid strategy should the United States pursue toward it? How does this compare with current U.S. foreign aid programs?

- Design an economic strategy for ensuring that the United States has an adequate supply of oil and other natural resources in the future.

- Put together an eight-person delegation to the next round of WTO trade talks. Defend your selections. What negotiating instructions would you give them?

- What measures would you use to create a ranking of how powerful a country's economy is? How high would the United States rank?

Student Website

www.mhcls.com/online

Internet References

Further information regarding these websites may be found in this book's preface or online.

International Monetary Fund (IMF)
http://www.imf.org
United States Agency for International Development
http://www.info.usaid.gov
United States Trade Representative
http://www.ustr.gov
World Bank
http://www.worldbank.org

As in so many areas of American foreign policy, the selection of U.S. international economic strategies during the cold war seems to have been a rather straightforward process and the accompanying policy debates fairly minor compared to the situation that exists today. At the most fundamental level, it was taken for granted that the American economy would best be served by the existence of a global free-trade system. To that end, international organizations were set up whose collective task was to oversee the operation of the postwar international economic order. Foremost among them were the General Agreement on Tariffs and Trade (GATT), the International Monetary Fund (IMF), and the International Bank for Reconstruction and Development (the World Bank). It was also widely accepted that many states would not be able to resist pressure from the Soviet Union or from domestic communist parties, due to the weak state of their economies and military establishments. Thus, containing communism would require foreign aid programs designed to transfer American economic and military expertise, goods and services, and financial resources to key states.

Events of the 1960s and 1970s shook the international economic system at its political and economic foundations. There followed a period of more than 20 years in which the international economic system was managed through a series of ad hoc responses to crises and the continued inability of foreign aid

programs to produce real growth in the less developed world. U.S. international economic policy during this period was often characterized as one of "benign neglect."

The adequacy of this response is questioned today. Policy makers and citizens today see the international economic order as highly volatile and perhaps even threatening. The focal point of their concern is with the process of globalization. The IMF defines globalization as the growing economic interdependence of countries through the increasing volume and variety of border transactions in goods, services, and capital flows. Most fundamentally, globalization is change inducing because of its ability to link activities around the world. From a policy perspective, the most significant aspect of globalization is that the international economic activity has become so large, rapid, and dense that it has outstripped the ability to governments and international organizations to manage it. Susan Strange described the situation as one of "casino capitalism" because, just as in a casino, a large element of luck determines the success or failure of international economic policies.

It is against this very changed backdrop of globalization that American international economic policy is now made and carried out. We can identify at least three major dimensions to American international economic foreign policy. They are trade, monetary policy, and foreign aid. Subsumed within them are a host of challenging issues and trade-offs such as economic growth, worker's rights, environmental protection, and global equity. The articles in this section highlight important issues encompassing questions in these areas.

The first reading, "America's Sticky Power," identifies economic power as a unique instrument of foreign policy having advantages that neither soft power nor military power possess. It attracts others to the U.S. voluntarily and then entraps them in a web of relations from which they cannot escape easily or without great cost. "Global Petro-Politics" presents a critical assessment of the American dependence on foreign oil. The third reading, "Africa and the Battle over Agricultural Protection," asserts that the issue of fairness in agricultural trade is for this decade what the problem of debt relief was for the 1990s.

America's STICKY Power

U.S. military force and cultural appeal have kept the United States at the top of the global order. But the hegemon cannot live on guns and Hollywood alone. U.S. economic policies and institutions act as "sticky power," attracting other countries to the U.S. system and then trapping them in it. Sticky power can help stabilize Iraq, bring rule of law to Russia, and prevent armed conflict between the United States and China.

By Walter Russell Mead

Since its earliest years, the United States has behaved as a global power. Not always capable of dispatching great fleets and mighty armies to every corner of the planet, the United States has nonetheless invariably kept one eye on the evolution of the global system, and the U.S. military has long served internationally. The United States has not always boasted the world's largest or most influential economy, but the country has always regarded trade in global terms, generally nudging the world toward economic integration. U.S. ideological impulses have also been global. The poet Ralph Waldo Emerson wrote of the first shot fired in the American Revolution as "the shot heard 'round the world," and Americans have always thought that their religious and political values should prevail around the globe.

Historically, security threats and trade interests compelled Americans to think globally. The British sailed across the Atlantic to burn Washington, D.C.; the Japanese flew from carriers in the Pacific to bomb Pearl Harbor. Trade with Asia and Europe, as well as within the Western Hemisphere, has always been vital to U.S. prosperity. U.S. President Thomas Jefferson sent the Navy to the Mediterranean to fight against the Barbary pirates to safeguard U.S. trade in 1801. Commodore Matthew Perry opened up Japan in

the 1850s partly to assure decent treatment for survivors of sunken U.S. whaling ships that washed up on Japanese shores. And the last shots in the U.S. Civil War were fired from a Confederate commerce raider attacking Union shipping in the remote waters of the Arctic Ocean.

The rise of the United States to superpower status followed from this global outlook. In the 20th century, as the British system of empire and commerce weakened and fell, U.S. foreign-policymakers faced three possible choices: prop up the British Empire, ignore the problem and let the rest of the world go about its business, or replace Britain and take on the dirty job of enforcing a world order. Between the onset of World War I and the beginning of the Cold War, the United States tried all three, ultimately taking Britain's place as the gyroscope of world order.

However, the Americans were replacing the British at a moment when the rules of the game were changing forever. The United States could not become just another empire or great power playing the old games of dominance with rivals and allies. Such competition led to war, and war between great powers was no longer an acceptable part of the international system. No, the United States was going to have to attempt something that no other nation had ever accomplished, something that many theorists of international relations would swear was impossible. The United States needed to build a system that could end thousands of years of great power conflicts, constructing a framework of power that would bring enduring peace to the whole world—repeating globally what ancient Egypt, China, and Rome had each accomplished on a regional basis.

To complicate the task a bit more, the new hegemon would not be able to use some of the methods available to the Romans and others. Reducing the world's countries and civilizations to tributary provinces was beyond any military power the United States could or would bring to bear. The United States would have to develop a new way for sovereign states to coexist in a world of weapons of mass destruction and of prickly rivalries among religions, races, cultures, and states.

In his 2002 book, *The Paradox of American Power: Why the World's Only Superpower Can't Go It Alone*, Harvard University political scientist Joseph S. Nye Jr. discusses the varieties of power that the United States can deploy as it builds its world order. Nye focuses on two types of power: hard and soft. In his analysis, hard power is military or economic force that coerces others to follow a particular course of action. By contrast, soft power—cultural power, the power of example, the power of ideas and ideals— works more subtly; it makes others want what you want. Soft power upholds the U.S. world order because it influences others to like the U.S. system and support it of their own free will [see sidebar: A Sticky History Lesson].

Nye's insights on soft power have attracted significant attention and will continue to have an important role in U.S. policy debates. But the distinction Nye suggests between two types of hard power—military and economic power—has received less consideration than it deserves. Traditional military power can usefully be called sharp power; those resisting it will feel bayonets pushing and prodding them in the direction they must go. This power is the foundation of the U.S. system. Economic power can be thought of as sticky power, which comprises a set of economic institutions and policies that attracts others toward U.S. influence and then traps them in it. Together with soft power (the values, ideas, habits, and politics inherent in the system), sharp and sticky power sustain U.S. hegemony and make something as artificial and historically arbitrary as the U.S.-led global system appear desirable, inevitable, and permanent.

SHARP POWER

Sharp power is a very practical and unsentimental thing. U.S. military policy follows rules that would have been understandable to the Hittites or the Roman Empire. Indeed, the U.S. military is the institution whose command structure is most like that of Old World monarchies—the president, after consultation with the Joint Chiefs, issues orders, which the military, in turn, obeys.

> ## Like Samson in the temple of the Philistines, a collapsing U.S. economy would inflict enormous, unacceptable damage on the rest of the world.

Of course, security starts at home, and since the 1823 proclamation of the Monroe Doctrine, the cardinal principle of U.S. security policy has been to keep European and Asian powers out of the Western Hemisphere. There would be no intriguing great powers, no intercontinental alliances, and, as the United States became stronger, no European or Asian military bases from Point Barrow, Alaska, to the tip of Cape Horn, Chile.

The makers of U.S. security policy also have focused on the world's sea and air lanes. During peacetime, such lanes are vital to the prosperity of the United States and its allies; in wartime, the United States must control the sea and air lanes to support U.S. allies and supply military forces on other continents. Britain was almost defeated by Germany's U-boats in World War I and II; in today's world of integrated markets, any interruption of trade flows through such lanes would be catastrophic.

Finally (and fatefully), the United States considers the Middle East an area of vital concern. From a U.S. perspective, two potential dangers lurk in the Middle East. First, some outside power, such as the Soviet Union during the Cold War, can try to control Middle Eastern oil or at least interfere with secure supplies for the United States and its allies. Second, one country in the Middle East could take over the region and try to do the same thing. Egypt, Iran, and, most recently, Iraq have all tried and thanks largely to U.S. policy—have all failed. For all its novel dangers, today's efforts by al Qaeda leader Osama bin Laden and his followers to create a theocratic power in the region that could control oil resources and extend dictatorial power throughout the Islamic world resembles other threats that the United States has faced in this region during the last 60 years.

As part of its sharp-power strategy to address these priorities, the United States maintains a system of alliances and bases intended to promote stability in Asia, Europe, and the Middle East. Overall, as of the end of September 2003, the United States had just over 250,000 uniformed military members stationed outside its frontiers (not counting those involved in Operation Iraqi Freedom); around 43 percent were stationed on NATO territory and approximately 32 percent in Japan and South Korea. Additionally, the United States has the ability to transport significant forces to these theaters and to the Middle East should tensions rise, and it preserves the ability to control the sea lanes and air corridors necessary to the security of its forward bases. More-over, the United States maintains the world's largest intelligence and electronic surveillance organizations. Estimated to exceed $30 billion in 2003, the U.S. intelligence budget is larger than the individual military budgets of Saudi Arabia, Syria, and North Korea.

Over time, U.S. strategic thinking has shifted toward overwhelming military superiority as the surest foundation for national security. That is partly for the obvious reasons of greater security, but it is partly also because supremacy can be an important deterrent. Establishing an overwhelming military supremacy might not only deter potential enemies from military attack; it might also discourage other powers from trying to match the U.S. buildup. In the long run, advocates maintain, this strategy could be cheaper and safer than staying just a nose in front of the pack.

STICKY POWER

Economic, or sticky, power is different from both sharp and soft power—it is based neither on military compulsion nor on simple coincidence of wills. Consider the carnivorous sundew plant, which attracts its prey with a kind of soft power, a pleasing scent that lures insects toward its sap. But once the victim has touched the sap, it is stuck; it can't get away. That is sticky power; that is how economic power works.

Sticky power has a long history. Both Britain and the United States built global economic systems that attracted other countries. Britain's attracted the United States into participating in the British system of trade and investment during the 19th century. The London financial markets provided investment capital that enabled U.S. industries to grow, while Americans benefited from trading freely throughout the British Empire. Yet, U.S. global trade was in some sense hostage to the British Navy—the United States could trade with the world as long as it had Britain's friendship, but an interruption in that friendship would mean financial collapse. Therefore, a strong lobby against war with Britain always existed in the United States. Trade-dependent New England almost seceded from the United States during the War of 1812, and at every crisis in Anglo-American relations for the next century, England could count on a strong lobby of merchants and bankers who would be ruined by war between the two English-speaking powers.

The world economy that the United States set out to lead after World War II had fallen far from the peak of integration reached under British leadership. The two world wars and the Depression ripped the delicate webs that had sustained the earlier system. In the Cold War years, as it struggled to rebuild and improve upon the Old World system, the United States had to change both the monetary base and the legal and political framework of the world's economic system.

The United States built its sticky power on two foundations: an international monetary system and free trade. The Bretton Woods agreements of 1944 made the U.S. dollar

the world's central currency, and while the dollar was still linked to gold at least in theory for another generation, the U.S. Federal Reserve could increase the supply of dollars in response to economic needs. The result for almost 30 years was the magic combination of an expanding monetary base with price stability. These conditions helped produce the economic miracle that transformed living standards in the advanced West and in Japan. The collapse of the Bretton Woods system in 1973 ushered in a global economic crisis, but, by the 1980s, the system was functioning almost as well as ever with a new regime of floating exchange rates in which the U.S. dollar remained critical.

The progress toward free trade and economic integration represents one of the great unheralded triumphs of U.S. foreign policy in the 20th century. Legal and economic experts, largely from the United States or educated in U.S. universities, helped poor countries build the institutions that could reassure foreign investors, even as developing countries increasingly relied on state-directed planning and investment to jump-start their economies. Instead of gunboats, international financial institutions sent bankers and consultants around the world.

Behind all this activity was the United States' willingness to open its markets—even on a nonreciprocal basis—to exports from Europe, Japan, and poor nations. This policy, part of the overall strategy of containing communism, helped consolidate support around the world for the U.S. system. The role of the dollar as a global reserve currency, along with the expansionary bias of U.S. fiscal and monetary authorities, facilitated what became known as the "locomotive of the global economy" and the "consumer of last resort. " U.S. trade deficits stimulated production and consumption in the rest of the world, increasing the prosperity of other countries and their willingness to participate in the U.S.-led global economy.

Opening domestic markets to foreign competitors remained (and remains) one of the most controversial elements in U.S. foreign policy during the Cold War. U.S. workers and industries facing foreign competition bitterly opposed such openings. Others worried about the long-term consequences of the trade deficits that transformed the United States into a net international debtor during the 1980s. Since the Eisenhower administration, predictions of imminent crises (in the value of the dollar, domestic interest rates, or both) have surfaced whenever U.S. reliance on foreign lending has grown, but those negative consequences have yet to materialize. The result has been more like a repetition on a global scale of the conversion of financial debt to political strength pioneered by the founders of the Bank of England in 1694 and repeated a century later when the United States assumed the debt of the 13 colonies.

In both of those cases, the stock of debt was purchased by the rich and the powerful, who then acquired an interest in the stability of the government that guaranteed the value of the debt. Wealthy Englishmen opposed the restoration of the Stuarts to the throne because they feared it would undermine the value of their holdings in the Bank of England.

A Sticky History Lesson

Germany's experience in World War I shows how "sticky power"—the power of one nation's economic institutions and policies—can act as a weapon. During the long years of peace before the war, Germany was drawn into the British-led world trading system, and its economy became more and more trade-dependent. Local industries depended on imported raw materials. German manufacturers depended on foreign markets. Germany imported wheat and beef from the Americas, where the vast and fertile plains of the United States and the pampas of South America produced food much more cheaply than German agriculture could do at home. By 1910, such economic interdependence was so great that many, including Norman Angell, author of *The Great Illusion*, thought that wars had become so ruinously expensive that the age of warfare was over.

Not quite. Sticky power failed to keep World War I from breaking out, but it was vital to Britain's victory. Once the war started, Britain cut off the world trade Germany had grown to depend upon, while, thanks to Britain's Royal Navy, the British and their allies continued to enjoy access to the rest of the world's goods. Shortages of basic materials and foods dogged Germany all during the war. By the winter of 1916-17, the Germans were seriously hungry. Meanwhile, hoping to even the odds, Germany tried to cut the Allies off from world markets with the U-boat campaigns in the North Atlantic. That move brought the United States into the war at a time when nothing else could have saved the Allied cause.

Finally, in the fall of 1918, morale in the German armed forces and among civilians collapsed, fueled in part by the shortages. These conditions, not military defeat, forced the German leadership to ask for an armistice. Sticky power was Britain's greatest weapon in World War I. It may very well be the United States' greatest weapon in the 21st century.

—W.R.M.

Likewise, the propertied elites of the 13 colonies came to support the stability and strength of the new U.S. Constitution because the value of their bonds rose and fell with the strength of the national government.

Similarly, in the last 60 years, as foreigners have acquired a greater value in the United States—government and private bonds, direct and portfolio private investments—more and more of them have acquired an interest in maintaining the strength of the U.S.-led system. A collapse of the U.S. economy and the ruin of the dollar would do more than dent the prosperity of the United States. Without their best customer, countries including China and Japan would fall into depressions. The financial strength of every country would be severely shaken should the United States collapse. Under those circumstances, debt becomes a strength, not a weakness, and other countries fear to break with the United States because they need its market and own its securities. Of course, pressed too far, a large national debt can turn from a source of strength to a crippling liability, and the United States must continue to justify other countries' faith by maintaining its long-term record of meeting its financial obligations. But, like Samson in the temple of the Philistines, a collapsing U.S. economy would

inflict enormous, unacceptable damage on the rest of the world. That is sticky power with a vengeance.

THE SUM OF ALL POWERS?

The United States' global economic might is therefore not simply, to use Nye's formulations, hard power that compels others or soft power that attracts the rest of the world. Certainly, the U.S. economic system provides the United States with the prosperity needed to underwrite its security strategy, but it also encourages other countries to accept U.S. leadership. U.S. economic might is sticky power.

How will sticky power help the United States address today's challenges? One pressing need is to ensure that Iraq's econome reconstruction integrates the nation more firmly in the global economy. Countries with open economies develop powerful trade-oriented businesses; the leaders of these businesses can promote economic policies that respect property rights, democracy, and the rule of law. Such leaders also lobby governments to avoid the isolation that characterized Iraq and Libya under economic sanctions. And looking beyond Iraq, the allure of access to Western capital and global markets is one of the few forces protecting the rule of law from even further erosion in Russia.

China's rise to global prominence will offer a key test case for sticky power. As China develops economically, it should gain wealth that could support a military rivaling that of the United States; China is also gaining political influence in the world. Some analysts in both China and the United States believe that the laws of history mean that Chinese power will someday clash with the reigning U.S. power.

Sticky power offers a way out. China benefits from participating in the U.S. economic system and integrating itself into the global economy. Between 1970 and 2003, China's gross domestic product grew from an estimated $106 billion to more than $1.3 trillion. By 2003, an estimated $450 billion of foreign money had flowed into the Chinese economy. Moreover, China is becoming increasingly dependent on both imports and exports to keep its economy (and its military machine) going. Hostilities between the United States and China would cripple China's industry, and cut off supplies of oil and other key commodities.

Sticky power works both ways, though. If China cannot afford war with the United States, the United States will have an increasingly hard time breaking off commercial relations with China. In an era of weapons of mass destruction, this mutual dependence is probably good for both sides. Sticky power did not prevent World War I, but economic interdependence runs deeper now; as a result, the "inevitable" U.S.-Chinese conflict is less likely to occur.

Sticky power, then, is important to U.S. hegemony for two reasons: It helps prevent war, and, if war comes, it helps the United States win. But to exercise power in the real world, the pieces must go back together. Sharp, sticky, and soft power work together to sustain U.S. hegemony. Today, even as the United States' sharp and sticky power

——————[Want to Know More?]——————

Joseph S. Nye Jr. introduced the concept of soft power in his seminal eassy "Soft Power" (FOREIGN POLICY, Fall 1990). His more recent *The Paradox of American Power: Why The World's Only Superpower Can't Go It Alone* (New York: Oxford University Press, 2002) is the best and most original book on how the United States can deploy different kinds of power.

The ancient Greek historian Thucydides is often credited with developing the basic doctrines of foreign policy realism in his classic *The History of the Peloponnesian War* (New York: Harper & brothers, 1836), but soft power played a major role in his account of the war between Athens and Sparta. Reading premodern histories, such as Livy's *History of Rome* (New York: Harper & brothers, 1958), with Nye's distinctions in mind will provide food for thought aobut the different forms that power can take.

For insight on the tangled relationship between Britian and the United States and U.S. global interests during the 18th and 19th century, see Walter Russell Mead's *Special Providence: American Foreign Policy and How It Changed the World* (New York: Knofp, 2001). Robert Jervis explains how the United States has always defined its interests globablly in **"The Comulsive Empire"** (FOREIGN POLICY, July/August 2003). Robert Skidelsky's *John Maynard Keynes: Fighting for Freedom, 1937-1946* (New York: Viking Press, 2001) describes the economic concerns of British and U.S. authorities as they looked to build a post-World War II global financial system. Charles P. Kindleberger's classic *A Financial History of Western Europe* (Boston: Allen & Unwin, 1984) illuninates Bretton Woods and a wide range of sticky-power issues. See also Carol C. Alderman's **"The Privatization of Foreign Aid: Reassessing National Largesse"** (*Foreign Affairs,* November/December 2003).

For links to relevant Web sites, access to the *FP* Archive, and a comprehensive index of related FOREIGN POLICY articles, go to `www.foreignpolicy.com`.

reach unprecedented levels, the rise of anti-Americanism reflects a crisis in U.S. soft power that challenges fundamental assumptions and relationships in the U.S. system. Resolving the tension so that the different forms of power reinforce one another is one of the principal challenges facing U.S. foreign policy in 2004 and beyond.

Walter Russell Mead is the Henry A. Kissinger senior fellow in U.S. foreign policy at the Council on Foreign Relations. This essay is adapted from his forthcoming book, Power, Terror, Peace, and War: America's Grand Strategy in a World at Risk *(New York: Knopf, 2004).*

Global Petro-Politics:
The Foreign Policy Implications of the Bush Administration's Energy Plan

"The United States cannot increase its intake of foreign oil by 50 percent, as called for under the Bush energy plan, without involving itself in the political, economic, and military affairs of the states from which all this petroleum is expected to flow. This involvement may take financial and diplomatic forms in most cases, but it will also often entail military action."

MICHAEL T. KLARE

The National Energy Policy proposal that President George W. Bush released on May 17, 2001 was developed with a single over-arching objective in mind: to increase the nation's aggregate supply of energy. "The goals of this strategy are clear: to ensure a steady supply of affordable energy for America's homes and businesses and industries," Bush affirmed. Without a substantial increase in energy supplies, he warned, the United States could face a significant threat to its national security and its economic well-being.

The perceived requirement for a substantial increase in energy supplies led Bush to advocate two steps that have produced considerable controversy in the United States: the extraction of oil from the Arctic National Wildlife Refuge (ANWR) in Alaska, and the relaxation of government oversight of energy-infrastructure improvements. The first, of course, aroused opposition because of the risk of major environmental damage to a pristine wilderness area; the second provoked controversy because of widespread suspicions that the administration had agreed to advocate such relaxation in deference to powerful figures in the oil, gas, and coal industries—many of whom, including former Enron chairman Kenneth Lay, had been major contributors to the Bush campaign. Both these concerns have helped focus public attention on the energy question and to foster congressional debate on key domestic aspects of the administration's plan. But they have also diverted attention from another critical aspect of the National Energy Policy (NEP): a growing reliance on imported energy to compensate for inadequate domestic supplies.

[The Bush energy plan] calls for policy-makers to devote as much effort to securing additional foreign supplies of energy as to increasing domestic production.

A THREAT TO NATIONAL SECURITY?

The United States is exceedingly fortunate among the major industrial powers in that it can supply a very large share of its total energy requirements from domestic sources. According to the United States Department of Energy (DOE), domestic energy production of 72.8 quadrillion British thermal units ("quads") accounted for 73 percent of total United States energy consumption in 2000. Furthermore, by drilling at the ANWR and increasing the use of coal and nuclear power, the United States can boost domestic production by another 18 quads over the next 20 years to 90.7 quadrillion BTUs. But the rub is this: consumption is rising at a faster rate than production, and so the nation will have to import an ever-increasing share of its total energy needs.[1]

This dependency is particularly acute in the case of petroleum, which accounts for about 35 percent of United States energy consumption and is absolutely essential for ground and air transportation. At present, the United States obtains about 53 percent of its petroleum requirement from foreign sources; by 2020 that figure is expected to rise to 62 percent. In practical terms, this means increasing America's intake of imported oil by 50 percent, from 24.4 million to 37.1 million barrels per day (mbd). Without these added imports, the United States would find it extremely difficult to sustain economic growth and fuel its immense fleet of cars, trucks, buses, and planes.

The Bush administration has explicitly characterized this dependency as a threat to national security. "On our present course," the NEP warns, "America 20 years from now will import nearly two of every three barrels of oil—a condition of increased dependency on foreign powers that do not always have America's interests at heart." To diminish this dependency, the administration intends to exploit every conceivable domestic source of energy, including the ANWR and other protected wilderness areas. Increased emphasis will also be placed on conservation and the development of alternative energy systems, including solar and wind power. But ultimately, the Bush plan relies on imports to provide a large share of the additional energy that the United States will require in the years ahead. Indeed, the NEP calls for policymakers to devote as much effort to securing additional foreign supplies of energy as to increasing domestic production.

The pressing requirement for ever-increasing supplies of imported energy will have a profound and lasting impact on American foreign policy.

The plan's reliance on increased acquisition of foreign energy is not immediately obvious from a casual reading of the NEP report. Only toward the end of the report, in the final chapter, does the significance of imported supplies become evident. Without actually specifying the amount of additional imported energy that will be required—an estimated 15.4 quadrillion BTUs in 2020, or as much energy as will be provided by all nuclear power plants and hydroelectric systems in the United States—the report lays out a detailed strategy for procuring these supplies from foreign producers around the world.

Growing American dependence on foreign sources of petroleum is the most important untold story arising from the release of the administration's energy plan. To obtain all the additional energy that will be needed, the United States will have to spend approximately $2.5 trillion on imported petroleum between now and 2020—assuming that prices remain at their current, moderate level—plus a comparable amount on imported natural gas. To ensure that these supplies are actually available, American firms will have to work with foreign producers to substantially increase their annual output. And, because many of these producers are located in areas of conflict and instability, the United States government will have to provide security assistance that could involve, on

some occasions, the deployment of American combat forces.

The pressing requirement for ever-increasing supplies of imported energy will have a profound and lasting impact on American foreign policy. Not only must officials ensure access to these overseas supplies, they must also take steps to make certain that foreign deliveries to the United States are not impeded by war, revolution, or civil disorder. These imperatives will govern United States policy toward all significant energy-supplying regions, especially the Persian Gulf area, the Caspian Sea basin, Africa, and Latin America.

TIED TO THE PERSIAN GULF

The Persian Gulf has been and will remain a major area of concern for United States foreign policy because it sits above the world's largest reservoir of untapped oil. According to BP Amoco, the major Gulf suppliers possess some 675 billion barrels of oil, or about two-thirds of known world reserves. The Gulf countries are also the world's leading producers on a day-to-day basis, jointly accounting for approximately 21 mbd in 1999, or about 30 percent of worldwide production.[2] And because the Gulf accounts for such a large share of global production, these countries usually determine the global price for petroleum products.

Although the United States obtains only about 18 percent of its imported petroleum from the Persian Gulf, it has a significant strategic interest in the stability of Gulf energy production because its major allies—especially Japan and the Western European countries—rely on imports from the region and because the Gulf's high export volume has helped keep world oil prices relatively low, thus benefiting the petroleum-dependent United States economy. With domestic production in decline, moreover, the United States will become increasingly dependent on imports from the Gulf. As a consequence, the NEP declares that "this region will remain vital to U.S. interests."

The United States has, of course, played a significant role in Persian Gulf affairs since World War II. As that conflict came to an end, President Franklin D. Roosevelt concluded an agreement with the king of Saudi Arabia, Abdul-Aziz ibn Saud, under which the United States agreed to protect the royal family against its internal and external enemies in return for privileged access to Saudi oil. At a later date, the United States also agreed to provide security assistance to the shah of Iran and to the leaders of Kuwait, Bahrain, and the United Arab Emirates (UAE). These agreements have led to the delivery of vast quantities of United States arms and ammunition to the Persian Gulf countries and, in some cases, to the deployment of American combat forces. (The United States security link with Iran was severed in January 1980, when the shah was overthrown by militant Islamic forces.)

American policy with regard to the protection of Persian Gulf energy supplies is unambiguous: when a threat arises, the United States will use whatever means are necessary, including military force, to ensure the continued flow of oil. This principle was first articulated by President Jimmy Carter in January 1980, following the Soviet invasion of Afghanistan and the fall of the shah, and has remained United States policy since. In accordance with the "Carter Doctrine," the United States has used force on several occasions: first, in 1987–1988 to protect Kuwaiti oil tankers from Iranian missile and gunboat attacks during the Iran–Iraq War, and then in 1990–1991 to drive Iraqi forces out of Kuwait (Operation Desert Storm).

Today the Carter Doctrine is as vital as ever. Between 1991 and 2001, the Department of Defense conducted a major expansion of United States military capabilities in the Persian Gulf, deploying additional air and naval forces in the region and "prepositioning" arms and ammunition for a powerful ground force.[3] These capabilities were all brought into play during the fall 2001 United States offensive against Al Qaeda forces in Afghanistan and in related operations in the greater Gulf area (although Saudi Arabia did impose some restrictions on the use of American airbases in its territory). The United States also continued to sell billions of dollars' worth of modern weapons to friendly regimes in the area, including Kuwait, Saudi Arabia, and the UAE. To further guard against a disruption in the oil flow, President George W. Bush pointedly warned the Iraqi government of dire consequences should it attempt to take advantage of any instability in the Gulf resulting from terrorist activity.

At this point, it appears that the threat from both Al Qaeda and Iraq has effectively been circumscribed, and that oil deliveries from the Gulf are relatively safe from disruption. But looking further into the future, American policymakers face two critical challenges: to ensure that Saudi Arabia and other Gulf producers increase oil production to the extent required by growing United States (and international) demand; and to protect Saudi Arabia itself from internal disorder.

The need to increase Saudi production is particularly acute. Possessing one-fourth the world's known oil reserves (an estimated 265 billion barrels), Saudi Arabia is the only country with the capacity to satisfy United States and international demand. According to the DOE, Saudi Arabia's net petroleum output must double over the next 20 years, from 11.4 million to 23.1 million barrels per day, to satisfy anticipated world requirements.[4] But expanding capacity by 11.7 mbd—the equivalent of total current production by the United States and Canada—will cost hundreds of billions of dollars and create enormous technical and logistical challenges. The best way to achieve the necessary increase, American analysts believe, is to persuade Saudi Arabia to open its petroleum sector to substantial United States oil-company investment. And, under the administration's energy plan, the president is enjoined to do exactly that. Any effort by Washington to apply pressure on Riyadh to allow greater American oil investment in the kingdom, however, is likely to meet with significant resistance from the royal family, which nationalized American oil holdings in the 1970s.

The administration faces yet another problem in Saudi Arabia: America's long-term security relationship with the regime has become a major source of tension in the country, as growing numbers of young Saudis turn against the United States because of its close ties to Israel and (what is seen as) its anti-Islamic bias. It was from this anti-American milieu that Osama bin Laden recruited many of his followers in the late 1990s and obtained much of his financial support. After September 11, the Saudi government cracked down on some of these forces, but grassroots opposition to the regime's military and economic cooperation with Washington remains strong. Finding a way to defuse this opposition while persuading Riyadh to increase its oil deliveries to the United States will be one of the most difficult challenges facing American policymakers in the years ahead.

Policymakers will also be paying close attention to Iran and Iraq, the second- and third-largest oil producers in the Gulf. Although both countries are currently barred from United States oil-company investment because of their support for terrorism and suspected pursuit of nuclear weapons, a future change in their political status could permit an American role in the development of their extensive petroleum reserves—something United States energy firms would undoubtedly welcome. Washington likely will continue to seek the emergence of friendly, cooperative governments in Baghdad and Teheran. If these efforts fail, the United States is fully prepared to counter any aggressive moves they might make with the full weight of its military power.

THE GEOPOLITICS OF ENERGY
IN THE CASPIAN SEA BASIN

Although the United States will remain dependent on oil from the Gulf because that is where most of the world's untapped reserves are located, it also would like to minimize this dependency to the greatest extent possible by diversifying the nation's sources of imported energy. "Diversity is important, not only for energy security but also for national security," President Bush declared on May 17, 2001. "Overdependence on any one source of energy, especially a foreign source, leaves us vulnerable to price shocks, supply interruptions, and in the worst case, blackmail." To prevent this, the administration's energy plan calls for a substantial United States effort to boost production in many parts of the world.

Among the areas that will receive particular attention from the United States is the Caspian Sea basin—the region consisting of Azerbaijan, Kazakhstan, Turkmenistan, and Uzbekistan, along with adjacent areas of Iran and Russia. According to the DOE, the Caspian basin houses proven reserves of 17.5 billion to 34 billion barrels of oil (bbl) and *possible* reserves of 235 bbl—an amount that, if confirmed, would make it the second-largest site of untapped reserves after the Persian Gulf.[5] To ensure that much of this oil will eventually flow to consumers in the West, the United States has made a strenuous effort to develop the area's petroleum infrastructure and distribution system. (Because the Caspian Sea is landlocked, oil and natural gas from the region must travel by pipeline to other areas; any efforts to tap into the Caspian's vast energy reserves must, therefore, entail the construction of long-distance export lines.)

The United States first sought to gain access to the Caspian's vast oil supplies during the Clinton administration. Until that time, the Caspian states (except for Iran) had been part of the Soviet Union, and so outside access to their energy reserves was tightly constricted. Once these states became independent, Washington waged an intensive diplomatic campaign to open their fields to Western oil-company investment and to allow the construction of new export pipelines. President Bill Clinton himself played a key role in this effort, repeatedly telephoning leaders of the Caspian Sea countries and inviting them to the White House for periodic visits. These efforts were essential, Clinton told Azerbaijan president Heydar Aliyev in 1997, to "diversify our energy supply and strengthen our nation's security."

The Clinton administration's principal objective during this period was to secure approval for new export routes from the Caspian to markets in the West. Because the administration was reluctant to see Caspian oil flow through Russia on its way to Western Europe (thereby giving Moscow a degree of control over Western energy supplies), and because transport through Iran was prohibited by United States law (for the reasons noted earlier), President Clinton threw his support behind a plan to transport oil and gas from Baku in Azerbaijan to Ceyhan in Turkey via Tbilisi in the former Soviet republic of Georgia. Before leaving office, Clinton flew to Turkey to preside at the signing ceremony for a regional agreement permitting construction of the $3-billion Baku-Tbilisi-Ceyhan (BTC) pipeline.

Building on the efforts of President Clinton, the Bush administration plans to accelerate the expansion of Caspian production facilities and pipelines. "Foreign investors and technology are critical to rapid development of new commercially viable export routes," the NEP affirms. "Such development will ensure that rising Caspian oil production is effectively integrated into world oil trade." Special emphasis is to be placed on completion of the BTC pipeline and on increasing the participation of United Sates companies in Caspian energy projects. Looking further ahead, the administration also hopes to build an oil and gas pipeline from Kazakhstan and Turkmenistan on the east shore of the Caspian to Baku on the west shore, thus increasing the energy outflow through the BTC line.

Until September 11, American involvement in the Caspian Sea basin and Central Asia had largely been restricted to economic and diplomatic efforts, accompanied by a number of military aid agreements. To combat the Taliban and al Qaeda in Afghanistan, however, the Department of Defense established military bases in Tajikistan and Uzbekistan. Although initially intended as temporary facilities to support United States troops committed to the Afghan war, these bases could form the kernel of a permanent American military presence in the Caspian area. Although nothing has been said about this publicly in Washington, such a presence would be consistent with development in the Persian Gulf, where United States efforts to protect the flow of oil have led to an expanded American military infrastructure.

Whether or not the American bases in Tajikistan and Turkmenistan acquire permanent status, Washington is certain to enhance its capacity to employ military force in the area. The Caucasus and Central Asia are no more stable that the Persian Gulf, and developing the Caspian as an alternative source of energy is pointless if its outflow of oil and gas cannot be secured. In recognition of the potential threat to Caspian energy supplies, the Department of Defense has conducted a series of joint military exercises with the forces of Kazakhstan, Kyrgyzstan, and Uzbekistan (the annual "CENTRAZBAT" exercises) and signed military cooperation agreements with other states in the area. These ties have been further strengthened since September 11.[6]

LOOKING TO AFRICA...

Although African states accounted for only about 10 percent of global oil production in 1999, the DOE predicts that their share will rise to 13 percent by 2020—adding, in the process, another 8.3 mbd to global supplies.[7] This is welcome news in Washington. "West Africa is expected to be one of the fastest-growing sources of oil and gas for the American market," the administration reported in 2001. Furthermore, "African oil tends to be of high quality and low in sulphur," making it especially attractive for American refiners.

The Bush administration expects to concentrate its efforts in two countries: Nigeria and Angola. Nigeria now produces about 2.2 mbd, and is expected to double its oil output by 2020—with much of this additional petroleum going to the United States. But Nigeria lacks the wherewithal to finance this expansion on its own, and existing legislation (not to mention widespread corruption) discourages investment by outside firms. The NEP thus calls on the secretaries of energy, commerce, and state to work with Nigerian officials "to improve the climate for U.S. oil and gas trade, investment, and operations." Yet by working this closely with the Nigerian government, Washington risks association with a regime that has been widely criticized for persistent human rights violations.

A similar picture is found in Angola. Here, too, the United States seeks to significantly expand oil production, now estimated at around 750,000 barrels per day. Several American energy firms have begun to explore for oil in deep-sea sites off Angola's Atlantic coast, and early indications are that these areas hold significant reserves of petroleum. But, again, deeper United States involvement in the oil industry could lead to close association with a regime that has been cited for egregious human rights violations.

Although American involvement in African energy development is certain to grow, it is unlikely that this will be accompanied—as in the Gulf and Caspian areas—by a direct American military presence. No matter how it is presented to the public, such a presence would inevitably conjure images of colonialism and invite opposition both at home and in Africa. But Washington is likely to provide Nigeria and other friendly countries with indirect forms of military support, including training, technical assistance, and the transfer of low-tech weaponry.

...AND LATIN AMERICA

The Bush administration plan also calls for a significant increase in United States oil imports from Mexico, Brazil, and the Andean countries. The United States already obtains a large share of its imported oil from Latin America—Venezuela is now the third-largest supplier of oil to the United States (after Canada and Saudi Arabia), Mexico is the fourth-largest, and Colombia is the seventh—and Washington hopes to rely even more heavily on this region in the future. According to Secretary of Energy Spencer Abraham, "President Bush recognizes not only the need for an increased supply of energy, but also the critical role the hemisphere will play in the Administration's energy policy."

In presenting these plans to governments in the region, American officials stress their desire to establish a common, cooperative framework for energy development. "We intend to stress the enormous potential of greater regional energy cooperation as we look to the future," Abraham told the Fifth Hemispheric Energy Initiative Ministerial Conference in Mexico City on March 8, 2001. "Our goal [is] to build relationships among our neighbors that will contribute to our shared energy security; to an adequate, reliable, environmentally sound, and affordable access to energy." However sincere, these comments overlook the fundamental reality: all this "cooperation" is aimed at channeling increasing amounts of the region's oil supplies to the United States.

The Bush energy plan emphasizes the acquisition of additional oil from Mexico and Venezuela. "Mexico is a leading and reliable source of imported oil," the NEP notes. "Its large reserve base, approximately 25 percent larger than our own proven reserves, makes Mexico a likely source of increased oil production over the next decade." Venezuela is critical to United States plans because it possesses large reserves of conventional oil (eclipsed only by those of Iran, Iraq, Kuwait, Saudi Arabia, and the UAE), and because it houses vast supplies of so-called heavy oil—a sludgelike material that can be converted to conventional oil through a costly refining process. According to the NEP, "Venezuelan success in making heavy oil deposits commercially viable suggests that they will contribute substantially to the diversity of global energy supply, and to our own energy supply mix over the medium to long term."

But United States efforts to tap into abundant Mexican and Venezuelan energy supplies will run into a major difficulty: because of a long history of colonial and imperial predation, these two countries have placed their energy reserves under state control and established strong legal and constitutional barriers to foreign involvement in domestic oil production. Thus, while they may seek to capitalize from the economic benefits of increased oil exports to the United States, they are likely to resist increased participation by American firms in their energy industries and any rapid increase in oil extraction. This resistance will no doubt prove frustrating to American officials, who seek exactly these outcomes. The NEP thus calls on the secretaries of commerce, energy, and state to lobby their Latin American counterparts to eliminate or soften barriers to increased United States oil investment. These efforts are likely to prove a major theme in United States relations with these two countries.

Energy considerations are also likely to figure in United States relations with Colombia. Although known primarily for its role in the illegal drug trade, Colombia is also a major oil producer and could play a more prominent role in future United States energy plans. Efforts to increase Colombian oil production have been, however, hampered by the frequent attacks on oil installations and pipelines mounted by antigovernment guerrilla groups. Claiming that these groups also provide protection to the drug traffickers, the United States, under "Plan Colombia," is assisting the Colombian military and police in their efforts to suppress the guerrillas. At no point has Washington explicitly tied these efforts to its energy policies, but United States officials no doubt believe that a substantial reduction in guerrilla activity will permit an eventual increase in oil production.

THE IMPLICATIONS

The foregoing provides but a foretaste of what American officials can expect to deal with in the years ahead if the United States continues to rely on imported petroleum to power its industries, heat its homes, and fuel its vehicles. The United States cannot increase its intake of foreign oil by 50 percent, as called for under the Bush energy plan, without involving itself in the political, economic, and military affairs of the states from which all this petroleum is expected to flow. This involvement may take financial and diplomatic forms in most cases, but will also often entail military action.

Perhaps Congress and the American people would agree that these efforts are indeed necessary to ensure a steady supply of energy. Certainly there have been few signs of dissent on this score. However, most public discussion of the Bush administration's energy plan has focused on its domestic rather than international consequences. This, unfortunately, has tended to obscure some of the important ramifications of the administration plan. There has been very little comment, for example, on the potential for increased military action attendant to the new policy. Ignoring these considerations could prove dangerous. In the interests of forging a sound and affordable energy plan. Congress should initiate a thorough and far-ranging examination on the foreign policy implications of the administration's proposed policy.

Notes

1. United States Department of Energy, "Annual Energy Outlook 2002." Accessed at <http://www.eia.doe.gov/oiaf.aeo>. Unless otherwise indicated, all energy statistics cited in this article are derived from this document or the *National Energy Policy* report, issued by the White House on May 17, 2001.

2. BP Amoco, *Statistical Review of World Energy* (June 2000).

3. For details see Michael Klare, *Resource Wars* (New York; Metropolitan Books, 2001), chap. 3.

4. Department of Energy, *International Energy Outlook 2001*, table D1.

5. Department of Energy, "Caspian Sea Region" (July 2001). Accessed at <http://www.eia.doe.gov/cabs/caspian.html>.

6. For background on these efforts, see Klare, *Resource Wars*, Chap. 4.

7. Department of Energy, *International Energy Outlook 2001*, table D1.

MICHAEL T. KLARE *is a professor of peace and world security studies at Hampshire College and the author of* Resource Wars: The New Landscape of Global Conflict *(New York: Metropolitan Books, 2001).*

Africa and the Battle over Agricultural Protectionism

Todd Moss and Alicia Bannon

In recent years, as African governments and development advocates have stepped up their campaign to reform the trade policies of rich countries, the issue of agricultural protectionism has come to the forefront. This is a highly divisive issue, with rich countries resisting poor countries' demands for major changes. In fact, the latest World Trade Organization (WTO) negotiations, the September 2003 Cancun meeting, failed largely because of the impasse over agriculture.

Critics highlight the hypocrisy of rich countries giving lip service to free trade while maintaining tariff barriers and paying subsidies to their farmers. Their argument that agricultural protectionism places an unfair burden on Africa is becoming a mainstream view. The *New York Times,* for example, argues that African farmers are "rightfully outraged that a nation [the United States] that enjoys all the benefits of open markets for its industrial products keeps putting up walls around its farmers."[1] The World Bank, the International Monetary Fund (IMF), and the Organization for Economic Cooperation and Development (OECD) have also come out strongly against current agricultural trade practices and advocate a major overhaul in order to benefit low-income countries.[2]

Several African countries have also become assertive on agricultural issues in international trade debates. South Africa played a lead role in the recent WTO negotiations, with Uganda, Botswana, and Kenya also becoming vocal players. Four West African countries—Burkina Faso, Mali, Chad, and Benin—have called on the United States to cut the $1-3 billion it spends each year subsidizing American cotton growers. More broadly, African politicians have used their bully pulpits to criticize unfair trade policies and their impact on Africa's long-term development. "The rich countries have a choice," says Ugandan president Yoweri Museveni, "either let Africa have real access to your markets for products, especially agriculture, or acknowledge that you prefer to keep us dependent on your handouts."[3]

Recently, development advocates and nongovernmental organizations (NGOs) have joined the campaign for reform of global agricultural markets. Oxfam and the World Council of Churches, among other organizations,

are taking an active role in lobbying trade negotiators on this issue.[4] In short, fairness in agricultural trade policy has become for this decade what debt relief was for the 1990s—central to the critique of U.S. and European policies toward the poor and a focal point for development advocacy.

The protectionist policies of rich countries are indeed a serious issue for Africa, where farming accounts for about 70 percent of total employment and is the main source of income for the vast majority of those living in or near poverty. The 30 member countries of the OECD spend a combined $235 billion per year to support their agricultural producers, but only about $60 billion on foreign aid (about one-fifth of which goes to Africa). Subsidies, tariffs, and nontariff barriers distort global prices and restrict access to rich-country markets. The global trading system discriminates against the world's poorest nations, making their products less competitive and undermining opportunities for growth, employment, and, ultimately, economic and social development. Additionally, intransigence on the part of rich countries over agricultural reform also indirectly harms poor countries due to its effects on broader trade negotiations. According to one estimate, unimpeded global trade would boost developing country income by about $200 billion a year in the long term.[5] The current stalemate over agriculture has frustrated trade liberalization and reform efforts in both multilateral and regional negotiations, hurting poor countries' prospects for export growth, and stalling progress on other important trade issues, like intellectual property rights.

Despite widespread criticism of current agricultural trade policies, rich countries continue to respond to entrenched interests. In fact, after introducing reforms to reduce subsidies in 1996, the United States has since increased its level of protectionism. The 2002 farm bill further increased federal subsidies—to some farmers by more than 80 percent. Across the Atlantic, France, Spain, Ireland, and Portugal have resisted changes to the European Union's broad agreement on farmer payments, known as the common agricultural policy (CAP). They effectively watered down a compromise reached last June that would have reduced protection levels. Among other things, France won a concession from the EU to maintain price guarantees for cereals, the largest single absorber of CAP funds. Why are rich countries so intransigent when it comes to agricultural protectionism?

Resisting Reform

There are significant political, institutional, and cultural reasons why agriculture enjoys a special status in the United States and Europe. One important barrier to reform is a classic public choice problem: while the benefits of agricultural protection are enjoyed by a small subset of farmers and agribusinesses, the costs are widely diffuse, making it difficult to mobilize energy for reform. Politically, producers of most major commodities are represented by strong lobbying groups, such as the National Cotton Council and the American Sugar Alliance in the United States, or the powerful French farmers union, the Fédération Nationale des Syndicats d'Exploitants Agricoles.

The influence of agricultural groups is often enhanced by institutional advantages. Although agriculture represents only 2 percent of the U.S. economy and less than a quarter of the population lives in rural areas, the American system of government gives rural states disproportionate representation in the Senate, often allowing farm interests to trump urban ones. The schedule of presidential primaries enables rural states like Iowa to project their concerns onto the public agenda, giving farming added prominence in national political debates. Additionally, agricultural interests are deeply and actively involved in the political process. The Center for Responsive Politics in Washington, D.C., reports that U.S. agribusiness donated $59 million to political campaigns in the year 2000, about the same as energy companies and more than three times what the defense sector gave.

Perhaps just as importantly, agriculture still plays an influential cultural role in the West, with many Americans and Europeans clinging to an idealized view of the small farmer and rural life. There is little doubt that British and French support for farmers is rooted in such romanticism. American national identity is partly based on the image of the rugged family farmer and (ironically) rural self-sufficiency. The desire on the part of the public to protect farmers also reflects general anxiety about job security among the population at large. Food security and (often unjustified) worries over food safety also play roles in Western support for protectionism. Thus, attempts to reform agricultural policy are easily painted by those who want to maintain the status quo as an assault on hardworking small farmers and on our national heritage, or even as a threat to national security.[6]

Despite these formidable opposition forces, agriculture is not invulnerable to reform. There are some indications, both at the global level and within the United States and the EU, that reforms are on the horizon. In part, this is because the campaign by African governments, the World Bank, and NGOs to increase awareness of the impact of agricultural protectionism on the incomes of African farmers is beginning to gain some attention.

While critics of developed countries' agricultural policies have largely focused on the United States, Europe is likely to be the most significant driver of agricultural reform. Specifically, EU expansion will force the Europeans to revisit the CAP. The average per capita income of the 10 new members of the EU is about half that of the other 15 members, and the new members are more than twice as reliant on agriculture. This will undoubtedly foster substantial new pressures for a major reform of the CAP as the current system becomes increasingly expensive and ultimately untenable—creating an opportunity for changes that could benefit Africa as well.

Such reform is critical to Africa's hopes. This is true not only because Europe's policies are arguably even more damaging to African agriculture than America's or Japan's, but also because prospects for global agricultural reform will largely depend on negotiations between the United States and the EU. The problem is that neither the United States nor the EU wants to make concessions unless the other also does so. As Rep. Charles Stenholm, the ranking minority member on the House Committee on Agriculture, has said: "I would be willing to eliminate cotton subsidies tomorrow if all the other countries would eliminate their subsidies for fibers, but we're not going to unilaterally disarm our farmers in that world market."[7]

This political deadlock affects not only multilateral talks like those at the WTO, but also bilateral and regional trade talks because the main barrier to reform is between the large economic trading blocs. Recent U.S. trade deals, such as the bilateral agreement with Australia and the Central American Free Trade Agreement (CAFTA) with El Salvador, Guatemala, Honduras, Nicaragua, and Costa Rica, illustrate this reality: agricultural issues have been deferred until future U.S.-EU agreement. Many of the changes in U.S. agricultural policy sought by the Latin Americans as part of the broader proposed Free Trade Area of the Americas will also depend on future U.S.-European negotiations.

What Protectionism Costs

Domestically, budgetary and fairness concerns could also lead to change. One of the main arguments in favor of reform is that current agricultural policies are hugely expensive. The U.S. Department of Agriculture paid out over $12 billion in subsidies in 2002, monies that come out of taxpayers' pockets.[8] The OECD estimates that the cost of U.S. market price supports for agricultural products—which include tariffs, quotas, and price guarantees—amounted to over $15 billion in 2002; such costs are borne by consumers through higher prices. To take just one example, the General Accounting Office estimates that the tariffs and quotas that are meant to protect U.S. sugar producers cost $1.9 billion in 1998, and led to a $900 million net loss to the economy.[9] Yet sugar producers account for less than one-half of one percent of all U.S. farms.

Such protectionism exacts an even higher price in Europe. The OECD estimates that EU market price supports in 2002 exceeded $57 billion. EU producer support costs (including subsidies, tariffs, and other protectionist measures) in 2002 came to over $100 billion, compared to about $40 billion for the United States. Oxfam recently estimated that British taxpayers alone pay £3.9 billion ($7 billion) per year to maintain the CAP.

Moreover, popular perceptions aside, small farmers are not the major beneficiaries of current agriculture policies. Eighty percent of U.S. subsidies go to agribusiness, and 10 percent of recipients collect about two-thirds of all subsidies. Seventy-eight farms in the United States received over $1 million each in subsidies in 2002.[10] Certain crops, like rice, peanuts, and cotton, receive most federal subsidies, while grains and livestock receive relatively little. Subsidy programs also favor large landowners and highly mechanized farms, which has arguably encouraged the consolidation of small farms. More broadly, on average only 25 percent of producer support actually goes to farmers, with other recipients, such as fertilizer suppliers, reaping many of the benefits.[11] Tariffs are another area where fairness issues come into play, because certain crops receive disproportionate support. For this reason, during the debate over CAFTA, American rice growers came out in favor of lifting trade barriers, while the heavily protected sugar growers were strongly opposed.[12]

Questions about regressive and unfair allocations of benefits are not limited to the United States. Such concerns are increasingly expressed in Europe as well. A recent Oxfam report that attracted a lot of press attention in Britain pointed out that current European agriculture policy "lavishes subsidies on some of Britain's wealthiest farmers and biggest landowners," creating "a perverse system of social welfare."[13] When the Duke of Westminster, one of Britain's wealthiest men, is receiving a farming subsidy of nearly £1,000 ($1,800) per day, agriculture policy has clearly strayed far from the ideal of supporting small farmers.

Despite the increased attention being given to the costs and fairness of existing agricultural policies,[14] the American and European publics are still largely uninformed about agricultural policy in practice. A recent University of Maryland/PIPA poll found that 46 percent of Americans incorrectly believe that farmers receive subsidies only in bad years. While those polled strongly supported emergency assistance for small farmers in bad years (77 percent in favor), a large majority (66 percent) opposed regularized annual subsidies. And fewer than one in ten of those polled supported regular subsidies for farms of 500 acres or more.[15] These findings suggest that popular support could be mobilized for substantial policy change. Indeed, were public preferences followed more

closely, the U.S. government would limit its agricultural support to emergency assistance for small farmers.

More broadly, protectionist policies are inherently biased against the vast majority of Americans and Europeans: consumers, urban and suburban dwellers, and producers in other economic sectors. Consumers are at times paying for agricultural protection twice over—once through direct subsidies financed by taxation and again through higher food prices due to trade barriers. Agricultural policy is also a means of redistributing resources from cities to rural areas. Although farmers are understandably loathe to acknowledge this, current protectionist measures are little different from welfare and other forms of state-sponsored entitlements directed at protecting certain segments of the population at the expense of the majority.

People employed in other sectors of the U.S. economy—such as manufacturing and services—are increasingly being asked to accept the job losses and changed working environments that result from globalization and normal economic evolution.[16] For the most part, policymakers have rightly avoided erecting trade barriers or subsidizing outmoded forms of industry in response to these pressures, recognizing that free trade and innovation bring net benefits to the economy as a whole. These groups may begin to resent the special protection afforded to farmers. Agricultural tariffs, for example, are four to five times higher than those applied to manufacturing goods.[17] Indeed, the U.S. Chamber of Commerce supports freer trade in agriculture, a position that stems from concerns that protectionist agricultural policies might prove an obstacle to securing trade agreements beneficial to American business.

Yet demands for reform of agricultural policy have generally been muted. Why has there been so little mobilization? First, as we have said, the public is not well informed about how agricultural protection works in practice, and its diffuse costs make its disadvantages less apparent. Second, the debates over protectionism in the United States and Europe are frequently muddled by competing issues, from protecting small farmers and the environment to promoting food security and safety. Finally, the various groups interested in reform are not traditional allies, so organization and infrastructure are lacking.

Advocates of change in the United States and Europe must recognize the political barriers they face and accept the fact that reform efforts will likely be slow and piecemeal. If they are to be successful, they must focus on the forms of protection that are most damaging and take aim at strategic "soft spots." Reform-minded political leaders and NGOs have a range of potential allies in the United States and Europe, including people whose main concern is African development. To be more effective, these advocates should consider targeting their arguments more carefully and building opportunistic alliances with those constituencies for whom agricultural reform is largely a domestic issue.

Broaden Cooperation, Narrow the Focus

Opponents of developed-country agricultural protectionism, particularly those concerned with the impact of such protectionism on sub-Saharan Africa, have focused on building alliances among developing countries —and to a lesser extent, with the Cairns Group of wealthier agricultural exporters, which includes Australia and Argentina. In criticizing U.S. and European agricultural trade barriers, both development advocates and African governments have focused almost exclusively on highlighting how the protectionist policies of wealthy countries—such as U.S. cotton subsidies—hurt Africans.

Given the political environment, however, this strategy by itself does not appear likely to make much headway. Reformers would likely have more success if they were to: (a) show how current policies adversely affect Americans and Europeans; (b) reach out to potential allies within the United States and the EU; and (c) narrow the focus of their criticism and their immediate goals.

The international debate tends to focus on the impact of agricultural protectionism on poor countries, ignoring domestic interests. Demands for reducing levels of protectionism are often couched in terms of a sacrifice rich countries should make for humanitarian reasons. But there is evidence that this strategy does not resonate with audiences in rich countries. In a recent poll of Americans, only 27 percent of respondents were aware that U.S. farm subsidies might contribute to poverty in the developing world. More significantly, 56 percent of those polled endorsed the view: "It is not our responsibility to take care of farmers in other countries."[18] Such responses reflect a deep-seated orientation toward national interest that will be very difficult to shift.

Domestic and international critics of protectionist policies rarely talk, much less collaborate. Africa-minded reformers have failed to reach out to domestic interest groups in the United States and Europe. Such groups span the political spectrum and include development advocates and aid organizations, fiscal conservatives, environmental and consumer watchdog organizations, agricultural producers in unprotected sectors, and producers in nonagricultural sectors. The Environmental Working Group in Washington, D.C., has criticized the distribution of U.S. agricultural subsidies, arguing for an increased emphasis on farmland conservation programs. Consumers Union has weighed in on the effects of protectionist policies on prices and consumption patterns. The National Taxpayers Union has complained about the cost of subsidies to taxpayers. The conservative Heritage Foundation includes farm subsidies in its Index of Dependency, a critique of large-scale federal benefit programs. Farm Aid says protectionist policies force small farmers off their land. Oxfam criticizes the agricultural policies of rich nations not only for their negative effects on African farmers but for their unfair domestic costs. Reformers would benefit from trying to harness the energy and clout of such groups to the common cause.

In addition to creating strategic alliances with such groups, advocates of change should also identify "soft spots" against which to launch their reform efforts. Critics of protectionism may have made a tactical mistake by demanding wholesale changes that would have a negative impact on some of the most protected and entrenched agricultural interests. For example, the U.S. cotton industry has become a favorite target: African countries focused on it during the Cancun meeting, and Oxfam views cotton as a "test case."[19] Cotton subsidies certainly have deleterious effects on farmers in developing countries. By one estimate, cotton growers in Francophone Africa lost about $700 million in income in 2001 because of lower prices.[20] But is this the best fight to pick? Cotton is produced by only a handful of African countries, so even a win might not be worth a great deal in the big picture. Even so, campaigners against cotton subsidies have demanded nothing less than the total elimination of supports. This past April, Brazil won a preliminary WTO challenge against the United States, successfully arguing that U.S. cotton subsidies violated current trade rules. Washington has indicated its willingness to consider cotton as part of a broader multilateral reform package. This creates an opportunity for African governments to win concessions, but making unrealistic demands will only spark stronger resistance to change. A more modest and conciliatory approach is perhaps more likely to promote serious policy changes.[21]

Critics should also set their sights on those forms of agricultural protection that are most damaging to African interests. Much of the debate on agricultural reform has emphasized reducing rich-country subsidies —in fact, the term "subsidy" is often used interchangeably with the term "protection." In reality, subsidies are only one form of protectionism, and not all subsidies present the same costs to African farmers.

Thus, while tariffs and direct subsidies are often grouped together, tariffs are arguably much more damaging to African countries and the global trade regime. Tariff peaks on commodities can approach 350 percent in the United States and top 500 percent in the EU, effectively barring entry into these markets. A World Bank study suggests that tariffs (in both rich and poor countries) have a greater impact on world prices than subsidies do, and that multilateral tariff reductions would be more beneficial than reductions in subsidies.[22] Similarly, a U.S. Department of Agriculture study found that agricultural tariffs have a global average rate of 62 percent, and that tariffs and tariff-rate quotas account for more than half of all agricultural price distortions.[23] The costs of tariffs are less obvious to the public than subsidies and are therefore less likely to generate domestic interest. However, this may be an area where it would be possible to build alliances with American consumers, who would benefit from lower prices, and with free trade advocates.

On subsidies, more targeted criticism would also have a greater impact. Subsidies take on many forms—from income supports to price supports to conservation programs that pay farmers to set aside land. Subsidies that give payments based on production tend to do the most damage to farmers in developing countries because they encourage overproduction in rich countries and lower prices for poor farmers. Ideally, subsidies could be separated—or in the lingo "decoupled"—from production, allowing rich countries to support their farmers while only minimally affecting international trade. No subsidy can be fully decoupled. However, some subsidies, like direct income support to farmers, are less trade distorting.

Critics of subsidy programs need to recognize that even small reforms may involve high political costs, and development advocates should gear their arguments against forms of protection that hurt African farmers the most. Strategically, reformers might do better to ask rich countries to shift toward less damaging subsidies, rather than demanding an end to subsidies altogether.[24]

Managing Expectations

African governments and other reform advocates need to recognize that a wholesale overhaul of U.S. and EU agricultural policies is unlikely. And they should keep in mind that whatever the potential gains to Africa from agricultural reform, they will be no substitute for development.

Agricultural protectionism is not the cause of poverty and underdevelopment in Africa, and its (partial) removal will not signal an end to the continent's problems. Hopes for huge gains in commodity prices are probably unrealistic. According to a U.S. Department of Agriculture study, global agricultural protectionism lowers agricultural prices by only about 12 percent.[25] The elimination of this distortion would no doubt be a good thing for Africa, but it would not solve the underlying problem of poverty.

Moreover, some African countries would also most likely be hurt by the removal of certain trade barriers, at least in the short term. For example, Mauritius currently benefits enormously from the EU sugar regime through privileged access to artificially higher prices. It has been actively lobbying against reform alongside British sugar producers and processors.[26] The removal of some agricultural protections would also raise food prices for Africa's food importers, which would have an adverse impact on both consumers and the overall terms of trade. One study suggests that certain African countries, such as Gabon, Algeria, and Tunisia, would be harmed by the (multilateral) reduction of tariffs and subsidies.[27]

More importantly, there is a risk for Africa that the attention on global agriculture will prove a distraction from continuing policy reform at home. The main constraints on African agriculture are domestic —weak infrastructure, low technology, poor skills, intra-African trade barriers, high taxes on agriculture, continued depen-dence on a small number of commodities, high transport costs, the spread of HIV/AIDS, and pricing and marketing policies that penalize farmers.[28] No matter what happens at the global level, African governments still need to think seriously about how to reform their own agricultural policies in order to boost their competitiveness.

One approach that remains underexploited is to develop policies that encourage production of less protected or unprotected commodities where African producers still retain relative advantage, such as fruits, vegetables, and perhaps organic food—especially to serve counterseasonal markets in the Northern Hemisphere. This approach is unlikely to work for all poor countries, as many lack the climate, soil quality, infrastructure, or policy environment to support a shift to niche products. There are also costs associated with switching products and the risk that these markets will prove more volatile than traditional sectors.[29] However, niche markets offer a potentially lucrative alternative for many poor farmers and one that does not require major changes in the global agricultural market nor overcoming powerful political actors. These markets also offer opportunities for diversification for countries that are heavily dependent on one or two primary commodities. Pineapples in Ghana, cut flowers in Uganda and Mozambique, green vegetables in Zambia, and mangoes in Mali are all encouraging examples of niche exports that are growing rapidly.[30]

Perhaps the biggest danger in the current debate over agricultural reform is that those with unrealistic expectations will end up disappointed, unnecessarily deepening Africa's sense of marginalization. There are already worrying signs of overestimating the gains that would come from the lifting of protective measures. Malian president Amadou Toumani Toure told the U.S. Congress last year: "These subsidies now most hinder our developments [*sic*]."[31] According to Uganda's Museveni, "the world . . . needs to encourage these positive trends in Africa by opening up their markets on a quotafree, tariff-free basis. This will, ipso facto, force the multinational investors to rush to Africa to invest there."[32]

Nonetheless, reformers ought to keep in mind the lesson learned from the debt relief campaign. Debt sustainability was (and still is) a very real problem for many African countries. Debt relief advocates built a broad coalition of politicians, NGOs, and civil society groups that forced the major powers to act. Yet reducing debt service obligations has not produced all the hoped for benefits, in part because the direct effects of debt were exaggerated and the benefits of debt forgiveness could only accrue in the context of other domestic reforms.

Distortions in global agriculture are a very real problem for many African countries. Advocates for change need to build a broad coalition to force the major powers to act, and to pursue a strategy based on the realities of the political forces aligned to protect the status quo. Yet given the strength of these forces and the importance of agriculture to Africa's future, the battle against agricultural protectionism must not be allowed to distract countries from necessary reforms at home and the wider war against poverty.

Notes

The authors wish to thank Sarah Lucas, Sheila Herrling, Kim Elliott, and Peter Timmer for their comments on this essay.

1. "The Fabric of Lubbock's Life," editorial, *New York Times*, October 19, 2003.

2. See, for example, "Declaration by the Heads of the IMF, OECD and World Bank," April 9, 2003, www.imf.org/external/np/sec/pr/2003/pr03150.htm.

3. Yoweri K. Museveni, "We Want Trade, Not Aid," *Wall Street Journal*, November 6, 2003. See also the comments of the presidents of Mali and Burkina Faso in Amadou Toumani Toure and Blaise Compaoré, "Your Farm Subsidies Are Strangling Us," *New York Times*, July 11, 2003.

4. "Statement from the International Civil Society Hearing on the WTO Agriculture Agreement," Geneva, February 21, 2003. See also "Dumping on the World: How EU Sugar Policies Hurt Poor Countries," Oxfam Briefing Paper 61, April 2004; and "Cultivating Poverty: The Impact of US Cotton Subsidies on Africa," Oxfam Briefing Paper 30, September 2002.

5. William Cline, *Trade Policy and Global Poverty* (Washington, D.C.: Center for Global Development, 2004).

6. For instance, soon after 9/11, the Agriculture Act of 2001 was renamed the Farm Security and Rural Investment Act in a particularly egregious attempt to redefine farm subsidies as a weapon in the war against terror.

7. Elizabeth Becker, "US Subsidizes Companies to Buy Subsidized Cotton," *New York Times*, November 4, 2003.

8. Environmental Working Group, "Farm Subsidy Database," www.ewg.org/farm/home.php.

9. "Sugar Program: Supporting Sugar Has Increased Users' Costs While Benefiting Producers" (Washington, D.C.: General Accounting Office, June 2000).

10. Environmental Working Group, www.ewg.org/farm/farmbill/stake.php.

11. Harry de Gorter, Merlinda Ingco, and Laura Ignacio, "Domestic Support for Agriculture: Agricultural Policy Reform and Developing Countries," World Bank Trade Note #7, September 10, 2003.

12. Scott Gold, "Louisiana's Deep-Rooted Trade Clash," *Los Angeles Times*, April 12, 2004.

13. "Spotlight on Subsidies: Cereal Injustice Under the CAP in Britain," Oxfam Briefing Paper 55, January 2004.

14. For some examples of this in the popular press, see www.nytimes.com/ref/opinion/harvestingpoverty.html, and www.guardian.co.uk/food.

15. Program on International Policy Attitudes (PIPA), "Americans on Globalization, Trade, and Farm Subsidies," Washington, D.C., January 22, 2004.

16. For example, see Charles Schumer and Paul Craig Roberts, "Second Thoughts on Free Trade," *New York Times*, January 6, 2004.

17. International Food Policy Research Institute, "Agriculture and Trade Facts," www.ifpri.org/media/trade/tradefacts.htm.

18. PIPA, "Americans on Globalization, Trade, and Farm Subsidies."

19. Kevin Watkins, "Cultivating Poverty: US Cotton Subsidies and Africa," speech at WTO public symposium, "Challenges Ahead on the Road to Cancun," June 17, 2003, p. 2.

20. Carlos A. Valderrama, head economist, International Cotton Advisory Committee, correspondence with authors, February 17, 2004.

21. For suggestions about priorities based on developing country export patterns, see Kim Elliott *Developing Countries, Agriculture and the Doha Round* (Washington, D.C.: Center for Global Development, forthcoming).

22. Bernard Hoekman, Francis Ng, and Marcelo Olarreaga, "Reducing Agricultural Tariffs versus Domestic Support: What's More Important for Developing Countries," Policy Research Working Paper 2918 (Washington, D.C.: World Bank, October 2002).

23. Mary E. Burfisher, ed., "The Road Ahead: Agricultural Policy Reform in the WTO—Summary Report," Agricultural Economic Report #797 (Washington, D.C.: Department of Agriculture, January 2001).

24. An example of possible misplaced attention is the criticism of "green box" subsidies, which are defined by the WTO as having a minimal impact on trade. While critics are justly concerned that the definitions are too broad, they have diverted attention from more damaging types of protectionism. For an example of this approach, see "EU Hypocrisy Unmasked: Why EU Trade Policy Hurts Development," Oxfam Briefing Note, May 5, 2003, p. 3.

25. Burfisher, "The Road Ahead."

26. Charlotte Denny, "Sugar Lobby Defends 'Scandalous' System," *Guardian* (London), February 23, 2004.

27. Hoekman et al, "Reducing Agricultural Tariffs versus Domestic Support."

28. For example, see Francis Ng and Alexander Yeats, "Good Governance and Trade Policy: Are They the Keys to Africa's Global Integration and Growth?" Working Paper 2038 (Washington, D.C.: World Bank, January 1999). For a discussion of reforms in the cotton sector, see Louis Goreux, "Reforming the Cotton Sector in Sub-Saharan Africa (Second Edition)," Africa Region Working Paper Series No. 62 (Washington, D.C.: World Bank, November 2003).

29. For a discussion of the challenges farmers face in transitioning from maize and cassava to pineapple in Ghana, see Markus Goldstein and Christopher Udry, "Agricultural Innovation and Resource Management in Ghana," Final Report to International Food Policy Research Institute, August 1999, www.ifpri.org.

30. For a successful case study of a mango export project in Mali, see "Linking Farmers to Markets: Exporting Malian Mangoes to Europe," Africa Region Working Paper Series No. 60, (Washington, D.C.: World Bank, August 2003).

31. Boosting Africa's Agricultural Trade: Hearing before the House Subcommittee on Africa (Committee on International Relations), June 24, 2003.

32. Yoweri Museveni, speech before the U.N. General Assembly, New York, November 11, 2001.

Todd Moss *is a research fellow and* **Alicia Bannon** *is a research assistant at the Center for Global Development, Washington, D.C. The views expressed here are those of the authors alone and do not represent the views of the CGD, its staff, or its board of directors.*

UNIT 7
U.S. Military Strategy

Unit Selections

Key Points to Consider

- Is military power an effective instrument of foreign policy today? What problems is it best and least capable of solving?

- Does arms control have a future? Can it make the United States more secure, or does it weaken U.S. security?

- How should we think about nuclear weapons today? What is their purpose? Who should they be targeted against? What dangers must we guard against?

- How great is the terrorist threat to the United States? What steps should the United States take to protect itself from terrorist attacks?

- Develop a list of "dos and don'ts" to guide American troops when they are called upon to act as occupation forces.

- Under what conditions should the United States engage in peacekeeping activities?

- Can nuclear proliferation be stopped? What strategy would you recommend?

Student Website

www.mhcls.com/online

Internet References

Further information regarding these websites may be found in this book's preface or online.

Arms Control and Disarmament Agency (ACDA)
http://dosfan.lib.uic.edu/acda/

Counterterrorism Page
http://counterterrorism.com

DefenseLINK
http://www.defenselink.mil/news/

Federation of American Scientists (FAS)
http://www.fas.org

Human Rights Web
http://www.hrweb.org

During the height of the cold war, American defense planners often thought in terms of needing a two-and-a-half war capacity: the simultaneous ability to fight major wars in Europe and Asia plus a smaller conflict elsewhere. The principal protagonists in this drama were well known: the Soviet Union and China. The stakes were also clear. Communism represented a global threat to American political democracy and economic prosperity. It was a conflict in which both sides publicly proclaimed that there could be but one winner. The means for deterring and fighting such challenges included strategic, tactical, and battlefield nuclear weapons; large numbers of conventional forces; alliance systems; arms transfers; and the development of a guerrilla war capability.

Until September 11, 2001, the political-military landscape of the post–cold war world lacked any comparable enemy or military threat. Instead, the principal challenges to American foreign policy makers were ones of deciding what humanitarian interventions to undertake and how deeply to become involved. Kosovo, East Timor, Somalia, Bosnia, Rwanda, and Haiti each produced its own answer that presented American policymakers with a new type of military challenge in the form of humanitarian interventions. The challenge of formulating an effective military policy to deal with situations where domestic order has unraveled due to ethnic conflict and bottled-up political pressures for reform remains. However, they are no longer viewed as first-order security problems in the post–cold war era.

With the terrorist attacks on the World Trade Center and the Pentagon, a more clearly defined enemy has emerged. Formulating a military strategy to defeat this enemy promises to be no easy task. President George W. Bush acknowledged as much in defining his war against terrorism as a new type of warfare and one that would not end quickly. To date the war against terrorism has led to two wars, one that brought down the Taliban government in Afghanistan and one that brought down Saddam Hussein in Iraq. It also brought forward a new national security strategy centered on preemption in place of deterrence. And, most unexpectedly from the point of view of the Bush administration, it has placed the American military squarely in the business of nation building and face-to-face with the problem of fighting counterinsurgencies.

The first set of essays in this unit examines the range of conflict situations that will confront American forces abroad and some of the key issues that need to be addressed in formulating a new military strategy for the United States. In "X + 9/11" Robert Hutchings makes a case for employing George Kennan's containment strategy that was originally presented in the "X" article in *Foreign Affairs* against terrorism. The next essay, "A Nuclear Posture for Today," is authored by a former head of the CIA and Deputy Secretary of Defense who rejects calls for abolishing nuclear weapons but insists that a new nuclear deterrence strategy is necessary.

With changes in the nature of the military threats confronting the United States has come a change in the arms control agenda. The old arms control agenda was dominated by a concern for reducing the size of U.S. and Soviet nuclear inventories. A much broader agenda exists today, and it is one with many more players at its core, it is the problem of dealing with weapons of mass destruction and the question of whether a national ballistic missile system is an important part of the solution to the problem. The final two essays examine this new agenda. "Double-edged Shield" takes a critical eye at proposals for relaxing export controls on missile defense technology. Next, Robert McNamara, who was Secretary of Defense in the Vietnam era, critiques the Bush administration's nuclear posture arguing that U.S. nuclear strategy is immoral, illegal, unnecessary and dangerous.

X + 9/11

Everything I needed to know about fighting terrorism I learned from George F. Kennan.

By Robert L. Hutchings

*G*eorge F. Kennan celebrated his 100th birthday earlier this year. The dean of U.S. diplomats is best known for his strategy of containment, which he first articulated in the so-called long telegram that he sent from Moscow in 1946—and soon thereafter unveiled in his 1947 article, "The Sources of Soviet Conduct," published under the pseudonym "X." Several conferences honoring Kennan have praised his enormous contribution to U.S. Cold War strategy, yet the most fitting tribute would be to apply his seminal theories to our present era—to examine the sources of terrorist conduct.

Containing the Soviet Union and fighting terrorism are strikingly different undertakings. Kennan examined the behavior of a sovereign state with defined borders, an established populace, a recognized government, and an official ideology. Terrorism, by contrast, does not operate within clear boundaries or abide by diplomatic niceties. Containment cannot deal with such an elusive adversary. But neither is war a fully adequate concept for addressing terrorism as an ongoing challenge. Terror is the tactic, not the adversary itself. To deal with terrorism over the longer term, we must go beyond the symptoms of the problem to address its underlying causes—which is precisely where Kennan's strategic logic takes us.

In his X article, Kennan argued that Soviet power was the product of both ideology and circumstance. Russia's antipathy toward the West was born of historical insecurity. In that context, communism was less a goal than a means—a way for Moscow to maintain control at home and spread its influence abroad. "This means that truth is not a constant but is actually created, for all intents and purposes, by the Soviet leaders themselves," Kennan wrote. "It is nothing absolute and immutable." This observation led Kennan to two conclusions: First, the United States was engaged in a long-term struggle, because the Soviet leaders—confident in their ideological infallibility and secure in their belief of ultimate triumph—were in no hurry to achieve their goals. But, Kennan was quick to add, this messianic conviction did not mean the Soviets were necessarily com-

mitted to a do-or-die struggle to the end. He did not assume that Soviet ideology was so powerful that it could not be overcome, or that the zealotry of the present generation of leaders would necessarily be passed to the next. If the Western powers remained vigilant, Kennan believed, the Soviet system would inevitably turn inward to deal with its inherent contradictions.

Kennan was not soft on communism. His containment strategy targeted the Soviet regime, whose aggressive impulses had to be kept in check. But he also argued for a strategy of engagement with the Russian people, whom he refused to consider permanent U.S. enemies. Kennan later lamented that containment came to be seen in almost exclusively military terms; what he had in mind was the full range of economic, political, psychological, military, and cultural tools at the United States' disposal.

Today, the United States and its allies again confront a seemingly implacable adversary. The challenge is to address and understand the sources of terrorist conduct, even as we counter the efforts of those who would attack us. Like the Soviets before them, Islamic militants are a product of both ideology and circumstance. Although the militants can trace their ideas to strains of puritanical Islam from the 14th century and to the Wahhabi and Salafi movements of the 18th and 19th centuries, much of their pathology is unrelated to religion. Al Qaeda is, to a large extent, a symptom of social dislocation.

The benefits of economic globalization have largely bypassed Arab countries, even as it has exposed them as never before to outside influences. In oil-rich states, elites have used their wealth and power to maintain authoritarian rule and avoid economic and political reform. It is no surprise that the citizens of these countries view the outside world through the prism of exploitation. Meanwhile, the pervasive exposure to Western mass culture has served both to attract and alienate these societies. It's an old story: The more modern and dynamic society undermines the traditional society's values, practices, and allegiances. The recurring response to such an existential crisis is a surge in millenarian beliefs and an inclination toward nihilism. As has been the case in countless struggles before, terrorism is the quintessential weapon of the weak against the strong.

Western nations should not assume that "we" and "they" have nothing in common. Al Qaeda leader Osama bin Laden and his followers deplore the materialism and vacuity of modern society. So do many in the West.

These conditions, however, need not be permanent. Hard as it may be to penetrate the anti-American sentiment prevalent in the Muslim world, the United States must undertake a strategy of engagement similar to what Kennan proposed for the Russian people. The two worlds are not as far apart as many think. A 2003 survey conducted by the Pew Research Center for the People and the Press reveals that citizens in Muslim countries place a high value on freedom of expression and the press, multiparty political systems, and equal treatment under the law.

Western nations should not assume that "we" and "they" have nothing in common. Al Qaeda leader Osama bin Laden and his followers deplore the materialism and vacuity of modern society. So do many in the West. Terrorists and their supporters rage against the inequities and degradation wrought by globalization. So do many thoughtful critics who would not dream of resorting to terrorism to achieve their goals. One of the core failings of communist ideology was that Karl Marx failed to understand that many of the class antagonisms he identified could be overcome peacefully rather than via class struggle. Similarly, the terrorist struggle is neither inevitable nor unending.

The most immediate task for Western governments is to continue to wage a broad-gauged campaign against al Qaeda and its leadership, while strengthening defenses against terrorist attack. But in the long term, the challenge is not only, or even principally, a military one. Indeed, many of the grievances that terrorists exploit—economic inequality, alienation brought on by globalization, and a sense of cultural humiliation—are remediable, at least potentially. Western countries have already advanced several elements of an engagement strategy, including the U.S.-sponsored Middle East Partnership Initiative, which funds programs that promote economic, educational, and political reform, and the European Union's Barcelona Process, which aims to create a free-trade zone with several Arab countries by 2010. The United States and its allies need to coordinate and sustain such efforts, and extend their engagement beyond pro-reform elites to nongovernmental activists and civil-society leaders. Just as the United States' cultural and exchange programs in Europe after World War II helped overcome old animosities, a new wave of programs should be put in place as a long-term investment in the future of the West's relationship with the Muslim world.

A policy of engagement with the Middle East also requires the development of a regional security framework. NATO could play a role in such an endeavor, by deepening and broadening its Mediterranean Dialogue, which currently encompasses seven Arab and North African states. What is needed over the longer term, however, is something broadly analogous to the Conference on Security and Co-operation in Europe (CSCE)—a region-wide framework that was founded in the 1970s to foster East-West cooperation and helped pave the way for the end of the Cold War. The CSCE was the logical culmination of Kennan's strategy for Europe, and it could be applied to the Middle East as well. Some elements of this security framework may include the participation of the United States; others may not.

Even as it wages a resolute campaign against international terrorism, America should not believe that it is engaged in a fight to the finish with radical Islam. This conflict is not a clash of civilizations, but rather a defense of our shared humanity and a search for common ground, however implausible that may seem now. Rapprochement is no more possible with Osama bin Laden than it was with Joseph Stalin back when Kennan was writing, and it will remain a distant hope for some years to come. Yet there is reason for optimism if we take the longer view, as Kennan did. "The issue … is in essence a test of the overall worth of the United States as a nation among nations," he wrote. "To avoid destruction the United States need only measure up to its own best traditions and prove itself worthy of preservation as a great nation."

It was good advice then. It is good advice now.

Robert L. Hutchings is chairman of the U.S. National Intelligence Council, which provides strategic analysis to the president and his national security council. This essay is adapted from a speech that can be read in July/August *Foreign Policy*.

A Nuclear Posture for Today

John Deutch

A THREAT TRANSFORMED

THE COLLAPSE of the Soviet Union was a dramatic geopolitical shift that should have led to major changes in the nuclear posture of the United States. The policy reviews undertaken by the Clinton administration in 1994 and the Bush administration in 2002, however, led to only minor alterations. As a result, the United States lacks a convincing rationale for its current nuclear force structure and for the policies that guide the management of its nuclear weapons enterprise.

The end of the Cold War did not mean that the United States could eliminate nuclear weapons altogether. Their existence is a reality, and the knowledge required to make them is widespread. But over the last decade, the nature of the nuclear threat has fundamentally changed, from large-scale attack to the use of one or a few devices by a rogue nation or subnational group against the United States or one of its allies. Countering the proliferation of nuclear weapons—by slowing the spread of nuclear capabilities among states, assuring that nuclear devices do not get into the hands of terrorist groups, and protecting existing stockpiles—has thus become as high a priority as deterring major nuclear attacks.

Unfortunately, the current U.S. nuclear posture does not reflect this shift. Washington still maintains a large nuclear arsenal designed for the Cold War, and it fails to take into account the current impact of its nuclear policies on those of other governments. In fact, with its overwhelming conventional military advantage, the United States does not need nuclear weapons for either war fighting or for deterring conventional war. It should therefore scale back its nuclear activity significantly. Policymakers should sharply decrease the number of warheads deployed with active military forces and make U.S. stockpile activities (of active and retired warheads and nuclear material) more transparent, setting a security standard for other nations. The United States should not, however, abandon effective nuclear forces, and it should even leave open the possibility of certain limited kinds of nuclear tests. A new U.S. nuclear posture, in short, should encourage international nonproliferation efforts without sacrificing the United States' ability to maintain a nuclear posture that deters attack.

DUAL PURPOSE

IN THE PAST, U.S. policymakers have considered many potential roles for nuclear weapons: massive retaliation, damage limitation in nuclear exchanges, or controlling escalation in more limited scenarios. Still, they have always understood that the purpose of nuclear weapons is to deter war, not to fight it. For deterrence to work, however, the threat of preemptive or retaliatory use must be credible. It follows that, regardless of the number or the mix of weapons in the nuclear arsenal, they must be maintained ready for use, not kept as "wooden cannon."

During the Cold War, a range of nuclear scenarios defined strategic deterrence of the Soviet Union. The number of weapons in the Single Integrated Operation Plan (SIOP), the nuclear-attack strategy drawn up by the military and approved by the president, depended on the number of attack options, the number of targets (military as well as urban and industrial), and the desired "expected damage" to each target. "Expected damage" depended on the "hardness" of the target, the probability of a weapon's reaching it, and the explosive yield and accuracy of the programmed weapon. It does not require much imagination to appreciate that such a calculation could justify acquiring several thousand strategic weapons, as was indeed the case. In the 1970s and 1980s, the United States and the Soviet Union also accumulated several thousand tactical nuclear weapons, smaller devices intended for regional or battlefield use.

Although the nature of today's threats calls into question the usefulness of the United States' large nuclear arsenal, nuclear weapons continue to play a key role in U.S. security. After all, there is no guarantee that geopolitical circumstances will not change dramatically, and the emergence of a more militant China or Russia's return to totalitarianism might compel the United States to place greater reliance on its nuclear forces. Moreover, Washington's commanding nuclear posture still works to limit the nuclear ambitions of other countries. U.S. allies, most notably Germany and Japan, have forsworn establishing their own nuclear programs in exchange for protection under the U.S. security umbrella. Were the United States to give up its arsenal, other countries might be tempted to develop their own.

The possession of weapons by current nuclear powers does not directly influence the ambitions of states or terrorist groups that already want their own. They believe, rightly or wrongly, that acquiring a nuclear weapon will improve their security situation. A change in the U.S. nuclear posture would certainly not have dissuaded any of the newest members of the nuclear club—Israel, India, and Pakistan from seeking the bomb. North Korea and Iran, meanwhile, are vastly more concerned by the United States' conventional power than they are by its nuclear forces. They would probably seek nuclear weapons even if the United States had none, perhaps even with greater determination.

At the same time, the United States relies on the cooperation of many nations to achieve its nonproliferation objectives, and in this regard the U.S. nuclear posture has important consequences. An effective nonproliferation effort requires restricting the transfer of nuclear materials and technology, encouraging effective inspection by the International Atomic Energy Agency, and strengthening standards for the protection of nuclear materials and facilities. Cooperation is also essential for establishing an international norm that forbids the nuclear ambitions of non-nuclear states. (This goal, in fact, raises a basic hypocrisy on the part of nuclear powers: they retain their own arsenals while denying others the same right. This contradiction prompted Washington unwisely to commit under Article 6 of the Nonproliferation Treaty [NPT] "to pursue good-faith negotiations" toward complete disarmament, a goal it has no intention of pursuing.)

Ultimately, Washington must strike a balance between conflicting goals: maintaining a modern nuclear weapons posture, on the one hand, and curbing the spread of nuclear weapons, on the other. The Bush administration has not struck this balance well. Some officials have made unfortunate policy statements about pre-emption, implying that the U.S. government might even consider a first nuclear strike. The administration's 2002 nuclear posture review unwisely treats non-nuclear and nuclear strike capabilities as part of a single retaliatory continuum. Policymakers have invoked technical and geopolitical uncertainty as an argument for modernizing the weapons complex and maintaining robust testing and production capabilities. Most unfortunately, the Bush administration has proposed work on a new warhead—a low-yield "robust nuclear earth-penetrator." Although it could have argued that some conceptual work on generic warheads is needed to preserve the competence of weapons designers, the administration has instead justified this weapon on the basis of its military utility, hinting at the possibility

of development and production in the future. The tone of this proposal ignores the indirect effect that new U.S. warhead research programs have on international attitudes toward nonproliferation.

HOW LOW CAN YOU GO?

TODAY, the U.S. nuclear arsenal should be managed with two purposes in mind: to deter a nuclear attack against the United States or its allies by retaining an overwhelming nuclear force with high "survivability," and to respond flexibly and precisely to a broad range of contingencies, including chemical or biological attack. The goal is to force any nation or subnational group that contemplates use of a weapon of mass destruction for an act of catastrophic terrorism to consider the possibility of U.S. nuclear retaliation and the complete destruction of its interests or sanctuary.

These purposes are not so different from those of the past, but the new nature of the threat means that many fewer weapons are needed to achieve them. In May 2001, President George W. Bush said at the National Defense University, "I am committed to achieving a credible deterrent with the lowest-possible number of nuclear weapons consistent with our national security needs, including our obligations to our allies." But just what is the "lowest possible number"?

The answer cannot be calculated using the classic SIOP method: there are no suitable target lists analogous to those drawn during the Cold War. But even a crude estimate of numerical requirements gives a sense of how much smaller the U.S. nuclear arsenal could be.

A fleet of nine Trident ballistic-missile-equipped nuclear submarines—half the size of the current fleet of 18 boats, which is capable of carrying about 3,000 warheads—would constitute a retaliatory force with sufficient survivability. Three partially loaded submarines would be on continuous station, each carrying 16 D-5 missiles with 8 nuclear warheads (a combination of the w76 and the w88), for a total of 384 warheads on alert. Another three would be in transit (carrying an additional 384 warheads in strategic reserve), and still another three would be in overhaul (and thus unarmed) at any given time. (Because each Trident can carry 24 missiles, such a deployment would add up to 1,728 accountable warheads under the counting rules of the Strategic Arms Reduction Treaty, suggesting that these rules may no longer be relevant to either the United States or Russia.) Another 200 operational nuclear warheads would complement the fleet, providing for flexible response. These would be placed on other delivery systems, such as land-based intercontinental ballistic missiles and cruise missiles on sea and air platforms that permit easier command and control.

Such a deployment—less than 1,000 warheads in total—would be smaller than the reduced target proposed by Bush as part of the Strategic Offensive Reductions Treaty: between 1,700 and 2,200 deployed strategic warheads by

2012. But for the sake of deterrence and response, this smaller nuclear force would be enough. China, the nation most likely to try to match the U.S. nuclear capability, is thought to have a total inventory of 400 nuclear weapons, including a small but growing ballistic missile force capable of reaching the United States.

In the past, all nuclear force reductions took place within U.S.-Russian arms control agreements. Given today's geopolitical realities, it is not necessary to wait for formal agreements before moving toward lower numbers. To be sure, the pace of reduction should consider Russian force levels as well as political developments there. But Washington's concern with Moscow's nuclear stockpile has as much, if not more, to do with security and the threat of "loose nukes" than with the threat of Russian attack.

Alarm over the security of nuclear stockpiles also points to the need to change the way nuclear warheads are counted. In the past, Washington counted only operational military warheads and delivery vehicles, the weapons that posed the most immediate threat. Now, however, preventing proliferation requires focusing not only on a country's deployed nuclear capability, but also on the security of its nuclear material and the intentions of those who control it. Accordingly, all nuclear weapons and material—including deployed warheads, warheads undergoing maintenance or modification, decommissioned warheads, and all weapons-grade highly enriched uranium and separated plutonium—should be counted as part of a nation's nuclear inventory.

This revised accounting scheme would do away with the anachronistic distinction between long-range strategic and short-range tactical weapons; today, all nuclear weapons are of equal concern. It would also drive home the importance of securing a country's entire nuclear inventory, including decommissioned warheads and nuclear-related materials (such as spent fuel and low-enriched uranium). Removing a warhead from the active force would shift it to a different accounting category, not drop it from the inventory altogether, because the device and its nuclear material would still require secure supervision.

Meanwhile, the United States should make its own total nuclear inventory known to the public, reporting the number of warheads and the amount of material in each category as an example to other governments. During the Cold War, there was good reason to keep this information secret. Now, however, greater transparency, consistent with proliferation concerns, would enhance U.S. security by giving allies comfort and prospective proliferators pause. Nations resisting disclosure would be inviting increased international scrutiny of their capabilities and intentions.

LOW-PROFILE MANAGEMENT

RESPONSIBILITY for managing the United States' nuclear weapons complex falls to the National Nuclear Security Administration (NNSA) of the Department of Energy (DOE). The NNSA's budget request for fiscal year 2005 was $6.6 billion, and this is expected to grow to $7.5 billion by 2009. The agency, which has some 35,000 employees, faces significant obstacles, including assuring the competence of its staff. The generation of scientists and engineers that developed, built, and tested nuclear weapons has long since retired. The current work force at the three main weapons laboratories—at Los Alamos, New Mexico; Livermore, California; and Sandia, New Mexico—has little direct experience designing or testing weapons. And the DOE's stringent response to recent unfortunate security lapses has hurt morale and clouded the atmosphere in the laboratories.

In 1992, the Exon-Hatfield-Mitchell amendment barred nuclear tests except those motivated by concern about the safety and reliability of weapons already in the stockpile. Since then there has been general agreement that there is no such need (affirmed by annual Defense Department reviews of nuclear safety and reliability), and the United States has observed a testing moratorium.

In the absence of a test program, the DOE has established a "stockpile stewardship program" designed to preserve the knowledge and technology required to extend the life of existing warheads. Advanced computing technology—bolstered by the DOE's impressive Accelerated Strategic Computing Initiative—has allowed modeling and simulations that can partially substitute for instrumented laboratory tests. The program also includes nuclear-weapons-related subcritical laboratory experimentation, conducted, for example, in the x-ray radiographic test facility at Los Alamos and the laser ignition facility at Livermore.

The premise behind the stockpile stewardship program is that computer simulation of the nuclear explosion sequence (beginning with chemical explosive detonation in the primary and ending with fission and thermonuclear burn in the secondary), confirmed with data from experimental facilities, can give technicians confidence in new or modified weapons. Scientists disagree, however, about whether this premise is correct. Some argue that the current program is enough to confirm the safety and reliability of existing weapons. The only way to prove the effectiveness of the strategy, however, is to demonstrate that computer codes can in fact predict the results of a nuclear explosion, as the program assumes. This suggests the need for a "scientific confirmation test," meant not to ensure stockpile security or to develop new weapons but to prove that the practical physics underpinning the nuclear program still holds. Accordingly, scientific confirmation should be added as an acceptable rationale for testing, in addition to the verification of the correction of a safety or reliability problem that cannot be verified by other means. Indeed, in the past, confidence in the stockpile came largely from development tests, rather than from tests specifically designed to confirm weapons reliability.

The NNSA program also includes several large and costly facilities intended to modernize the production infrastructure. These include a new tritium extraction facility at Los Alamos, a pit disassembly and conversion facility at the Savannah River Laboratory in South Carolina, and plans for a modern pit facility. Each individual project may be justified, but the quantity, size, and timing of such developments contribute to an impression that the U.S. weapons complex is growing and that the United States is not, in fact, reducing the role of nuclear weapons.

A more realistic U.S. nuclear posture would require a smaller but still high-quality weapons research and engineering program and a consolidated production complex. The existing stockpile stewardship program's approach is reasonable, but confirmation that physics knowledge remains adequate may require (and, from a technical point of view, ideally would require) occasional "scientific confirmation tests." Careful timing and management of such tests could mitigate the adverse international reaction they would inevitably cause. Meanwhile, conceptual work on the design of new warheads should not be precluded per se, but if it is proposed and performed there must be no ambiguity about future development. Greater transparency with regard to the activities of the NNSA would also help convince domestic and international audiences that Washington is striking the right balance in managing its nuclear weapons.

RETHINKING ARMS CONTROL

A NEW U.S. nuclear posture should include consideration of several current and prospective arms control measures. The most controversial is the Comprehensive Test Ban Treaty (CTBT), which would permanently ban all future nuclear tests, with no provision for withdrawal. The United States has not ratified the CTBT (nor have India, Iran, Israel, North Korea, and Pakistan), but 109 nations (including the United Kingdom, France, Russia, and China) have.

Proponents of the CTBT see its potential for strengthening international norms against nuclear weapons as vital to nonproliferation efforts. They argue that it is especially worthwhile because, with the stockpile stewardship program in place, the United States does not need testing to confirm stockpile safety or reliability. Opponents respond that the CTBT has verification problems, that testing has no direct effect on either the pace or the likelihood of success by determined proliferators such as North Korea and Iran, and that, given the uncertainty of future requirements for new weapons, forgoing forever the possibility of new tests is a mistake.

Both sides in this debate have strengths and weaknesses. Opponents of the CTBT are correct that testing should be allowed if the assurance of stockpile safety or reliability requires it. However, they exaggerate the treaty's verification problems: only very low-yield tests (or tests that insulate the explosion from the surrounding earth) have much of a chance of escaping detection. CTBT advocates, meanwhile, are correct that the treaty would bolster international nonproliferation norms, even if their

assertion that no test will ever again be necessary to assure stockpile safety is dubious. (In fact, some CTBT advocates may oppose testing precisely because they believe that confidence in the reliability of nuclear weapons will erode without it—to the point that nuclear weapons will lose their deterrent value and become irrelevant.) Those who attempt to sidestep the issue by claiming that a future president could invoke the supreme national interest to renounce the treaty are implying that it is better to accept a treaty despite major reservations than to work to craft one that resolves difficult issues.

There is, fortunately, a sensible middle ground in this dispute: a CTBT of limited term. Former national security officials Brent Scowcroft and Arnold Kanter have proposed entering into the CTBT for a five-year term (since all agree that U.S. nuclear tests will not be necessary anytime soon), with possible five-year extensions, after ratification by the Senate. Such a compromise would have the advantage of strengthening nonproliferation efforts and thus be preferable to having no CTBT—while leaving open the possibility of not extending the treaty if geopolitical circumstances or stockpile considerations change. A similar approach worked with the NPT, which was ratified in 1969 for a 25-year period, with review conferences every five years, and then made permanent in 1995. Opponents argue that it would be difficult or impossible at this stage to change the terms of the internationally negotiated CTBT. But the CTBT does not enter into force until 44 countries, including the United States, have ratified it, so the choice is whether the United States prefers a renewable five-year CTBT to no CTBT at all.

The U.S. nuclear posture must change to meet a transformed nuclear threat.

A second still-unratified arms control treaty is the fissile material production cutoff treaty, originally proposed by President Bill Clinton at the United Nations in 1993; it would prohibit new production of separated plutonium or highly enriched uranium. This is an attractive measure, because the United States and other nuclear states have ample amounts of weapons-usable material. The ban would prohibit any state from undertaking new production, thus serving basic nonproliferation objectives, and would limit the total amount of material that must be kept secure.

The UN Conference on Disarmament has been deliberating the cutoff treaty for several years. On August 4, 2004, the U.S. ambassador to the UN, John Danforth, announced that the Bush administration, although supportive of the ban, does not believe that effective verification is feasible. This and earlier statements by the Bush administration imply that alleged verification shortcomings will be a barrier to an agreement. But with a new nuclear posture, opposition to this treaty would be inexplicable. No arms control treaty is perfectly verifiable; there is always a risk that a violation will go undetected. Verification could be enhanced if signatory countries agreed to inspections. Traditionally, the United States and other nuclear weapons states have not accepted such inspections, but there is now little reason for the United States to resist them. Here again, transparency is in the interest of the United States. A signatory violating the treaty would be stigmatized as a proliferator before the international community. And a state that refused to sign the treaty would be signaling its interest in acquiring material suitable for making a bomb.

Arms control advocates have proposed two other major changes to U.S. nuclear policy: pledging "no first use" and de-alerting nuclear forces. Even with a changed nuclear posture, however, the arguments for such reforms are not convincing.

Since 1978, Washington has committed to not using nuclear weapons against non-nuclear states that are signatories to the NPT, unless they attack the United States with the backing of a nuclear state. Successive U.S. administrations, however, have also maintained a policy of "strategic ambiguity," refusing to rule out a nuclear response to a biological or chemical attack. Supporters of a stronger no-first-use policy argue that strategic ambiguity sends the wrong signal to other governments: even the United States, with its overwhelming conventional military advantage, sees value in leaving open the possibility of first use. And this impression, they argue, undermines nonproliferation. They underestimate, however, just how much strategic ambiguity aids deterrence by keeping potential adversaries uncertain about a U.S. response.

De-alerting nuclear forces would mean increasing the amount of time between the decision to launch a nuclear weapon and its actual launch, in order to prevent accidental or unauthorized attacks, avoid misunderstanding, and add time to negotiate in a crisis. During the Cold War, a prompt launch capability was necessary to assure the survivability of land-based forces. Those who support de-alerting U.S. nuclear forces correctly argue that such a concern is no longer relevant. But they underestimate the practical obstacles to de-alerting submarine-launched warheads. If warheads were removed from the submarines, maintaining a continuous sea-based deployment would not be possible; the ships would need to be kept close to port, near the warheads, where they would be more vulnerable. Alternatively, communications to submarines on station could be managed to lengthen the time to launch, but it is hard to see how this could serve as a verifiable confidence-building measure. Such a step would be easily reversible anyway, making its usefulness quite limited.

Finally, the United States should make clear that any reduction is not a first step toward the abolition of the U.S. nuclear force. The U.S. nuclear posture should be consistent with foreseeable U.S. security interests. In the distant future, depending on the state of the world, a move to even lower—or potentially back to higher—levels might make sense.

Even with the Cold War over, nuclear weapons remain far more than empty symbols; they cannot simply be eliminated, despite the hopes of some arms-control advocates and the stated goals of the NPT. Nonetheless, the U.S. nuclear posture must change to meet a transformed nuclear threat. The U.S. nuclear force must be strong enough to deter and to survive attack even as it serves, as much as possible, to advance Washington's nonproliferation goals. Instead of treating nonproliferation and the maintenance of a nuclear deterrent as mutually exclusive, the United States must shape and manage its nuclear force in a way that does both.

JOHN DEUTCH is Institute Professor at the Massachusetts Institute of Technology. He served as Deputy Secretary of Defense, Chairman of the Nuclear Weapons Council, and Director of Central Intelligence during the Clinton administration and as Undersecretary of Energy during the Carter administration.

DOUBLE-EDGED SHIELD

The United States is considering relaxing export controls
so it can share missile defense technology with its friends—
a move that could help its enemies.

Sarah Chankin-Gould & Ivan Oelrich

"**T**HE GRAVEST DANGER our Nation faces lies at the crossroads of radicalism and technology," declares the White House in its National Security Strategy. "We will build defenses against ballistic missiles and other means of delivery. We will cooperate with other nations to deny, contain, and curtail our enemies' efforts to acquire dangerous technologies."

In principle, defending the homeland from missile attack and denying adversaries offensive missile technology should be complementary goals. Yet a growing chorus of missile defense proponents both within and outside the Bush administration now argues that current efforts to limit the exports of ballistic missile technology are stifling international efforts to cooperate on building an effective missile defense system. In December 2002, just six months after the United States withdrew from the Anti-Ballistic Missile Treaty—an agreement that President George W. Bush called a "Cold War relic"—the White House issued a document, National Security Presidential Directive (NSPD)-23, that appeared to place the Missile Technology Control Regime (MTCR) in its crosshairs.[1]

A voluntary, nonbinding arrangement that currently includes 34 countries, the MTCR was formed in 1987 and relies on strong export controls to limit transfers of equipment and technology to retard missile proliferation. A list of controlled items appears in the MTCR Annex and is divided into two categories. Category I items, which face the strictest export controls, are complete missile systems capable of carrying a 500-kilogram payload at least 300 kilometers (parameters that reflect the weight of a primitive nuclear weapon and a strategically important range). Category II items, which are considered for export on a case-by-case basis, are missile-related components in-cluding propellants, structural materials, specific types of computers, launch support equipment, and flight control and navigation equipment.

The problem, as the Bush administration sees it, is that many of those Category II items are essential components of a ballistic missile defense system. And working with foreign countries to develop and deploy that technology has emerged as a key element of the White House's strategy. In part, the administration is motivated by a belief that missile defenses are of such benefit that it has a moral requirement to share them. And, in part, it is motivated by the desire to demonstrate that missile defense is not a self-serving plan meant to increase U.S. military dominance. Of course, missile defense cooperation also brings with it the advantage of gleaning expertise from partners' technological capabilities.

Thus, NSPD-23 suggests that the time has come to reconsider the onerous export controls imposed by the MTCR. "As part of our efforts to deepen missile defense cooperation with friends and allies, the United States shall seek to eliminate unnecessary impediments to such cooperation," the security directive notes. "The secretaries of Defense and State shall review existing policies and practices governing technology sharing and cooperation on missile defense, including U.S. export control regulations and statutes, with this aim in mind."

Although originally scheduled to be completed within six months, these export control reviews are still a work in progress. The administration has offered no explanation for the delay. If that review process culminates in a decision to dilute MTCR export controls, it is a decision that the United States will come to regret. The technology that the White House labels as purely "defensive" has many applications that could aid would-be adversaries in the development of offensive ballistic missiles. Worse still, that technology could provide other countries with the means to design countermeasures that would thwart the very missile defense program the Bush administration seeks to deploy.

Slow but steady

Proponents of the MTCR are the first to admit that it has several shortcomings. As a voluntary arrangement that relies on the "good faith" of its members, it contains no prescribed sanctions against countries or companies that violate its guidelines. The dual-use nature of missile technology, which is also used for space launch vehicles, makes regulation inherently difficult. Perhaps the MTCR's biggest problem is one of perception: Like all arms control regimes, its failures are obvious, while its accomplishments—the absence of proliferation—are harder to recognize and get credit for.

Yet, the MTCR is not without success stories, like that of Argentina's Condor ballistic missile development program, which the regime brought to a halt. And some missile nonproliferation failures can even be seen as successes for the MTCR. North Korea's trade in its grossly outdated Scud missiles is possible only because interested buyers cannot get access to more modern alternatives, even illicitly.

Moreover, the United States has worked successfully to strengthen the regime's export controls. In 2002, members expanded the MTCR's mandate, pledging to prevent proscribed technologies from falling into the hands of terrorist organizations. And, one year later, regime members added "catchall" provisions to the export controls, enabling states to control items destined for missile programs, even if they are not specifically regulated by the regime. Also, in recognition of the growing threat of biological and chemical weapons, new controls were adopted regulating the export of unmanned aerial vehicles (UAVs) "designed or modified" for aerosol delivery.

Yet, since NSPD-23 became public, debate among analysts and experts about the role of the MTCR has intensified, and calls to eliminate regime controls that might impede missile defense cooperation are gaining wider currency. In October 2003, the *Washington Post*'s Bradley Graham described the MTCR as a "stumbling block" to missile defense cooperation.[2] Last year, Steven Lambakis, a senior analyst at the Virginia-based National Institute for Public Policy, opined in *Defense News* that "while big steps have been taken to internationalize the U.S. missile defense program, we are about to stub our toe on a bureaucratic stone called the Missile Technology Control Regime. This stone needs to be removed because the risks of remaining defenseless against a missile attack far outweigh the risks of discarding the MTCR's outmoded guidelines." For Lambakis and like minded people in and outside of the administration, it is "ironic" that the MTCR "now targets all missile types, even defensive missiles."[3]

Critics of the MTCR often cite the Arrow—Israel's missile defense system that was developed with U.S. funds and assistance—as "Exhibit A" to illustrate the supposed absurdity of the regime. Due to MTCR restrictions, the United States could not build and ship complete Arrow interceptor missiles to Israel because they are Category I missiles. The solution: Boeing produced 51 percent of the components stateside, then shipped them to Israel for assembly. Israel Aircraft Industries produced the other 49 percent. In 2003, when the United States and Israel (a non-MTCR country) were ready to test the Arrow system, they hit another bump in the road. U.S. export control officials worried that after Israel shipped Arrow missiles to the United States for testing, a return shipment to Israel of any untested missiles would be prohibited by the MTCR. The problem was a legal technicality, and was resolved through a legal technicality—Israel retained legal possession of the missiles throughout the testing process.

Echoing the sentiment of MTCR critics, journalists Amy Svitak and Gopal Ratnam wrote in *Defense News*: "The problem faced by the Arrow testers highlights the friction between two goals in U.S. policy: curbing the spread of ballistic missile technology and cooperating with allies to develop an international missile defense system." Yet the Arrow argument is fundamentally irrelevant. Looking beyond the controversy, it is clear that the MTCR worked exactly as it should: The restrictions prompted the careful examination of a missile technology transfer, and they did not prevent cooperation on missile defense. The aerospace industry may complain that these regulations are a burden, but that is the price of a consistent and strong export policy on sensitive missile technology.

The buddy list

With the exception of Russia, an MTCR member, the Bush administration has not yet identified potential missile defense partners. The founding members of the MTCR—Canada, France, Germany, Italy, Japan, and Britain—are probable contenders, as is Australia. (Although Canada has recently declined to participate in the North American missile defense system.) But, beyond these countries, the White House's concept of "friends and allies" is vague. A second tier of countries is likely to include Israel, Taiwan, and South Korea—perhaps even Pakistan and Egypt.[4]

Yet when it comes to sharing missile defense technology, especially with non-NATO countries, there may be such a thing as too many friends. As Henry Sokolski, the executive director of the Washington-based Nonproliferation Policy Education Center, has pointed out, it is difficult for the United States to hold others accountable for their missile exports, when they can argue that the United States transfers missile defense and UAV technologies to a number of "non-security treaty" countries, including the United Arab Emirates, Saudi Arabia, India, Pakistan, Taiwan, Israel, and Egypt.

Another concern is that weapons can outlast alliances. When the French sold Exocet missiles to Argentina in the late 1970s, they did not foresee that their British allies would face those very missiles in the Falkland Islands war in 1982. And the United States has had reason to regret its sale of F-14 fighter planes to the shah of Iran. Similarly, some of the estimated 2,000 Stinger surface-to-air missiles transferred to mujahideen in Afghanistan in the 1980s to fight the Soviets might now be in the hands of Taliban and Al Qaeda fighters.

The gravest danger in sharing missile technology is that of secondary or tertiary proliferation—equipment and technology may end up where it's not supposed to. Even the closest and most reliable U.S. allies, Britain and Australia, have exhibited shortcomings in their efforts to stop the pass-through of sensitive equipment. Britain, for example, has an arms embargo proscribing weapons sales to Iran, but no trade embargo. In 2002, the BBC exposed the British Department of Trade and Industry's approval of the sale of beryllium, a material used in nuclear weapons, to Iran, because the transfer was not considered an arms sale.[5] The more countries the United States shares technology with, the more the proliferation risk grows. And the less advanced a nation's missile program, the bigger the boon U.S. missile defense technology would be. This concern is not merely theoretical. In Pakistan—a country that is one of the most recent additions to the U.S. "friends" list—A. Q. Khan's recently exposed illegal nuclear underground network depended on knowledge stolen from countries such as Germany and the Netherlands.

As for Russia, the arsenal it inherited from the Soviet Union is in itself reason enough to court Moscow's cooperation on security issues. But this effort is not without serious risks. In its June 2002 *Unclassified Report to Congress on the Acquisition of Technology Relating to Weapons of Mass Destruction and Advanced Conventional Munitions,* the CIA identified Russia, North Korea, and China as "key suppliers" in the global proliferation chain. It is not unthinkable that Russia might share U.S. missile defense technology with China. Moscow has already directly assisted Beijing's weapons program, which has also benefited from technology and know-how gleaned from its dealings with the West. Often these sales begin legally, but are diverted for military purposes. In 1994, for example, McDonnell Douglas sold machine tools to the China National Aero-Technology Import and Export Corporation for use in the Trunkliner commercial aircraft program, but a number of these tools were diverted to the Nanchang Aircraft Manufacturing Company—a producer of cruise missiles.[6] China, in turn, has shared critical military technology with Pakistan, Iran, Libya, and North Korea. The technology that the United States shares with its small circle of friends could over time become the possession of a wide array of adversaries.

Making missiles easy

Is it possible to export technology that is useful only for missile *defense,* but would not aid development of a missile *offense*? Wishful thinking. Strip away the semantics surrounding this debate, and you are left with the bare reality that a missile is a rocket equipped with a guidance system that can be pointed in any direction.

Rockets use either liquid- or solid-propellant; the technologies for each are very different. A major danger of looser export controls on missile defense-related technology is that it would allow a proliferator to move from liquid- to solid-fuel rockets. In general, liquid propellants are more efficient at lifting payloads because they contain more energy for a given weight than do solids. But volatile liquid fuel is difficult to store long-term. Solid fuel can stay stable for years and be used on a moment's notice. Because of these differences, space launch vehicles tend to use liquid propellants, while solid rockets are strongly preferred by the military.

In principle, a defensive ballistic missile interceptor could use either solid or liquid propellants. In practice, solid propellants are required. An interceptor needs to do more than get a certain payload to a certain place—it needs to get the payload there fast if it is to meet the oncoming missile halfway through its flight. While a liquid propellant rocket could be designed for rapid acceleration, the technical obstacles are formidable. Solid fuel rockets have a higher acceleration rate and allow for a more efficient interceptor design.

In their efforts to develop ballistic missiles, nascent proliferators will almost certainly start out with the militarily less desirable (but technologically less sophisticated) liquid-propellant rockets. However, if those countries gained access to missile defense technology, they could gain the know-how to speed the shift from liquid- to solid-propellant offensive missiles. That's bad news from the perspective of missile defense proponents. For starters, solid-fuel rockets are more mobile, making them harder to locate and destroy on the ground. Secondly, launch preparation is simpler and faster, reducing the window for intelligence to provide advance warning. And, finally, since solid-fuel missiles possess faster acceleration, they are much harder to hit.

Indeed, defensive rocket technology would even improve the offensive capabilities of nations that already possess long-range, solid-fuel rockets. The performance demands of a defensive missile exceed those of an offensive missile by almost any measure. Technologies essential to missile defense, such as high-temperature nozzles, filament-wound rocket motor casings, and high-energy propellants, can all be applied to offensive missiles to give them longer range, greater speed, and larger payloads.

Similarly, the performance demands for guidance and control in defensive missiles are greater than those of offensive missiles. An offensive missile targets an entire city; a defensive interceptor targets a solitary reentry vehicle, perhaps only a meter wide. Moreover, while the target of an offensive missile is typically a fixed point, the interceptor must strike a moving target—hitting a bullet with a bullet, as the saying goes. Loosening the MTCR restrictions on exports of guidance and control systems would likely allow potential adversaries to enhance their targeting systems.

Even components of missile defense that have no apparent offensive capabilities could pose a long-term threat. The current U.S. defensive missile design provides an example. Radar detects and tracks the attacking missile. The interceptor is launched and, with information from the radar, is guided to a target "box." Once inside this space, the interceptor's homing vehicle will pick up the enemy warhead on its infrared sensor, and, based on those sensor readings, the homing vehicle will guide itself to a collision with the warhead. (It remains to be seen whether this system will actually work as planned, but it is described here as it is meant to function.) This infrared homing sensor has no lethal applications. The United States could export that technology with complete confidence it would not show up in the next generation of offensive missiles. But, exporting the guidance technology or homing vehicle would allow another nation to determine exactly how sensitive the sensor is, what wavelengths of light it detects, its field of view, and its agility. In effect, the United States would deliver to its potential adversaries the precise technical specs required to build decoys or countermeasures to outwit U.S. interceptors. Missile defense already pushes the boundaries of what is physically possible and technically feasible, and anything that helps the attacker build countermeasures will make ballistic missile interception impossible.

The best defense

Those who portray the MTCR as an impediment to homeland security would do well to remember the underlying nature of the threat: If the crux of national defense is an evolving missile defense system, then the key to success is to evolve that defense faster than enemies make technological advances. The MTCR has done that by slowing the proliferation of ballistic missile technology, thus delaying advances in enemy technology while the United States continues to improve its defense capabilities.

What are the best options for sharing ballistic missile defenses? If exporting defensive missile technology, components, and complete systems will aid the attackers at least as much as the defenders, there is no gain in weakening the MTCR's controls, and much to be lost. If sharing missile defense with the world is important, then the United States should, along with other MTCR nations, form a consortium to share not technology or missiles, but the service.[7] By installing and maintaining complete missiles, the United States could extend the umbrella of missile defense over its allies—without the risks associated with technology transfers. The defended nation would operate the launchers, even conduct live firings and test intercepts, but would not be allowed to disassemble the missile, which would remain under the formal ownership of the consortium. To remove any hint that the United States is motivated by profits, this service should be highly subsidized by the missile supplier. To allay fears that the missile supplier could apply political pressure by threatening withdrawal of the missiles, no member could veto the consortium's services.

The best defenses are multilayered; for ballistic missile defenses, one would ideally have boost-phase, midcourse, and terminal defenses for maximum protection. But the real first layer of defense is export controls. If the United States weakens those controls for the sake of an unproven missile defense, it risks a regime that, though flawed, does work.

Notes

1. Available at www.fas.org/irp/offdocs/nspd/nspd-23.htm.

2. Bradley Graham, "U.S. Controls Hamper Foreign Role in Missile Defense; Bush-Ordered Review of Restrictions Is Running Late and Into Disagreements on Exceptions," *Washington Post,* October 19, 2003, p. A27.

3. Steven Lambakis, "MTCR Could Cripple Missile Defense," *Defense News,* vol. 19, no. 7, February 16, 2004, p. 37.

4. Henry Sokolski, "Missile Nonproliferation and Missile Defense," Heritage Lectures, no. 761, July 12, 2002.

5. "UK 'Sells' Bomb Material to Iran," BBC Radio, September 23, 2002.

6. "China's Missile Imports and Assistance," chart prepared by the Center for Nonproliferation Studies, Monterey Institute of International Studies, for the Nuclear Threat Initiative.

7. There are several proposals for internationalizing the nuclear fuel cycle so that only a handful of nations will have the ability to enrich uranium or reprocess plutonium. These suppliers would provide uranium, probably at or below market rates, to the world's reactors, but the uranium would remain under the ownership and control of the international suppliers' consortium. Similarly, MTCR nations could provide ballistic missile defense services.

Sarah Chankin-Gould *is an alumna of the Herbert Scoville Junior Peace Fellowship. Ivan Oelrich is the director of the Strategic Security Project at the Federation of American Scientists.*

Apocalypse Soon

Robert McNamara is worried. He knows how close we've come. His counsel helped the Kennedy administration avert nuclear catastrophe during the Cuban Missile Crisis. Today, he believes the United States must no longer rely on nuclear weapons as a foreign-policy tool. To do so is immoral, illegal, and dreadfully dangerous.

Robert S. McNamara

It is time—well past time, in my view—for the United States to cease its Cold War-style reliance on nuclear weapons as a foreign policy tool. At the risk of appearing simplistic and provocative, I would characterize current U.S. nuclear weapons policy as immoral, illegal, militarily unnecessary, and dreadfully dangerous. The risk of an accidental or inadvertent nuclear launch is unacceptably high. Far from reducing these risks, the Bush administration has signaled that it is committed to keeping the U.S. nuclear arsenal as a mainstay of its military power—a commitment that is simultaneously eroding the international norms that have limited the spread of nuclear weapons and fissile materials for 50 years. Much of the current U.S. nuclear policy has been in place since before I was secretary of defense, and it has only grown more dangerous and diplomatically destructive in the intervening years.

Today, the United States has deployed approximately 4,500 strategic, offensive nuclear warheads. Russia has roughly 3,800. The strategic forces of Britain, France, and China are considerably smaller, with 200-400 nuclear weapons in each state's arsenal. The new nuclear states of Pakistan and India have fewer than 100 weapons each. North Korea now claims to have developed nuclear weapons, and U.S. intelligence agencies estimate that Pyongyang has enough fissile material for 2-8 bombs.

How destructive are these weapons? The average U.S. warhead has a destructive power 20 times that of the Hiroshima bomb. Of the 8,000 active or operational U.S. warheads, 2,000 are on hair-trigger alert, ready to be launched on 15 minutes' warning. How are these weapons to be used? The United States has never endorsed the policy of "no first use," not during my seven years as secretary or since. We have been and remain prepared to initiate the use of nuclear weapons—by the decision of one person, the president—against either a nuclear or nonnuclear enemy whenever we believe it is in our interest to do so. For decades, U.S. nuclear forces have been sufficiently strong to absorb a first strike and then inflict "unacceptable" damage on an opponent. This has been and (so long as we face a nuclear-armed, potential adversary) must continue to be the foundation of our nuclear deterrent.

In my time as secretary of defense, the commander of the U.S. Strategic Air Command (SAC) carried with him a secure telephone, no matter where he went, 24 hours a day, seven days a week, 365 days a year. The telephone of the commander, whose headquarters were in Omaha, Nebraska, was linked to the underground command post of the North American Defense Command, deep inside Cheyenne Mountain, in Colorado, and to the U.S. president, wherever he happened to be. The president always had at hand nuclear release codes in the so-called football, a briefcase carried for the president at all times by a U.S. military officer.

What is shocking is that today, more than a decade after the end of the Cold War, the basic U.S. nuclear policy is unchanged.

The SAC commander's orders were to answer the telephone by no later than the end of the third ring. If it rang, and he was informed that a nuclear attack of enemy ballistic missiles appeared to be under way, he was allowed 2 to 3 minutes to decide whether the warning was valid (over the years, the United States has received many false warnings), and if so, how the United States should respond. He was then given approximately 10 minutes to determine what to recommend, to locate and advise the president, permit the president to discuss the situation with two or three close advisors (presumably the secretary of defense and the chairman of the Joint Chiefs of Staff), and to receive the president's decision and pass it immediately, along with the codes, to the launch sites. The president essentially had two options: He could decide to ride out the attack and defer until later any decision to launch a retaliatory strike. Or, he could order an immediate retaliatory strike, from a menu of options, thereby launching U.S. weapons that were targeted on the opponent's military-industrial assets. Our opponents in Moscow presumably had and have similar arrangements.

The whole situation seems so bizarre as to be beyond belief. On any given day, as we go about our business, the president is prepared to make a decision within 20 minutes that could launch one of the most devastating weapons in the world. To declare war requires an act of congress, but to launch a nuclear holocaust requires 20 minutes' deliberation by the president and his advisors. But that is what we have lived with for 40 years. With very few changes, this system remains largely intact, including the "football," the president's constant companion.

I was able to change some of these dangerous policies and procedures. My colleagues and I started arms control talks; we installed safeguards to reduce the risk of unauthorized launches; we added options to the nuclear war plans so that the president did not have to choose between an all-or-nothing response, and we eliminated the vulnerable and provocative nuclear missiles in Turkey. I wish I had done more, but we were in the midst of the Cold War, and our options were limited.

The United States and our NATO allies faced a strong Soviet and Warsaw Pact conventional threat. Many of the allies (and some in Washington as well) felt strongly that preserving the U.S. option of launching a first strike was necessary for the sake of keeping the Soviets at bay. What is shocking is that today, more than a decade after the end of the Cold War, the basic U.S. nuclear policy is unchanged. It has not adapted to the collapse of the Soviet Union. Plans and procedures have not been revised to make the United States or other countries less likely to push the button. At a minimum, we should remove all strategic nuclear weapons from "hair-trigger" alert, as others have recommended, including Gen. George Lee Butler, the last commander of SAC. That simple change would greatly reduce the risk of an accidental nuclear launch. It would also signal to other states that the United States is taking steps to end its reliance on nuclear weapons.

We pledged to work in good faith toward the eventual elimination of nuclear arsenals when we negotiated the Nuclear Non-Proliferation Treaty (NPT) in 1968. In May, diplomats from more than 180 nations are meeting in New York City to review the NPT and assess whether members are living up to the agreement. The United States is focused, for understandable reasons, on persuading North Korea to rejoin the treaty and on negotiating deeper constraints on Iran's nuclear ambitions. Those states must be convinced to keep the promises they made when they originally signed the NPT—that they would not build nuclear weapons in return for access to peaceful uses of nuclear energy. But the attention of many nations, including some potential new nuclear weapons states, is also on the United States. Keeping such large numbers of weapons, and maintaining them on hair-trigger alert, are potent signs that the United States is not seriously working toward the elimination of its arsenal and raises troubling questions as to why any other state should restrain its nuclear ambitions.

A PREVIEW OF THE APOCALYPSE

The destructive power of nuclear weapons is well known, but given the United States' continued reliance on them, it's worth remembering the danger they present. A 2000 report by the International Physicians for the Prevention of Nuclear War describes the likely effects of a single 1 megaton weapon—dozens of which are contained in the Russian and U.S. inventories. At ground zero, the explosion creates a crater 300 feet deep and 1,200 feet in diameter. Within one second, the atmosphere itself ignites into a fireball more than a half-mile in diameter. The surface of the fireball radiates nearly three times the light and heat of a comparable area of the surface of the sun, extinguishing in seconds all life below and radiating outward at the speed of light, causing instantaneous severe burns to people within one to three miles. A blast wave of compressed air reaches a distance of three miles in about 12 seconds, flattening factories and commercial buildings. Debris carried by winds of 250 mph inflicts lethal injuries throughout the area. At least 50 percent of people in the area die immediately, prior to any injuries from radiation or the developing firestorm.

Of course, our knowledge of these effects is not entirely hypothetical. Nuclear weapons, with roughly one seventieth of the power of the 1 megaton bomb just described, were twice used by the United States in August 1945. One atomic bomb was dropped on Hiroshima. Around 80,000 people died immediately; approximately 200,000 died eventually. Later, a similar size bomb was dropped on Nagasaki. On Nov. 7, 1995, the mayor of Nagasaki recalled his memory of the attack in testimony to the International Court of Justice:

> Nagasaki became a city of death where not even the sound of insects could be heard. After a while, countless men, women and children began to gather for a drink of water at the banks of nearby Urakami River, their hair and clothing scorched and their burnt skin hanging off in sheets like rags. Begging for help they died one after another in the water or in heaps on the banks.... Four months after the atomic bombing, 74,000 people were dead, and 75,000 had suffered injuries, that is, two-thirds of the city population had fallen victim to this calamity that came upon Nagasaki like a preview of the Apocalypse.

Why did so many civilians have to die? Because the civilians, who made up nearly 100 percent of the victims of Hiroshima and Nagasaki, were unfortunately "co-located" with Japanese military and industrial targets. Their annihilation, though not the objective of those dropping the bombs, was an inevitable result of the choice of those targets. It is worth noting that during the Cold War, the United States reportedly had dozens of nuclear warheads targeted on Moscow alone, because it contained so many military targets and so much "industrial capacity." Presumably, the Soviets similarly targeted many U.S. cities. The statement that our nuclear weapons do not target populations per se was and remains totally misleading in the sense that the so-called collateral damage of large nuclear strikes would include tens of millions of innocent civilian dead.

This in a nutshell is what nuclear weapons do: They indiscriminately blast, burn, and irradiate with a speed and finality that are almost incomprehensible. This is exactly what countries like the United States and Russia, with nuclear weapons on hairtrigger alert, continue to threaten every minute of every day in this new 21st century.

NO WAY TO WIN

I have worked on issues relating to U.S. and NATO nuclear strategy and war plans for more than 40 years. During that time, I have never seen a piece of paper that outlined a plan for the United States or NATO to initiate the use of nuclear weapons with any benefit for the United States or NATO. I have made this statement in front of audiences, including NATO defense ministers and senior military leaders, many times. No one has ever refuted it. To launch weapons against a nuclear-equipped opponent would be suicidal. To do so against a nonnuclear enemy would be militarily unnecessary, morally repugnant, and politically indefensible.

I reached these conclusions very soon after becoming secretary of defense. Although I believe Presidents John F. Kennedy and Lyndon Johnson shared my view, it was impossible for any of us to make such statements publicly because they were totally contrary to established NATO policy. After leaving the Defense Department, I became president of the World Bank. During my 13-year tenure, from 1968 to 1981, I was prohibited, as an employee of an international institution, from commenting publicly on issues of U.S. national security. After my retirement from the bank, I began to reflect on how I, with seven years' experience as secretary of defense, might contribute to an understanding of the issues with which I began my public service career.

At that time, much was being said and written regarding how the United States could, and why it should, be able to fight and win a nuclear war with the Soviets. This view implied, of course, that nuclear weapons did have military utility; that they could be used in battle with ultimate gain to whoever had the largest force or used them with the greatest acumen. Having studied these views, I decided to go public with some information that I knew would be controversial, but that I felt was needed to inject reality into these increasingly unreal discussions about the military utility of nuclear weapons. In articles and speeches, I criticized the fundamentally flawed assumption that nuclear weapons could be used in some limited way. There is no way to effectively contain a nuclear strike—to keep it from inflicting enormous destruction on civilian life and property, and there is no guarantee against unlimited escalation once the first nuclear strike occurs. We cannot avoid the serious and unacceptable risk of nuclear war until we recognize these facts and base our military plans and policies upon this recognition. I hold these views even more strongly today than I did when I first spoke out against the nuclear dangers our policies were creating. I know from direct experience that U.S. nuclear policy today creates unacceptable risks to other nations and to our own.

To launch weapons against a nuclear power would be suicide. To do so against a nonnuclear enemy would be militarily unnecessary, morally repugnant, and politically indefensible.

WHAT CASTRO TAUGHT US

Among the costs of maintaining nuclear weapons is the risk—to me an unacceptable risk—of use of the weapons either by accident or as a result of misjudgment or miscalculation in times of crisis. The Cuban Missile Crisis demonstrated that the United States and the Soviet Union—and indeed the rest of the world—came within a hair's breadth of nuclear disaster in October 1962. Indeed, according to former Soviet military leaders, at the height of the crisis, Soviet forces in Cuba possessed 162 nuclear warheads, including at least 90 tactical warheads. At about the same time, Cuban President Fidel Castro asked the Soviet ambassador to Cuba to send a cable to Soviet Premier Nikita Khrushchev stating that Castro urged him to counter a U.S. attack with a nuclear response. Clearly, there was a high risk that in the face of a U.S. attack, which many in the U.S. government were prepared to recommend to President Kennedy, the Soviet forces in Cuba would have decided to use their nuclear weapons rather than lose them. Only a few years ago did we learn that the four Soviet submarines trailing the U.S. Naval vessels near Cuba each carried torpedoes with nuclear warheads. Each of the sub commanders had the authority to launch his torpedoes. The situation was even more frightening because, as the lead commander recounted to me, the subs were out of communication with their Soviet bases, and they continued their patrols for four days after Khrushchev announced the withdrawal of the missiles from Cuba.

The lesson, if it had not been clear before, was made so at a conference on the crisis held in Havana in 1992, when we first began to learn from former Soviet officials about their preparations for nuclear war in the event of a U.S. invasion. Near the end of that meeting, I asked Castro whether he would have recommended that Khrushchev use the weapons in the face of a U.S. invasion, and if so, how he thought the United States would respond. "We started from the assumption that if there was an invasion of Cuba, nuclear war would erupt," Castro replied. "We were certain of that.... [W]e would be forced to pay the price that we would disappear." He continued, "Would I have been ready to use nuclear weapons? Yes, I would have agreed to the use of nuclear weapons." And he added, "If Mr. McNamara or Mr. Kennedy had been in our place, and had their country been invaded, or their country was going to be occupied ... I believe they would have used tactical nuclear weapons."

We must move promptly toward the elimination—or near elimination—of all nuclear weapons.

I hope that President Kennedy and I would not have behaved as Castro suggested we would have. His decision would have destroyed his country. Had we responded in a similar way the damage to the United States would have been unthinkable. But human beings are fallible. In conventional war, mistakes cost lives, sometimes thousands of lives. However, if mistakes were to affect decisions relating to the use of nuclear forces, there would be no learning curve. They would result in the destruction of nations. The indefinite combination of human fallibility and nuclear weapons carries a very high risk of nuclear catastrophe. There is no way to reduce the risk to acceptable levels, other than to first eliminate the hair-trigger alert policy and later to eliminate or nearly eliminate nuclear weapons. The United States should move immediately to institute these actions, in cooperation with Russia. That is the lesson of the Cuban Missile Crisis.

A DANGEROUS OBSESSION

On Nov. 13, 2001, President George W. Bush announced that he had told Russian President Vladimir Putin that the United States would reduce "operationally deployed nuclear warheads" from approximately 5,300 to a level between 1,700 and 2,200 over the next decade. This scaling back would approach the 1,500 to 2,200 range that Putin had proposed for Russia. However, the Bush administration's Nuclear Posture Review, mandated by the U.S. Congress and issued in January 2002, presents quite a different story. It assumes that strategic offensive nuclear weapons in much larger numbers than 1,700 to 2,200 will be part of U.S. military forces for the next several decades. Although the number of deployed warheads will be reduced to 3,800 in 2007 and to between 1,700 and 2,200 by 2012, the warheads and many of the launch vehicles taken off deployment will be maintained in a "responsive" reserve from

which they could be moved back to the operationally deployed force. The Nuclear Posture Review received little attention from the media. But its emphasis on strategic offensive nuclear weapons deserves vigorous public scrutiny. Although any proposed reduction is welcome, it is doubtful that survivors—if there were any—of an exchange of 3,200 warheads (the U.S. and Russian numbers projected for 2012), with a destructive power approximately 65,000 times that of the Hiroshima bomb, could detect a difference between the effects of such an exchange and one that would result from the launch of the current U.S. and Russian forces totaling about 12,000 warheads.

In addition to projecting the deployment of large numbers of strategic nuclear weapons far into the future, the Bush administration is planning an extensive and expensive series of programs to sustain and modernize the existing nuclear force and to begin studies for new launch vehicles, as well as new warheads for all of the launch platforms. Some members of the administration have called for new nuclear weapons that could be used as bunker busters against underground shelters (such as the shelters Saddam Hussein used in Baghdad). New production facilities for fissile materials need to be built to support the expanded force. The plans provide for integrating a national ballistic missile defense into the new triad of offensive weapons to enhance the nation's ability to use its "power projection forces" by improving our ability to counterattack an enemy. The Bush administration also announced that it has no intention to ask congress to ratify the Comprehensive Test Ban Treaty (CTBT), and, though no decision to test has been made, the administration has ordered the national laboratories to begin research on new nuclear weapons designs and to prepare the underground test sites in Nevada for nuclear tests if necessary in the future. Clearly, the Bush administration assumes that nuclear weapons will be part of U.S. military forces for at least the next several decades.

Good faith participation in international negotiation on nuclear disarmament—including participation in the CTBT—is a legal and political obligation of all parties to the NPT that entered into force in 1970 and was extended indefinitely in 1995. The Bush administration's nuclear program, alongside its refusal to ratify the CTBT, will be viewed, with reason, by many nations as equivalent to a U.S. break from the treaty. It says to the nonnuclear weapons nations, "We, with the strongest conventional military force in the world, require nuclear weapons in perpetuity, but you, facing potentially well-armed opponents, are never to be allowed even one nuclear weapon."

If the United States continues its current nuclear stance, over time, substantial proliferation of nuclear weapons will almost surely follow. Some, or all, of such nations as Egypt, Japan, Saudi Arabia, Syria, and Taiwan will very likely initiate nuclear weapons programs, increasing both the risk of use of the weapons and the diversion of weapons and fissile materials into the hands of rogue states or terrorists. Diplomats and intelligence agencies believe Osama bin Laden has made several attempts to acquire nuclear weapons or fissile materials. It has been widely reported that Sultan Bashirud-din Mahmood, former director of Pakistan's nuclear reactor complex, met with bin Laden several times. Were al Qaeda to acquire fissile materials, especially enriched uranium, its ability to produce nuclear weapons would be great. The knowledge of how to construct a simple gun-type nuclear device, like the one we dropped on Hiroshima, is now wide-spread. Experts have little doubt that terrorists could construct such a primitive device if they acquired the requisite enriched uranium material. Indeed, just last summer, at a meeting of the National Academy of Sciences, former Secretary of Defense William J. Perry said, "I have never been more fearful of a nuclear detonation than now…. There is a greater than 50 percent probability of a nuclear strike on U.S. targets within a decade." I share his fears.

A MOMENT OF DECISION

We are at a critical moment in human history—perhaps not as dramatic as that of the Cuban Missile Crisis, but a moment no less crucial. Neither the Bush administration, the congress, the American people, nor the people of other nations have debated the merits of alternative, long-range nuclear weapons policies for their countries or the world. They have not examined the military utility of the weapons; the risk of inadvertent or accidental use; the moral and legal considerations relating to the use or threat of use of the weapons; or the impact of current policies on proliferation. Such debates are long overdue. If they are held, I believe they will conclude, as have I and an increasing number of senior military leaders, politicians, and civilian security experts: We must move promptly toward the elimination—or near elimination—of all nuclear weapons. For many, there is a strong temptation to cling to the strategies of the past 40 years. But to do so would be a serious mistake leading to unacceptable risks for all nations.

Robert S. McNamara *was U.S. secretary of defense from 1961 to 1968 and president of the World Bank from 1968 to 1981.*

UNIT 8

The Iraq War and Beyond

Unit Selections

Key Points to Consider

- How important are allies and/or the United Nations in the reconstruction of Iraq?

- How important is Iraq to the security interests of the United States?

- Make a list of dimensions along which you would measure the success or failure of the reconstruction of Iraq? How would you rate the situation today along these dimensions?

- How quickly should the United States undertake another "Iraq War?" What words of advice would you give policy makers about to embark on such a war?

- When and under what conditions should the United States leave Iraq?

- What should U.S. foreign policy be toward Iran?

Student Website

www.mhcls.com/online

Internet References

Further information regarding these websites may be found in this book's preface or online.

White House: Renewal in Iraq
http://www.whitehouse.gov/infocus/iraq/

The Iraq War, from its planning through its conduct, and post war occupation and reconstruction has been the single defining feature of the George W. Bush administration's foreign policy. The Iraq War has come to sharply divide the American public. For its supporters, the Iraq War is the second campaign of the first war of the twenty-first century, the war against terrorism. For its detractors, the Iraq War has served to detract the United States from more critical threats emanating from terrorist groups such as al Qaeda and has isolated the United States from its traditional allies. Conflicts of opinion extend beyond the war to questions about the handling of intelligence and decision-making procedures prior to the terrorist attacks of September 11, 2001. Because it is so central to American foreign policy, we have organized a separate section around evaluations of the Iraq War and its implications for American foreign policy.

In order to better understand the chain of events that led the authors of these essays to take the positions they did, we present a timeline of the Iraq War beginning with President Bush's 2002 State of the Union address. While rumors that the Bush administration was determined to go to war with Iraq, after the defeat of the Taliban in Afghanistan, were widespread in Washington they took on a new intensity following this speech.

- **January 29, 2002**: In his State of the Union address Bush identifies Iraq, North Korea, and Iran as an "axis of evil" and promises that the U.S. would not allow "the world's most dangerous regimes to threaten us with the world's most destructive weapons."
- **September 12, 2002**: Bush addresses the opening session of the United Nations and challenges it to confront the "grave and gathering danger" of Iraq or become irrelevant.
- **September 17, 2002**: The Bush administration releases its national security strategy that replaces deterrence with preemption.
- **October 10, 2002**: Congress authorizes the use of force against Iraq.
- **November 27, 2002**: Weapons inspections resume in Iraq following a unanimous November 8th Security Council resolution calling for tougher arms inspections in Iraq.
- **December 21, 2002**: Bush approves deployment of U.S. forces to the Persian Gulf.
- **February 14, 2003**: UN Weapons Inspector Hans Blix asserts that progress has been made in Iraq.
- **February 24, 2003**: The U.S., Great Britain, and Spain introduce a resolution at the Security Council authorizing the use of military force against Iraq. France, Germany, and Russia oppose the resolution.
- **March 17, 2003**: Bush presents Saddam Hussein with a 48-hour ultimatum to leave Iraq.
- **March 19, 2003**: Operation Iraq Freedom begins with a decapitation strike aimed at Iraqi leadership targets in Baghdad.
- **March 21, 2003**: Major fighting in Iraq begins.
- **April 9, 2003**: Baghdad falls.
- **May 1, 2003**: President Bush declares an end to major combat operations
- **May 19, 2003**: Thousands in Baghdad peacefully protest U.S. presence.
- **May 23, 2003**: UN Security Council lifts sanctions and gives U.S. and Great Britain authority to control Iraq until an elected government is in place.

- **July 9, 2003**: Secretary of Defense Donald Rumsfeld admits that the cost of the war was underestimated by one-half. He now places it at $3.9 billion/month and acknowledges that far more troops than anticipated will be needed for the occupation.
- **July 17, 2003**: U.S. combat deaths in Iraq reach the level of the Persian Gulf War.
- **December 13, 2003**: Saddam Hussein is captured.
- **April 29, 2004**: Photos aired of torture and mistreatment of Iraqi prisoners by U.S. personnel at the Abu Graib prison.
- **June 8, 2004**: UN Security Council passes resolution ending formal occupation and outlining a role for the UN in post-transition Iraq.
- **June 28, 2004**: U.S. transfers power to the new Iraqi government.
- **September 8, 2004**: U.S. casualties reach 1,000 dead. One month later a report estimates Iraqi war-related casualties to be as high as 10,000.
- **October 6, 2004**: U.S. top weapons inspector issues report concluding that Iraq destroyed its illegal weapons months after the 1991 Persian Gulf War.
- **December 1, 2004:** U.S. announces that it plans to expand military presence in Iraq to 150,000 troops.
- **January 30, 2005**: Iraq holds first multiparty election in 50 years.
- **April 28, 2005**: Prime Minister Ibrahim al-Jaafari and his cabinet are approved by the National Assembly,
- **June 16, 2005**: Agreement reached on increasing Sunni participation in drafting of a new constitution.

The first reading in this section, "Lifting the Veil," provides findings from recent public-opinion polls from the Middle East. The author concludes that defeating terrorism will require defeating the rage that fuels it. The article provides an assessment of past U.S. foreign policy toward Iraq. "The Sorcerer's Apprentice," provides a highly critical overview written from the political right of American foreign policy toward Iraq under George W. Bush and his predecessors in office. The final two articles address the current and future security concerns the U.S. will face in the region. In "The Ethics of Exit," five observers give us their views on whether or not it is time for the United States to leave Iraq. "Taking on Tehran," directs our attention to the difficult question of how the United States should respond to the aggressive and anti-American foreign policy of Iran.

Lifting the Veil
Understanding the Roots of Islamic Militancy

Henry Munson

In the wake of the attacks of September 11, 2001, many intellectuals have argued that Muslim extremists like Osama bin Laden despise the United States primarily because of its foreign policy. Conversely, US President George Bush's administration and its supporters have insisted that extremists loathe the United States simply because they are religious fanatics who "hate our freedoms." These conflicting views of the roots of militant Islamic hostility toward the United States lead to very different policy prescriptions. If US policies have caused much of this hostility, it would make sense to change those policies, if possible, to dilute the rage that fuels Islamic militancy. If, on the other hand, the hostility is the result of religious fanaticism, then the use of brute force to suppress fanaticism would appear to be a sensible course of action.

Groundings for Animosity

Public opinion polls taken in the Islamic world in recent years provide considerable insight into the roots of Muslim hostility toward the United States, indicating that for the most part, this hostility has less to do with cultural or religious differences than with US policies in the Arab world. In February and March 2003, Zogby International conducted a survey on behalf of Professor Shibley Telhami of the University of Maryland involving 2,620 men and women in Egypt, Jordan, Lebanon, Morocco, and Saudi Arabia. Most of those surveyed had "unfavorable attitudes" toward the United States and said that their hostility to the United States was based primarily on US policy rather than on their values. This was true of 67 percent of the Saudis surveyed. In Egypt, however, only 46 percent said their hostility resulted from US policy, while 43 percent attributed their attitudes to their values as Arabs. This is surprising given that the prevailing religious values in Saudi Arabia are more conservative than in Egypt. Be that as it may, a plurality of people in all the countries surveyed said that their hostility toward the United States was primarily based on their opposition to US policy.

The issue that arouses the most hostility in the Middle East toward the United States is the Israeli-Palestinian conflict and what Muslims perceive as US responsibility for the suffering of the Palestinians. A similar Zogby International survey from the summer of 2001 found that more than 80 percent of the respondents in Egypt, Kuwait, Lebanon, and Saudi Arabia ranked the Palestinian issue as one of the three issues of greatest importance to them. A survey of Muslim "opinion leaders" released by the Pew Research Center for the People and the Press in December 2001 also found that the US position on the Israeli-Palestinian conflict was the main source of hostility toward the United States.

It is true that Muslim hostility toward Israel is often expressed in terms of anti-Semitic stereotypes and conspiracy theories—think, for example, of the belief widely-held in the Islamic world that Jews were responsible for the terrorists attacks of September 11, 2001. Muslim governments and educators need to further eliminate anti-Semitic bias in the Islamic world. However, it would be a serious mistake to dismiss Muslim and Arab hostility toward Israel as simply a matter of anti-Semitism. In the context of Jewish history, Israel represents liberation. In the context of Palestinian history, it represents subjugation. There will always be a gap between how the West and how the Muslim societies perceive Israel. There will also always be some Muslims (like Osama bin Laden) who will refuse to accept any solution to the Israeli-Palestinian conflict other than the destruction of the state of Israel. That said, if the United States is serious about winning the so-called "war on terror," then resolution of the Israeli-Palestinian conflict should be among its top priorities in the Middle East.

Eradicating, or at least curbing, Palestinian terrorism entails reducing the humiliation, despair, and rage that drive many Palestinians to support militant Islamic groups like Hamas and Islamic Jihad. When soldiers at an Israeli checkpoint prevented Ahmad Qurei (Abu al Ala), one of the principal negotiators of the Oslo accords and president of the Palestinian Authority's parliament, from traveling from Gaza to his home on the West Bank, he declared, "Soon, I too will join Hamas." Qurei's words reflected his outrage at the subjugation of his people and the humiliation that Palestinians experience every day at the checkpoints that surround their homes. Defeating groups like Hamas requires diluting the rage that fuels them. Relying on force alone tends to increase rather than weaken their appeal. This is demonstrated by some of the unintended consequences of the US-led invasion and occupation of Iraq in the spring of 2003.

On June 3, 2003, the Pew Research Center for the People and the Press released a report entitled *Views of a*

Changing World June 2003. This study was primarily based on a survey of nearly 16,000 people in 21 countries (including the Palestinian Authority) from April 28 to May 15, 2003, shortly after the fall of Saddam Hussein's regime. The survey results were supplemented by data from earlier polls, especially a survey of 38,000 people in 44 countries in 2002. The study found a marked increase in Muslim hostility toward the United States from 2002 to 2003. In the summer of 2002, 61 percent of Indonesians held a favorable view of the United States. By May of 2003, only 15 percent did. During the same period of time, the decline in Turkey was from 30 percent to 15 percent, and in Jordan it was from 25 percent to one percent.

Indeed, the Bush administration's war on terror has been a major reason for the increased hostility toward the United States. The Pew Center's 2003 survey found that few Muslims support this war. Only 23 percent of Indonesians did so in May of 2003, down from 31 percent in the summer of 2002. In Turkey, support dropped from 30 percent to 22 percent. In Pakistan, support dropped from 30 percent to 16 percent, and in Jordan from 13 percent to two percent. These decreases reflect overwhelming Muslim opposition to the war in Iraq, which most Muslims saw as yet another act of imperial subjugation of Muslims by the West.

The 2003 Zogby International poll found that most Arabs believe that the United States attacked Iraq to gain control of Iraqi oil and to help Israel. Over three-fourths of all those surveyed felt that oil was a major reason for the war. More than three-fourths of the Saudis and Jordanians said that helping Israel was a major reason, as did 72 percent of the Moroccans and over 50 percent of the Egyptians and Lebanese. Most Arabs clearly do not believe that the United States overthrew Saddam Hussein out of humanitarian motives. Even in Iraq itself, where there was considerable support for the war, most people attribute the war to the US desire to gain control of Iraqi oil and help Israel.

Not only has the Bush administration failed to win much Muslim support for its war on terrorism, its conduct of the war has generated a dangerous backlash. Most Muslims see the US fight against terror as a war against the Islamic world. The 2003 Pew survey found that over 70 percent of Indonesians, Pakistanis, and Turks were either somewhat or very worried about a potential US threat to their countries, as were over half of Jordanians and Kuwaitis.

This sense of a US threat is linked to the 2003 Pew report's finding of widespread support for Osama bin Laden. The survey of April and May 2003 found that over half those surveyed in Indonesia, Jordan, and the Palestinian Authority, and almost half those surveyed in Morocco and Pakistan, listed bin Laden as one of the three world figures in whom they had the most confidence "to do the right thing." For most US citizens, this admiration for the man responsible for the attacks of September 11, 2001, is incomprehensible. But no matter how outrageous this widespread belief may be, it is vitally important to understand its origins. If one does not understand why people think the way they do, one cannot induce them to

think differently. Similarly, if one does not understand why people act as they do, one cannot hope to induce them to act differently.

The Appeal of Osama bin Laden

Osama bin Laden first engaged in violence because of the occupation of a Muslim country by an "infidel" superpower. He did not fight the Russians in Afghanistan because he hated their values or their freedoms, but because they had occupied a Muslim land. He participated in and supported the Afghan resistance to the Soviet occupation from 1979 to 1989, which ended with the withdrawal of the Russians. Bin Laden saw this war as legitimate resistance to foreign occupation. At the same time, he saw it as a *jihad*, or holy war, on behalf of Muslims oppressed by infidels.

When Saddam Hussein invaded Kuwait in August 1990, bin Laden offered to lead an army to defend Saudi Arabia. The Saudis rejected this offer and instead allowed the United States to establish bases in their kingdom, leading to bin Laden's active opposition to the United States. One can only speculate what bin Laden would have done for the rest of his life if the United States had not stationed hundreds of thousands of US troops in Saudi Arabia in 1990. Conceivably, bin Laden's hostility toward the United States might have remained passive and verbal instead of active and violent. All we can say with certainty is that the presence of US troops in Saudi Arabia did trigger bin Laden's holy war against the United States. It was no accident that the bombing of two US embassies in Africa on August 7, 1998, marked the eighth anniversary of the introduction of US forces into Saudi Arabia as part of Operation Desert Storm.

Part of bin Laden's opposition to the presence of US military presence in Saudi Arabia resulted from the fact that US troops were infidels on or near holy Islamic ground. Non-Muslims are not allowed to enter Mecca and Medina, the two holiest places in Islam, and they are allowed to live in Saudi Arabia only as temporary residents. Bin Laden is a reactionary Wahhabi Muslim who undoubtedly does hate all non-Muslims. But that hatred was not in itself enough to trigger his *jihad* against the United States.

Indeed, bin Laden's opposition to the presence of US troops in Saudi Arabia had a nationalistic and anti-imperialist tone. In 1996, he declared that Saudi Arabia had become an American colony. There is nothing specifically religious or fundamentalist about this assertion. In his book *Chronique d'une Guerre d'Orient*, Gilles Kepel describes a wealthy whiskey-drinking Saudi who left part of his fortune to bin Laden because he alone "was defending the honor of the country, reduced in his eyes to a simple American protectorate."

In 1996, bin Laden issued his first major manifesto, entitled a "Declaration of Jihad against the Americans Occupying the Land of the Two Holy Places." The very title focuses on the presence of US troops in Saudi Arabia, which bin Laden calls an "occupation." But this manifesto also refers to other examples of what bin Laden sees as the oppression of Muslims by infidels. "It is no secret that the people of Islam have suffered from the oppression, injustice, and aggression of the alliance of Jews and Christians and their collaborators to the point that the blood of the Muslims became the cheapest and their wealth was loot in the hands of the enemies," he writes. "Their blood was spilled in Palestine and Iraq."

Bin Laden has referred to the suffering of the Palestinians and the Iraqis (especially with respect to the deaths caused by sanctions) in all of his public statements since at least the mid-1990s. His 1996 "Declaration of Jihad" is no exception. Nonetheless, it primarily focuses on the idea that the Saudi regime has "lost all legitimacy" because it "has permitted the enemies of the Islamic community, the Crusader American forces, to occupy our land for many years." In this 1996 text, bin Laden even contends that the members of the Saudi royal family are apostates because they helped infidels fight the Muslim Iraqis in the Persian Gulf War of 1991.

A number of neo-conservatives have advocated the overthrow of the Saudi regime because of its support for terrorism. It is true that the Saudis have funded militant Islamic movements. It is also true that Saudi textbooks and teachers often encourage hatred of infidels and allow the extremist views of bin Laden to thrive. It is also probably true that members of the Saudi royal family have financially supported terrorist groups. The fact remains, however, that bin Laden and his followers in Al Qaeda have themselves repeatedly called for the overthrow of the Saudi regime, saying that it has turned Saudi Arabia into "an American colony."

If the United States were to send troops to Saudi Arabia once again, this time to overthrow the Saudi regime itself, the main beneficiaries would be bin Laden and those who think like him. On January 27, 2002, a *New York Times* article referenced a Saudi intelligence survey conducted in October 2001 that showed that 95 percent of educated Saudis between the ages of 25 and 41 supported bin Laden. If the United States were to overthrow the Saudi regime, such people would lead a guerrilla war that US forces would inevitably find themselves fighting. This war would attract recruits from all over the Islamic world outraged by the desecration of "the land of the two holy places." Given that US forces are already fighting protracted guerrilla wars in Iraq and Afghanistan, starting a third one in Saudi Arabia would not be the most effective way of eradicating terror in the Middle East.

Those who would advocate the overthrow of the Saudi regime by US troops seem to forget why bin Laden began his holy war against the United States in the first place. They also seem to forget that no one is more committed to the overthrow of the Saudi regime than bin Laden himself. Saudi Arabia is in dire need of reform, but yet another US occupation of a Muslim country is not the way to make it happen.

In December 1998, Palestinian journalist Jamal Abd al Latif Isma'il asked bin Laden, "Who is Osama bin Laden, and what does he want?" After providing a brief history of his life, bin Laden responded to the second part of the question, "We demand that our land be liberated from the enemies, that our land be liberated from the Americans. God almighty, may He be praised, gave all living beings a natural desire to reject external intruders. Take chickens, for example. If an armed soldier enters a chicken's home wanting to attack it, it fights him even though it is just a chicken." For bin Laden and millions of other Muslims, the Afghans, the Chechens, the Iraqis, the Kashmiris, and the Palestinians are all just "chickens" defending their homes against the attacks of foreign soldiers.

In his videotaped message of October 7, 2001, after the attacks of September 11, 2001, bin Laden declared, "What America is tasting now is nothing compared to what we have been tasting for decades. For over 80 years our *umma* has been tasting this humiliation and this degradation. Its sons are killed, its blood is shed, its holy places are violated, and it is ruled by other than that which God has revealed. Yet no one hears. No one responds."

Bin Laden's defiance of the United States and his criticism of Muslim governments who ignore what most Muslims see as the oppression of the Palestinians, Iraqis, Chechens, and others, have made him a hero of Muslims who do not agree with his goal of a strictly Islamic state and society. Even young Arab girls in tight jeans praise bin Laden as an anti-imperialist hero. A young Iraqi woman and her Palestinian friends told Gilles Kepel in the fall of 2001, "He stood up to defend us. He is the only one."

Looking ahead

Feelings of impotence, humiliation, and rage currently pervade the Islamic world, especially the Muslim Middle East. The invasion and occupation of Iraq has exacerbated Muslim concerns about the United States. In this context, bin Laden is seen as a heroic Osama Maccabeus descending from his mountain cave to fight the infidel oppressors to whom the worldly rulers of the Islamic world bow and scrape.

The violent actions of Osama bin Laden and those who share his views are not simply caused by "hatred of Western freedoms." They result, in part at least, from US policies that have enraged the Muslim world. Certainly, Islamic zealots like bin Laden do despise many aspects of Western culture. They do hate "infidels" in general, and Jews in particular. Muslims do need to seriously examine the existence and perpetuation of such hatred in their societies and cultures. But invading and occupying their countries simply exacerbates the sense of impotence, humiliation, and rage that induce them to support people like bin Laden. Defeating terror entails diluting the rage that fuels it.

Henry Munson is Chair of the Department of Anthropology at the University of Maine.

The Sorcerer's Apprentices

The U.S. has a long history bungling it in Iraq.

By Angelo M. Codevilla

TODAY'S IRAQ, THE BIBLICAL LAND OF UR, used to interest Americans only as history and exotica—the Marsh Arabs at the mouth of the Tigris and Euphrates, north of the fabled location of the Garden of Eden, above that Baghdad and Mesopotamia, the land of Abraham, of Babylon, of Israel's Babylonian captivity, and of the Arabian Nights. There, in the third century B.C., Xenophon's 10,000 Athenians fought the anabasis up the Euphrates Valley, through the Kurds, and over to the Black Sea. After the Islamic conquest and the great Mongol invasion, the area was a sleepy part of the Ottoman Empire, until Woodrow Wilson broke that up. Modern Iraq was born of the Versailles settlement of 1919 that brought forth so many other botches.

Iraq was not a good idea in the first place. American and British Wilsonians decided to re-create something like the Babylonian Empire: Sunni Mesopotamian Arabs from the Baghdad area would rule over vastly more numerous southern Sh'ia Arabs, and Arabophobe Kurds. Why the ruled should accept such an arrangement was never made clear. But before a local Mesopotamian ruler could be found, the British made matters worse by "parachuting" in a foreign imperial client. During the War, Britain had fought the Turks in the Middle East largely through Lawrence of Arabia's alliance with the Hashemites—descendants of the Prophet and traditional rulers of the Hejaz area of southwestern Arabia, including Mecca. But the Brit-

ish had also allied with their rivals, the house of Saud, rulers of the central region of Nejd which, joined to the Wahabi sect, aspired to control the whole peninsula, especially Mecca. In their war for Arabia and Islam, the Saudis promptly showed how impotent were the post-war British to protect their clients. And so it happened that on the floor of the U.S. Senate, Henry Cabot Lodge spoke as follows:

> "The following dispatch appeared recently in the newspapers: 'HEDJAZ AGAINST BEDOUINS. The forces of emir Abdullah recently suffered a grave defeat, the Wahabis attacking and capturing Kurma, East of Mecca. Ibn Savond is believed to be working in harmony with the Wahabis. A squadron of the Royal Air Force was ordered recently to go to the assistance of the king.' Under Article 10 [of the Treaty proposed for ratification] if king Hussein appealed to us for aid and protection, *we should be obliged* to send American soldiers to Arabia ... in order to protect his independence against the assaults of the Wahabis."

Lodge scorned Britain's "fair creations" in Arabia by comparing them to "the Mosquito king" that it had set up in Central America. He argued that there is no logical end to such games. The British proved him right. Having failed to protect the Hashemites in Arabia they set them up as alien rulers elsewhere—Abdullah the lesser in Palestine and Hussein the greater (and his son Faisal) in his consolation prize, Iraq. This added to the regime's unpopularity. If America had helped Britain to defeat the Wahabis, Iraq might have been less frail with a native ruler. But the Americans who most supported the Versailles treaty were least eager to help Britain maintain its empire. Still, no one could have wiped away the problems that required Britain to use 100,000 troops to keep Iraq together in the interwar period.

From the beginning, while what one might call the right wing of American policy makers hoped to see the British Empire continue but was unwilling to help it do so, the left wing pushed for the British Empire to fade way, believing it would leave behind rulers even more open to fruitful relations with America. They imagined reaping the benefits of empire without bearing its burdens. And so the pattern of American policy was set for Iraq as well as for the other cripples that came forth from the wreckage of empires in the twentieth century: some Americans wanted nothing to do with them, others wanted to impose their will, while others yet thought that the locals would adopt democracy and become equal members of the world community. Few American policy makers measured the ends they sought against the means they were willing to commit. All seemed more interested in getting discrete actions approved despite their domestic opponents. If policy is a complex of measures reasonably conceived and brought to term, there has been no policy. Instead, clashing priorities have produced results that none wanted.

TODAY'S PROBLEMS in the Persian Gulf began in 1953 with the joint British-American sponsorship of the military coup that overthrew Iran's leftist Prime Minister Mossadegh and placed power in the hands of the young Shah. Some Americans believed that Iran's Shah, plus Iraq's and Jordan's British-sponsored monarchs, would be enough to lead their region to every kind of progress while fighting Communism. Other Americans in the State Department, and even more in the CIA, were less concerned with stability and fighting Communism but even more committed to fostering what they thought was progress in the region. They sought to act as the world's truest revolutionaries. In Egypt, the CIA sponsored a set of young army officers led by Colonel Nasser and allied with the Muslim Brotherhoods that overthrew the compliant but too conservative King Faruk. Americans sponsored Egyptian-type movements throughout the region because they thought that Western-sponsored kings were not nationalistic or socialistic enough. Among the fortunes these Americans advanced were those of the Ba'ath, a national socialist movement founded in Syria in 1943 under Nazi influence.

Not surprisingly, even as the two strands of American policy fought one another with words and budgets in Washington, their proxies in the Middle East fought one another with knives and guns. After Nasser's American-aided success against Britain, France and Israel, the CIA-supported Ba'ath parties took power in Syria, Iraq, and almost succeeded in doing so in Jordan. Almost immediately, they wrecked the structure that other Americans had built in the region. Nasser had merely received Soviet aid, but Abdul Karim Kassem, immediately after taking power in Baghdad in 1958, aided the Soviet Union by killing the American-sponsored Central Treaty Organization (CENTO), which had joined Turkey, Iraq, Iran, and Pakistan (West and East). CENTO had made Containment a geographic reality by anchoring NATO in the West to the Southeast Asian Treaty Organization (SEATO) in the East. Iraq's withdrawal left a gap that frightened those at State and CIA who cared most about anti-Communism and embarrassed those whose creature Arab national socialism was.

The latter group, however, believed that the problem had just been that the wrong faction of the Ba'ath had come to power. They would fix that. Out of their magic bag they picked six contacts, including a 22-year-old thug named Saddam Hussein, and sent them to assassinate Abdul Karim Kassem in October 1959. They botched it. The CIA then set up Saddam in luxurious exile in Cairo, where he continued to be handled both through Egyptian intelligence and directly from the U.S. Embassy.

The radio of the Islamic revolution was run by the KGB out of Soviet Baku.

By 1963, Kassem had made enough enemies within the Ba'ath that the CIA needed only join a native coup against him. The CIA's gunman, Saddam, contributed enough to the coup's success that he became the head of the new ruling faction's secret police. As such, he oversaw the new regime's murder of some 4,000 people, described to gullible Americans as "Communists," but killed in fact for having been too close to Kassem. The CIA congratulated itself on a success that seemed to show the efficacy of its subtle covert action and to justify its dealing with people like Saddam. But their assumption that the likes of Saddam would follow the CIA's agenda and be subordinate to the CIA's authority rather than serve themselves was hallucinogenic smoke. By the late '60s, Saddam had become the power, while Iraq's President Abu Bakr was increasingly a figurehead.

Disappointing Americans who fancied themselves his handlers, Saddam never exhumed CENTO. Instead, Iraq and Syria's Ba'athist regimes became close military and political allies of the Soviet Union. By 1970 they had isolated Iran's Shah, now America's only surrogate. Iraq had become the Shah's chief challenger and was harboring his chief problem, the Ayatollah Khomeini.

American statesmen were of many minds about this. Some thought that Ba'athist Iraq posed less danger to the Shah and to the American order in the Persian Gulf than it presented opportunity to improve relations with progressive Arabs. They voiced Sunni Arab desires for some substantial Arab power to exist in the region to shield fragile

Saudi Arabia and the weak Gulf states against Shi'ite Iran. And they argued that supporting Iraq was necessary to quiet Turkish worries about the Kurds. Nevertheless Arabists at State and CIA compromised with those who feared that the rise of pro-Soviet forces in the region would sweep away the Shah, and agreed to a plan of moderate pressure: the CIA would arm Iraq's Kurds, actualize their latent threat to the Baghdad regime, and thus force it to cease bothering Iran. By 1975 this plan to straddle Sunni and Shi'a, the conservative Shah and the progressive Ba'ath, seemed to have worked to perfection. Iraq sent Khomeini off to Paris. In exchange, the Americans left the Kurds to their fate. Saddam gassed and otherwise slaughtered them by the thousands. Henry Kissinger's reaction to this, that foreign policy was not to be confused with humanitarianism, amounted to retail Machiavellianism and wholesale naïveté

By 1978, Saddam's secret services were contributing logistics, cash, and Shi'ite agents to the coalition that destroyed the Shah. Although the Ayatollah Khomeini was indispensable to it, so were Soviet line organizations. Notably, Yasser Arafat's Palestine Liberation Organization provided the bulk of the street fighters. The radio of the Islamic revolution was run by the KGB out of Soviet Baku. Indeed, overthrowing the American order in the Gulf had become so dear to progressives around the world (including State and CIA) that President Carter himself was persuaded to help ease the Shah out of office in the hope that his doing so would ingratiate America with Khomeini and with progressive Arabs. Hopes for this rose in 1979 when Saddam took power directly in Iraq. But his attitude toward America turned harder than ever. Then Iranian revolutionaries took American embassy personnel hostage. Paris's Le Figaro announced "Open Season On Americans!" U.S. policy was a self-inflicted shambles.

S ADDAM'S INVASION OF IRAN on September 22, 1980, gave American factions more opportunities to make thing worse. Though those who had championed the Shah hated Khomeini, they continued to see Iran as a bulwark against Soviet and Arab expansion. Among them were Secretary of State Al Haig and NSC staffers Howard Teicher and Oliver North. They did not object to Israel selling Iran parts for its American weapons. With these munitions, Iran turned back Saddam. But when, in 1981, Israel used American-supplied aircraft and intelligence to destroy Iraq's Osirak nuclear reactor, the pro-Arab progressive elements at State and CIA, led by Assistant Secretary of State Richard Murphy, enlisted CIA deputy director Bobby Ray Inman and Defense Secretary Caspar Weinberger to tilt U.S. policy toward Saddam.

To Congress they argued that Israel had recklessly fouled a sophisticated effort, already showing success, to bring Iraq out of the Soviet orbit into the "family of nations" and to make of it America's point of reliance in the oil-rich region for the post-Shah era. To prevent Israel from doing such a terrible thing again, the CIA cut Israel's access to

U.S. intelligence and began instead to supply Iraq with satellite photos. To muted congressional guffaws, the State Department took Iraq off the list of states that abet terrorism. In 1982, with the help of George Shultz, Haig's replacement as Secretary of State, this group turned President Reagan to its view. In December 1983, Reagan's special ambassador, Donald Rumsfeld, told Saddam that his defeat would be against U.S. interests. George Bush made calls to smooth the flow of U.S. weapons, credits, and intelligence to Iraq. The U.S. even tried to help Saddam build an oil pipeline along the Israeli border. And so the tide of battle turned again—not because of any Machiavellian design to exhaust two bad regimes, but because of contradictory U.S. policies.

When Bush became President, he felt that America owed Saddam a debt for his having bombed Iran.

There were more turns yet to come. By late 1985 the administration's cold warriors convinced Reagan that, from the perspective of what he valued most, the U.S.-Soviet conflict, the real disaster for America would be Iran's defeat by Iraq's Soviet-backed force. With new U.S. help, Iran advanced. At the same time, National Security Adviser Robert McFarlane pressed Reagan to trade U.S. arms to Iran in exchange for the release of American hostages in Lebanon and for the chance at reestablishing something like the old geopolitical relationship between America and Iran. But as some hostages were released, others were taken—a supply-side hostage policy. But the tilt toward Iran had not undone the pipeline of weapons flowing from the U.S. to Iraq. And after the 1986 revelation that revenues from arms sales to Iran had financed the Nicaraguan war in violation of law forced the departure of the pro-Iranians (McFarlane, John Poindexter, and North) from the National Security Council, the tilt toward Iraq went further yet. Vice President Bush advised Saddam to bomb with increased vigor.

When Bush became President, he felt that America owed Saddam a debt for ever having bombed Iran. In 1989, Bush ignored Pentagon warnings that Iraq was building nuclear weapons. In October, Secretary of State James Baker met with his Iraqi counterpart Tariq Aziz and specifically excluded specific concerns about Iraq's development of weapons of mass destruction. Until the eve of Saddam's invasion of Kuwait in August 1990, the CIA continued to share intelligence with the dictator and opposed congressional efforts to limit the resources flowing to him. All told, U.S. taxpayers guaranteed $5 billion in never-repaid loans to Saddam. When U.S. ambassador April Glaspie met with Saddam on the eve of the 1990 invasion of Kuwait and expressed no U.S. objection to it on the supposition that he would not take "all" of Kuwait, she was faithfully implementing Bush's expressed hope to "bring him into the family of nations." That hope was not backed by means reasonably calculated to effectuate it, chiefly because it is impossible to imagine what might have accomplished such a thing.

Neither were the hopes that the Bush team attached to the Gulf War of 1990-91 so calculated. A half-million American troops, and a battle won so spectacularly that America could do whatever it wished, did not make up for an unrealistic and self-contradictory vision. Bush wanted Saddam defeated, humbled, possibly removed from power. But, following State and CIA, he also wanted Iraq to remain a unified nation under control of the Ba'ath party. The problem was, thoroughly defeating Saddam would also deprive the Ba'ath party of power, and without Ba'ath power (there was no other) the Iraqi state's components-remember that Iraq is not a nation but an empire made more restive by Saddam's brutalities—would go their own unpredictable ways. And so, after a military campaign that consisted of killing untold thousands of Iraqis who did not matter while sparing the few who did, the Bush team faced the choice it should have faced before making war: to accept either the uncertain costs of undoing the Iraqi regime, or the certain problems of merely reducing its military force. Since State and CIA had soured only on Saddam without questioning their commitment to the regime, to Iraq itself, or even to the cavalier way in which they related ends and means, and since Bush accepted uncritically their judgment as well as the priorities of Saudis, Turks, Jordanians, et al., he saved Saddam and called it victory.

Victory gives the winner his preferred version of peace, turns the page, and lets him go on to other matters. But Saddam did not treat America as if it had won. The Gulf War had made Iraq a continuing test of America's competence in the world and Saddam did not make that test easy for America's leaders. To neighboring states and peoples he presented the fact that he had fought and survived a mighty onslaught as proof of his potency, and of his leadership in a common cause: opposition to America—foreign, envied, apparently mighty, but ultimately impotent. American elites in the 1990s for once were united—in missing the magnitude of Saddam Hussein's political achievement. Thanks to their forbearance, this ex-CIA agent, this atheist, this bloody persecutor of Muslims, this tyrant, glutton of the finest Western food, drink, and whores that billions can buy, managed to convince millions of poor, hungry, powerless, devout people that he represented their fondest hopes, that America stood between them and those hopes, that America was beatable, and that they should make war against America.

This politics, not any military power, was Saddam's weapon of mass destruction—all the more effective because America exposed itself by pursuing contradictory wills of the wisp. And that, with means disproportionate to ends. Indispensable to Saddam's success was the U.S. government's ignorance of his mind due in part to the CIA's habit of relying on sources controlled by Iraqi intelligence

(see Laurie Mylroie in this issue). A decade after the Gulf War, never mind after the 2003 war, we still speculate but do not know what he thought he was doing.

Two BUSHES AND ONE CLINTON spent the decade after the Gulf War trying to bring Israelis and Arabs together, protect Saudi Arabia, and sanction Iraq economically lest it produce certain weapons. Saddam turned all these efforts to his credit and America's detriment, while at the same time fostering acts of terror. In Palestine, his money, propaganda, and henchmen made sure that no local Arab could afford to be less demanding of Israel or less damning of America than he. Quickly, he made the Saudis realize that relying on Americans for protection against other Arabs was a deadly self-indictment. At this writing we do not know how thoroughly Iraqi secret services backed up Iraqi foreign policy of fostering Islamic resentment amongst Saudis. But appeasing Saddam—trying to prove in countless ways how truly Arab, meaning by now anti-American, the royal family really was—became a political necessity that overshadowed Saudi relations with America.

Saddam used economic sanctions to strengthen his grip on his people, by shifting privations to peoples who opposed him while giving his supporters even greater relative advantages. The U.S. government could not deny Saddam's charge that starvation and disease from sanctions were killing innocents. Nor could it tell itself that the sanctions were doing more than raising the price of Saddam's pursuit of nuclear, chemical, and biological weapons. Textbooks teach that because economic resources are fungible, those who are subject to sanctions (other than total blockades on small countries) are forced only to pay higher prices for whatever they want. But neither Bushes nor Clintons were much on reading. Secretary of State Colin Powell even proposed "smart sanctions"—as conceivable as sharp balloons. By the late '90s, Saddam was more important than he had been before the Gulf War.

Hundreds OF YEARS FROM NOW, textbooks will still cite U.S. Iraq policy to define divorce between ends and means. All means of coercion—diplomacy, economic pressure, subversion, and military action itself—are effective to the extent that the plan of which they are part exerts force upon the target greater than the sacrifices demanded of it. In the decade alter the Gulf War, Bushes and Clintons had hopes about Iraq, and discrete actions. But no coherent, success-oriented plan. How could they have one? On one hand they wanted the Ba'athist regime to remain. On the other, they wanted Iraq to change the role it was playing—successfully—in world politics. And their means were half-measures advertised as such.

U.S. diplomacy, consisting of demands that Iraq grant more access to U.N. weapons inspectors, resembled a Kabuki show. Iraqis would delay and complicate. Americans said darkly that all means of enforcement were under consideration. But the end of the Gulf War had made plain to Saddam the internal contradictions of American policy and the limits they imposed. And so the inspection ritual would limp forward, with economic sanctions as the only American hammer. As more time passed, however, these became more trouble for America than for Saddam. The subversion consisted on the one hand of helping disaffected Kurds, but not enough to give them a chance to establish independence. Never mind of threatening the regime. When, in 1996, Saddam's army invaded the Kurdish enclave, America advertised its impotence by sending five cruise missiles against air defense sites hundreds of miles away. On the other hand, subversion consisted of placing hopes and money on the CIA's favorite Ba'athist henchmen, who were really working for Saddam. There was an independent set of Iraqi opponents of the regime, the Iraqi National Congress, supported by the U.S. Congress. But State and CIA conducted covert actions against it.

The subversion consisted on the one hand of helping disaffected Kurds, but not enough to give them a chance to establish independence.

One of many examples of U.S. military action should suffice as the clearest proof of fecklessness. In 1993, after discovering an Iraqi plot to kill former President Bush, Clinton sent some 23 cruise missiles to destroy the headquarters of Iraq's intelligence service—at night, killing mostly cleaning women. Clinton intended "to send a message to those who engage in state-sponsored terrorism, to deter further violence against our people ... our intent was to target Iraq's capacity to support violence against the United States and other nations and to deter Saddam Hussein from supporting such outlawed behavior in the future."

Meanwhile, the Clinton administration endorsed the CIA's judgment that terrorism came not from states like Iraq, but from "loose networks" of renegade individuals. The chasm between words and reality sent a real message: America would not threaten Saddam's core interests. He was free to spread hate and contempt of America to the world.

Laurie Mylroie describes Iraq's role in anti-American terrorism. Such descriptions are necessarily incomplete and suggestive because terrorism, like all forms of indirect warfare, depends for its success on hiding the state's role as much as possible. While there is room to dispute Iraq's responsibility for any given act of international terror, no one denies that dealing death was Saddam Hussein's indispensable tool in international as in domestic relations, nor that Iraqi intelligence ran camps for training foreign Arab terrorists, nor that Saddam publicly supported the PLO and other longtime allies in the anti-Western cause. The point here is that surely the most effective aid that he received in con-

cealing his hand in this business came from disputes amongst Americans about what ought to be done about Iraq.

SEPTEMBER 11 inflamed those disputes to the point of allowing the dispute itself to overshadow America's interest, never mind that of the Iraqi people. Instinctively, George W. Bush is said to have believed that Saddam "probably was behind [the attacks] in the end." Due to Deputy Secretary Paul Wolfowitz, the Department of Defense long held that, as The New York Times columnist Thomas Friedman later wrote, "98 percent of terrorism is what governments make happen or let happen." Hence, the war on terror should aim at changing hostile regimes. Ba'athist Iraq headed the list. State and CIA differed. CIA director Tenet argued that Osama bin Laden's al Qaeda was responsible—no one else—and agreed with Secretary of State Powell that only targets in Afghanistan should be hit in retaliation. Both State and CIA argued against trying to topple Afghanistan's Taliban regime. Bush agreed with them. And when two weeks of bombing mud huts in October 2001 showed that the only way of hurting al Qaeda was to create an Afghan regime hostile to it, State and CIA convinced Bush to try defeating the Taliban without producing a victory for their internal enemies, the Northern Alliance. Only after another week of derisory bombing showed the absurdity of this did Bush override State/CIA and order support of the Alliance. Much more strongly did these agencies oppose any sort of action against the Iraqi regime. Such action would alienate everyone they cared about: the Europeans, the United Nations, the Arab world, The New York Times, and of course America's Best And Brightest.

Powell convinced him that the clever way to obtain popular support for regime change was to pretend that the objective was something else: disarming Iraq of Weapons of Mass Destruction.

Bush somehow decided to take the Pentagon's advice and do "regime change" in Iraq, but he did not thereby break with the premises of his earlier decisions, or with their proponents. Nothing that happened on September 11 had changed the Bush team's primary objective in the Middle East—maintaining the status quo—or its evaluation of what the status quo required, namely, the good graces of Saudi Arabia and Egypt. That meant not touching Iraq, for that would suggest that Bush was somehow dissatisfied with their regimes as well. Yet, having decided to act against Iraq, he did not explain to himself or to others what he meant to do. Indeed, Secretary of State Powell convinced him that the clever way to obtain popular support for regime change was to pretend that the objective was something else: disarming Iraq of Weapons of Mass Destruction. Contradictory premises mixed with the tangled wed of dissimulation to produce a mess.

That Saddam Hussein possessed or was trying to possess such weapons was conventional wisdom. That is why the emphasis seemed clever. For example, Senator John Kerry, palimpsest of the Democratic Left, was saying, as late as January 2003: "Without question, we need to disarm Saddam Hussein. He is a brutal, murderous dictator, leading an oppressive regime.... He presents a particularly grievous threat because he is so consistently prone to miscalculation.... And now he is miscalculating America's response to continued deceit and his consistent grasp for weapons of mass destruction.... So the threat of Saddam Hussein with weapons of mass destruction is real..." By the same token, President Clinton had often talked about using force to disarm Saddam, e.g., in February 1998: "One way or the other, we are determined to deny Iraq the capacity to develop weapons of mass destruction and the missiles to deliver them. That is our bottom line." "If Saddam rejects peace and we have to use force, our purpose is clear. We want to seriously diminish the threat posed by Iraq's weapons of mass destruction program."

Bush thought that merely matching the expressed views of the factions whose support he was seeking, acknowledging their authority, and stating that his decision depended on their support would deliver that support. With it, he could make war and get "regime change." This proved too clever by half because those factions were playing Iraq to look good to their constituencies even more than he was to look good for his. So, whereas in the summer of 2002 polls had been running heavily in favor of overthrowing Saddam, by January 2003 opposition to attacking Iraq, and to President Bush, had risen sharply. Common sense would not have expected otherwise. To ask support of anyone, never mind of opponents, for a course of action on which one claims not to have decided oneself, giving the impression that one's decision is contingent on such support, is to beg for opposition.

More important, once President Bush had given the American people the impression that America needed the United Nations' blessing to go to war, many Americans took him at his word and disapproved of war without those blessings. Besides, his enemies charged, when Bush said "disarmament" of Iraq he really meant "regime change." What he really meant was a matter of dispute to which he contributed. On October 21, 2002, he endorsed Colin Powell's proposal that if Saddam truly disarmed, that would constitute regime change and the regime could stay in power. But by March 2003, Saddam's departure was the point. And, late in the game, he defined the operation with the title "Iraqi freedom." This was less cynicism than a reflection of the shifting balance of power within the administration.

True democracy would require elections not prejudiced by the power of Iraqi political personages chosen by the Pentagon.

What would the actual purpose of U.S. military operations be? The answer, crucial for planning, was manifold and contradictory. An operation meant strictly to "disarm" would be an armed scavenger hunt—highly dangerous unless preceded by destruction of enemy armed forces. Destruction of enemy forces that left the regime intact made even less sense. So any operation would have to destroy the armed forces and the regime. But what would replace it? Here Washington's factions showed their differences, and plans for operations reflected them long before the first bombs fell on March 20, 2003.

One group in the Pentagon wanted to arm Iraqi exiles and Kurds, recognize them as a provisional government, and run a military operation to put them in power. Essentially, America would empower the enemies of America's enemies and step back as they dealt summarily with the Ba'athist regime's vast infrastructure. This would have required few U.S. troops during the battle and, by definition, no American would take a hand in the inevitable settling of scores. At the other end of the spectrum, State and CIA having long argued that the weapons, not the regime, were the problem, were less concerned with eliminating America's enemies. Because they wanted to change Ba'athist Iraq as little as possible, they wanted no anti-regime locals in the fight at all. Afterward, they wanted to pick and choose among Saddam's entourage while making sure to suppress any separatist tendencies among southern Shi'ites and northern Kurds. This required an extensive, long-term U.S. occupation force.

President Bush, typically, chose both and added idealism. Iraq, he decided, would be governed by Iraqis, but not yet. True democracy would require elections not prejudiced by the power of Iraqi political personages chosen by the Pentagon. So American military forces would run Iraq for a long time with the help of Iraqi "technocrats" chosen by, well, by fights between State, CIA, and Pentagon, and during this time set up absolutely free and impartial elections. Despite freedom and impartiality, the occupation and elections would have to guarantee the territorial integrity of the country, prohibit religious fundamentalism, establish the rights of women, etc. How, no one could explain.

Saddam knew all this as well as the rest of the world. We do not know what he thought about it. But we now know what he did. Americans puzzled in January when Saddam emptied his jails of common criminals. Political prisoners were long dead. No one guessed that Saddam put the criminals on the street as part of a plan for after the war—to augment regime loyalists in killing Americans and their collaborators. A few Americans puzzled at why Saddam did not take the opportunity to invite the U.S. forces or anyone else to come—peacefully—and take whatever they thought were forbidden weapons. In Washington, even fewer paid much attention to the widely reported fact that the regime was apparently moving lock, stock, and barrel out of the palaces and ministries that Washington had publicly designated as targets of its "Shock and Awe" campaign. No one knew, of course, that Saddam had gathered over $1 billion for his post-war operations in Iraq. All sides in Washington also missed Saddam's decision to take his regime underground, expose the army and nonessential cadres to destruction, and to wage his fight after what America considered the war.

As "SHOCK AND AWE" was getting under way on March 21, Defense Secretary Donald Rumsfeld said that the Iraqi regime was "starting to lose control" because "their ability to see what is happening on the battlefield, to communicate with their forces, and to control their country is slipping away." But the regime had not tried to see, communicate, or control. It was long gone. Gradually, U.S. planners realized that they would have to convince Iraqis that the regime had quit. Saddam would endeavor to convince them of the opposite. The real fight was just beginning. The shooting would be in Baghdad. But the issue would be decided in Washington—just like Vietnam.

The U.S. armed forces were ordered to arrest anyone who tried governing. Anarchy, anyone?

By April 9, the Bush team's decision not simply to crush the enemy, but to export good government, coupled with its failure to decide who would govern, began to haunt the operation. The U.S. armed forces were ordered to arrest anyone who tried governing. Anarchy, anyone? Running Iraq would require favoring some local claimants to power over others chosen by Washington. But the State Department and the CIA favored some Iraqis and the Defense Department others. The Bush team counted on rival Iraqis and Americans to sort things out. It also counted on no resistance from the remnants of the regime. Nonsense.

By mid-May, embarrassment at apparent chaos led Bush to order U.S. forces into action to restore order. But whose order? In June, U.S. forces, at who knows whose direction, raided the offices of the Pentagon-allied Iraqi National Congress. "Well, they won't be pro-American anymore, I guess," mused one of the soldiers who carried out the dumb order. Meanwhile, remnants of the regime, along with religiously motivated fighters from throughout the Arab world (so much for the State/CIA canard that secular and religious terrorists do not cooperate) began a campaign of ambushes

that has killed some 12 American soldiers per week, as well as Iraqi officials who cooperate with Americans. Iraqis learned that whereas no one would kill them for being anti-American, some would kill them for not being anti-American. And the Americans learned that they did not know who the killers were.

By fall 2003, U.S. military operations had come down to garrison duty plus something like the search and destroy tactics of Vietnam, against mostly insignificant persons. That meant soldiers barging around the country, reasonably afraid for their lives, treating mostly innocent people as if they were enemies because they do not know who was who. Captured regime bigwigs have given no useful intelligence, betting that no harm will come to them from siding with Saddam, and much harm would come from siding against him. That calculus is all the more indicative of bad things for America because it is so reasonable. Americans eager to anticipate attacks could only rely on low-level informants. Quite simply, Americans were strangers, short timers, not fearsome, and not about to become anything else, who did not know the difference between Ahmed and Abdul, and were not about to find out—except the hard way.

The fighting was limited to a small part of Iraq—the area inhabited by the Sunni Mesopotamians who have ruled Iraq since 1919. Southern Shi'ites and northern Kurds, grateful to America for liberating them from Saddam and the Mesopotamians, not only do not fight Americans, but fear being placed once again under Sunni Arabs. Left to their own devices, they would either make some sort of separation from them or a war of reprisal and intimidation against them. Probably both. But the Americans prevent them from doing either. U.S. policy prefers to have Americans shot at.

By FALL 2003, the Americans were scrambling to put an Iraqi face on the occupation. Hard bargaining between State and Defense produced a 25-member provisional governing council with some authority except over what really counts: the capacity to make war against the forces that, among other things, killed one member of that council and wounded another. The war they would make would be more like that which the Lebanese militias made against the PLO in 1982—the kind of war that settles matters in the region. The kind of massacre war that Americans do not and should not make.

The only meaningful choice that Americans can make in Iraq at the end of 2003 is whether or not to step aside and let the enemies of the Mesopotamians have at their former rulers. Absent that, serving on an American-sponsored governing authority may amount to signing one's own death warrant, as such service turned out to be in Vietnam. Friendly Iraqis were facing the same deadly choice as had the Vietnamese: succumb to the enemies that the Americans won't let you fight as you would like, or be thrown to the wolves by Americans who regard you insufficiently faithful to their domestically driven agenda. The other alternative is for such friendly Iraqis to survive by becoming unfriendly.

Of course Iraq had chemical and biological weapons! Some U.S. Special Forces who had found their hiding places in 2002 had become contaminated and quite sick.

Meanwhile, back in America, President Bush's inability to succeed in Iraq lowered his chances of re-election. The President had told Bob Woodward:

"I'm the commander, see, I don't need to explain why I say things. That's the interesting thing about being the President. Maybe somebody needs to explain to me why they say something, but I don't feel like I owe anybody an explanation."

But in fact he did explain why he made war on Iraq primarily in terms of Weapons of Mass Destruction. That mistake was sure to become an embarrassment. Of course Iraq had chemical and biological weapons! Some U.S. Special Forces who had found their hiding places in 2002 had become contaminated and quite sick. But since these substances are almost as easily unmade as they are made, and since the pieces for making them do not have to be kept together, turning their discovery into the test of legitimacy of U.S. policy always amounted to leading with America's political chin. Saddam did in fact get rid of them. None of Bush's resident geniuses ever understood what little role they ever played in his quiver. Later, Bush explained the war in terms of the numerical measures of good government that he was bringing to Iraq. But as in Vietnam, this won't do. Mostly, failure to kill those who kill Americans requires not explanation, but termination.

Failure to focus on killing America's enemies, as well as on the desire of most Iraqis to be rid of the kind of American expertise that foisted Saddam on them in the first place, is precisely the result of the dysfunctional interplay of overblown personalities and domestic agendas that passes for foreign policy in today's Washington.

Angelo M. Codevilla is professor of international relations at Boston University and a senior editor of The American Spectator.

The Ethics of Exit

Iraq's first democratic elections in decades have passed, and a new Iraqi government is getting on its feet. Is it time for the United States and its allies to leave? What is the U.S. obligation and when is it discharged? In this **FP Roundtable,** *five leading experts argue over what it will take for the United States to bid Iraq a proper farewell.*

Avoiding Betrayal

Lawrence F. Kaplan

Critics of the decision to go to war would do well to recognize that we are no longer debating the merits of invading Iraq; we are debating the merits of abandoning Iraq. Now that the United States has turned that country inside out and created conditions that Iraqis do not have the means to remedy alone, a premature withdrawal would hardly right what most advocates of doing so consider to be the wrongs of the past. And greater wrongs do exist.

One is indifference; another is betrayal. If we "bring the troops home" before stability is returned to Iraq, the United States would be guilty of both.

Aside from the staggering moral calculation involved in leaving to its fate a country the United States has invaded and destabilized, how would a U.S. withdrawal from Iraq at this early date work in practical terms? It wouldn't. The result would be a strategic catastrophe. Preventing Iraq from coming apart at the seams means preventing the country from becoming what Afghanistan was until recently —a vacuum filled by terrorist organizations, which is what one National Intelligence Council report suggested Iraq is now fast becoming. Only an Iraqi government that possesses a relative monopoly on the means of violence can prevent this outcome. Alas, Iraq's security forces are nowhere near their goal of fielding sufficient numbers of police, national guard, and soldiers. In the meantime, then, either the U.S. military will fill the gap or no one will.

This would seem to be a rather obvious truth. It certainly is to Iraq's leaders. Prime Minister Ibrahim al-Jaafari predicts, "If the United States pulls out too fast, there would be chaos," while his colleague, Mowaffak Al-Rubaie, calls the prospect "a recipe for disaster." Yet from the vantage point of the United States, whose troops continue to bleed in Iraq, it isn't so obvious. Hence, Americans must ask themselves exactly what they owe Iraq. If U.S. policy truly has a moral component, which I believe it does, the answer must be something better—or, at the very least, not worse—than what went before. That does not mean garrisoning Iraq in perpetuity. But it does mean staying until, at a minimum, Iraqis have the ability to subdue forces unleashed by our actions.

Lawrence F. Kaplan *is senior editor at* The New Republic *and senior fellow at the Hudson Institute. These essays are drawn from a recent conference by Notre Dame's Kroc Institute and Fordham University's Center on Religion and Culture.*

Get Out Now

George A. Lopez

The new Iraqi authorities must be able to challenge the insurgency on nationalist, political, and religious grounds. But Iraqi leaders will not have the cultural and political space to do so unless the United States takes several difficult steps.

First, the United States must announce and execute a phased withdrawal of troops to be completed by February 2006. For this action to be credible, the United States must also scale down its embassy, making it equivalent in size to others in the region. Next, the United States must dismantle the military bases now under construction to remove the image of an Iraqi government dependent on U.S. force.

There are two principal objections to this strategy. The tactical objection is that an announced deadline provides insurgents with a substantial advantage in their own planning. In the political realm, critics assert that these steps constitute a "cut and run" strategy that will be interpreted by both our allies and enemies as a sign of weakness.

The first claim is not credible. U.S. leaders have been consistently incorrect about the scope, motivations, and strategies of the insurgency. During the past two years, the administration has announced that attacks would ebb after the capture of Saddam Hussein, after the handover of authority by the Coalition Provisional Authority to the Iyad Allawi interim government, after the reconquest of Fallujah, and after the January election. Instead, the insurgency has intensified and solidified. It is now apparent that the pervasive U.S. presence motivates quite disparate dissenters to spread anarchy. Announced deadlines will provide Iraqi authorities the best bargaining leverage they can have in this environment.

The fear that aggressive withdrawal will signal U.S. weakness misses the point. Iraq's desire to be rid of the occupiers is clear. A January 2005 Zogby opinion poll found that 82 percent of Sunnis and 69 percent of Shiites favor U.S. withdrawal "either immediately or after an elected government is in place." Withdrawing in the face of such strong national consensus is not a policy of weakness but one of appropriate deference to the wishes of the Iraqi people. And through its subsequent actions, the United States ultimately will be able to determine how that withdrawal is judged. A continued commitment to economic aid and to the political choices Iraqis make for themselves will provide ample positive data for history. A U.S. withdrawal would be a victory of good sense over exaggerated fears.

George A. Lopez is senior fellow at the Joan B. Kroc Institute for International Peace Studies at the University of Notre Dame.

A Job Half Done

Kenneth R. Himes

With great efficiency and military skill, the United States won an unjust war in Iraq. Then, with poor planning and inept management, the administration put at risk a just peace. Given this shoddy scorecard, should the United States simply withdraw from a place it never should have invaded?

Just war theorists are used to inquiring into the justice of a war's cause (*jus ad bellum*) and its conduct (*jus in bello*). Now we must probe the *jus post bellum*: What obligations does the occupier have and when are they discharged?

St. Augustine, one of the founding figures of the just war tradition, helped us understand that peace is not simply the absence of conflict. This understanding suggests that America's work is only half done—if that. The invasion has created a moral obligation for the victors to maintain a measure of social order, while reestablishing the government and institutions of the defeated nation. The moral imperative during the occupation is Iraqi well-being, not American interests.

Accordingly, the United States and its allies must not depart until basic social institutions are in place or until it is clear that occupying forces are either unwanted or unable to contribute to the creation of those institutions. For those Americans eager for their country to get out of Iraq, it is tempting to argue that the U.S. presence is the cause of the insurgency and that withdrawal is already ethically proper. But that is only half correct: The insurgents will oppose any non-Sunni-dominated government, and the present Iraqi security forces are still unable to maintain order.

The United States should do all it can to see that a political regime, with the approval of a majority of Iraqis, assumes sovereign authority promptly. The January elections gave the next government a healthy chance at legitimacy, but the United States must still ensure the stability of the new government. When an independent and representative government of Iraq assumes power and tells the United States to leave, it should withdraw speedily. If it asks foreign forces to continue their presence or provide other forms of assistance, the United States must be open to the request. An unjust war must not become an excuse for leaving behind an unjust peace.

Kenneth R. Himes *is chair of the theology department at Boston College.*

Tightly Tied to the New Iraq
Jean Bethke Elshtain

To wage a just war, states must aim to punish aggressors or remedy a massive injustice. The goal is a more just situation than the one that existed before the resort to armed force, and the occupying power is obliged to do everything it can to prevent a worse outcome. Given this rough and ready framework of evaluation, what does an ethical exit require?

First, the country that has committed to, and completed, military operations must assess its degree of responsibility for the postwar situation. If its role was minor, its responsibility is proportionately diminished. In the case of Iraq, of course, the United States and its allies bear the heaviest burden. The United States in particular has a direct responsibility for postwar Iraq that no other country or organization shares. This state of affairs is obviously not ideal. A major power should bring as many allies on board as possible when it commits to war. Given what we know of U.N. stalling and ineptitude where dictatorial regimes are concerned, however, the formal involvement of the international community will often be impossible. The international community has a huge stake in the outcome and should help rather than hinder, but ultimate ethical responsibility lies with the powers that unseated Saddam Hussein.

The countries responsible for the postwar situation bear a major burden in repairing infrastructural and environmental harm that is the direct result of military operations. Civilian affairs teams should first concentrate on the basic necessities of life—water and electricity, and then schools, hospitals, and other basic institutions of civic order. Repairing the political infrastructure is just as essential to creating a just peace. That means leaving the people in the invaded country, as well as the wider international environment, in better shape than before the intervention. Installing legitimate authority in Iraq is a delicate balancing act.

The occupying powers must also provide defense and security. If a country has been disarmed, the occupying power has taken on responsibility for its security and protection from external and internal enemies. How long this provision will be, and how extensive, will depend on the threats it faces and the speed with which Iraq can rebuild its own defense and internal security capability.

Finally, the occupying powers must react if yet another Saddam-type regime of fear begins to emerge. Even as the United States protected postwar Western Europe—including a new democratic state in West Germany—throughout the Cold War and decades of bipolarity, so the United States must remain tightly tied to a new Iraq. Just as the Allies would never have permitted a Nazi state to reemerge in Germany, so must the United States show vigilance with Iraq, should internal forces of stability and decency falter and collapse. The Iraqi people must not be victimized again.

Jean Bethke Elshtain is professor of social and political ethics at the University of Chicago's Divinity School.

An Islamic Solution
Sohail H. Hashmi

As the United States struggles for the best way to get out of Iraq, the Muslim world should contemplate how to get in. Muslim civil, political, and religious leaders must move beyond the resentment and hostility engendered by the Iraq war. Not one Muslim state committed troops to the "coalition of the willing," and few have assisted beyond token measures in the postwar stabilization of the country. Animosity toward the United States and its policies in the region has grown steadily in the Muslim world. Perhaps most significant, some Islamic scholars have not only condemned the American invasion but issued fatwas calling on Muslims to assist the insurgency.

After the January elections in Iraq, however, Muslims cannot afford to continue harping on the wrongs of the war. Islamic ethics require that they help their Iraqi brethren build a more peaceful and prosperous country. As the Koran commands, "Let not enmity of any people divert you from justice. Be just: That is closest to piety."

Above all, Islamic ethics require that Muslims refrain from materially or morally assisting murderers and terrorists masquerading as mujahideen. Because many Muslims sympathize with the insurgents' goal of driving the United States out of Iraq, they tacitly accept the atrocities these insurgents are committing. Kidnapping, torture, beheading, and the random killing of civilians through suicide bombings are not the work of mujahideen. They are the acts of criminals and should be firmly denounced as such by all Muslims.

Muslim troops approved by the Arab League and the Organization of the Islamic Conference should replace American, British, and other European forces as interim peacekeepers until Iraqi security forces are properly trained. This force cannot come from countries neighboring Iraq, which might have their own designs on its territory, but it could draw on troops from Morocco, Egypt, Pakistan, or Bangladesh.

The drafting of the country's constitution will undoubtedly stoke old controversies within and outside Iraq about the compatibility of Islam and democracy.

These disputes should not be allowed to divert attention from a central moral principle: the right of the Iraqi people to self-determination. The constitution that best provides for the security, welfare, and justice of all Iraqi citizens—Sunni and Shia, Muslim and non-Muslim—will inherently be an Islamic constitution. A successful Iraqi democracy will benefit all Arabs and all Muslims; a collapse of the Iraqi experiment into civil war will help no one.

Muslim leaders have an obligation to avoid the mistakes they committed in the lead-up to the U.S. intervention in Iraq, not just in 2003 but in 1991 as well. They had an obligation to isolate and to remove the brutal regime of Saddam Hussein when he attacked Iran, terrorized his own people, and invaded Kuwait. Yet for decades, Arab leaders either did nothing or actively supported Saddam. Their action and inaction made U.S. intervention all too easy.

Now that Saddam is facing trial for crimes against humanity, he should be tried under both international and Islamic law. Iranians and Kuwaitis should be allowed to participate in the trial, not just as aggrieved citizens of a foreign country but as Muslims victimized by a dictator who disguised himself as a Muslim ruler. One famous *hadith*, or saying of the prophet Muhammad, states: "The highest form of jihad is speaking truth to the tyrant." Holding Saddam accountable under Islamic law will help other victims speak truth to their tyrants.

Sohail H. Hashmi *is associate professor of international relations at Mount Holyoke College.*

Taking on Tehran

Kenneth Pollack and Ray Takeyh

THE TICKING CLOCK

EVEN AS the United States struggles to fix the troubled reconstruction of Iraq, the next big national security crisis has already descended on Washington. Investigators from the International Atomic Energy Agency (IAEA) have discovered that Iran is trying to acquire the capability to enrich uranium and separate plutonium, activities that would allow it to make fissile material for nuclear weapons. Revelations of Iran's massive secret program have convinced even doubtful European governments that Tehran's ultimate aim is to acquire the weapons or, at least, the ability to produce them whenever it wants.

It is an open question whether the United States could learn to coexist with a nuclear Iran. Since the death of Ayatollah Ruhollah Khomeini in 1989, Tehran's behavior has conveyed some very mixed messages to Washington. The mullahs have continued to define their foreign policy in opposition to the United States and have often resorted to belligerent methods to achieve their aims. They have tried to undermine the governments of Saudi Arabia and other U.S. allies in the Middle East; they have waged a relentless terrorist campaign against the U.S.-brokered Israeli-Palestinian peace process; and they have even sponsored at least one direct attack against the United States, bombing the Khobar Towers—a housing complex filled with U.S. troops—in Saudi Arabia in 1996. Although Tehran has been aggressive, anti-American, and murderous, its behavior has been neither irrational nor reckless. It has calibrated its actions carefully, showed restraint when the risks were high, and pulled back when threatened with painful consequences. Such calculations suggest that the United States could probably deter Iran even after it crossed the nuclear threshold.

There is no question, however, that the United States, the Middle East, and probably the rest of the world would be better off if they did not have to deal with a nuclear Iran. The hard part, of course, is making sure that Tehran never gets to that point. It appears to have made considerable progress in many aspects of its nuclear program, thanks to extensive assistance from Chinese, Germans, Pakistanis, Russians, and perhaps North Koreans. Iran's clerical regime has also shown itself willing to endure considerable sacrifices to achieve its most important objectives.

Yet there is reason to believe that Tehran's course can still be changed, if Washington takes advantage of the regime's vulnerabilities. Although Iran's hard-line leadership has maintained a remarkable unity of purpose in the face of reformist challengers, it is badly fragmented over key foreign policy issues, including the importance of nuclear weapons. At one end of the spectrum are the hardest of the hard-liners, who disparage economic and diplomatic considerations and put Iran's security concerns ahead of all others. At the opposite end are pragmatists, who believe that fixing Iran's failing economy must trump all else if the clerical regime is to retain power over the long term. In between these camps waver many of Iran's most important power brokers, who would prefer not to have to choose between bombs and butter.

This split provides an opportunity for the United States, and its allies in Europe and Asia, to forge a new strategy to derail Iran's drive for nuclear weapons. The West should use its economic clout to strengthen the hand of Iranian pragmatists, who could then argue for slowing, limiting, or shelving Tehran's nuclear program in return for the trade, aid, and investment that Iran badly needs. Only if the mullahs recognize that they have a stark choice—they can have nuclear weapons or a healthy economy, but not both—might they give up their nuclear dreams. With concern over Iran's nuclear aspirations growing, the United States and its allies now have a chance to present Iran with just such an ultimatum.

THE GREAT DIVIDE

IRAN'S CONSERVATIVE BLOC is riddled with factions and their contradictions. But whereas reformers and conservatives differ over domestic issues, the divisions within the conservative faction chiefly relate to critical foreign policy issues. Stalwarts of the Islamic revolution launched by Ayatollah Khomeini in 1979 still control Iran's judiciary, the Council of Guardians (the constitution's watchdog), and other powerful institutions, as well as key coercive groups such as the Revolutionary Guards and the Islamic vigilantes of the Ansar-e-Hezbollah. The hardliners consider themselves the most ardent Khomeini disciples and think of the revolution less as an antimonarchical rebellion than as a continued uprising against the forces that once sustained the U.S. presence in Iran: Western imperialism, Zionism, and Arab despotism. Ayatollah Mahmood Hashemi Shahroudi, the chief of the judiciary, said in

2001, "Our national interests lie with antagonizing the Great Satan. We condemn any cowardly stance toward America and any word on compromise with the Great Satan." For ideologues like him, international ostracism is the necessary price for revolutionary affirmation.

The pragmatists among Khomeini's heirs believe that the regime's survival depends on a more judicious international course. Thanks to them, Iran remained a regular player in the global energy market even at the height of its revolutionary fervor. Today, these realists gravitate around the influential former president Hashemi Rafsanjani and occupy key positions throughout the national security establishment. One of the group's leading figures, Muhammad Javad Larijani, a former legislator, argues, "We should not have what I would call an obstinate policy toward the world." Instead, the pragmatic conservatives have tried to develop economic and security arrangements with foreign powers such as China, the European Union, and Russia. In reaction to the United States' overthrow of two regimes on Iran's periphery—in Afghanistan and Iraq—they have adopted a wary but moderate stance. Admonishing his more radical brethren, Rafsanjani, for example, has warned, "We are facing a cruel and powerful U.S. government, and we have to be cautious and awake."

In a similar vein, the issue of Iraq is also fracturing the theocratic regime. In the eyes of Iran's reactionaries, the Islamic Republic's ideological mission demands that the revolution be exported to its pivotal Arab (and majority Shiite) neighbor. Such an act would not only establish the continued relevance of Iran's original Islamic vision but also secure a critical ally for an increasingly isolated Tehran. In contrast, the approach of Tehran's realists is conditioned by the requirements of the nation-state and its demands for stability. For this cohort, the most important task at hand is to prevent Iraq's simmering religious and ethnic tensions from engulfing Iran. Instigating Shiite uprisings, dispatching suicide squads, and provoking unnecessary confrontations with the United States hardly serves Iran's interests at a time when its own domestic problems are deepening. As a result, Tehran's mainstream leadership has mostly encouraged Iraq's Shiite groups to participate in reconstruction, not to obstruct U.S. efforts, and to do everything possible to avoid civil war. Hard-liners, meanwhile, have won permission to provide some assistance to Muqtada al-Sadr's Mahdi Army and other Shiite rejectionists.

Teetering between the two camps is Iran's supreme religious leader, Ayatollah Seyed Ali Khamenei. As the theocracy's top ideologue, he shares the hard-liners' revolutionary convictions and their confrontational impulses. But as the head of state, he must safeguard Iran's national interests and temper ideology with statecraft. In his 16 years as supreme leader, Khamenei has attempted to balance the ideologues and the realists, empowering both factions to prevent either from achieving a preponderance of influence. Lately, however, the Middle East's changing political topography has forced his hand somewhat. With the American imperium encroaching menacingly on Iran's frontiers, Khamenei, one of the country's most hawkish thinkers, is being forced to lean toward the pragmatists on some issues.

THE NUCLEAR CARD

MORE THAN any other issue, the pursuit of nuclear weapons has exacerbated tensions within Iran's clerical estate. The theocratic elite generally agrees that Iran should maintain a nuclear research program that could eventually allow it to build a bomb. After all, now that Washington has proved willing to put its provocative doctrine of military pre-emption into practice, Iran's desire for nuclear weapons makes strategic sense. And Tehran cannot be entirely faulted for rushing to acquire them. When the Bush administration invaded Iraq, which was not yet nuclearized, and avoided using force against North Korea, which already was, Iranians came to see nuclear weapons as the only viable deterrent to U.S. military action.

Although Iranian leaders agree on the strategic value of a strong nuclear program, they are divided over just how strong it should be. Conservative ideologues press for a nuclear breakout in defiance of international opinion, whereas conservative realists argue that restraint best serves Iran's interests. The ideologues, who view a conflict with the United States as inevitable, believe that the only way to ensure the survival of the Islamic Republic—and its ideals—is to equip it with an independent nuclear capability. Ali Akbar Nateq-Nuri, a conservative presidential candidate in 1997 and now an influential adviser to Khamenei, dismissed Tehran's recent negotiations with the Europeans, noting, "Fortunately, the opinion polls show that 75 to 80 percent of Iranians want to resist and [to] continue our program and reject humiliation." In the cosmology of such hard-liners, nuclear arms have not only strategic value, but also currency in domestic politics. Iranian conservatives see their defiance of the Great Satan as a means of mobilizing nationalistic opinion behind a revolution that has gradually lost popular legitimacy.

In contrast, the clerical realists warn that, with Iran under intense international scrutiny, any act of provocation by Tehran would lead other states to embrace Washington's punitive approach and further isolate the theocratic regime. In an interview in 2002, the pragmatic minister of defense, Ali Shamkhani, warned that the "existence of nuclear weapons will turn us into a threat to others that could be exploited in a dangerous way to harm our relations with the countries of the region." The economic dimension of nuclear diplomacy is also pushing the pragmatists toward restraint, as Iran's feeble economy can ill afford the imposition of multilateral sanctions. "If there [are] domestic and foreign conflicts, foreign capital will not flow into the count," Rafsanjani has warned. "In fact, such conflicts will lead to the flight of capital from this country."

IT'S THE ECONOMY, STUPID

DESPITE ample natural resources, Iran continues to suffer double-digit rates of inflation and unemployment. A million young Iranians enter the job market every year, but the economy produces less than half that many jobs. The clerics' penchant for centralization has bred an inefficient command economy with a bloated bureaucracy. Extensive subsidies for basic commodities, such as wheat and gasoline, waste tens of billions of dollars but do little to alleviate poverty. Massive foundations that are philanthropic only in name monopolize key sectors of the economy, operating with little competition, regulation, or taxation. Inefficient state-owned enterprises drain the government budget, and a vast gray market of commercial entities has been spun off from government ministries. The recent increase in oil prices is not a long-term solution to Iran's woes; the economy's flaws run much too deep. Twenty-five years after Iran's revolution pledged to deliver a more just society, the Islamic Republic has spawned an economy that benefits only an elite group of clerics and their cronies and stifles private enterprise.

Reform is possible, but it would require selling off public enterprises and scaling back the government's onerous subsidies. Iran's clerical elite is too implicated in corrupt arrangements and too fearful of losing its prerogatives to endorse measures that would fundamentally alter the structure of the economy. Concerns that an aggressive privatization program would unleash popular dissatisfaction are discouraging reform. Any attempt to restructure the public sector would exacerbate an already inflamed unemployment crisis. The reactionary Council of Guardians is unlikely to countenance privatizing key sectors such as the banking industry, as such measures run counter to Iran's constitution. And a serious campaign against corruption would alienate the regime's remaining loyalists.

Iran's technocrats recognize the country's deepening economic predicament. Muhammad Khazai, the deputy minister of economy and finance, has acknowledged that Iran will need $20 billion in investment every year for the next five years if it is to provide sufficient jobs for its citizens. The oil industry—the lifeblood of Iran's economy—faces an even more daunting challenge. The National Iranian Oil Company estimates that $70 billion is needed over the next ten years to modernize the country's dilapidated infrastructure and is counting on foreign oil companies and international capital markets to provide approximately three-quarters of those massive investments. Given the clerical elite's inability to reform the economy, foreign investments have become critical to Iran's economic revival. Khazai insists, "We should be thinking of drawing foreign investments and [of] prepar[ing] the ground for [an] inflow of foreign capital."

The leadership in Tehran is divided over how to balance its nuclear ambitions with its economic needs.

Some officials have gone so far as to suggest that Iran's economic difficulties cannot be redressed if Tehran continues to have such a tense relationship with the United States. The exasperated head of the Management and Planning Organization, Hamid Reza Baradaran Shoraka, has noted that among the major obstacles to the country's development are the economic sanctions imposed by Washington. Continued antagonism toward the United States would hardly ensure that these sanctions are lifted.

As a result, the realists have tried to leverage Iran's nuclear intentions to secure a more favorable security and economic relationship with the United States. Like the North Korean leadership, Iran's clerical oligarchs are hoping to use Tehran's nuclear ambitions to force negotiations with and extract concessions from Washington. In a press conference in September, the powerful secretary of the Supreme National Security Council, Hasan Rowhani, acknowledged that Tehran had held constructive talks with U.S. officials on the war in Afghanistan and suggested that "such negotiations on the nuclear file [are] not totally out of [the] question." Fearful that Iran's feeble economy could not withstand more multilateral sanctions, Iran's pragmatists are willing to back down on the nuclear question to help save the economy.

So far, these competing pressures have resulted in inconsistent government positions. Even as it has agreed to suspend efforts to acquire nuclear capabilities, the Iranian government has insisted that it would never give up its nuclear weapons program and, in fact, has prodded it along. Meanwhile, in an attempt to head off international sanctions, Khamenei has temporarily sided with the realists. Despite calls by clerical firebrands and the Iranian parliament to discard the Nonproliferation Treaty (NPT), in October 2003 he agreed that Tehran would sign the NPT's Additional Protocol, including provisions for a fairly intrusive inspection regime. Last November, Tehran also accepted a deal brokered by France, Germany, and the United Kingdom to suspend uranium-enrichment activities and forgo completion of the nuclear fuel cycle.

A NEW APPROACH

WITH TEHRAN DIVIDED over how to balance its nuclear ambitions with its economic needs, Washington has an opportunity to keep it from crossing the nuclear threshold. Since the economy is a growing concern for the Iranian leadership, Washington can boost its leverage by working with the states that are most important to Tehran's international economic relations: the western European countries and Japan, as well as Russia and China, if they can be persuaded to cooperate. Together, these states must raise the economic stakes of Iran's nuclear aspirations. They must force Tehran to confront a painful choice: either nuclear weapons or economic health. Painting Tehran's alternatives so starkly will require dramatically raising both the returns it would gain for compliance and the price it would pay for defiance.

Washington and its allies must confront Tehran with a painful choice: either nuclear weapons or economic health.

In the past, dissension among the United States and its allies allowed Tehran to circumvent this difficult choice. Throughout the 1990s, the United States pursued a strategy of pure coercion toward Iran, with strong sanctions and a weak covert action program. In the meantime, the Europeans refused even to threaten to cut their commercial relations with Tehran, no matter how bad its behavior became. Iran played Europe off against the United States, using European economic largesse to mitigate the effects of U.S. sanctions, all the while making considerable progress with its clandestine nuclear program.

Today, the situation is different. A fortunate result of Iran's unfortunate nuclear progress is that Tehran will now have a much harder time hedging. Revelations that Iran has moved closer toward producing fissile material over the past two years could help forge a unified Western position. In the 1990s, Europeans could ignore much of Iran's malfeasance because the evidence was ambiguous. But with the IAEA recently having uncovered so many of Iran's covert enrichment activities—and with Tehran subsequently having admitted them—it will be far more uncomfortable, if not impossible, for Europeans to keep looking the other way. It is still unclear just how seriously Europe takes Iran's nuclear activities, but in public and private statements, European officials no longer try to play them down. Moreover, when during negotiations with the EU in November Tehran requested that 20 research centrifuges remain active, the Europeans refused. Such resolve marked a drastic departure from Europe's fecklessness during the 1990s. That Tehran quickly complied was a sure sign that it fears incurring the wrath of its economic benefactors.

It may now be possible to fashion a multilateral policy that can persuade Tehran to abandon its nuclear program. Working together, the United States and its allies should lay out two dramatically diverging paths for Iran. On one course, Iran would agree to give up its nuclear program, accept a comprehensive inspection regime, and end its support for terrorism. In exchange, the United States would lift sanctions and settle Iran's claims over the assets of Shah Mohammed Reza Pahlavi. The West would also consider bringing Iran into international economic organizations such as the World Trade Organization, granting Iran increased commercial ties, and perhaps even providing it with economic assistance. Western nations could sweeten the deal by agreeing to assist Iran with its energy needs (the ostensible reason for its nuclear research program) and to forswear direct military attack. The United States could also help create a new security architecture in the Persian Gulf in which Iranians, Arabs, and Americans would find cooperative ways to address their security concerns, much as Washington did with the Russians in Europe during the 1970s and the 1980s. If, on the other hand, Iran decided to stay its current course, U.S. allies would join Washington in imposing precisely the sort of sanctions the mullahs fear would scuttle Iran's precarious economy. These sanctions could take the form of everything from barring investment in specific projects or entire sectors (such as the oil industry) to severing all commercial contacts with Iran if it proved utterly unwilling to address Western demands.

UPPING THE ANTE

IN AN IDEAL WORLD, the Iranians would agree to work out all their differences with the West in a single grand bargain. Such a comprehensive deal would serve Washington well, as it would be the fastest way to resolve current disputes and the surest platform from which to build a new, cooperative relationship. In fact, under the presidencies of Ronald Reagan, George H.W. Bush, and Bill Clinton, Washington repeatedly offered such an approach. But conservative ideologues in Tehran repeatedly quashed the efforts of any Iranian who attempted to take up the United States' conciliatory offers. The Clinton administration made nearly a dozen unilateral gestures toward Iran, including the partial lifting of sanctions, to enable the reformist government of President Muhammad Khatami to participate in such negotiations. But these overtures triggered a conservative backlash that eventually debilitated Khatami's government.

Even if a grand bargain seems unlikely given Iran's complicated domestic politics, a policy of true "carrots and sticks" remains a viable option. In this case, Western nations would lay out the same two paths for Iran but would do so as statements of a joint policy, rather than as the goals of bilateral negotiations with Tehran. Officials from the United States, European countries, and Japan as well as from any other country willing to participate, including China and Russia would explicitly define what they expect Iran to do and not do. To each of these actions, the allies would attach positive and negative inducements (the "carrots" and the "sticks"), so that Tehran could clearly understand both the benefits it would gain from ending nuclear and terrorist activities and the penalties it would suffer for refusing to end them.

Such an effort will not be easy. The United States and its allies will have a hard time defining clear benchmarks to measure Iran's compliance, and they will likely disagree over how much to reward or punish Tehran at each step. But the approach can work, so long as a few critical measures are applied.

First, the strategy requires that both the potential rewards and the potential penalties be significant. Iranian hard-liners will not abandon their nuclear program easily. Although the mullahs are not as stubborn as North Korean leader Kim Jong Il continues to be—they would not knowingly allow three million fellow citizens to die of starvation just to preserve their nuclear program—they unquestionably are willing to tolerate considerable hardship to keep their nuclear hopes alive. In order to change Tehran's behavior, therefore, the inducements will have to be potent: big rewards that could revive the economy or heavy sanctions that would surely cripple it.

Second, Tehran must be presented with the prospect of serious rewards, not just punishments; Washington must be willing to make concessions to Iran in return for real concessions from it. The most obvious reason for this condition is that the Europeans insist on it. European diplomats have consistently said that they can persuade their reluctant governments to threaten serious sanctions for Iran's continued misbehavior only if the United States agrees to reward compliance with real economic benefits.

The carrots, moreover, need to be as big as the sticks. Only the prospect of significant bonuses will provide ammunition to pragmatists in Tehran who argue that Iran should revise its nuclear stance to secure the benefits necessary to revitalize its troubled economy. Current levels of trade and investment from Europe and Japan have not been adequate to solve Iran's deep-seated economic problems. The pragmatists' case will become convincing only if Tehran's compliance with Western demands can help the Iranian economy do better than it does now. Granting enough economic concessions to maintain the status quo probably would not sway undecided Iranians; significantly more generous incentives might.

Washington must raise dramatically the returns Tehran would gain for compliance and the price it would pay for defiance.

The painful experience of trying to make the Iraq sanctions stick during the 1990s suggests another prerequisite for the approach that must be adopted with Tehran. One of the lessons learned from Iraq was that, although many governments threatened Saddam Hussein with sanctions if he defied the international community, few imposed them when he did. Spelling out in advance all of the steps Tehran is expected to take or to avoid, as well as the specific rewards and punishments they would incur, is the best way to prevent Iran and U.S. allies from reneging on their commitments as they have in the past.

Last, all incentives must be applied in graduated increments, so that small steps, positive or negative, would bring Tehran commensurate gains or sanctions. For Iranians to even consider forgoing their nuclear ambitions, they will need to see tangible gains from the start, as well as be able to point to a pot of gold at the end. Conversely, Tehran probably will not change course if it does not systematically suffer increasingly severe consequences for its reticence. Without immediate and automatic penalties, it is likely to act as it did throughout the 1990s, dismissing the West's promises and warnings as empty rhetoric while continuing to advance its program under the status quo.

THE LEAST BAD OPTION

THERE IS, of course, no guarantee that such an approach will persuade Tehran to end its nuclear projects or its support for terrorism. Even if Iran does halt these projects, the strategy is far from perfect: at the very least, it will require Washington to live for some time longer with a regime it abhors. But by setting out clearly the rewards Iran would accrue for cooperating and the penalties it would suffer for bucking, a carrots-and-sticks policy would force Iran's leadership to confront the choice it never wanted to make: whether to shelve its nuclear program or risk the crippling of its economy. Because Iran's economic woes have been a major factor in popular discontent with the regime, there is good reason to believe that, if forced to make such a choice, Tehran would grudgingly opt to save its economy and look for other ways to deal with its security and foreign policy aspirations.

This approach also is the best available, for it has a much greater chance of succeeding than the alternatives. Invading Iran simply should not be an option; Washington should not try

to deal with Tehran's nuclear program and its support for terrorism as it did with the Taliban and Saddam's regime. The United States is now in the thick of reconstruction in Afghanistan and Iraq, leaving it with very limited forces available to invade another country. Iran's mountainous terrain and large, nationalistic population would likely make any military campaign daunting. Postwar reconstruction would be even more complex and debilitating there than it has been in Afghanistan and Iraq.

Although most Iranians want a different type of government than they have and a better relationship with the United States, it would be foolhardy to believe that Washington could solve its problems with Tehran's nuclear ambitions by staging a coup or inciting a popular revolution to topple the current regime. Young Iranians seem to have a better image of the United States than their elders did, but their greater open-mindedness should not be confused with a desire to see U.S. interference in Iranian politics, something Iranians have responded to with ferocity in the past. Furthermore, although many Iranians may want a different government, they have shown little inclination to do what would be necessary to dislodge the current one. Most are weary of revolutions: when they had the chance to start one, amid student demonstrations in the summer of 1999, few heeded the call. There is good reason to believe that this regime's days are numbered, but little to think that it will fall soon enough or that the United States can do much to speed its demise. Advocating regime change might be a useful adjunct to a new Iran policy, but it will not solve Washington's immediate problems with Iran's nuclear program and its support for terrorism.

Likewise, at present, the costs, uncertainties, and risks of waging an air campaign to destroy Iran's nuclear sites are too great to make it anything but a measure of last resort—the hopes of some in the Bush administration notwithstanding. Because Tehran has managed to conceal major nuclear facilities, it is unclear by how much even successful bombing could set back the country's nuclear development. Moreover, no matter how little damage it suffered, Iran would likely retaliate. It has the most capable terrorist network in the world, and the United States would have to stand ready for a full onslaught of attacks. Perhaps even more important, a U.S. military campaign would probably prompt Tehran to unleash a clandestine war on U.S. forces in Iraq. The Iranians are hardly omnipotent there, but they could make the situation far more miserable and deadly than it already is. Without better intelligence about Iran's nuclear program and better protection against an Iranian counterattack, the idea of a U.S. air campaign should be kept on the shelf as a last-ditch option.

Iran today is at a crossroads. It might restrain its nuclear ambitions to the parameters set out in the NPT, or it might rashly cross the threshold, brandishing the bomb as a tool of revolutionary diplomacy. It might play a positive role in rebuilding a stable Iraq, or it might be a dogmatic actor that exacerbates Iraq's sectarian and ethnic cleavages. As difficult as the U.S. predicament is in Iraq today, Tehran could make it much worse: it could dramatically inflame the insurgency and destabilize its already insecure neighbor. Since the demise of Saddam Hussein, Iran has dispatched clerics and Revolutionary Guards to

Iraq and released funds to establish an intricate network of influence there. It is still unclear what the theocracy's specific goals are, but there is concern that they could be at odds with those of the United States.

Much now depends on Washington's conduct, the security environment that emerges in the region, and the extent to which Washington and its allies can force Tehran to choose between its nuclear ambitions and its economic well-being. Given Iran's economic frailty and shifting power dynamics within its leadership, a strategy offering strong rewards and severe penalties has a reasonable chance of discouraging Tehran from its nuclear plans, especially if the Europeans and the Japanese are willing to participate in full. In fact, it is the only plan that has any real prospect of success at present. Rather than continue to criticize everyone else's Iran policy, the United States should stop making perfect the enemy of good enough. Washington has a chance to curb Tehran's alarming behavior, with the help of its allies and without resort to force. If it does not seize the opportunity now, at some point soon it will likely wish it had.

KENNETH POLLACK *is Director of Research at the Saban Center for Middle East Policy at the Brookings Institution and the author of* The Persian Puzzle: The Conflict Between Iran and America. **RAY TAKEYH** *is a Senior Fellow in Middle East Studies at the Council on Foreign Relations.*

Iran's Nuclear Calculations

Ray Takeyh

As the Bush administration energetically addresses the issue of nuclear proliferation in the Middle East, Iran has suddenly emerged as one of Washington's foremost concerns. Over the years, many Western analysts have assumed that Iran's nuclear program was largely limited to the Bushehr installation near the Persian Gulf that operates under the oversight of the International Atomic Energy Agency (IAEA). The ostensible purpose of this installation is to provide Iran with an alternative source of energy to gas and oil. Western concerns were not so much that Bushehr would produce a nuclear bomb, but that under the cover of a civilian research program Iran was gathering sufficient knowledge and expertise to achieve a nuclear weapons capacity.

Over the past year, a series of revelations has shocked the Washington establishment and forced a revision of previous intelligence assessments. The first shock came last August when U.S. intelligence reported that Iran had built extensive facilities for the enrichment of uranium in Natanz, approximately 200 miles south of Tehran. The Natanz installation currently contains 160 centrifuges, needed for this purpose, with another 1,000 under construction. The plan is to have 5,000 operational centrifuges within two years. This would give Iran the capacity to produce several nuclear bombs a year.

In addition, it appeared that Tehran was completing another facility at Arak in central Iran for the production of heavy water, needed for the production of plutonium. Although initial CIA assessments were that Iran could achieve a nuclear arms capacity within five to eight years, the sophisticated nature of these installations indicates that it may be able to do so within three years. The more alarming aspect of the recent discoveries is that, increasingly, much of the technology for assembling a nuclear device is being indigenously produced.

But despite these seemingly dire developments, it is not inevitable that Iran will be the next member of the exclusive nuclear club. In Tehran's corridors of clerical power, there is in fact a subtle debate going on regarding the wisdom of crossing the nuclear threshold. What the Islamic Republic decides to do in this respect will depend to a great extent on the nature of its evolving relationship with the United States and the security architecture of the Persian Gulf. An imaginative U.S. policy can still influence the outcome of Iran's deliberations, stacking the scales in favor of those within Iran who seek to remain within the confines of the Nuclear Non-Proliferation Treaty, to which Iran is a signatory.

Contrary to Western assumptions, Iran's nuclear calculations are not derived from an irrational ideology, but rather from a judicious attempt to craft a viable deterrent capability against an evolving range of threats. Despite its dogmatic rhetoric, continuing support of international terrorism, and defiant opposition to the Israeli-Palestinian peace process, Iran has evolved during the past decade into a largely circumspect and cautious regional power whose strategic doctrine is predicated on preserving its independence and safeguarding its vital interests. This transformation reached its apex with the election of the moderate cleric Muhammad Khatami to the presidency in 1997. The new president set the tone early on by noting that "making enemies is not a skill; real skill lies in the capacity to neutralize enemies."[1] Under Khatami's stewardship, Iran has sought to advance its interests through a pragmatic diplomacy emphasizing trade, reconciliation with erstwhile foes such as Saudi Arabia, and mutual security compacts. The crude tactic of brandishing nuclear threats is inconsistent with Iran's current international orientation and should not be presumed to be the motivation behind its nuclear policy.

On the surface, Iran has ample incentives to acquire nuclear weapons, given its dangerous and unstable neighborhood. However, despite persistent chaos on its frontiers, Iran's nuclear program has always been conditioned by a narrower but more existential set of threats. Instability in Afghanistan and Central Asia may be an important concern for Iran's defense planners, but it is hard to see how nuclear weapons can ameliorate the handling of these crises. Since the inception of the Islamic Republic, negating the Iraqi and American challenges has been the most significant task for Iran's national security establishment. These two states have dominated Iran's threat perceptions and determined its defense priorities.

Here, it is important to set the Israeli question in its proper context with respect to Iran's unconventional weapons aspirations. To be sure, even a cursory survey of the clerical regime's declarations would lead one to conclude that the Islamic Republic perceives nuclear-armed

Israel as an existential threat not just to itself but to the entire Islamic world. However, the invocation of the Israeli military threat is largely rhetorical, employed by the clerical regime as a means of mobilizing regional and domestic opinion behind a range of policy initiatives. In the clerical cosmology, Israel is seen less as an imminent military threat than as an ideological threat, with Zionism transgressing onto sacred Muslim land. However disturbing the Zionist threat may be to Iranian clerics, it does not drive Tehran's pursuit of nuclear weapons. Despite its rhetorical fulminations and aggressive posturing, Iran has opted for a low-intensity challenge to Israel by fueling terrorist actions against the Jewish state while avoiding direct military confrontation.

While the Israeli-Palestinian arena may be peripheral to Iran's core interests, the critical Persian Gulf area constitutes Tehran's most serious strategic concern. The Gulf is Iran's most important outlet to international petroleum markets and essential to the country's economic stability. During the past two decades, Saddam Hussein's Iraq has presented a formidable threat to Tehran, as the Iraqi dictator sought supremacy in the Gulf and waged a merciless eight-year war against his neighbor in which he employed chemical weapons against Iranian troops. The war ended in 1988 with an uneasy cease-fire, which led neither to genuine peace nor greatly improved relations. The border between the two states remained unsettled, and both sides continued to sponsor proxy wars against each other. The fear of a revived Iraq, free of the straitjacket into which it had been forced in 1991 after its defeat in the Gulf War, shaped Iran's defense posture. With Saddam's downfall and the impending dismantling of the Iraqi weapons of mass destruction infrastructure, however, the existential threat posed by Iraq has been eliminated. Any successor regime in Baghdad is likely to adhere to Iraq's non-proliferation commitments (it is a signatory to the Nuclear Non-Proliferation Treaty) and may even cultivate favorable ties with the Islamic Republic.

With Saddam gone, America has emerged as the foremost strategic problem for Iran and the primary driver of its nuclear weapons policy. The Bush Doctrine, which pledges the preemptive use of force as a tool of counter-proliferation, combined with the substantial augmentation of American military power on Iran's periphery, has intensified Tehran's fears of "encirclement" by the United States—or even worse, of being its next target. President Bush's characterization of Iran as a member of the "axis of evil," and Secretary of Defense Donald Rumsfeld's more recent rhetorical support for regime change, has aggravated an already strained relationship. Iran's leadership clearly sees itself as being in Washington's cross hairs, and it is precisely this perception that is driving its accelerated nuclear program. As Khatami confessed in early April, "They tell us that Syria is the next target, but according to our reports, Iran could well follow."[2]

In the menacing shadow of the American colossus, Iran's strategic planners have drawn sobering lessons from Operation Iraqi Freedom. The clerical oligarchs certainly noticed that Saddam's much bruited repositories of chemical weapons did not prove a deterrent against an American president determined to effect regime change. As an Iranian official confessed, "The fact that Saddam was toppled in twenty-one days is something that should concern all countries in the region."[3] In the meantime, developments on the Korean peninsula offered their own lessons. The North Korean model suggests that a presumed nuclear capability may not only avert a pre-emptive American strike but generate its own set of economic rewards and future security guarantees.

The paradox of the post–September 11 Middle East is that although Iran's security has improved through the removal of Saddam and of the Taliban in Afghanistan, its feelings of insecurity have intensified. The massive projection of American power in the region and the enduring antagonism between Washington and Tehran constitute Iran's foremost strategic dilemma and its primary motivation for the acquisition of the "strategic weapon." However, as with nearly every other important issue currently being debated in the Islamic Republic, the notion of crossing the nuclear threshold is hardly a settled topic. A more adroit American diplomacy can have an impact on the parameters of this debate.

To Go Nuclear or Not?

It is often assumed that the Islamic Republic has already made its decision and is relentlessly pursuing a determined nuclear strategy. Ascribing such cohesion and efficacy to a fractious, polarized polity is too simple. While much of the political debate in Iran is conducted in public, nuclear discussions are largely held in secret. Nonetheless, at times of intense international crisis, such as the recent American war in Iraq, the veil of secrecy lifts and the contours of the debate seep into the pages of newspapers and specialized journals that often act as surrogates for the various clerical factions.

The first sustained exposure of Iranian nuclear deliberations came when Pakistan test-fired its first nuclear weapon in 1998. The debate in Tehran focused not so much on whether Iran should pursue a robust nuclear research program but on the wisdom of crossing the nuclear weapons threshold. The respected journal *Payam-e-Emrouz* set the parameters of the debate in stark terms by suggesting that "the dangerous regional situation in which our country exists reminds us that more than any other time we have to be thinking of our national interests."[4] The proliferation of weapons of mass destruction on Iran's frontiers, it was argued, mandated development of a more effective deterrent power.

However, the notion that this necessitated the possession of nuclear weapons did not go unchallenged. The journal *Farda,* with connections to the Foreign Ministry, argued against the proposition: "Does deployment of nuclear weapons—if possible and of the weak kind such as those of Pakistan— bring us security or insecurity against large countries such as the U.S.? Certainly the answer is insecurity since Iran does not have the superior military technology of the U.S. and these weapons cannot play a deterrent and security role against the U.S. On the other hand, Iran has befriended the small countries of the region and at least for now has no critical problems. Deploying such weapons not only cannot solve any problems for Iran; it will further add to its problems."[5]

In essence, the opponents of a nuclear breakout suggest that such a move may accentuate Iran's strategic vulnerabilities by undermining its carefully cultivated ties with the Gulf states and the international community. The argument that Iran's existing international relationships and longstanding commitment to the nonproliferation treaty act as a constraint on its nuclear activities should not be easily dismissed. The Islamic Republic has invested considerable effort in recent years in fostering favorable ties with most of its neighbors, as well as with Europe and Asia. To be sure, given the recent projection of U.S. power in Afghanistan and Iraq, the case for achieving a nuclear deterrent has become measurably more compelling. As one of Iran's leading reformist politicians, Mostafa Tajazadeh, said on the eve of the U.S. invasion of Iraq, "It is basically a matter of equilibrium. If I don't have a nuclear bomb, I don't have security."[6] Others within the Iranian leadership are frustrated by what they view as an American double standard that would maintain U.S. strategic supremacy but deny nuclear capability to regional powers. In the words of the prominent conservative columnist Amir Mohebian, "The Americans say in order to preserve the peace for [their] children, [they] should have nuclear weapons and [we] should not."[7]

However, all is not lost, as those calling for restraint continue to press their case. The opponents of a nuclear breakout, including reformist politicians and officials in the Foreign Ministry, maintain the necessity of adhering to the broad confines of the international nonproliferation regimes as the best means of ensuring Iran's fundamental interests. As Ali Reza Aghazadeh, an important Khatami advisor on nuclear issues, affirmed recently, "Peace and stability cannot be achieved by means of nuclear weapons."[8]

While the events in Iraq have caused considerable consternation among the clerical oligarchs, the developments on the Korean peninsula offer a window of opportunity for an Iranian officialdom that is still prone to come to an arrangement over its nuclear weapons program. Iran's planners may be opting for a variation of the North Korean strategy, namely threatening to cross the nuclear threshold as a means of fostering better relations with the United States, including a resumption of economic ties. The economic dimension is particularly important as, in the last decade, Tehran has grudgingly come to realize that Iran's tense relations with the United States preclude its effective integration into the global economy and ac-

cess to needed technology. Foreign Ministry spokesman Hamid Raza Asefi first unveiled this strategy in March, claiming, "We are ready for discussions and negotiations, but we need to know what benefits the Islamic Republic would get from them."[9] Assadollah Saburi, the deputy head of Iran's Atomic Energy Organization, dangled the prospect of Iran's acceptance of additional IAEA inspection protocols, but said, "We do not want to increase our commitment in the face of [trade] sanctions that are currently imposed."[10] Given the economic and diplomatic cost of financing a clandestine nuclear weapons infrastructure, Iran's officialdom may be prepared for a grand deal, which would involve agreeing to limits on Iran's nuclear activities in exchange for the United States allowing Iran access to such international lending institutions as the International Monetary Fund and permitting American investments in Iran, particularly in the petroleum sector. At any rate, the real significance of these declarations is that there still exists in Iranian official circles a propensity to negotiate and bargain.

The ultimate fate of Iran's nuclear program rests on the outcome of the intense power struggle going on inside the country. While there is currently consensus across the political spectrum with respect to the necessity of sustaining a nuclear *research* program, no such agreement is evident on the issue of actually crossing the nuclear weapons threshold. It is here that the internal factions matter, as the conservatives would be more prone than the reformers to violate Iran's treaty commitments and imperil important regional relationships for the sake of acquiring nuclear arms. The hardliners—with their suspicions of the United States and indeed of the entire international order—have always pressed for a revolutionary foreign policy. A prominent figure of the right, Ayatollah Muhammad Yazdi, represents this worldview: "The enemy [the West] wants to westernize the country, eliminate the Islamic regime, and the Koran with whatever methods [it has at its disposal]."[11] This notion is echoed by another influential hardliner, the former head of the Revolutionary Guards, Mohsen Rezai, who deprecates the reformers' approach as "submissive policies, weakness and giving unilateral concessions in the name of détente."[12] The truth is that given its ideological precepts, its suspicions and paranoia, the Iranian right does not find international isolation and dogmatic confrontation with the West necessarily objectionable.

Moreover, conservatives are wary of international treaties and diplomacy when it comes to preserving the vitality of the Islamic Republic. As Ali-Akbar Hashemi Rafsanjani, Iran's powerful former president, said in the aftermath of Iran's war with Iraq, "The war taught us that international laws are only scraps of paper."[13] Indeed, President Khatami's declared policy of détente came under intense criticism, with the commander of the Revolutionary Guards, Yahya Rahim Safavi, pointedly asking: "Can we withstand America's threats and domineering attitude with a policy of détente? Will we be able to protect the Islamic Republic from international Zionism by signing conventions banning the proliferation of chemical and nuclear weapons?"[14]

Since the mid-1990s, when the reform movement began in intellectual and political circles, reformers have endorsed a foreign policy of engagement and integration in the global society. Khatami has led the charge by insisting on a "new paradigm of interaction among nations and cultures in a world that longs for peace and security." This pragmatic reformist diplomacy calls for protecting Iran's interests through an interlocking set of commercial and strategic ties with critical international actors such as the European Union and the Gulf states. As Khatami has also noted, Iran must respect "the right of other nations to self-determination and access to the necessary means of honorable living."[15] The Bush administration, which has been dismissive of the reform movement, would be wise to recognize that the contest in today's Iran is not just about the nature of domestic Islamic rule but also about what type of international orientation the theocracy will pursue in the future. While the reformers may not yet have been successful in liberalizing the Islamic Republic, in the realm of foreign affairs they have been quietly effective in restraining the impetuous impulses of the hardliners.

What Can Washington Do?

Thwarting Iran's nuclear ambitions has been the aim of successive U.S. administrations. Over the years, Washington has scored some impressive gains and managed to delay and frustrate Tehran's quest for nuclear technology. The Reagan administration succeeded in obtaining Europe's agreement to rigorous export controls with respect to dual-use technologies and in getting Germany to abandon its cooperation with Iran's nascent nuclear research program. During the Iran-Iraq War, Iran's nuclear research program remained largely dormant and was not reactivated until the early 1990s. Given Europe's continued unwillingness to participate, Iran turned to the Russian Federation, with which it signed a nuclear cooperation agreement in 1995.

The Russian Federation is helping Iran rebuild its two nuclear reactors at the Bushehr installation, which suffered from neglect during the Iran-Iraq War, and has provided the Islamic Republic with fuel fabrication technology and, possibly, even uranium enrichment centrifuge plants. Throughout the late 1990s, both the Bush and Clinton administrations attempted to deter Russia from this course by means of warnings, selective sanctions, and promises of expanded economic ties. A number of compacts were negotiated between the United States and Russia, most notably the December 1995 accord hammered out by Vice President Al Gore and Prime Minister Viktor Chernomyrdin, in which Russia agreed to limit its cooperation with Iran to work on one unit of the Bushehr plant. Russia in essence agreed not to provide

additional reactors or fuel-cycle assistance to Iran. By the year 2000, this arrangement had unraveled. The recent meeting between Presidents Bush and Putin at the G-8 summit in Evian, France, has not fully resolved the dispute. President Putin seemingly accepted the need for the international community to check Iran's nuclear ambitions, but his economic advisor, Andrei Illarionov, emphasized: "Iran is a neighbor. We want to have good relations with it, including in the field of civilian nuclear energy."[16]

Persuading Russia to alter its policy has proven difficult because Moscow has compelling economic and geopolitical reasons for cooperating with Iran. On the economic front, Russia's own nuclear research and aerospace industries have few domestic customers and must look elsewhere for business if they are to survive. Over 300 Russian firms have participated in the construction of the Bushehr facility, which has provided approximately 20,000 jobs for Russians.[17] But Russia has another incentive for continued cooperation with Iran. As with his predecessor, Boris Yeltsin, Vladimir Putin appreciates Iran's influence in the Islamic realm and seeks favorable ties with Tehran as a means of preventing Iranian mischief in the unsettled states of Central Asia. The fact that Tehran has largely stayed out of the Islamist struggle in Chechnya and has been restrained in promoting its ideology in the former Soviet Republics is a testimony to the success of Russia's diplomacy.

This was the situation that the Bush administration inherited and quickly proceeded to make worse. Given that Iran's nuclear ambitions stem, in large part, from seeing the United States as a threat, Washington's conduct has a material impact on Tehran's proliferation tendencies. Thus far, the Bush administration has exacerbated Iran's strategic anxieties and further fueled its desire for acquiring nuclear arms. President Bush's earlier denunciation of Iran as a member of the "axis of evil" and more recent statements by administration officials such as Undersecretary of State John Bolton, who called on Tehran to "draw the appropriate lesson from Iraq,"[18] only buttress the position of those within the Islamic Republic's hierarchy who insist that the only way to negate the American challenge is through the possession of nuclear weapons. In the meantime, the administration's focus on missile defense, its withdrawal from the Anti-Ballistic Missile Treaty, and its relative disdain for European opinion in the run-up to the war with Iraq have limited its capacity to gain Russian cooperation regarding Iran.

Moreover, since Iran is increasingly producing much of its nuclear infrastructure on its own, attempts to derail Tehran's nuclear activities by pressuring external actors will yield limited results. It is time for the Bush administration to remove its ideological blinders and recognize that America's central role in Iran's strategic conception gives it a unique opportunity to diminish Tehran's zeal for nuclear arms. Washington should take up Iran's recent offer, made by the Foreign Ministry, that it would adhere to additional IAEA protocols if the United States were to relax its trade sanctions against Iran. Indeed, the United Nations Security Council could be the venue for such a discussion.

A more forthcoming U.S. policy of easing economic restrictions on Iran would be wise for two reasons. It would help induce Tehran to conform to nonproliferation standards, and it would also help the reformers rehabilitate Iran's economy and thus consolidate their power base. Given the fact that two decades of sanctions and coercion have failed to modify Iran's objectionable policies—its sponsorship of terrorism, opposition to the Arab-Israeli peace process, and pursuit of an ambitious nuclear weapons research program—a more adroit diplomacy and economic engagement may prove more effective in pushing Iran in the right direction.

While holding out the prospect of dialogue and cooperation, Washington should also begin assembling a new "coalition of the willing" designed to exert pressure on Iran should it prove uncooperative. The European Union and Russia should be induced to make it clear to Tehran that crossing the nuclear threshold will force them to impose rigorous economic sanctions. At a time when Iran is in dire need of foreign investment, such a step would make a significant impression on Tehran. The timing is propitious for Washington to make such a move since the recent revelations of Iran's nuclear status appear to have led many Europeans to move in the direction long desired by the United States. Dominique de Villepin, the much maligned French foreign minister, has taken the lead on this issue, telling Tehran that "it is essential to continue confidence-building measures, in particular by signing the additional protocols of the Nuclear Non-Proliferation Treaty."[19] At the same time, Washington should press the Gulf states (particularly Saudi Arabia), with which the United States has close security and economic ties, to make it clear to Tehran that continued favorable relations will be contingent on Iran's adherence to its nonproliferation commitments.

Today, Iran stands at a strategic crossroads and will soon have to make fundamental decisions regarding its nuclear program. Shrill rhetoric of the "axis of evil" variety and imperious presidential doctrines are unlikely to prevent nuclear proliferation. A more clever diplomacy of carrots and sticks, offering to integrate Iran into the global economy while holding out the stark threat of multilateral pressures, can best dissuade it from taking the nuclear road.

Notes

1. Islamic Republic News Agency (IRNA), February 28, 2000.
2. Agence France Presse (AFP), April 11, 2003.
3. Reuters, April 19, 2003.
4. "It Happened in the Neighborhood," *Payam-e-Emruz*, no. 24, June/July 1999.
5. "Answer to Questions," *Farda*, no. 10, May 1999.
6. Karl Vick, "Iranians Assert Right to Nuclear Weapons," *Washington Post*, March 11, 2003.
7. Ibid.
8. Afsane Bassir Pour, "Interview with Ali Reza Aghazadeh," *Le Monde*, March 13, 2003.
9. AFP, March 16, 2003.
10. Nazila Fathi, "Business as Usual," *New York Times*, March 19, 2003.
11. AFP, October 25, 2002.
12. Ali Taheri, "Former Guard Commander Castigates Khatami's Submissive Foreign Policy," *Entekhab*, April 30, 2003.
13. IRNA, October 19, 1988.
14. *Jameeh*, April 27, 1998.
15. IRNA, November 11, 2001.
16. AFP, June 4, 2003.
17. Anton Khlopkov, "Iranian Program for Nuclear Energy Development: The Past and the Future," *Yadenry Kontrol Digest*, vol. 6 (summer 2001), p. 19.
18. AFP, April 10, 2003.
19. AFP, April 24, 2003.

Ray Takeyh teaches at the National Defense University, where he is director of studies of the Near East and South Asia Center. The views expressed here are the author's own.

From *World Policy Journal*, Summer 2003, pp. 21–28. © 2003 by the World Policy Institute. Reprinted by permission.

Index

Test Your Knowledge Form

We encourage you to photocopy and use this page as a tool to assess how the articles in *Annual Editions* expand on the information in your textbook. By reflecting on the articles you will gain enhanced text information. You can also access this useful form on a product's book support Web site at *http://www.mhcls.com/online/*.

NAME:

DATE:

TITLE AND NUMBER OF ARTICLE:

BRIEFLY STATE THE MAIN IDEA OF THIS ARTICLE:

LIST THREE IMPORTANT FACTS THAT THE AUTHOR USES TO SUPPORT THE MAIN IDEA:

WHAT INFORMATION OR IDEAS DISCUSSED IN THIS ARTICLE ARE ALSO DISCUSSED IN YOUR TEXTBOOK OR OTHER READINGS THAT YOU HAVE DONE? LIST THE TEXTBOOK CHAPTERS AND PAGE NUMBERS:

LIST ANY EXAMPLES OF BIAS OR FAULTY REASONING THAT YOU FOUND IN THE ARTICLE:

LIST ANY NEW TERMS/CONCEPTS THAT WERE DISCUSSED IN THE ARTICLE, AND WRITE A SHORT DEFINITION:

We Want Your Advice

ANNUAL EDITIONS revisions depend on two major opinion sources: one is our Advisory Board, listed in the front of this volume, which works with us in scanning the thousands of articles published in the public press each year; the other is you—the person actually using the book. Please help us and the users of the next edition by completing the prepaid article rating form on this page and returning it to us. Thank you for your help!

ANNUAL EDITIONS: American Foreign Policy 06/07

ARTICLE RATING FORM

Here is an opportunity for you to have direct input into the next revision of this volume.
We would like you to rate each of the articles listed below, using the following scale:

1. **Excellent: should definitely be retained**
2. **Above average: should probably be retained**
3. **Below average: should probably be deleted**
4. **Poor: should definitely be deleted**

Your ratings will play a vital part in the next revision.
Please mail this prepaid form to us as soon as possible.
Thanks for your help!

RATING	ARTICLE
_____	1. Grand Strategy in the Second Term
_____	2. Hegemony on the Cheap
_____	3. Reaganism v. Neo-Reaganism
_____	4. The Eagle Has Crash Landed
_____	5. Some Hard Truths about Multilateralism
_____	6. Exploiting Rivalries: Putin's Foreign Policy
_____	7. The United States and Russia in Central Asia: Uzbekistan, Tajikistan, Afghanistan, Pakistan, and Iran
_____	8. America as European Hegemon
_____	9. China's Response to the Bush Doctrine
_____	10. Japan: America's New South Korea?
_____	11. The U.S. and Latin America Through the Lens of Empire
_____	12. Libya: Who Blinked, and Why
_____	13. Darfur and the Genocide Debate
_____	14. The Paradoxes of American Nationalism
_____	15. Doctrinal Divisions: The Politics of U.S. Military Interventions
_____	16. Missed Signals
_____	17. The Return of the Imperial Presidency?
_____	18. In Defense of Striped Pants

RATING	ARTICLE
_____	19. Checks, Balances, and Wartime Detainees
_____	20. "Misunderestimating" Terrorism: The State Department's Big Mistake
_____	21. Words vs. Deeds: President George W. Bush and Polling
_____	22. The Pros From Dover
_____	23. America's Sticky Power
_____	24. Global Petro-Politics: The Foreign Policy Implications of the Bush Administration's Energy Plan
_____	25. Africa and the Battle over Agricultural Protectionism
_____	26. X + 9/11
_____	27. A Nuclear Posture for Today
_____	28. Double-edged Shield
_____	29. Apocalypse Soon
_____	30. Lifting the Veil: Understanding the Roots of Islamic Militancy
_____	31. The Sorcerer's Apprentices
_____	32. The Ethics of Exit
_____	33. Taking on Tehran
_____	34. Iran's Nuclear Calculations

(Continued on next page)

BUSINESS REPLY MAIL
FIRST CLASS MAIL PERMIT NO. 551 DUBUQUE IA

POSTAGE WILL BE PAID BY ADDRESEE

McGraw-Hill Contemporary Learning Series
2460 KERPER BLVD
DUBUQUE, IA 52001-9902

**NO POSTAGE
NECESSARY
IF MAILED
IN THE
UNITED STATES**

ABOUT YOU

Name   Date

_____

Are you a teacher? ☐   A student? ☐
Your school's name

_____

Department

_____

Address   City   State   Zip

_____

School telephone #

_____

YOUR COMMENTS ARE IMPORTANT TO US!

Please fill in the following information:
For which course did you use this book?

_____

Did you use a text with this ANNUAL EDITION?   ☐ yes ☐ no
What was the title of the text?

_____

What are your general reactions to the *Annual Editions* concept?

_____

Have you read any pertinent articles recently that you think should be included in the next edition? Explain.

_____

Are there any articles that you feel should be replaced in the next edition? Why?

_____

Are there any World Wide Web sites that you feel should be included in the next edition? Please annotate.

_____

May we contact you for editorial input?   ☐ yes ☐ no
May we quote your comments? ☐ yes ☐ no